Thomas Mellon
and His Times

D0213389

Thomas Mellon
and His Times

THOMAS MELLON

Foreword by David McCullough
Preface to the Second Edition by Paul Mellon
Edited by Mary Louise Briscoe

University of Pittsburgh Press
Pittsburgh and London

Published by the University of Pittsburgh Press, Pittsburgh, Pa. 15260
Copyright © 1994, University of Pittsburgh Press
Foreword copyright © 1994, David McCullough
Preface to the second edition copyright © 1994, Paul Mellon
Introduction, afterword, and notes copyright © 1994, Mary Louise Briscoe
All rights reserved
Manufactured in Canada
Printed on acid-free paper
Second printing, 1995
Paperback edition, 1996

LIBRARY OF CONGRESS CATALOGING-IN-PUBLICATION DATA

Mellon, Thomas, 1813–1908.
    Thomas Mellon and his times / Thomas Mellon. — 2nd ed. / preface
by Paul Mellon; foreword by David McCullough; edited by Mary Louise
Briscoe.
        p.   cm.
    Includes bibliographical references and index.
    ISBN 0-8229-3777-8 (cl.)—0-8229-5512-5 (pbk.)
    1. Mellon, Thomas, 1813–1908   2. Capitalists and financiers—
United States—Biography.   3. Mellon family.   I. Briscoe, Mary
Louise.   II. Title.
HC102.5.M377A3   1994
332'.092—dc20
[B]   94-11892
                                        CIP

A CIP catalogue record for this book is available from the British Library.

Eurospan, London

Contents

Foreword

David McCullough

IT IS ONLY AT THE LAST, in the final chapter of this remarkable autobiography, that its author gets around to telling us what he looks like—his height, weight, color of eyes, and so forth—and it is a tribute to the book he has written that by then such details seem hardly necessary. For we *know* this man, so vivid, so unmistakable is his point of view, so distinctive is the voice of the storyteller. We would recognize him at once were he to walk into a room, no matter his height or the color of his eyes.

There he would stand in his seventy-third year, as he was in 1885 when he finished the book—Thomas Mellon of Pittsburgh, founding father of Mellon Bank, unbending, unblinking, a gentleman of the old school in stiff collar and frock coat, and clearly not one of "festive disposition," as he would say.

"I have for many years been rated as a millionaire, and perhaps justly so," he also modestly observes near the close of his story. In the dollar of the day that meant vastly more than it does now, and one feels this too would show, though in his bearing only, never in any kind of "display." The Judge, as he was known, deplored display.

He is well worth our time and interest, this starchy old Presbyterian, quite as much now as when he took up his pen for the exclusive benefit of family and a select circle of friends. We enter in these pages a time and an America more distant and different than perhaps we can ever know. A contemporary of Abraham Lincoln, he is the immigrant farm boy from a place called Poverty Point, Pennsylvania—an eager, earnest book-reader and rail-splitter like Lincoln, who at age seventeen suddenly takes command of his destiny, throws down his ax, and runs ten miles to stop his father from buying a farm for him and thereby fixing a life for him that he doesn't want. The whole episode, like the name "Poverty Point," could be from a Victorian novel, or a scene in an old Henry Fonda movie, except that it is entirely real, and, as he writes, "my feet were light under the circumstances." His outlook has been transformed, his ambition focused by the *Autobiography of Benjamin Franklin* and like that classic work, this his own life-rendering bears down mightily on such virtues as industry and thrift as the sure paths to success.

The story he unfolds is amazing. He himself is amazing, in his irrepressible earnestness, candor, his observations on life and especially on life and work. Indeed, if there is a prevailing theme for Thomas Mellon, it is work—hard, persevering, everlasting work—from farm to college to the practice of law to service on the bench to banking, and the overall deadly serious business of not just making money but *keeping* it. The whole objective is "to work oneself up in the world," with accent on the verb. And whatever he undertakes, it is "with all my might."

The reader is treated to no end of opinion, and the bias of the social commentary expressed is at times appalling by our standards. He loathes Irish Catholics, socialism, Mormon missionaries, not to say the general "rowdyism and rudeness" of the common American democracy. Poverty, he writes, is a "misfortune to the weaklings who are without courage or ability to overcome it." The "poor Indians" have "gone down" because "stupidity and ignorance always suffer."

Nor is he ever short on advice, on everything from how to pick a lawyer to the control of the passions. In the choosing of a wife, he instructs, character, temper, disposition, taste, and something called "inclination" must be "ascertained with certainty and considered carefully," while ancestry, health, and "position" should be allowed their due weight. As for physical beauty, romance, love, such influences are to be regarded as dubious at best.

On occasion, the old gentleman can be quite funny, more so than probably he knew and particularly on the subject of matrimony. Describing his own courtship of Miss Negley, he recounts the mounting impatience he felt as with lessons in botany, evenings spent admiring her scrapbooks, she denied him opportunity to express his intentions. But then he adds that at least "she never inflicted music upon me."

It may be said with certainty of Thomas Mellon that they truly don't make them that way anymore, and a great part of the pull of the book, and reason to applaud this new edition, is the chance to hear him out, to keep company with such a strong, authentic personality from an era characterized by many of like outlook. Once encountered he is not forgotten. And if there is a single most important surprise in store for the reader it is to discover what a wonderfully well written book it is, what a skilled storyteller is at hand.

There is eyewitness history—accounts of Pittsburgh's Great Fire of 1845 and the financial panic of 1873. There are deft sketches of people he knew and of his travels south and abroad. (In the time-honored way of American travelers, he loves to compare what he's seeing to the standard of back home. Hillsides in Ireland look like "our Pittsburgh Southside"; the Thames at London he judges to be about the size of the Monongahela.)

And as with all autobiographies there is much that goes unsaid, much left out, which also reveals something about the author. He tells us notably little about his wife, for example. Were she to walk into a room, we would be hard put to recognize her from the few fragments he provides. It is striking, too, how little he has to say about—of all things—banking. Compared to all he writes about the law and his time on the bench, the advent of Mellon Bank and his part in it adds up to not a lot here, as if that part of the story doesn't much interest him.

There is scarcely a word about the great national figures of the time or the great issues—nothing of Lincoln, nothing of slavery or westward expansion—except as they relate to finance or family enterprises. In writing of the Civil War, his primary distress is over those Mellon "interests at stake in money and property." His only expressed passion on the titanic struggle is over the prospect that any son of his might be fool enough to want to go off and fight in it. He appears to be without sympathy or feeling for the causes at stake. In this, to be sure, he is representative of many of comparable station in society—those who hired substitutes for their sons or for themselves—but he is also the exact antithesis of many others of wealth and prominence. No less a looming figure than John A. Roebling, for example, another immigrant who had "made good" beginning in Western Pennsylvania, ordered his son to enlist exactly because of his own, the father's, passionate love of the Union, his hatred of slavery.

Thomas Mellon hates war, he hates the waste of it, "the humbuggery, imbecility and petty tyranny of upstart subordinate officers." He hates taxes. He is outraged over the rising extravagance of government, the rising crime rate, the rising cost of living, the declining quality of education, the decline of moral standards overall, and in much of this he sounds quite in tone with the laments of our own time. An insistent old grouch he may be, yet we find ourselves, again and again, nodding in agreement: "Hollow pretexts now take the place of earnest regard for public good. . . . Professions of reform in party platforms are attendant, but no reform comes of it."

To a major degree his is a dark view of the American chronicle. It is a book shadowed with foreboding and a sense of loss and impoverishment, which is all the more striking, of course, coming from a man of such abundant wealth and high station.

It is with growing fascination that we watch him circle and at last center on the dominating paradox of the very industrial-financial bonanza in which he himself has played a lead part. The famous moneylender, the founder of the great banking house that has so much to do with all that Pittsburgh has become, and thus with the whole rise of industrial America, turns out to be a closet Jeffersonian.

He sees in the advance of the machine and factories and the big city work force the demise of all that he holds dear in American life as once characterized the rural world of his boyhood. Then working people were "individualized" in character and condition. "Small proprietors who own their own tools and work on their own materials are better contented and make better citizens," he insists, recalling the weavers, tinners, wheelwrights, and blacksmiths in and about Poverty Point. Like Jefferson, he sees "a better moral atmosphere" in rural democracy. With the rise of industrialization, the massing of population in big cities, American freedom is at stake. His condemnation of the mill towns growing along the Monongahela beside the giant new Carnegie steel plants, could hardly be more harsh had they been written by a radical reformer of the day:

> And the crowding of men and families of the same occupation together has a demoralizing effect; it dwarfs individuality, reduces all to a common level in a monotonous condition, and creates a caste feeling and discontent with their lot. The stimulus to improvement by the moral effect of associating with others of different occupations and of other conditions is removed. The employ-

ees and their families in the larger manufacturing and mining establishments are often designated each by his number, and live in numbered tenements, and are all subjected to the same routine, and treated alike: too much like the soldiers of an army or the inmates of a prison.

In truth, he despised the Carnegie mills and all that they and others like them bespoke of the future—he the owner of coal mines and industrial real estate, he the lifelong champion of the creed of Progress. Better that it would all vanish, he seems to be saying. He is like Henry Ford in a later day, who would lament the loss of the America he knew before the advent of the automobile and would spend millions of his automobile fortune to create a facsimile of that older, preindustrial America at Dearborn, Michigan.

This is the paradox we all feel running like a fault line through the American experience.

Even his money and the very solid comforts of his way of life, the great material rewards he has reaped, are worrisome to Thomas Mellon. It is not from a large bank account that he has "derived the most enjoyment," but from the work to attain it, "from the struggles necessary to remove obstacles in my way, and the satisfaction resulting from overcoming such as seemed insuperable." Don't work for the payoff, he is telling us, the work *is* the payoff, the pleasure therein.

He wants wealth for his children, and yet that very wealth, he knows, may have a detrimental effect on them: "It requires a higher nature than the average youth possesses to resist the temptations of wealth and ease." One wonders what his response might have been had he even vaguely imagined the magnitude of industrial productivity and power that would one day be concentrated at Pittsburgh, or the far larger fortune and influence his sons would gather in their time.

Even as it was, even in 1885, more than twenty years before his death, he feels himself "a stranger in a strange land," so dramatically has everything changed.

What sustains him, above all, is love of family, and much of what is most appealing about the book—and about him—is in those portions devoted to his home life. He is truly, as he says, a family man, and in what he writes about his children, his trust in them and they in him, their importance to him, the seriousness with which he takes the responsibility of being their father, there is no mistaking the depth of his feelings. Those passages recounting the loss of those who died are profoundly moving and the most endearing side of him that he reveals. Here after all is a very human fellow being.

"All through those busy years of professional and judicial labors," he writes, "my heart was in my home; it was there I was happy, and there my feelings centered." It was also, we come to appreciate, why he wrote the book in the first place.

Preface to the Second Edition

Paul Mellon

THIS AUTOBIOGRAPHY of my grandfather was privately printed in 1885 in a limited edition for friends and family only. In his preface, he called it a "memento of affection" and entreated his descendants to "handle and preserve it with care." As one of those descendants, born the year before he died, I have always felt a strong personal interest in my grandfather's life and have treasured his book. I equate his actions with my own decision to reject the life my father hoped *I* would lead—a century after he rejected the life his father hoped he would lead. I have also followed his example by writing my own autobiography—in which I quote extensively from his.

I have always felt that my grandfather's book deserved a wider readership than that represented by his descendants alone, although he himself felt that the book should remain private and admonished against making it available for "sale in the bookstores." It seemed to me that by now it would be a greater act of grandfilial piety to disobey his command than to obey it. By chance, as I was considering how it might be published, I learned that the University of Pittsburgh Press had come to the same conclusion; that is, that it should be made available to a much wider audience. We have combined our forces, and the present volume is the result.

The University of Pittsburgh Press has had a longtime interest in the history of Pittsburgh and western Pennsylvania. Thomas Mellon was brought as a child from County Tyrone, in Ulster, to Westmoreland County in the early nineteenth century and grew up to become a prominent citizen of Pittsburgh. His autobiography provides a vivid eyewitness account of the economic life of the city during the period when it was making the transformation from an overgrown village (though still full of marvels for ten-year-old Thomas when he first saw it) to a great world center of industry. He made his own fortune largely through old-fashioned investments, particularly real estate, but he also contributed to the city's industrial growth. The bank he founded in 1870 was an important source of capital for some of Pittsburgh's early industrialists, notably Henry Clay Frick, who took out a number of loans in order to build coke ovens. Andrew Carnegie was my grandfather's friend and wrote to him praising his book.

Since my grandfather's origins were humble, he provides an abundance of fascinating details about the more mundane aspects of nineteenth-century American life—everything from farming practices to courting customs—which, because they were unremarkable at the time, often went unreported. Such details are precious to the historian and indeed to anyone interested in our nation's past.

Thomas Mellon lived a very long life. He was born in 1813, before the battle of Waterloo and not long after the founding of our republic, and lived until 1908. He came to America when James Monroe was president and almost outlived the presidency of Theodore Roosevelt. As he himself was aware, America altered tremendously during the long period in which he lived, and he devoted a fascinating chapter of his book to describing some of the changes he had witnessed. I have always been impressed by the great surge in the speed and ease of travel that he describes. His emigrant's voyage from Ireland to Saint John, New Brunswick, took "a trifle over twelve weeks." It took another two weeks from New Brunswick to Baltimore by sail, and then a further three weeks to travel—by Conestoga wagon—to the still largely unpopulated Westmoreland County. When in his old age he made a sentimental journey to Ireland in 1882, his trip, now by steamship, took only nine days—fewer days than his first transatlantic journey had taken weeks. And even this was not the end of the wonders he witnessed. During his lifetime he saw the invention of the telephone, electric lighting, the automobile, and human flight, and as well witnessed the full flowering of travel by rail.

In the pages of his autobiography my grandfather stands out, I think, as a vivid personality. He was a man of strong feelings and firm opinions, salted by occasional glints of wry humor. There is proof, moreover, that he was capable of second thoughts. Early copies of the book contained a chapter on "vexatious litigations," in which he provided perhaps not entirely objective accounts of some of his legal battles. Apparently he thought better of such frankness, for in later copies the chapter was eliminated (but largely restored here). In our more enlightened times, some of his prejudices will surely (and rightly) seem unattractive and bigoted. On the other hand, his views on American political life at that period may strike many readers as particularly apropos of our own.

Thomas Mellon said that the turning point of his young life came after reading the autobiography of Benjamin Franklin, undoubtedly the first great American autobiography. This book is thus a literary descendant of Franklin's, and I trust will not be found unworthy of its ancestor.

Introduction

Mary Louise Briscoe

IN 1823, when Thomas Mellon was ten years old, he walked to Pittsburgh from his father's small farm outside the city, near the present-day Murrysville-Export area. A neighbor who accompanied him part of the way told the boy that he would "see more there in a day than at Poverty Point in a lifetime." Once in the city, young Thomas understood. He later recalled viewing the mansion of Jacob Negley and other holdings of this great landowner: "The whole scene . . . impressed me with an idea of wealth and magnificence I had before no conception of. . . . [The thought occurred to me] whether I might not one day attain in some degree such wealth, and an equality with such great people."

Highly intelligent, ambitious, and living in a time of unparalleled economic growth in the United States, Thomas Mellon (1813–1908) far more than achieved his childhood goal. When he died at the age of ninety-five, he was an almost mythic figure in the legal and financial history of Pittsburgh. History would show him to be the founder of a family that was to have great influence on the national and international economy and the worlds of art and philanthropy. In 1936, only twenty-eight years after his death, the Mellons were considered one of the four wealthiest families in the United States—along with the Rockefellers, DuPonts, and Fords.

His surviving sons included Andrew W. Mellon, secretary of the treasury under presidents Harding, Coolidge, and Hoover and founder of the National Gallery of Art, and Richard Beatty Mellon, who became president of Mellon Bank. One of his grandsons, William Larimer Mellon, was the prime organizer of Gulf Oil Corporation. Another, Richard King Mellon, was the major force in the urban renaissance of industrial Pittsburgh after the Second World War. A third grandson, Paul Mellon, is a great collector and benefactor of art museums and other institutions.

Thomas Mellon's newspaper obituaries reflected a reverence for his accomplishments as well as a sense of disbelief that he was gone. His prominence as an immigrant from a farm in Ulster who had become a successful lawyer, judge, banker, landowner, coal operator, financier, and civic leader—as well as his longevity—had by 1908 transformed him into an institution rather than an individual. Perhaps he knew that he had outlived his time. When he privately printed his autobiography *Thomas Mellon and His Times* in 1885, he wrote: "To the general public which surrounds me now, I am a stranger in a strange land." He was to live twenty-three more years.

Thomas Mellon and His Times is unique among the very few accounts written by the great American entrepreneurs of the nineteenth century. This man who was gifted with ambition and the fiscal judgment to match it also turned out to be an excellent writer with a keen sense of narrative, an occasionally wintry sense of humor, and a dead-honest view of himself and his family. One need not always like him to respect his striking ability as an autobiographer, especially in this age of ghost-writing and self-congratulatory personal accounts.

Thomas was very clear that his autobiography was "for his family and descendants exclusively," as the original title page notes. In the preface, he writes that the book contains "nothing which it concerns the public to know, and much which if writing for it I would have omitted." But he did not hesitate to give the book to friends and business associates. When Andrew Carnegie received an inscribed copy, he responded with characteristic charm, as well as his appreciation of Benjamin Franklin's autobiography and his own ambitions as a writer: "Is it not a remarkable coincidence that Franklin should have inspired you to write it. If I can make the third in the trio, you will be right in the prediction as to the time I shall be remembered."[1] In 1920, Carnegie's autobiography was published by Houghton Mifflin Company.

Others, especially Thomas's wife and sons, were not initially so enthusiastic. There are stories that Andrew and Richard attempted to retrieve some of the copies their father had distributed, apparently hoping to keep family matters within the family.[2] If the stories are true, perhaps their father's directness disturbed his sons. He admitted—indeed castigated himself—that he had failed to anticipate the Panic of 1873 and overextended the new family bank.

Thomas is always careful not to credit either himself or any member of his family with too many virtues, which may not have pleased his children. For example, after observing that his sons Thomas and James had accumulated between them $100,000 by the time they were twenty-one years old, he cautions: "I do not wish it understood, however, that the remarkable success of those two boys at such an early age was due to great talent or extraordinary abilities." Whatever his son Andrew's concern may have been, he seems to have overcome it by 1900 when he gave a copy to his prospective father-in-law, Alexander McMullen, an Englishman who was somewhat perplexed by Thomas Mellon's impersonal account of his courtship of Sarah Jane Negley, and who told his wife that "the Mellons must be a strange family."[3] Years later, when Andrew was secretary of the treasury, he had a standing offer of twenty-five dollars for stray copies, not to suppress the book, he said, but because it had become one of his favorite presents for special friends, including President Calvin Coolidge on his retirement in 1929.[4]

For Thomas Mellon, an extremely private man, the autobiography was intended to serve an educational purpose. In his preface he writes of wanting to present his thoughts and feelings, his views and methods, his accomplishments and failures, a sense of his identity that would be more than "the outward and changeable husk or envelope in which he was contained." He hopes that his family and descendants will be able to learn from his experience. "It may," he writes, "serve to impress on [them] the truth of that important rule of life which demands labor, conflict, perseverance, and self-denial to produce a character and accomplish purposes worth striving for."

As a farm boy of fourteen Thomas had first read the autobiography of Benjamin Franklin which, readers of this book will discover, became one of the most important influences in his life. In 1871, when Thomas Mellon erected the first building that would house T. Mellon and Sons' Bank at 512-514 Smithfield Street, a life-sized cast-iron statue of Benjamin Franklin was placed above the main entrance to the four-story building. It remained there until a new building was erected on the same site in 1924, a visual reminder of Franklin's influence on the bank's founder and the values that he hoped to represent in his business.[5] Mellon often advised young men to pattern their lives after

Franklin, and at one point had a private edition of one thousand volumes of Franklin's autobiography printed so that he could personally distribute them. William Larimer Mellon, who received a copy from his grandfather on his twenty-first birthday, remembers that Franklin's name was frequently on Thomas Mellon's lips: "The boys in our family literally were brought up on Franklin. . . . Franklin became a sort of genie of the Mellon family. I cannot exaggerate this influence."[6]

Benjamin Franklin's autobiography, published twenty-five years before Thomas Mellon arrived in western Pennsylvania, had become widely read among the literate public in America and England, one of the first life stories to attain such prominence. Franklin's work is a narrative of success, self-improvement, and public service in which he ultimately associates his personal identity and development with that of the young nation he served. He envisioned his autobiography as a work that would encourage "more writings of the same kind . . . and [induce] more men to spend lives fit to be written." Like all of Franklin's projects, it was intended to influence the development of the new American nation.[7]

Thomas Mellon's audience was more modestly defined, but his autobiographical impulse was nonetheless quite similar to Franklin's. His narrative voice is that of a thoughtful, confident, practical man who has earned a certain authority by virtue of his experience, yet is candid about his mistakes and can recall with ease the simple pleasures of his childhood, the great fun of schoolboy pranks, or the anxieties of adolescence. His work resonates with Protestant morality combined with a rich sentiment for the land and family values that is characteristic of his Scotch-Irish Presbyterian background. As Paul Mellon has written, his grandfather's writings "convey an engaging quality of self-examination mixed with fierce puritanism."[8] Although he had little interest in formal religion, he followed his wife's wishes when she gathered her somewhat reluctant family into the carriage on Sunday mornings to drive to services, and until they died Thomas and Sarah Jane, like their older sons, were leading supporters of the East Liberty Presbyterian Church, which was on the same site as the first log church in Negleystown built by Sarah Jane's father, Jacob Negley.

The theme of education is strong throughout his narrative, for it was his own education, much of it informal, that enabled Mellon to make his decision at the age of seventeen to leave the family farm in Westmoreland County for a new and different life in Pittsburgh. He credits much of what he learned to those lessons of hardship and survival that he derived from the struggles of his immigrant family.[9] His early formal schooling was limited to those few months each year when he was not needed to help with the farm work, but he read widely, encouraged by his mother and by his Uncle Thomas—so affectionately described in the family history section, chapter 3—who sent him trunkloads of books and periodicals from Philadelphia. When he began thinking of giving up farm life and going to college, he wrote to Uncle Thomas about his uncertain future, making it clear that this break in family tradition was extraordinarily difficult for him. "Strange and unreasonable as it may seem," he wrote, "there are some of my relations who care not how soon I might fail in this undertaking."[10] Among his own siblings—three sisters and one brother—only Thomas Mellon would master the difficult transition from an agrarian to an industrial society, straining to apply the values of family life on a farm which he firmly believed in.

Thomas Mellon's grandfather Archibald had immigrated to western Pennsylvania in 1816, the same year that Pittsburgh was incorporated as a city. It had a population of 6,000 (10,000 including the suburbs of Birmingham, Allegheny, Bayardstown, and Lawrenceville), with 960 houses, eight churches, three banks, three market houses, a Masonic Hall, a courthouse, and a jail. When Thomas Mellon and his parents arrived in Westmoreland County in 1818, the Pennsylvania Road had been completed to Pittsburgh and the National Road to Wheeling, West Virginia. By 1828, when Mellon was studying at County Academy of Greensburg, Pittsburgh was already a smokey industrial city of the steamship era at the hub of commerce going upstream as well as down.

The mid-nineteenth century was an exciting and volatile period in Pittsburgh. Other entrepreneurs, younger than Thomas, had their beginnings then. Thirteen-year-old Andrew Carnegie arrived from Scotland in 1848, working his first job as a bobbin-boy in a cotton factory at $1.20 per week. In 1852 eight-year-old Henry John Heinz began to sell radishes and other surplus vegetables from the family garden and by 1869 was marketing horseradish he grew in a tiny plot on the banks of the Allegheny River in Sharpsburg. In 1859 Edwin L. Drake discovered oil in Titusville and by 1871 Pittsburgh had sixty petroleum refineries that produced 36,000 barrels a day. George Westinghouse, still a boy in upper New York State during the 1850s, would by 1869 receive a patent for the air-brake that would transform the railroad industry. Henry Clay Frick was born in 1849, and when he was twenty-one, he would receive a $10,000 loan from T. Mellon and Sons' Bank which enabled him to buy coal land near Connellsville and build fifty beehive coke ovens.

By early 1873 there were ninety organized banks and about a dozen private banks in the city, almost half of which went out of business during the Panic of 1873. Thomas Mellon opened his bank three years before the crisis, but it survived, and he went on to establish his sons in the careers that would eventually develop one of the greatest family fortunes in America.

Convinced of the moral value of work, Mellon admits he had little time for pleasure or social amenities before his marriage, but he takes pains to describe himself as a man in whom "the tender passion and love of children and domestic life was always strong." Although chapter 12 gives a rather businesslike description of his courtship of Sarah Jane Negley, his early letters reveal that there was a time in his life when he had a more romantic view of female society. At twenty-one, he writes freely to his friend John Coon about a number of girls, "the sweet creatures," and in another letter he notes it is valuable to be in the social company of women because it helps to refine a man's character.[11] One can only speculate about the change in his view during the next nine years, but by the age of thirty he had decided that marriage should come first, love second. Although Sarah Jane does not figure prominently in his book, she looms large in the background of Mellon's life. Theirs was a Victorian marriage, American style.

The fact that the young Mellons took the honeymoon described in chapter 13 may in itself reveal more about them than the absence of detail about their courtship and marriage, for it was in many ways a grand adventure. While Thomas Mellon was not a man to discuss his personal feelings, travel did excite him, and those passages describing such adventures are among the most interesting in his narrative, with a surprising and often sensual feeling for the landscape around him.

In recalling his honeymoon, Thomas Mellon vividly portrays travel conditions in the early nineteenth century. While it is difficult to imagine him sleeping on an eighteen-inch plank in the common room of a canal boat, it is important to remember that the young married couple was traveling on the best accommodations available for cross-country journeys in their time. And they traveled alone in a time when wedding trips were typically family affairs on which the newlyweds, accompanied by a mother, sisters, or cousins, went to visit relatives who had been unable to attend the ceremony. Private romantic honeymoons did not become popular with Americans until mid-century, when travel for pleasure became more accessible.

Thomas was a devoted and intense father, and his children were the center of his life. Concerned for their education, he built a one-room schoolhouse on the family estate so that he would have more direct control over their instruction. As his sons grew, he watched carefully to identify their strengths and encourage their individual development. Just as his father had taught him to plough and split rails, so he taught his sons basic entrepreneurial skills when each was in his early teens. Although Mellon had to rely on his college education to improve his life, he did not think it necessarily appropriate for his children, and none of them earned college degrees. Only James Ross and Andrew attended college, James Ross at Canonsburg Academy for one year, and Andrew at Western University for three. Family history differs about why Andrew left Western three months before graduation when he was only seventeen, either because of his health or because he was more interested in working full-time at the bank with his father.

The passages in which Thomas describes the illness and deaths of his three young children are the most emotional in the book, and they reveal the depth of his feeling. He was agonized to watch his only daughters, Emma and Rebecca, die in early childhood of heart disease and dysentery, but it was to the death of his son Selwyn that he was never reconciled. The boy contracted diphtheria at the age of nine and lingered for eight days before dying. Years later Thomas wrote that "Time has brought me consolation in all other deaths but this: for Selwyn I cannot be comforted." During their long lives, Thomas and Sarah Jane lived to see two more of their eight children die, both after the period covered by *Thomas Mellon and His Times:* George in 1887 and Thomas Alexander in 1899. Andrew, James, and Richard lived into the 1930s.

The home at 401 Negley Avenue was the real and symbolic center of family life for the Mellons. James Ross Mellon recalled:

> Our home was happy and I cannot recall in all my young life of any discord between my mother and father. They were always quiet and kind to the children; always finding some work for us to do, and remunerating us in some way for all we did for them. In their last days I recall seeing them sitting one at each side of the fire-place in the evenings like two doves, quiet and love-able.[12]

William Larimer Mellon describes his grandmother as a warm, caring woman who spent a great deal of her time on church and charity work and controlled the household through her wrathful housekeeper, Mrs. Cox, an excellent cook who smoked a clay pipe and seems to have intimidated every family member except Thomas himself. But it was Sarah Jane who baked the weekly bread every Saturday and loved to have all her boys, with their families in later years, come for dinner on Sundays and holidays.

When Thomas Mellon retired as judge in 1869 after a decade on the Court of Common Pleas, he was already a wealthy man and his two older sons were well established in business. The 1860s brought industrial prosperity to Pittsburgh, when the population reached 86,000, real estate value more than doubled, and the production of glass, iron, and steel accelerated at an astonishing rate. Yet in the early days of the Civil War, there was little business in court, so Mellon used the time to take pleasure in reading—older writers such as Bacon, Descartes, Berkeley, Locke, and Hume, and the new and controversial works by Darwin, Spencer, Wallace, Huxley, and Argyle, among others. After serving his ten-year term, he declined reelection and was anxious to get more involved in business opportunities that the booming prosperity of Pittsburgh had helped to make possible: "One had only to buy anything and wait, to sell at a profit: sometimes, as in real estate for instance, at a very large profit in a short time."

The judge opened T. Mellon and Sons' Bank in a rented room in 1870; Andrew was then fourteen, Richard eleven, and George nine, hardly of age to be involved in the business venture. Andrew, however, still a student at Western University in 1870, went to the bank with his father every morning, his job being to help a trusted employee unlock the safe at the start of the business day. Andrew's assignment was typical of his caring father, who encouraged his sons to develop independently from their earliest years according to their individual talents in education as well as in business.

The patriarch of the Mellon clan officially retired from active business at T. Mellon and Sons' Bank in 1882 at the age of sixty-nine, passing the responsibility for management of the bank on to his son Andrew, who was then twenty-seven. Mellon kept an office in the bank where he went daily to look after his other business affairs, which included keeping an eye on his sons George and Richard who at age twenty-two and twenty-four had established the Mellon Brothers Bank in Bismarck in the Dakota territory.

Eight years later, in 1890 on February 3, the birthday they shared, Thomas and Sarah Jane placed by indenture all their real property in Andrew's hands, and this was followed over the years by their personal property. He, in turn, executed "A Declaration of Trust" indicating that his purpose as sole owner was to manage the estate in consultation with his three brothers.[13] In a long memorandum dated August 25, 1898, Thomas explained that he had only acquired wealth for the independence it offered. Now he was parting with it, "until nature should grant me the final divorce," for the same reason: "to promote my freedom from the care and responsibility [of] retaining it." He did so with "full confidence in the sound judgment and other good qualities of our children." Whatever the actual value of the judge's assets, the appraised value of property belonging to the judge and his wife at the time was $2,457,548—or approximately seventy million in today's dollars.[14]

The judge, realistic as always, would have been aware of the perils of his age—he was eighty-eight—and obviously intended that this transfer would guarantee flexibility of action concerning the Mellon assets, thereby promoting the interests of the family. "There was something reminiscent of the Biblical patriarchs in Grandfather's deep feelings of obligation toward the members of his family," writes William Larimer Mellon, "and in his anxiety to set all his sons on their courses in life, establishing each one somewhat farther along the way than his own bleak start." Although Thomas was a demanding father and scrutinized his sons closely, he had a deep pride in their accomplishments. On Christmas Day, 1878, he wrote to them: "I wish to give you all some acknowledgment of the great pleasure and satisfaction it affords a father to see his children well doing and agreeable. It is my greatest happiness, and repays all the labor and care of my life."[15]

Although much has been written about the Mellon family, Thomas's son Andrew is the one best remembered for his entrepreneurial genius in Pittsburgh's financial and industrial growth and his influence on the national and international economy. Writers and historians have been fascinated by the powerful wealth of the Mellon empire and the impact of it on family members, on Pittsburgh, and on American history and culture at large. Histories of the entire family by Burton Hersh and David Koskoff devote only a chapter to the life of Thomas Mellon,[16] and because there is no biography, most of what we know of him is available only in this previously unpublished autobiography, a scattering of family letters, and those memories of the man and his legend recorded in the early twentieth century by family members and associates.[17] *Thomas Mellon and His Times* is thus an invaluable source on the life of the powerful and respected patriarch, but it is also a rare, lively, candid, and rich memoir of a self-made nineteenth-century entrepreneur, a man who came to this country as a five-year-old Ulster emigrant and lived through the years of America's rise from a frontier to an industrial power.

Editorial Note: All spelling, capitalization, and punctuation in the original text have been retained in this edition. The original edition was divided into two parts: Part I, "Family History," and Part II, "Auto-biography," which have been reversed in this edition for ease of reading. Some passages have been omitted in several chapters, primarily in the family history section, including much of a legendary account of the origin of Ireland and its inhabitants starting with Noah and the Scythians, a portion of his animadversions on the character, religion, and living habits of those he refers to as "the Celtic Irish," and several sections that merely repeat points often made elsewhere in the text. We trust we have retained enough on these subjects to give a candid account of Thomas Mellon's beliefs and prejudices, which show him to be a thoroughgoing representative of his time, place, and heritage.

Acknowledgments

Paul Mellon provided access to unpublished letters and manuscripts from the family archives that were essential to this project. Thomas Mellon Schmidt and James Ross Mellon II provided many family photographs and much helpful advice on a variety of textual details. Additional help was provided by Rachel Larimer Mellon Walton, James Mellon Walton, and Ian Rawson.

As editorial consultant, Alan Williams's help with the preparation of the manuscript was invaluable. Eric Lindquist, Paul Mellon's archivist, provided and verified a number of details in Mellon family history.

During my travels to Northern Ireland, Eric Montgomery, chairman of the Ulster-American Folk Park and secretary of the Scotch-Irish Trust of Ulster, was, with his wife, Joan, an enthusiastic and generous host. Mr. Montgomery, John Gilmour, director of the Ulster-American Folk Park, and his staff provided material on the region of Thomas Mellon's birthplace. Brian Trainor, director of the Ulster Historical Foundation in Belfast, provided genealogical research on the Wauchobs, Thomas Mellon's mother's family who settled in Kinkitt.

Helpful in the search for family history and period photographs were Mary M. Weibel, at Mellon Bank, for material in the Mellon Bank archives; George Tabor, Andrew W. Mathieson, and Mary Ellen Cunningham at Richard K. Mellon and Sons; the archival staffs at the Westmoreland County Historical Society and the Kansas City Public Library; Marilyn Holt at the Pennsylvania Department of the Carnegie Library, Pittsburgh; Charles Aston at the Hillman Library of the University of Pittsburgh; Audrey Iacone and Carolyn Schumacher at the Historical Society of Western Pennsylvania; and Jill Clark at the Sewickly Public Library. I am especially thankful to James V. Burke at the University of Pittsburgh's University Center for Instructional Resources for his superb and timely copying of historical photographs.

I am grateful to Edward K. Muller, Van Beck Hall, R. J. Gangwere, and C. Hax McCullough, Jr., for reviewing portions of the text, and to Carol Lynch and Cindy Hoffman for their help in preparing the manuscript.

Many thanks to those who verified historical photos and documents and in various other ways contributed to the completion of this book, including: Rosine Bucher, Gene Klebingot, and Bruno Krsul at Soldiers and Sailors Memorial Hall, Pittsburgh; Brian Butco, Wilma D. Hutchings, Walter Kidney, William Pettit, Peggy Tucker Thompson, John D. C. and Aida Craig Truxall, Susan Scott Tucker, Helene Snyder Smith, and Barbara Widdoes.

I am also grateful to Frederick A. Hetzel, Director of the University of Pittsburgh Press, and Kathy McLaughlin, Production Editor, for their careful and imaginative suggestions about all aspects of this edition—and to Fred for his commitment for the past thirty years to *Thomas Mellon and His Times* as a major American autobiography.

Some Events in the Life and Times of Thomas Mellon

———————— ➤ ● ◆ ————————

1813   Born at Camp Hill Cottage in Omagh, County Tyrone, Ireland
        on February 3

1816   Grandfather Archibald Mellon emigrated to Western Pennsyl-
        vania
        Pittsburgh incorporated as a city, population 6,000

1818   Immigrated with parents to Poverty Point, Westmoreland
        County, Pennsylvania
        First bridge spanning Pittsburgh's three rivers built on
        Smithfield Street

1819   The Panic of 1819

1823   First visit to Pittsburgh, for which he traveled 42 miles
        round-trip on foot

1825   Erie Canal opened

1827   Read Franklin's autobiography

1828   Studied during winter months at County Academy
        of Greensburg

1830   Decided to reject farm life, declining to accept the farm
        property his father was about to buy him

1832   Studied for two years at Tranquil Retreat Academy in
        Monroeville, boarding at school and walking home for
        weekends

1833   Parents moved to farm near Monroeville

1837   Graduated from Western University

1838   Taught Latin at Western University for several months; began studying law in the office of Judge Charles Shaler; appointed assistant deputy prothonotary in March; admitted to the bar December 15

1839   Opened law office in Pittsburgh at Fifth and Market in June

1843   After brief courtship, married Sarah Jane Negley on August 22

1844   Son Thomas Alexander born

1845   The Great Fire of Pittsburgh

1846   Son James Ross born

1847   Daughter Sarah Emma born

1850   Built family home at 401 Negley
        Death of his daughter, Sarah Emma

1851   Daughter Annie Rebecca born

1852   Death of his daughter, Annie Rebecca
        The Pennsylvania Railroad opened from Philadelphia to Pittsburgh, November 29

1853   Son Samuel Selwyn born

1855   Son Andrew William born

1858   Son Richard Beatty born

1859   Elected Judge, Court of Common Pleas
        Edwin L. Drake established the first oil well in Titusville

Andrew Carnegie, age 24, was promoted to his first management position, head of the Pittsburgh division of the Pennsylvania Railroad

1860   Son George Negley born

1862   Death of his son, Samuel Selwyn

1869   Decided not to seek reelection as judge; returned to private business
George Westinghouse organized Westinghouse Air Brake Company to manufacture air brakes for steam railways

1870   Opened first bank in January

1871   Purchased 512–514 Smithfield Street for T. Mellon and Sons' Bank
Loaned $10,000 to Henry Clay Frick to buy coal fields and establish his first coke ovens

1873   The Crash of 1873

1874   Andrew Carnegie introduced the Bessemer process for making steel in Pittsburgh, erecting the Edgar Thomson Steel Works in Braddock

1877   Purchased the failing Ligonier Valley Railroad, putting sons Richard and Thomas in charge of development

1880   Elected to Select Council of Pittsburgh, serving until 1887

1882   Officially retired from active business, leaving Andrew as bank manager; traveled to Ireland, Scotland, and England with son George, visiting family home in Camp Hill, Robert Burns country, London

1885   Completed autobiography on August 22, his forty-second wedding anniversary

1887   Richard joined Andrew in management of the bank
        Death of his son, George

1890   With Sarah Jane, transferred all real property to Andrew

1890–   Lived in Kansas City intermittently for five years,
1895   starting new business ventures, and left Sarah Jane
        in Pittsburgh

1892   The Homestead Steel Strike

1899   Death of his son, Thomas Alexander

1908   Died on his birthday, February 3

1909   Death of Sarah Jane, January 19

Thomas Mellon
and His Times

Preface to the First Edition

IS A KNOWLEDGE of our ancestors of any use to us? Is there any benefit to be derived from knowing their character and habits, and what manner of men they were of? We may have inherited no worldly possessions from them, but never can ignore the legacies of good or bad qualities they are sure to have left us by heredity. To what extent in this way may not the shading of our mental, moral, and physical character and habits be due to them? In what proportions have our different ancestors contributed to our make up? Science teaches that we are but reproductions of those going before us: each individual but a new edition of a work published long ago, with some slight modifications—additions or subtractions, improving or impairing the original text. Some of our inherited qualities may be very good, others very bad; some should be cultivated, others repressed: and if we knew just how we came by them, and how they cropped out or were manifested in our predecessors, we might deal with them all the more intelligently.

The natural affection for ancestors, and for pictures of remote ancestors, may therefore be a wise provision. But in this direction we can obtain little assistance from a family portrait. An old picture may be a very poor likeness of the original, and at best can show nothing of his true character or qualities; but still natural affection clings to it, and imagination supplies those traits we would flatter in ourselves. How much more satisfactory would it not be if we could have a true representation of our ancestor's course through life from first to last, as in a panorama: showing his thoughts and actions, his good and bad qualities, what were his feelings on trying occasions; how he bore prosperity or adversity; what were his views on the current affairs of his day; what

3

his motives and methods, and what he accomplished or wherein he failed; how he performed his duties as a citizen and fulfilled his domestic relations. Such a picture would bring him home to us in his working clothes, and reveal the hidden ties between his nature and our own. It would represent to us that identity which through life he regarded as himself, and not a mere presentation of the outward and changeable husk or envelope in which he was contained, and through which it is never easy to read the contents.

I was thus led to reflect whether such a picture was possible. The nearest approach to it would be a true narrative of the ancestor's life, written by himself; no other could do the work so well, as no other could know the facts and circumstances so accurately.

Besides the utility and pleasure such a picture would afford, however poorly executed, there is another consideration in its favor. Every one who has spent a long and active life in varied pursuits must have had many experiences which rightly or wrongly he conceives would be beneficial to those coming after him to know. His better judgment may tell him it is useless, as it is seldom any one recalls another's experience when the occasion for it arises—the magnetic needle to guide each man's course must be within himself; but still it is a natural desire to give others the benefit of what we know. And when the time approaches for closing the book of all our experience, we may imagine ourselves still anxious for a few last words with those dearest to us. Might it not therefore be the preferable course to put into some lasting form beforehand all we may deem worth saying, rather than leave it to the hurry and confusion of the final parting?

At first I scarcely hoped to ever have the leisure to attempt anything of the kind in my own case; but still the inclination led me to try, and to make notes and procure materials from time to time as best I could. And at last the desired opportunity came. In the evening of life, with a competence for all reasonable wants, and sons both able and willing to manage my affairs as well as I could myself, further necessity for constant attention to business details was removed, and the following pages are the result. They have been prepared in the hours and half hours snatched from business for a period of over a year past: a rather desultory method of composition, which will account for incidental irregularities of style; but they contain nothing which it concerns the public to know, and much which if writing for it I would have omitted.

And besides the purposes previously indicated, I cherish the hope that, should an old copy of the book happen to fall into the hands of some poor little boy among my descendants in the distant future, who, inheriting a share of my spirit and energy, may be desirous of bettering his condition, it may tend to encourage and sustain his commendable ambition. It may show him that industry and perseverance will overcome what without them would be insuperable; and that the more insurmountable the obstacles in his way, the greater will be his satisfaction in overcoming them. It may serve to impress on him the truth of that important rule of life which demands labor, conflict, perseverance and self-denial to produce a character and accomplish purposes worth striving for. And it may tend to assure him that such a course carries with it more real satisfaction and pleasure than a life of ease and self-indulgence.

It may also not be amiss here to remind others of my descendants that whilst family pride founded on ancestry, without good qualities in themselves to sustain it, is a sure sign of weakness and degeneracy: yet just enough such pride to produce self-respect, in connection with average good qualities, is a valuable preservative against low associations and bad habits.

And finally, let me entreat those of my descendants into whose hands this memento of affection may fall, to handle and preserve it with care, remembering that it is committed to them for safe-keeping not only for themselves but for their descendants likewise, and that it will not be for sale in the bookstores, nor any new edition published; and remembering also what satisfaction it may afford a descendant of theirs and mine, many generations hence, to read the history of one of his remote ancestors as related by the ancestor himself. I advise this not on account of any intrinsic merit in the book itself, but because it may in time become a valued ancestral relic, and for that reason its defects be overlooked for the sake of the author.

AUTOBIOGRAPHY

———◆ ● ◆———

*"The web of our life is of a mingled yarn,
good and evil together."*

Chapter 1

———— ◆ • ◆ ————

Childhood

I WAS BORN IN 1813, on the 3d of February, at the Camp Hill Cottage on my father's farm, Lower Castletown, parish of Cappaigh, county Tyrone, Ireland.[1] The small farm of twenty-three acres on which the cottage stands was a part of my grandfather's larger farm, which he cut off and allotted to my father in view of his approaching marriage. The cottage itself was built by my father with the assistance of his brother Archy, chiefly by the labor of their own hands. It is a nice little place on the bank of the river Strule, about a half mile below Cappaigh bridge. The river here is about two hundred feet wide, and after receiving Cappaigh Burn and the Morn and Derg waters, empties into Lough Foyle at Londonderry, some twenty miles below our place. It was here I first saw the light, and where I remained till in my fifth year; and what has ever seemed strange to me is the fact that its picture has always remained fresh in my mind, with all its details of location and scenery. So much so that when my son James visited Ireland fifty-six years after I left it, I was able to give him a plot and description of it so correct that he recognized it at sight; and when I revisited it myself in 1882, sixty-four years after I had left it, there was not the slightest correction to be made in my mental map. It was all there in every particular, as I had seen it when a child and still remembered it, except the spring well on the croft brae, which it surprised me not to find until the owner of the place informed me he had displaced it by subdrainage to improve the land for cultivation.

The vivid and permanent impression which that place and its surroundings made upon my mind at so early a period affords me an interesting subject of speculation. Why is it, a memory not very tenacious in other respects in after life should receive such clear impressions, even to the minutest details of form and landscape, at so early a period, and retain them fresh and unimpaired ever afterwards? It must not only be true, as metaphysicians teach, that we learn more in the first five years of life than in any ten years afterwards, but also that we retain whatever we learn in those five years incomparably better than anything we learn at a later date. There is this about it, perhaps: the fact of the objects being all fresh in my mind, and at once permanently cut off from view afterwards, may have acted in a manner to preserve the impression distinct and unconfused, similar to the effect of closing the camera suddenly on receiving the impression on the metallic plate.

I remember also many incidents of my early Irish life quite clearly.

On one occasion, when my father and mother went to the neighboring market town, they left me and the dog to keep house, giving me strict orders to remain inside with the door bolted, and to let no one in on any account; and after seeing that I had bolted it securely on the inside, they left to return at noon. Beggars were numerous at the time, mostly thieves—tramps we call them here. It was a bright summer day, but gloomy in the house. I stood the solitary confinement very well for a while, but at length hours seemed to stretch out into days, and I saw from the window a plaything which I coveted greatly, and the longer I looked the more I desired to have it. There could be no harm in opening the door just long enough to run out and get it. No tramps were in sight. My good resolution was unable to resist the temptation. I disobeyed commands and fell from duty. I remember the trepidation of heart to this day with which I drew the bolt and peeped out to see that the coast was clear. Then I made the plunge, secured the coveted object, and turned to re-enter; but there an entirely unexpected obstacle presented itself. It was my first experience of the truth that "the way of the transgressor is hard." The dog which was shut up with me had a stricter sense of duty, even if his discretion was poor. He was a remarkably sagacious and faithful watch dog, such as were highly prized at that time, robbery in the neighborhood being of almost nightly occurrence. What stock he was of I cannot say; all that I remember is that he was greatly valued by my father. He had been shut up with me as a reserve force against tramps; and, as my misfortune proved, was literally faithful to his trust, and no respecter of persons. He would not let me recross the threshold, nor come outside himself.

The dog and I had always been the best of friends; he had been my constant companion in the hunt after water rats, and, according to report, had once saved my life by dragging me out of a ditch filled with water into which I had stumbled. At first I was indignant, but found threats useless. Then I tried coaxing; but after exhausting all manner of blandishments upon him he was still inexorable. There he stood in the centre of the doorway with his fore feet on the sill, showing his teeth and growling vigorously at every effort on my part to enter. This performance went on till I became desperate. Tramps might appear any moment or, what was nearly as bad, the time was approaching for the return of my parents who might thus find me unfaithful to my charge. I well remember how this thought tormented me; and in desperation, like the old man in the fable, I resolved to try what virtue there was in stones, hurling them at him with all the force and rapidity I could muster. But all to no purpose: what blows he could not dodge he received with patience, but did not flinch a jot. At last one went wide of the mark and smashed through a pane of glass in the front window. This capped the climax of my distress. I remembered no more, but when my parents returned they found the dog at his post in the open doorway, holding the fort; and found me lying asleep in the front yard near by, with my face all smeared with tears and dust.

I remember another rather ludicrous occurrence in which I figured shortly afterwards. Mark Mellon, a neighbor and relative, called to complain about our cattle breaking into his oats field. Mark was very negligent about repairing fences, but quite ready to complain of trespass. My father was not at home; and when he and my mother got into a heated altercation, I hastened to the back room where my father kept his arms and uniform—he was an officer in a local militia company at the time—and, taking his sword from where it stood behind the door, I ran out and in great excitement presented it to my mother. This circumstance changed the contention into merriment, and they parted in good humor.

I also well remember numerous visits to my grandfather's place a very short distance down the lane, and the good times I had with my uncles and aunts there; and the tribulations and conflicts I was often involved in with a flock of geese belonging to a family who lived on the way between the two places. I always supplied myself with a long rod or brush; but at hatching time, and when the goslings were young and the geese cross, the ganders were often too bold to respect my switch, and if they attacked me there was nothing for it but to run till I could procure some one to escort me past them.

But the time came when my grandparents and the residue of the family, excepting my father, concluded to follow those who had gone before to America. I remember well the procession on the occasion of their departure. They had sold the farm and farm stock—all except such household goods as were packed to take along—and their neighbors and friends were on hand to see them off and bid them farewell. The jaunting car with the female portion of the family going before, and the carts with the goods following, then a long escort on foot, resembled a funeral procession more than anything else, and was pretty much the same in feeling. At the top of a hill on the road, about a mile distant, was the place of parting. That was the last point from which the old homestead could be seen: a homestead which had sheltered the family and their ancestors for so many generations. It was sad to look back upon it for the last time. After a great deal of tear shedding and hand shaking, and good wishes and blessings, the kind hearted crowd turned homeward, and the little emigrant party continued their solitary way onward with sad hearts.

The Scotch-Irish, as well as the Celts, are an exceedingly tender hearted people. The occasion of whole families emigrating to America in those days was frequent. It was regarded as a final parting—as much so indeed as could be effected by death, as no return was expected; and on such occasions the whole country round about assembled to bid the departing ones godspeed and farewell, which always produced an outburst of emotion on both sides. They so much resembled funerals that they were called "living wakes," to distinguish them from the other class.

My parents and I were with the returning crowd: they with sad hearts, I without any due appreciation of the gravity of the occasion. Uncle Samuel and my father alone of the family now remained behind. My father was regarded as provided for; comfortably fixed or comparatively so as to his neighbors. He had a wife and child to care for, and it was deemed best for him not to give up certainty for hope, or incur the risks of emigration to seek his fortune in the New World. Samuel remained behind only to settle up some business which could not be closed in time to accompany the others; but he expected to be able to leave also in a few months. Then none but my father would remain. It was not the rule for families in affluent circumstances to emigrate, or for any one reasonably provided for to do so. Whilst my grandfather was in comfortable circumstances so long as his family remained single and under his own roof, yet they were too numerous to give each a start in the world for a new family. Armour, the oldest son, had already married and would have been given the Camp Hill farm instead of my father, but he married against the will of his parents; and although the lady was respectable there was a slight unpleasantness which induced him to leave with his young wife to join his uncle John in America. He did not find his uncle in Westmoreland county where he expected to meet him; but he remained there, and almost the entire family followed and settled in the same neighborhood some years afterwards, as heretofore related.[2]

People born and raised in the New World can hardly realize in imagination the conditions of life in the Old. In the New World hitherto young people may marry with little or no provision or calculation for the support of a family. If without property or income, the opportunities for employment and for procuring the means of living are so abundant that they can ignore the fear of starvation and want; but it is not so in the old country. There the wages of labor are so low, and opportunities of remunerative employment so scarce, that to maintain a wife and children on the ordinary wages of a laborer or mechanic is hardly possible; and to rise above a laborer's condition is equally difficult. Among the middle classes, farms are divided into the smallest portions which will produce the necessaries of life of the cheapest kind under rigid economy; and without such a farm, or some business equally lucrative, a man who would marry without means to emigrate would have want and starvation staring him in the face.

But returning to my life in Ireland: Although it was a settled point when my grandparents left that we should remain permanently at the old place, my father soon began to entertain thoughts of following his family. Letters from America were eagerly looked for, and gazetteers and books of geography descriptive of the country and its resources eagerly read. I well remember the long winter nights which were spent by my parents perusing and discussing descriptions of different parts of America, and the products of the land, and opportunities for bettering the condition of settlers there. In the course of two years they had

fully made up their minds to leave. Then came much talk and consultation about selling the farm, and disposing of the stock and settling
up affairs. It all resulted in the aggregation of about two hundred
guineas in gold coin, equal to one thousand dollars. These were carefully stitched in a belt which my mother fastened around her waist,
with which to sink or swim as the case might be in our voyage over the
stormy sea. At last there was a busy time of preparation. My uncle Joe
Wauchob came over from Kinkitt and took me away with him on his
return home. He was to meet my parents with me at an appointed time
and place on their way to Derry. I rode behind him on his horse, and I
remember it was very rough, as he dashed along rapidly; but he
stopped at a public house in Newtonstewart, where he partook of some
refreshments, and from there rode home harder than ever. It was all I
could do to keep my seat by holding on to him; and, as a safeguard
perhaps, he kept hold of me by the arm. It was a Tam O'Shanter ride,[3]
and I must have been badly scared and shaken up when we arrived at
his house because my aunt took him to task for treating the child so
roughly, as she said; which he excused as being the right thing to accus-
tom the lad to hardships. I remained there about two weeks and had a
good time frolicking with my cousin John and his sister Elinor, about
my own age. In a spirit of mischief we made frequent excursions across
the cotter's potato garden, which annoyed him greatly; but he ended
our sport by seizing and imprisoning us under a creel. The punishment subdued us. A creel is a large, square basket, holding a cart load
of farm vegetables or other matter, and used as a cart or car bed.

The appointed day arrived however, and I was delivered over to my
parents as agreed on. I remember very well our journey to Derry,
which we entered by the bridge across the Foyle. We were to go aboard
ship the next day but were prevented by an event of a serious nature.
My father's trouble and worriment incident to the settlement of affairs
and the labor of packing up and preparing to leave, had brought on a
fever which did not develop until after we arrived in Derry. For a few
days he had complained of pains in his limbs, and a ringing sound in
his ears; but on the day we were to go on board a high fever had set in,
and the ship's surgeon excluded him on the ground of illness. This was
a serious disappointment; but not so serious as our apprehensions
regarding the illness. Our means were not such as to justify the expense
of costly board or lodging and medical treatment; and indeed, my

father had become so ill that a hotel or boarding house would not have cared to admit him. The physician pronounced it a dangerous and probably a protracted attack.

My mother was equal to the emergency however; I remember going with her from place to place until she found two suitable upstairs rooms which she engaged as lodging rooms. She then had her baggage removed, and bedding unpacked and adjusted; and had my father conveyed from the lodging house where we had stopped, and placed as comfortably as circumstances would allow in this new temporary home in Derry. She then procured an attentive and skillful physician recommended by Mr. Buchanan, the owner of the vessel in which we had taken passage. This Buchanan was the uncle of the late President of the United States of that name. Here my father lay in a helpless and at last almost hopeless condition for nearly four weeks. But the physician's care, and my mother's nursing, finally brought him through. At one time he was so low that the physician gave him up, and my mother wrote a letter to his father's family in America, informing them of our distress and asking their advice: whether in case of his death they would advise her to go on with me and join them, or to return to her own people at Kinkitt. The turn came however and he began to convalesce; and I remember, after he was able to walk out of doors with a cane, his usual stroll with me by the hand was along the top of Derry walls, where I thought it very strange to be able to look down into the chimney tops. And I remember of our examining Roaring Meg, and the other celebrated old guns which had done such execution in the siege of Derry.[4] Derry must have been supplied with hydrants at that time much resembling those in present use, as I was greatly surprised at one which stood on the pavement near our lodging house. There was a pool of water at and around its base, which was the only supply visible to me; and how so large a supply of water could be obtained from so small a source, and why the water of its own accord flowed up and out of the spout, were mysteries which excited my curiosity. I remember very well also the appearance of an old woman who sat at the open gate of the city wall, beside a stand of candies and sea *dulce*.[5] Her table afforded an irresistible temptation to my scarce half-pennies.

But time wore on, and at last we were in condition to embark, and did so in one of the same line of ships. Our destination was St. Johns, New Brunswick. England at that time was in no friendly mood towards the United States, and would clear no ships except to ports in her own dominions. We were a trifle over twelve weeks on the voyage, many instances of which I remember but they are not worth relating now.

All I remember of St. Johns is seeing fields covered with fish split open to dry. And here I first saw and tasted the cucumber, and saw negroes.

We soon obtained passage in a coasting vessel and reshipped for Baltimore, which we reached in about two weeks. The day we arrived in the bay below Baltimore was exceedingly hot to our fresh experience, as nothing like it ever prevails in Ireland. We were quarantined there for a whole tedious, hot day; and, while lying there, my father with others went on shore in the ship's yawl and brought back a lot of fine, red, ripe peaches. This was our first taste of the peach; and, whilst agreeable, the flavor was remarkably strange to my palate, such as I shall never forget; but it lost its novelty afterwards.

At last we landed in Baltimore at Fell's Point, on or about the 1st of October, 1818; and here I may regard my childhood as ended, and boyhood commenced.

Chapter 11

———— ◆ ◆ ◆ ————

Boyhood

I REMEMBER BUT LITTLE of Baltimore on the occasion of our arrival there. We remained but a day or two. The weather was hot and disagreeable to unacclimated comers such as we were, and we left as soon as transportation could be procured for ourselves and baggage. Here we parted with our particular friends the Galeys, who had been our neighbors at home and our companions on the voyage, Denny and Peggy, and their son Robert. Robert was of my age, and my playfellow on the ship; and twenty-five years afterward we were thrown together again on life's journey, and have been constant friends ever since. Mr. Galey obtained immediate employment from a widow lady of Maryland to superintend her plantation, and we separated, they for their Maryland home, and we for the backwoods of Western Pennsylvania—such it was then considered.

We had come to Baltimore in preference to New York or Philadelphia, because it was at that time regarded as of easier access from the sea; and as having the advantage of better roads and transportation across the mountains to the Western country. Pittsburgh dealt chiefly with Baltimore then. My father chartered a Conestoga wagon and team: such was the name given to the heavy four horse wagon with long bed and white canvas cover, used in those days for transportation of goods and emigrants between the seaports and the West.[1] The teamster was to carry our baggage and ourselves for a stipulated price from Baltimore to Greensburg, in Westmoreland county. It was a long, tedious trip, mostly over mud roads badly cut up—especially in the mountains, as wagons and teams were very numerous before the introduction of turnpikes or canals. Still, the October weather was fine; the

17

orchards were numerous, with the ripe, tempting fruit strewing the grass under the trees; and a generous welcome to help ourselves was always easily obtained from the owners. To my young mind the luxuriant vegetation and luscious fruit gave the country the appearance of a paradise. Another wagon and family was in company, destined for Pittsburgh. We slept by night in the wagon; and evening and morning prepared our food at a camp fire by the side of the road, as was then the custom of emigrants. On some occasions in the mountain regions the wagons halted over night where it suited best, regardless of an inn or other stopping place; the driver had a supply of oats on hand, and a horse trough lashed on the rear end of the wagon, and at such times would take his meals with us and spread his mattress under a tree.

We were three weeks on this tedious journey. At last our spirits began to rise as we approached Youngstown, which was near where our friends had settled; and there we received the glad news that my uncles Samuel and Archy were on the road only a mile or so ahead of us, constructing a section of the Greensburg and Stoystown turnpike.[2] It was in the evening; the wagon stopped in the town for the night, and we walked on and soon came in sight of the long board shanty usual for boarding and lodging laborers on public works. As we approached it we saw my grandmother milking a cow before the door, and my grandfather sitting on a log nearby smoking his pipe. When we came up and their attention was attracted, it was at first with bewildered amazement they beheld us, then in joyful recognition. What increased their surprise was that they had only a few days before received my mother's sad letter, which she had written in Derry when the physician had informed her that he had no hope for my father's recovery. Letters traveled slowly in those days, frequently much more so than passengers. Such had been the case in this instance; and at the time my father appeared on the scene his relatives in this country were mourning his death. He appeared to his father and mother, as they expressed it, as one risen from the dead. It was a happy reunion all round.

The Greensburg and Stoystown Turnpike Company had been chartered a year or so before by the legislature, and the construction of the road let to contractors. My uncles Samuel and Archy, impecunious but enterprising as are most young Scotch-Irishmen, had taken two miles of it near the present monastery.[3] Here they had built the shanty already mentioned for their men, and had lodging rooms in one part of it for themselves; and some thirty or forty laborers, and a proportionate number of carts were at work on the job. It was but five miles from the farm at the Crabtree where my grandfather and his family had settled; and he and my grandmother were in the habit of visiting their boys engaged in making turnpike every week or so with a fresh supply of provisions. It was thus we happened to meet them as we did. We had our goods and baggage unloaded there the next morning after our arrival, and dismissed the team; and, accompanied by grandfather and grandmother, we walked across to the Crabtree place. I have remembered that walk all my life. My parents and grandparents seemed so much to enjoy each other, it was like a walk for pleasure; distance and fatigue were forgotten in the joy of reunion and social conversation. We stopped in a grove of trees by the way and had luncheon. The spot is impressed on my memory ever since. I never pass it that I do not stop to recall the occasion and the parties to it.

Arrived at the old stone mansion house at the Crabtree, my grandfather's new home, now the residence of Captain Cook, there was another surprise and joyful meeting with my aunts Margaret and Annie, and uncle John. Here we remained until the following April. Grandfather and uncle John had not yet taken in their corn and pumpkins, or gathered the apple crop; and my enjoyment was great accompanying them in this work, and riding back and forth in the farm wagon. The only drawbacks to my pleasure were the burs and Spanish needles, which manifested a remarkable facility in getting into my clothes and hair when among the weeds. I was soon taught also to have a wholesome fear of snakes, as this land was not under the protection of either Moses or St. Patrick. These annoyances were new, as nothing of the kind existed in Ireland. Here also I met with Indian corn prepared as food in mush and otherwise, and well remember the sensation of a peculiarly wild flavor or taste which it produced at first, although I soon became very fond of it. Here also, towards the end of March, we encountered the first storm of thunder and lightning I had ever experienced. I had seen lightning and heard thunder in Ireland, but nothing to be compared with this. Atmospheric changes there are so frequent and moderate they do not produce such convulsions as take place here. It was late at night after a warm evening; my father had gone to Greensburg to negotiate with Mr. John Shaeffer, a merchant of that place, for a farm, and had not yet returned; which made the situation the more alarming, as it appeared to my mother he could not escape with his life, returning through the woods in such a conflict of the elements. The blinding glare of sharp lightning flashes through the uncurtained windows of our bed room, followed by peal after peal of deafening thunder, was a situation truly terrific to my mother and me, who were wholly unaccustomed to such a scene. While it lasted it produced a degree of alarm in both of us which I can never forget. The storm however, like many other threatened disasters, passed over without harm; my father soon returned and we were again happy. It had overtaken him on his way, but he obtained shelter in a vacant school house.

Vegetation in this country seemed to me wilder and more luxuriant, and the crops in some respects more abundant than in Ireland; and in this I think I was correct.

An incident which occurred during this stay at the Crabtree place serves to disclose a prominent feature of my grandfather's character. He was sociable and remarkably pleasant company, and his wit and humor were always attractive to young people whom he could hold in a continual state of mirth and enjoyment. In person he was tall, vigorous and active, but without any disposition to display or boast of his power in that respect. On the occasion in question we were all engaged in sugar making at the sugar camp on the Crabtree meadow; and uncle John, then about twenty, with some other boys had been trying their agility in a foot race from the one end to the other of the meadow, about a quarter of a mile. Uncle John, who much resembled his father in size and appearance, had won the race, and seemed rather elated over his speed of foot. Grandfather however lowered his pretensions by suggesting *he* could beat him over the same course, although then approaching close towards the age of sixty. They started, and grandfather did win by considerable odds.

My father had spent the winter searching for a farm; and had nearly closed for one at Elder's Ridge in Indiana county, but finally purchased from Mr. Shaeffer the John Hill tract on one of the tributary streams of Turtle creek, in Franklin township, about one mile north of the mills then belonging to Duff, now Stork.[4]

It was in the second week of April, 1819, that we journeyed from the Crabtree to our new home, twelve miles distant. This was in the style of a regular flitting. My father had procured a team, three cows, a wagon and some household furniture; and my grandfather and uncle John accompanying with their team, we set out over as bad roads as that part of Westmoreland county can produce—and in this line Westmoreland county is unsurpassed. When arrived at the top of Duff's hill we halted to rest the teams and take a view of what was to be our future home. There it lay in view, spread out before us; and the sight was not unattractive, surrounded by high hills and stretching up to the top of one of them which had been selected as the best location for an orchard. It presented a cozy and homelike appearance, with its pleasant stream and meadow and the alternation of woodland and clear field; and though in a remote and unfrequented part of the county, the cross roads at the lower end of it removed any undue appearance of solitude. The orchard on its hill top, though half a mile distant, presented a most inviting and cheerful appearance. It was surrounded on three sides by uncleared woodland; but all around the fence and between the apple trees had been set with peach trees which were in full bloom and attracted our special attention, presenting an almost unbroken surface of the bright and beautiful peach blossom.

We soon arrived and took possession. The house had been vacant for some time and was in a dilapidated condition, rather rough and primitive at best: a log cabin of two apartments, with one outside door and two windows; and wooden chimney constructed in the centre with stonelined fireplace, then plastered with clay mortar to the top, to protect the wooden structure from fire. The floor was of puncheons—logs split in two and hewed smooth on the flat side, and laid with that side up; the upper floor or loft composed of a few loose boards, and the roof of lap boards. It was a true specimen of the farm house of its day.

Uncle John returned the next morning, but grandfather remained for a week to assist in putting things in order about the house and barn. Hinges, bolts and latches were all constructed of wood. Besides, many other repairs were needed, and grandfather was very expert with the carpenter tools then in use, namely, the auger, hatchet and saw. Rough and uncouth as was this new residence, it is wonderful how much satisfaction and contentment it afforded us. It was the consummation of our anxious hopes to be again quietly settled in a home of our own. The cares and apprehensions of the great journey were now at an end, we had gained our object; were in possession of a farm seven times larger than the one we had left, which when paid for would be clear of rents and tithes and subject to but nominal taxes. The prospect before us now was greatly superior to that we had left behind; but there were hardships yet to come which we did not foresee. We were to experience hard times and encounter a mountain of labor and privation which few others would have overcome. It was only the remarkable industry and indomitable courage and energy of my parents which sustained them under the difficulties they were about to meet with, and carried them through to final success. This remained my home for fifteen years, during that period of life which is by far the most important to a young man—the period when he is a *"hobble-de-hoy,"* neither a man nor a boy; the veally stage of existence, when sentiments and habits are emerging out of chaos and crystallizing into form. It is the period when slight influences produce lasting effects for good or evil. Here were implanted in my nature those root principles of right and duty, tenacity of purpose, patient industry and perseverance in well doing which have accompanied me through life. It was during these fifteen years I underwent that long and anxious mental conflict of deciding the question of a vocation, or what I should follow for a living when I grew up.

Yet all the labors and cares of that period had their compensations. It was a happy home. No home can be unhappy to a boy with kind parents and good health. His work may be severe, with few indulgences and little time for play or recreation; but with good health and kindness at home, the exuberance of boyish spirits, and the anticipation of a better time coming will supply the necessary pleasure and enjoyment. I have no doubt the ragged newsboy derives more satisfaction from the few extra pennies of a good day's sale of his papers, and the encouragement of his poor mother, than the boy pampered and indulged in all the ease and luxury wealth can afford. Such is the compensatory rule of Providence, operating in our nature. It is with no unpleasant feeling, therefore, that I recur to that period; and it still recalls bright and happy memories, mingled with occasions of anxiety and alarm. When I recur to it now at a time over fifty years later, it seems of greater extent than nearly twice that length of time of my active business life.

The unlooked for labor and hardships which we were to encounter resulted from the memorable change of affairs which came on so unexpectedly in 1819–20; and which, as it played so important a part in our history and the history of the time, may as well be described in this connection.

The war of 1812, as every war of any magnitude has done before or since, had unduly stimulated business and inflated prices of all kinds. The war itself had ended in 1815, after the battle of New Orleans; but the impetus it had given to trade and business caused them to go on increasing in magnitude until they assumed proportions which neither the means at command nor the demand for products and improvements could sustain. In all such conditions the check post is reached at last; and on this occasion it was reached in 1819, just as the great collapse of 1873 was reached at a like interval after the war of the Rebellion.

After we were fairly housed at our new home, the next thing in order was to procure seed and farm utensils and put in a spring crop. In those days no manufactories of agricultural implements existed. The plow and wagon maker was as necessary a trade in every neighborhood as was the blacksmith; and it required both to supply the farmer with his tools. Hence haste was made to the wagon maker, and the remarkably long plow, with wooden mould-board of the period procured, and taken to the blacksmith, where it was shod with the old-fashioned iron plow share and cutter; and one field was plowed for corn and another for oats. It was important to have the crop in in due time. Prices of farm products were good and business of every kind prosperous. After the hand money was paid on the farm, and a moderate amount of farm stock and seed and utensils were purchased, the little stock of coin which had been so carefully stowed away and brought over in my mother's belt was nearly exhausted.

As illustrative of the existing inflation and subsequent depression of prices, I may mention that the price of wheat at the time was a dollar and a quarter; rye a dollar; oats seventy cents, and corn the same per bushel; and other farm products in like ratio. Wages of labor and goods of all kinds were equally high, and the price of lands no less inflated, at the time of our purchase. Farm lands in the suburbs of Pittsburgh were selling at one thousand dollars per acre, and vacant town lots on Fourth street, between Wood and Smithfield, at two thousand dollars each, as the records of deeds show.[5] When my father had his land prepared for the seed he applied for it to Jacob Kline, a wealthy German farmer. Mr. Kline expressed himself disposed to be generous and obliging to his new neighbor. He had about one thousand bushels of oats in his granary which he was holding for seventy-five cents per bushel, but would let my father have the small quantity he needed for seed at sixty-five, as a favor: declaring at the same time that he would hold the residue until he got seventy-five, or shovel it into the dunghill. And singularly enough as it turned out, Mr. Kline kept his word: for oats and everything else soon afterwards declined all at once so much so that the crop, the seed of which cost sixty-five cents, when harvested and threshed and carried to market in the following winter was sold for twelve cents per bushel; and Mr. Kline's stock on hand, after being kept for two years in confident expectation of a change of times and a return of old prices, was attacked by an insect of some kind and the substance of the grain eaten out to such an extent that it had actually to be shoveled into the dunghill. This collapse did not affect oats alone, but everything else in the same proportion. As I remember and compare it with the collapse of 1873 in which I had greater interests at stake, I find a great similarity between the causes and effects of both. Prior to 1819 the construction of turnpike roads had been extensively engaged in. Blast furnaces and iron forges were dotted all along the western foot of the mountains; and the transportation of metal and goods back and forth between them and Pittsburgh was lively. Money, especially paper money, was abundant; every county town had its bank of issue. But even this did not supply the demand; and nearly every furnace and turnpike company and corporation of any kind issued their own notes, which were called "shinplasters," but passed as current as the best. Such inflation of the currency gave further impetus to new projects, and only added fuel to the flame which was consuming the vitality of legitimate business pursuits. The end came at last, the bubble burst, and all went down with a crash. No bank or banker outside of the city withstood the shock; and but two banks withstood it there. The shinplasters disappeared with the parties who had issued them. We had no more furnace money, no more of "Blair's Gap" or any other turnpike money; and the spread eagle on the ample notes of the Westmoreland Bank of Greensburg, Pennsylvania, disappeared. All the merchants, manufacturers and dealers in Pittsburgh, with the exception of about a dozen, went under and took the benefit of the insolvent laws; and it was nearly ten years before business and prices began perceptibly to recuperate.

And since then I have lived to see several crashes of the same kind, especially that of 1873, over fifty years afterwards, resulting from the same cause—excessive extension of credit and consequent expansion of values. Shinplasters and wildcat bank money had been prohibited; but in the inflation which preceded the collapse of 1873 "accommodation paper" had taken their place, and produced the same effect. Public and private banks of loan and deposit had accumulated. A banking house was established in nearly every ward of the cities, and in nearly every town and village throughout the State: a circumstance which is regarded by political economists as a bad omen for the future of trade. High rates of interest on general and special deposits drew money to the banks which was loaned out to unsafe enterprises on accommodation paper. The impetus given to business of all kinds by the war of the Rebellion went on increasing under this stimulus for some years unimpaired, just as it had done in the war of 1812. The vitals of trade were destroyed by the canker worm of credit; bloated inflation spread and increased until the decayed carcass dropped dead. The effect of this collapse in 1873 was as disastrous as that of 1819; but owing to the greater extent and resources of the country was not of as long duration. Both occasions have been commonly referred to as "panics"; but a panic is only the scare consequent upon the collapse of credit which in each case, and in all similar conditions, becomes inevitable. After the collapse of 1819, my father's farm was not worth half the deferred payments that remained against it; and the prospect of making those payments was, to all appearance, hopeless.

Real estate fell to zero everywhere; the lots on Fourth street already mentioned fell from two thousand to four hundred. The square between Diamond street and Fifth avenue, opposite the Howard block on Smithfield street, then owned by David Pride, only brought four hundred dollars at Sheriff's sale, and was purchased by Thomas Liggett, in whose family it still remains. During the preceding inflation many lots on Market street between the Market House and the Monongahela river had been leased by Samuel Ewalt and others, on perpetual lease, with rents reserved equal to six per cent. interest on what was then the value of the lot, and the lessees had built substantial brick business houses upon them; but after the collapse they could not be let for half the ground rent, and the lessees in most instances abandoned them, the ground rent landlords taking possession and renting them when and for what they could.[6] Any prospect of an increased value enabling the lessee to reclaim under his lease, appeared so improbable that few of the ground rent landlords cared to go to the expense, or took the precaution, to extinguish the lessee's title by judicial sale; and the consequence was that when the value did increase, some fifteen years afterwards, to such an extent as to attract the attention of lessees or their heirs, numbers of suits were entered, calling on the landlords to account for the rents theretofore received, and asking a restoration of the property on being paid the balance of rent in arrear. These suits were mostly successful. Some cases of this kind were in controversy as late as the time of my admission to the bar, in 1840.

So, too, farm lands in the suburbs which had been held before at one thousand, fell to one hundred. A fifteen-acre lot with a good brick mansion house on it, and improved with a fine orchard and shrubbery of all kinds, owned and occupied by Mr. Miltenberger, a wealthy ironmaster, until the collapse, was offered to my father for fifteen hundred dollars. It included the ground where the Fifth avenue Market House now stands, and extended from Fifth avenue, then called the Fourth street road, to the Bluff above the Monongahela river. The effect on real estate was in all respects similar to that in 1873, when lots at the East End selling readily at twelve hundred to eighteen hundred dollars in 1872, fell to prices ranging from two to six hundred, and sales could seldom be made at that.

It was in this season of depression my parents had to meet the deferred payments on their farm. I include both, because they showed equal interest and worked together with equally untiring energy, industry and perseverance. They had put their money into the land which, though small in amount, was their all, and looked on the place as their home. No matter how great the difficulties or discouraging the prospect, they entertained no thought of giving up the struggle. To apply for an extension of time on the payments was useless, because the collapse had broken up Shaeffer, the party from whom they purchased, and his estate was in the hands of the law. Each *gale*, as it was called, had to be met strictly on the day it was due, in each and every year. A particular clause in the contract rendered payment on the day important; it stipulated for payment on the day appointed, "in money and bags and oats at market prices." If therefore the day passed without payment or a tender, the stipulation as to trade would be lost, and the whole have to be paid in money. This was of moment to us because, whilst money was an impossibility, bags and oats still retained market prices, however low. Bags were a particular article of merchandise in much demand, and well known to the trade of those days. They were extensively used for the package of grain and salt and other commodities requiring transportation. Flax was used in their construction instead of hemp; and an acre or so of flax was then raised on almost every farm and manufactured by the females of the family into table and bed linen, towels and shirting, besides being put to numerous other uses. It was homespun and coarse, but durable; and the tow of the flax was usually converted into bagging and made into bags of the regulation size, containing three bushels each. For this flax industry nearly every farm house had a loom and spinning wheels; and it was this industry that saved us the forfeiture of our land. During the four years after the panic in which deferred payments were to be made, wheat averaged forty cents per bushel, rye thirty-three, corn twenty-five, and oats twelve cents; butter six to ten cents per pound, eggs six cents per dozen, and good large chickens twelve cents per pair. But the average market price of bags was fifty cents; and on the first day of each April two pack horses went to Greensburg loaded with several bales of bags and a few bushels of oats. My father was a strict constructionist of his contract, and supposed payments had to be made in all the articles named; hence he had money and bags and oats, but the great preponderance was in bags.

The advantage lay in this: money had disappeared, and barter was the order of the day, and regulated the market price. Bags averaged fifty cents when thirty could not have been obtained in cash. A bank note was rarely seen in our neighborhood, unless in the hands of a stranger; and the few coins in circulation were of the kind presenting the old-fashioned Spanish pillars on their face.

My parents worked on and on incessantly through all the stress of those hard times, without flagging in their exertions or defaulting on a payment—manifesting our family trait of indomitable perseverance, and not asking credit nor going into debt for anything they could possibly do without, and then only for what they could certainly pay for on the day appointed. Their labor was incessant: farm work during the day, and spinning and weaving at night. And in these four busy years I was no idle spectator myself. A thousand things in the farm work and linen and bag making could be done by a boy of my age, and resort to my assistance was not neglected. Pleasure and recreation had small scope in the family, but the more restricted in opportunity the more intense it was in quality when obtained. Sundays afforded regularly recurring and highly enjoyed rest and recuperation to all. With me other occasions of recreation were extremely rare. When I think of our family relations and recall to memory the thoughts, feelings and motives of action of those days, I am inclined to believe it would be better for society if young people were more generally brought up under similar hardships and restraints. It produces a degree of energy, industry, determination, self-reliance and self-denial which can hardly be otherwise obtained. The boy acquires an interest and assumes a responsibility in the success of family affairs, and forms a closer intimacy with his parents. At meals or by the fireside, or in other intervals of leisure with my parents, we would hold free intercourse and discuss the conditions of the stock or plans of farm work and future prospects with eager gratification. In this way I was led to assume cares and enter into the spirit of our affairs and feel a zeal for their success which would not have been inspired if I had been treated with the indifference and disregard which those boys are usually subjected to whose services are not in demand. I am sure that the consideration thus shown me, and the trust and confidence thus placed in me produced a degree of earnest thought and purpose at the time unattainable under other conditions, and to which I have been much indebted for success in after years.

I have often noticed the same results since in the families of farmers and gardeners in straitened circumstances: all the members of the family, old and young, working together and discussing and expressing their opinions on family affairs and interests. Talk to the six year old boy, and he tells you of the condition of *our* crops, *our* cattle, the strength and value of *our* team, and what *we* are going to do next, with as much pride and confidence as if he was an equal partner in the concern.

As a general rule parents, especially such as are in easy circumstances or engaged in extensive enterprises, hold their children at too great a distance from them. They underrate their capacity for comprehension and judgment, and do not admit them close enough in their confidence. The boy readily perceives and sympathizes with his father in his cares and troubles and plans and projects. This feeling must be encouraged by kindness and confidence, to make him feel that he is regarded as of sufficient importance to be relied on. Under this treatment he seldom fails to appreciate the regard shown for him, or to fulfill the parents' hopes. His pride and self esteem sustain him in the line of duty; and he can be influenced and confirmed in the way of well doing better by this than by any other method that I have ever observed. Make your child a partner in your joys and sorrows, your hopes and fears; impart your plans and purposes; stand not on your dignity, but let yourself down to his capacity, if need be, and show your trust in him. You will be surprised to find how much a five or ten year old boy can understand of the ways of men, and how readily he will enter into your views. Your feelings will attach him, and you will be gratified at the strength of character and good resolution you will inspire in him by such treatment. It produces a bond of affection between you that is not easily broken, and affords you an opportunity of insight into your child's nature which is not otherwise attainable. I experienced the benefit of such training myself, and applied it in raising my own family with the most satisfactory results. Unfortunately, however, there are some children of such low and ignoble natures that kindness is wasted on them; but these are exceptions, and in most cases of the kind force or severity will be found equally as ineffectual. But I must resume my narrative.

Those years of all work and no play were not attended with such hardships and discomforts as may be imagined. If periods of pleasure and relaxation were few, they were the more enjoyable. Family relations so near and dear, with all the members intently engaged in one common purpose, was itself an abundant source of happiness. The industrious pursuit of worthy objects contains pleasure in itself. But these four years of imperative payments had their ending at last, and the time came when we could breathe more freely and look to the future with greater confidence.

Being out of debt, attention was turned to improvements. Scotch-Irish instinct never feels safe without a competence laid up for old age or misfortune. This desire was now measurably gratified, but the habit of industry and thrift was not extinguished. The farm needed improvement by new buildings and otherwise. Whilst our log cabin was moderately comfortable, we longed for something better. Our barn was a like primitive structure, in a dilapidated condition; and the fences were bad and overgrown with brushwood to be grubbed out. Besides this, in many nooks and corners in the fields and meadow were thickets of briers and brambles. All these needed labor. Our first attention was given to building. The fashionable farm house of the period was the square log, two-story shingle-roof dwelling, with one-story kitchen at the rear or end. With the aid of a chopper and hewer we soon had the materials for such a building on the ground. My department was to drag the logs with the team from the woods where they were dressed to the place where the building was to be erected; and after its erection to haul the stone from the fields, where they had been piled up in clearing the ground for the plow, to the new house for the chimneys which my father built with his own hands. And in less than a year we had as fine a six-roomed dwelling as the best of our neighbors, and that fall and winter as good a square log double barn as was to be seen thereabouts. And in less than seven years from the time of our possession we had the farm in first rate order and were beginning to accumulate money.

But as I was now twelve years of age, I may consider my boyhood ended.

Chapter III

━━━ ◆ • ◆ ━━━

Material Progress

MY PARENTS WERE of a class who never wearied in well doing; and no sooner had they the farm paid for and improved than they began to look out for new acquisitions. Money was scarce, but very little of it went far in the purchase of land at that time. Business had not recovered from the great collapse, and land was cheap. We had the finest apple and peach orchard in the neighborhood, but no market for either.

Every farmer of consequence had his own distillery to convert his rye into whiskey. There were no excise laws, and no tax on whiskey. The Whiskey Insurrection[1] had frightened the politician from interfering with the farmer's interests in that direction. Rye was the crop best suited to the quality of the land in our section. Our rye and other grain products of the farm were not extensive, but my father conceived the idea of converting his surplus apple and peach crop into whiskey. The cause of so much distilling in the country at the time was the lack of transportation. The crop could be transported at least cost when reduced to spirits. It must be recollected we had neither canal nor railroad, and wretchedly bad turnpikes; so it was my father improvised a distillery.

Two rocks projected on the opposite sides of the ravine above our spring and spring house, and not forty feet apart at the top. It was an easy matter to project poles enough from the one to the other to support a roof. On these poles a straw roof was placed, and by enclosing the two sides a convenient still house was produced, with little labor and no cost. Here a second-hand still and the necessary vessels for distilling purposes were provided, and the ripe apples and peaches, as they dropped from the trees, were drawn down in sled loads from the orchard on the hill a short distance above. Before this many hundreds of bushels of peaches had rotted under the trees every year, but now all were utilized. This was part of our employment every season from 1821 to 1824; and my share in it, gathering the apple and peach crops from the ground, was part of my hardest labor.

There was something peculiar about the apple and peach crops of those times: a failure of either was unusual, and neither blight nor disease affected the trees. Those peach trees grew and flourished and bore crops for upwards of twenty years without apparent exhaustion, and most of the apple trees are in good condition yet. Indeed, three of the peach trees were still alive when I was there in 1876. In the darkness of color and roughness of the bark they rather resembled old plum trees. I attribute the fruitfulness and longevity of this orchard to its peculiar location and the freshness of the ground when it was planted. The ground was newly cleared for it, and the location exceptionally good— a rich, dry, stony hilltop. Our distillery was operated at suitable times, as crops demanded; and the work on the canal ten miles distant, which commenced soon afterwards, afforded a ready market for the peach and apple brandy.[2] And it was not long till money accumulated for the purchase of another farm.

Accordingly, in 1826 the M'Closky farm was purchased, distant about a mile and a half from the homestead. To farm this under our own supervision brought additional labor. I was put to the plow in my twelfth year, and could soon handle it with facility although with much effort and fatigue. Afterwards for some years I did the home plowing as well as that of the M'Closky farm, and a good deal of plowing on farms in the neighborhood besides, where we were in the habit of taking fields on shares from such of our neighbors as had them to spare or were without labor to cultivate them. It was whilst thus engaged in plowing I read the most of Shakespeare's plays. They had come to me separately in pamphlet form among some books and papers sent by my uncle Thomas, and were in convenient shape to carry in the pocket to read whilst the horses rested or during the recess for dinner.

I never took to Shakespeare, however, so warmly as to Pope and Burns and Goldsmith, and the other English and Scotch poets. The fine sentiments of Shakespeare seemed to cost too much sifting among the quarrels of kings and vulgar intrigues of their flunkies, and the obsolete manners of a rude age.

It was about my fourteenth year, at a neighbor's house, when plowing a field we had taken on his farm for buckwheat, that I happened upon a dilapidated copy of the autobiography of Dr. Franklin. It delighted me with a wider view of life and inspired me with new ambition—turned my thoughts into new channels. I had not before imagined any other course of life superior to farming, but the reading of Franklin's life led me to question this view. For so poor and friendless a boy to be able to become a merchant or a professional man had before seemed an impossibility; but here was Franklin, poorer than myself, who by industry, thrift and frugality had become learned and wise, and elevated to wealth and fame. The maxims of "poor Richard" exactly suited my sentiments. I read the book again and again, and wondered if I might not do something in the same line by similar means. I had will and energy equal to the occasion, and could exercise the same degree of industry and perseverance, and felt no misgiving except on the score of talent. But a want in this respect I supposed might only limit my field of operations, and I might well spare a vast amount of Franklin's success and still be fully compensated for the effort. I soon had an electric machine constructed of big-bellied bottles and glass fruit jars, which in its effects astonished the neighbors. But I never carried my researches in that direction any further, concluding that other and more useful practical branches of knowledge would suit my purposes better. After that I was more industrious when at school, and more constant than ever in reading and study during leisure hours. I regard the reading of Franklin's Autobiography as the turning point of my life.

We were now in the way of material progress. Industry and thrift, with reasonable judgment to guide, will always prosper. My father's next purchase was a house and lot in Newlansburg, and another in New Salem, neither of much value but still an acquisition. His next purchase, in 1831, was the Moore farm, across the turnpike opposite my uncle Archy's place, about half way between our home farm and New Salem. This new acquisition was without buildings, and it fell to my lot to have most to do with their erection.

But for some two or three years before this my mind had been gradually undergoing a change. My heart was becoming alienated from farm work. The more I read and the more I saw I was the more convinced that I might do better, and that in both mind and body I was better fitted for some other occupation or pursuit. I never was robust and able-bodied to such a degree as renders heavy farm work easy or agreeable; and the more I read the more I wanted to know. And all this time my uncle of Philadelphia was plying me with remittances of books and papers of the most miscellaneous variety on all imaginable subjects, such as he picked up from time to time at book auctions in the city. From this source fuel was being constantly added to the flame of my ambition to rise above the condition of a common farmer. My mother had been from the beginning let into the secret of my new aspirations, and shared my hopes and fears. She was my most confidential adviser at all times. Her moderate counsels neither inflated my hopes nor depressed my spirits, but were always prudent and wise, encouraging me when despondent by promising me her assistance in every way she could, if I concluded on attempting a college education: because that was regarded by both of us as necessary to a professional or literary life. I had no capital to become a merchant or to enter upon any other such business, and the pursuit of knowledge was more in accord with my desires; and my mother was incited by a lurking hope that if I inclined to learning I would eventually enter the ministry. I did not for some time disclose my wishes to my father. I knew they would displease him, and I could expect no encouragement from him. He looked upon farming as the best, safest, most worthy and independent of all the occupations of men; and any one who forsook it for something else was regarded as led astray by folly and nonsense.

We were now on the flood tide of prosperity, or what he regarded as such. His pride and expectation was to have a farm well stocked to give me at the proper time; and I knew that to propose a different course would appear to him as underrating his plans and kind intentions, and would meet with the most strenuous opposition. For me to abandon the honest and noble pursuit of an independent farmer, and become a doctor or teacher or miserably dependent preacher; or what was in his eyes worst of all, to enter the tricky, dishonest profession of the law, was a proposition which seemed to him too preposterous to contemplate. I knew that nothing could induce him to acquiesce in such a course. Hence I was backward in breaking the matter to him; and when I did my worst fears were realized. He could not be reconciled to it, and would not entertain the subject. It was grievous to me to give him so much evident annoyance; but the resolution he came to was, that if I could not continue a respectable, industrious young man, but would abandon my present course of well doing to run after some delusion of fancy, he would be no party to such folly. If I took that course it would be without his assistance. Then if I failed, which he regarded as certain, there would be something for me to fall back on so long as he was possessed of property or means; whereas if he helped me now in a career of folly or profligacy, my share in his property would be spent and I would end my days in poverty. Such was his course of reasoning; which did not annoy me so much on account of the means it deprived me of in my project as it did on account of the pain and disappointment it gave him. His firmness staggered my resolution; and for a year or so I was wavering and undecided, almost indeed won over to his side. Farming has many attractions. I understood it well, and was neither indolent nor lazy; and any one who understands his business thoroughly is apt to take a delight in it.

I therefore worked on, pleased in the growth of crops and improved methods of cultivation, and trying to discover new spheres of interest and profit in that line. But as reading was kept up at every spare interval, the longing desire for some different pursuit of a more intellectual character could never be got rid of. I had now reached a time of life when a want for the society and companionship of other young men of like age begins to be felt; and my habit of reading had created a taste which unfitted me for enjoying the company of those around me. They were for the most part rude and coarse, though clever and good natured, and wholly uncultivated. With them my literary aspirations found no sympathy; which brings me to another subject.

Chapter IV

Our Neighbors

IT IS IN PLACE NOW to advert to our neighbors. There were three or four families of Scotch-Irish stock like ourselves, but with the exception of one old lady they had all been born in this country. All the rest were of German descent, known as Pennsylvania Dutch.[1] These Dutch were our nearest neighbors, and by far the most numerous throughout that district. As a general rule they were good farmers in comfortable circumstances, but without the ambition or energy to better their condition which inspired my parents. The English element of the neighborhood, as it was known, when not spurred by necessity for the most part possessed as little push or ambition as the Dutch. No kinder, cleverer or more obliging neighbors than these Dutch people could be desired. Their old women rivaled each other in medical skill in the virtues of all manner of roots, herbs, barks and gums. Their garrets were laboratories well provided with bunches of these remedies; and every ailment which flesh is heir to found a simple cure and attentive doctress free of charge. The nearest professional doctors were Postlewaite of Greensburg, and Marchand of Jacksonville, equally too far off and expensive to be called in unless in the case of such a calamity as the cutting of an artery or the bite of a mad dog. Hydrophobia was Marchand's specialty. Minor surgical operations, such as the drawing of a tooth or setting of a broken limb, were promptly attended to free of charge, by Major Ament, our blacksmith;[2] and births only required the attention of the nearest midwife, a functionary who could be improvised of almost any elderly lady in the neighborhood. Then all our neighbors were kind hearted and obliging. If any one fell short of getting his farm work done in season, as putting in the seed or harvesting the crop at the proper time, they were always ready to collect together and help him out of the difficulty, even if the party was himself to blame: as I remember to have happened on one occasion, when a neighbor who was subject to the habit, got on a protracted drunk when he ought to have been harvesting his wheat. To save his crops the neighbors, my father among the rest, collected and cut it and placed it in shuck, to be housed when he got sober.

For the social virtues, and all the qualities which go to make up the good citizen and kind neighbor, the Dutch were all that could be desired. There were two points in their character, however, wherein they did not altogether come up to the Scotch-Irish standard of morality—sexual intercourse and religious observances, and on account of this my parents did not approve of close social intimacy with them. Although not as a general rule immoral or licentious, the sentiments of many of them regarding sexual intercourse were rather loose, and organized religious worship could hardly be said to exist.

Their ancestors were German Lutheran or German Reformed, but the distinction had been lost. Both sects had a representation in the county at an early day. The Rev. Michael John Steck had come to the country in 1792, and preached at six different points, the chief of which was Greensburg, till 1819. Then his son, Rev. John Michael Steck, took his place, and continued preaching till 1848. For the German Reformed, Rev. Mr. Weber officiated prior to 1820, and after him Rev. Nicholas Hacke preached from 1820 till 1872, officiating in numerous congregations throughout the county, with headquarters at Greensburg. The visits of any of these pastors to the Manor Meeting House, the station nearest our neighborhood, were so far apart that the times of meeting were usually forgotten, and church-going among our Dutch neighbors had nearly become obsolete when Peter Hill, our nearest neighbor and a leader among them, commenced its revival shortly before we left the place.

The history of religion in the county, as between the Dutch and English at that time showed a marked difference. Indifference as to creeds and dogmas and formal exercises characterized the Dutch. This is shown by their long continued satisfaction with their pastors, the weakness of age never being regarded as a disqualification for the pulpit, and in one instance the office remaining in the same family for two generations. Whilst with the English or Scotch-Irish element, a con-

stant critical inspection into the ability and performances and sentiments and opinions of their pastors was always in progress, resulting in
church disputes and frequent changes. In the Dutch mind there was
more repose and contentment; in the English more earnestness and
activity. As a consequence, it may be inferred the English possessed
more general intelligence. The old and wise men among our Dutch
neighbors possessed abiding confidence in the folk-lore of their ancestors. They would admit that the active practice of witchcraft had generally ceased, but most of them claimed having had, at one time or
another, personal experience of its effects.

Many of them had in their youth been great hunters; even in our
day, Peter Hill and other old Germans were accustomed to make their
annual winter excursion into the then wilderness of Clarion and Forest
counties, and would each bring home a sled load of venison. And they
all expressed undoubting belief that no matter how unerring the aim,
if some one with an evil eye or possessed of the power of sorcery
should happen to put a spell on their gun, no game could be killed
until the spell was taken off. This was done by marking a human figure
on a tree to represent the witch, and shooting a silver bullet into it with
the gun supposed to be affected. The bullet was usually the smallest silver coin battered into the proper shape. Old Philip Drum and our
neighbor Peter, who were great hunters, usually took the precaution of
ridding their guns of these sorceries before setting out on the hunt;
taking it for granted that if the gun was not affected the purification
would do no harm.

They also had equal faith in a right time and a wrong time in the
moon for the performance of most farm labors. They professed to
know of their own knowledge that if the best spring well was cleaned
out in the decline of the moon, it would certainly go dry. The signs of
the Zodiac in the Dutch almanac afforded an indispensable guide for
farm work; because if hogs were slaughtered in the wrong sign every
housewife knew the bacon would decrease and not increase as it
should, in the process of cooking; and a fence built in the wrong sign
would rot sooner than it would otherwise have done. Besides, to plant
potatoes or spread manure on the land except in the right sign was
absolute folly. Our neighbors generally entertained these beliefs and
only pitied the presumptuous ignorance of such as ourselves who disregarded them. Science had not as yet greatly disturbed their thoughts,

but Major Ament had some pride of knowledge in that direction, and liked to discuss such matters with those whose intelligence he respected; and as I had acquired some reputation for the reading of books, he invariably introduced the subject of the earth's motion whenever I went to his shop or took a grist to his mill. We differed decidedly as to whether or not the earth turned upside down. That it did so was a proposition too absurdly preposterous for the Major to entertain. It could only be believed by one who did not know the difference between standing on his head or his heels, as evidently must be the case once a day if the earth turned clear over. He held to the rational theory as he regarded it, that the earth was round in the manner of his millstone, with the flat side up, and turned on its axis just as the millstone turned on the spindle; and the people existed on the upper surface and were whirled around, always retaining an erect posture. He allowed the attraction of gravitation was a good thing to keep them from flying off the earth at a tangent; but gravitation would never account for either man or woman not discovering the fact of being turned heels upward. This was to the Major a self-evident and unanswerable argument.

With like scope of comprehension at the time gas was first spoken of as a lighting agency, one of our German neighbors happened to be in Pittsburgh and hearing some men conversing on the subject at the place where he stopped he inquired into the nature and quality of gas, and how it could produce light from pipes in the ground. He was informed that gas was simply the light of the sun stored up in the coal, and after being extracted from it in a volatile form was carried through the town in pipes, wherever required. He was highly indignant that townsmen should regard country people so verdant as to believe such stuff; and the company to whom he related the circumstance fully agreed with him in the shallow conceitedness of townsmen underrating the intelligence of country people. I was present at the gathering where he related it, and much hilarity was indulged in at the absurdity of the idea of bottling up sunshine for lighting purposes.

As religious services were unattainable most of the time to our Dutch neighbors, they spent their Sundays in rest and recreation, congregating at each others' houses, the old people smoking their pipes and discussing the general gossip of the neighborhood; whilst the young people in groups romped on the lawn or made excursions into the orchards, or went for chestnuts or wild grapes into the woodlands. Even after our neighbor Peter had effected an embryo church organization amongst them it did not mend matters much as regarded Sunday observance. But the following extract from a former publication of mine will explain the religious situation of the time more particularly:

"*The religious ideas and habits, over fifty years ago, in that part of Westmoreland county (Franklin township), where I was raised.*

"Rev. Father Wynal, of the Lutheran persuasion, was nursing an embryo congregation among the Germans. He resided near Saltsburg, in Indiana county, but came over and preached to them every fourth Sunday, holding the services in the dwelling of our nearest neighbor, Peter Hill. The congregation has since developed into that now worshiping in a comfortable brick edifice known as Hill's Church, with Mr. Snyder as pastor. Well, at the time to which I refer, when Mr. Wynal was the pastor, and old Peter Hill, as honest a man and good a neighbor as need be, was its contributor, treasurer, trustee and entire session, the Sunday on which *preaching was to be* at Peter's was regarded as a holiday by the surrounding German population. They gathered from all quarters. The services lasted from nine till twelve A.M., when Peter's wife, Hetty, née Geiger (for he was married twice, and had in all twenty-five children), with the assistance of her neighbor women would have an ample dinner cooked, which was not only free but welcome to all who had *come to meeting*. The dinner being over, the younger men would spend the afternoon in games of *corner* ball and pitching quoits on the green in front of the house, whilst the pastor and Peter and the old men sat smoking their pipes on the porch, looking on at the sport with marked satisfaction. Evidently, it occurred to neither pastor nor people that there was anything wrong or sinful in the performance. Times change, however, and religious observances as well as other habits change according to the prevailing fashion; for the same congregation would not now spend Sunday afternoon in that way.

"At the same time, we of Scotch Presbyterian proclivities had a similar gathering every third Sunday at Duff's Tent. Duff's Tent was a place in the woods with benches made of split logs, and an eight by ten, box-shaped structure boarded up and roofed, for a pulpit, and for a pastor we had the Rev. Hugh Kirkland, a fresh graduate from the theological school of Glasgow, Scotland, and zealous in the strictest ideas of the Scotch Kirk. He regarded the sanctity of Rouse's Version of David's Psalms, and the enormity of Sabbath breaking as of vital importance, and he preached on few topics except 'To prove the Roman Catholic Church to be the Antichrist and whore of Babylon;' or 'The desecration of the Sabbath by the Lutherans;' or 'The damnable heresies of the Methodists in denying the doctrines of innate depravity and predestination, and persisting in singing the carnal songs of Watt instead of the Psalms of David.' This kind of preaching, however, did not bring forth good fruit, even in the Scotch Presbyterian soil in which it was sown. My father allowed the Methodists the use of a vacant house on his place to hold their meetings on one or two occasions, and several of the Kirkland flock attended a Methodist meeting to hear the Rev. Bascomb, a celebrated preacher of the time. Mr. Humes, one of them, joined in singing the Methodist hymns. This Rev. Kirkland regarded as an indignity to his teaching, and in his next sermon took occasion to animadvert severely on the conduct of those who, after being washed from their sins had, like the sow, again betaken themselves to wallowing in the mire. He was too pointed in his remarks to leave room for doubt as to whom they applied, and this raised a row; but the straw that broke the camel's back was the starting of a Sabbath school. George and Michael Haymaker and some other young people of his flock undertook to open a Sabbath school in the school house at Newlansburg, near by. This was too great a sacrilege for the good man to bear! He could not brook the desecration of the Sabbath day by such worldly employment as school teaching, and as a majority of his flock inclined to favor the Sabbath school, he shook the dust from his feet and departed."

The Scotch-Irish and other English speaking residents of the neighborhood surpassed the Germans in respect for religious worship and social purity. Hence, though few in numbers, much more attention was given by them to the maintenance of religious ordinances. Soon after our arrival in the neighborhood a log meeting house was erected as a substitute for Duff's Tent in the woods, and served the purpose until the congregation was absorbed into other organizations in the neighboring villages.

Besides its religious peculiarities our neighborhood was not destitute of legendary history. It had been the haunt of bears and wolves whose dens in the rocks could yet be pointed out. One of these was in the ravine immediately below the garden fence of the log cabin we first occupied. It extended into a rocky point at the foot of the garden, on which was located a primitive graveyard of the early settlers of the neighborhood. Such burying places, irrespective of churches or religious sects, were scattered over the country. After places for religious worship were located, these were abandoned. Such was the one in a little grove at the foot of our garden, affording the last resting place of some twenty of the earliest settlers, old and young. The graves were entirely neglected until in the year 1884, when the descendants of some of these ancestors, although living in a distant county, had the place enclosed by a substantial fence. A notable circumstance about it was the longevity of a common rosebush. It was planted in 1817, at the head of a grave of a young woman, a daughter of the first settler, John Hill, and was still in good condition bearing its annual crop of flowers commemorating the life it represented, when the place was enclosed in 1884. It had survived the ravages of cattle and other adversities for sixty-seven years, and was still in a healthy condition. Under this secluded spot was the bears' cave, far below the resting place of the dead, however. It is now nearly filled, and its entrance closed with rubbish. On the other side of the ravine a few paces further up was our spring, elevated on a shelf of the rock, affording a perennial fountain of clear, pure water from which we drew our household supplies. The whole ravine and its borders were covered with brushwood—prominent in which was the luscious June berry and wild plum; and thickly inhabited by different species of wild bird: affording a quite romantic retreat of a Sunday for reading and reflection.

But the early settlers had suffered most from a more dangerous foe than bears or wolves—the wild Indian. The old people yet living when we came there were never tired of relating the local horrors of the settlement: how certain families were massacred and burned in their cabins; how at one time when the Indians had come suddenly upon the settlement and the children were at school, the teacher dismissed them to hide in the woods and thickets as best they could, and fled to take his chances for life or death under similar conditions. They were scarcely in their hiding places before the savage yell was heard resounding through the woods, and the school house was in flames. And old Mrs. Duff would relate how Providence interposed to save the lives of her and her husband and family on another occasion by moving them one Sunday afternoon to take a walk over the hill to the corn field; where they had scarcely arrived ere they heard the savage war-whoop, and soon saw the smoke of their burning cabin from their place of concealment in the tall corn.

Then there was the murder of the entire Klingensmith family near Grapeville, where a father, mother and five children were slaughtered and a sixth child, a boy, carried off prisoner. He remained with the Indians for twenty years, when he returned to the neighborhood but had outgrown his identity, and being unknown and unrecognizable was unable to recover the farm which his father had owned. In disgust he returned to the Indians, married a squaw and was never heard of afterwards. Then there was the battle of Bushy Run, and the burning of Hannastown with all its horrors, to be talked over.[3] Such incidents formed an exhaustless source of conversation among the old people; but it is all now forgotten. Singularly enough, many of these old people were descendants of those who had escaped from similar atrocities in the massacres in Ulster by the native Irish, in 1641.

Such were our good, kind neighbors and their legends. In the half century which has elapsed since my residence among them they have all dropped out, except a very few who were then mere children. Emigration and death soon make great changes in local population. I have been in the habit of revisiting this old tramping ground of my childhood at intervals ever since, and on each successive occasion found those who recognized me becoming fewer and fewer, till at last no more remain who knew me when a boy. The rocks and glens, the meadows and streams, and such of the buildings and other landmarks as remain are still my friends and acquaintances, or seem to me so when I visit them; and appear as if they remembered and were glad to welcome me. Every object revives some thoughts of the past; some hopes or fears, or plans for future execution which possessed me long ago in the same locality. Association of ideas has a wonderful tenacity. It interests me now on such visits, when alone with these silent friends, to run over in memory the history of the plans and projects and companions associated with them in boyhood. Many, indeed most of the

air castles I indulged in building at that early date have been successfully completed; and whilst the enjoyment anticipated from them at
the time has not been altogether disappointed, yet it is curious to compare the difference between the anticipation and realization. As between Pessimist and Optimist philosophy, I unhesitatingly adopt the
doctrine of the latter, that life is worth living. But neither of these doctrines is true in the extreme: the middle course—Meliorism—is the
truest and best.

Chapter v

---◆ ● ◄---

First Visit to the City

IT WAS IN 1823. I was then nine years of age,[1] and had been
looking forward with eagerness for an opportunity to visit the city and
see the wonders I had heard related of it. Among them was a steam
grist mill reported to be in operation at Negleystown, afterwards called
East Liberty, and now the East End. This wonderful curiosity, as it was
regarded, I could take in on the way. Early in the spring my father had
consented to my going between the first and second corn hoeings; and
when the long looked for time finally arrived, preparation had been
made for the expense of the journey by the sale of a bag of rye, which I
was allowed to transport on a pack-horse to Murraysville and sell for
the highest price I could get. The price obtained was thirty-three cents
per bushel. It was paid in silver, ninety-nine cents, and appeared in my
eyes, taking the bulk and weight of the rye required to produce it into
account, a pretty large sum for spending money. A distant relative, the
widow Dunford, resided in Bayardstown, near the city. There I was to
lodge. Bayardstown was where is now the Ninth ward.

The journey was made on foot, without satchel, comb or brush.
Three days was the limited time, and therefore little baggage was needed. The way was not difficult to find, and soon after leaving home I fell
in with a neighboring farmer with his wagon, going to market; and his
conversation tended for a time to shorten the tediousness of the journey. I still remember one remark he made, for it acted as a thorn in the
flesh. When he learned I was going to see the city, he observed that I
would see more there in a day than at Poverty Point in a lifetime. This
reflection on the character of our neighborhood I did not at all relish. I
was not aware then that it deserved the appellation; but afterwards,

45

when better acquainted with the quality of lands elsewhere, although our immediate neighborhood was a fair average of the lands in Franklin township, I found the truth very nearly justified his invidious remark. The dissatisfaction however which it created in my mind caused me very soon to part company with him; which was the more easily done because I could walk much faster than he drove.

Nothing else of the journey impressed itself on my memory so as to be reproduced now until I came to the residence of Reece Jones, the tobacconist, in later years the residence of George Finley, on Frankstown avenue a short distance east of the present Lincoln school house, and then about a mile east of the village of Negleystown. Frankstown avenue was then known as the Frankstown State Road. The northern turnpike leaving the Greensburg at Wilkinsburg, and passing through Murraysville and New Salem, had not yet been constructed and opened through; and the old State Road from Pittsburgh by way of Frankstown in the mountains, was still used by mail stages and Conestoga wagons.

The Jones place was the first neat and trim suburban country residence of a well-to-do citizen I had seen since leaving Baltimore in 1818; and its beauty made a strong impression, although at the present time it would be considered a rather plain affair. What chiefly attracted my notice was the front fence along the road for several hundred feet, the palings of which were entirely of barrel staves, all bowed out in the middle, and evidently having been used for barrels or casks rather at some former time. I did not know then that Mr. Jones was a tobacconist; and why a man should take such pains to procure staves for palings was the query.

But the greatest of all the wonders I expected to see was near by. After leaving the Jones place I could hear the puffing of Negley's steam mill. It was quite a curiosity to know how steam could operate a grist mill. I was well acquainted with the mode of operation of the water mills of our neighborhood: the large wheel some sixteen feet in diameter, with its square boxes called buckets all around the outside, which were filled and driven by the force and weight of the water from the forebay. I had no other idea of the application of power to drive machinery, and supposed the steam was allowed to escape against the buckets or boxes, and drove the wheel the same as by water power.

When I arrived at the mill however, I discovered quite a different state of affairs; and indeed it was nearly as different from the modern steam engine as from the great wheel of the water mill. The cylinder stood on end on a solid stone foundation in a pit; the piston attached to an immense horizontal beam, which was permanently attached by hinges at one end to perpendicular beams in the framework of the building. To the other or movable end was attached the pitman, which worked the crank of the fly-wheel. The steam was supplied by two immense boilers without flue or cylinder, consuming five times more coal than would produce the same amount of steam in modern boilers. The whole affair, as regarded the steam and its application, was primitive and rude.

After I had gratified my curiosity by close inspection of everything and was about to leave, the engineer, intentionally perhaps and without warning, displayed a feature of the steam power which I had not discovered: its ability in sound as well as force. He touched the safety valve, producing a report that hastened my departure considerably.

But notable objects were only beginning to appear. The very large sign reaching across the entire front of a small frame building with "Negley's Store" in great gilt letters, the only store of the village, looked unusually conspicuous. After passing through the village I resorted to the neighboring hillside, so as to take in at one view the whole of the beautiful scenery which the East Liberty valley presented. So much level and well cultivated country was new to me. My standpoint, or rather resting place, was the old quarry west of Negley avenue, near its junction with Penn avenue. Here I sat down and contemplated the whole scene. The first object which excited my admiration was the great meadow, the largest I had ever seen. It was bounded by what is now Penn avenue, Negley avenue, Collins avenue and Stanton avenue, and comprised about one hundred acres. The Negley mansion house and orchards appeared to be included in it; and it was not marred by division fences except on the line of what is now Highland avenue. It presented an uninterrupted surface of tall green grass; and as the breezes passed over it, causing it to undulate in light and shade like the waves of the sea, it left an abiding impression of natural beauty. There was the steam mill in one direction at the northeast corner of what is now Penn and Collins avenues, with the pillar of black smoke rising from its chimney and the white puffs of escaping steam; and this great meadow, and the land on either side of it as far as I could see—all belonging to Jacob Negley as I was told in the village—and the great brick mansion in the other direction towards the river. It was one of the finest mansions about the city anywhere.

The whole scene was new to me, and impressed me with an idea of wealth and magnificence I had before no conception of. I remember wondering how it could be possible to accumulate such wealth, and how magnificent must be the style of living and what pleasures they must enjoy who possessed it. I remember also of the thought occurring whether I might not one day attain in some degree such wealth, and an equality with such great people; and of picturing to my imagination how nice their children must look in their fine clothes, when riding about in their carriage. It appeared magnificent! and I inferred the happy condition of its possessors must be magnificent also. My thoughts on the occasion serve to show how greatly mistaken people are regarding each others' condition. The young and the inexperienced or ignorant conceive those who are wealthy, or in a condition of life regarded higher than their own, to be proportionately happier and proportionately elevated above them: whereas poor humanity has its cares and sorrows, its burdens and labors under all conditions; the difference is rather in quality than quantity. Nature, in her wise compensatory process, equalizes all conditions. If I had known on that day what I learned many years afterwards, I would have seen the possessors of all this magnificent show of wealth laboring under still greater difficulties and anxiety of mind than my parents in the struggle to pay for their farm. At this very time Jacob Negley was inextricably involved in debt and maintaining an almost hopeless struggle against fate; and with the labor of his wife and children was staving off the evil day when the Sheriff would despoil him of his possessions: a catastrophe which soon overtook him however, when he sunk beneath the waves of adversity, died broken-hearted and left a widow and children to battle with the storm. The panic of 1819–20 had ruined him.

While sitting on the grassy slope of that hillside and contemplating the great meadow and beautiful scenery around me, I remember also of a wish crossing my mind to become acquainted with the boys and girls of this fine house and plantation, that I might see how they regarded school, work and other matters interesting to boys and girls. Were they good readers, or could they write and cipher as well as I could? I felt some satisfaction in the thought that however fine they might be, I might equal them in that respect. My memories of this occasion are only interesting in view of what took place eighteen years afterwards. It did not occur to me then that I was one day to become so well acquainted with this family that one of these little girls should become my wife; and that the home where I would pass the most and happiest days of my life was to be within a few steps of the spot where I was then sitting!

After leaving this memorable resting place in my journey no unusual object presented itself till I came in sight of the Allegheny river. Fields and woodlands obstructed the view till I arrived at the arsenal wall. Immediately west of the arsenal there was a deep ravine and thicket of willows and brushwood, with three small frame houses beyond fronting on the turnpike. From the embankment of the road I could see the great river. Just below, on the south side of the road and not far east of the junction of Butler street and Penn avenue, was the country seat of Malcolm Leech, then a prominent Pittsburgh merchant, who when a boy had emigrated from our neighborhood in Ireland. He had also accumulated much wealth, which was another encouraging circumstance; for why might not one poor boy accomplish what another had done? Leech's family were not of the type, however, to benefit by paternal thrift. After his death they soon squandered what he left them.

At the foot of the hill was a brick tavern painted yellow, which remains until this day, standing cornerwise to Penn Avenue. All else between East Liberty and Bayardstown was agricultural land, with rich fields of wheat and corn on either side of the two-mile lane or turnpike, now Penn avenue. The city line, including Bayardstown, was about where Seventeenth street now is. Bayardstown was then but a suburb, with considerable unimproved land lying between it and the city proper. I soon found my way to the cotton factory of James Adams, then in full operation where St. Philomena's German Catholic Church now stands, at the corner of Liberty and Fourteenth streets. This was my objective point. Here I expected to find the son of our lady relative, Mrs. Dunford, with whom I was to lodge. Her son James, with whom I was intimate, had been often at our house. I found him in the engine house of the factory. The meeting was gladsome, and he showed me a much larger and finer steam engine and machinery than I had seen at Negleystown; and what was still more wonderful to me, the operations of all the spinning jennies and power looms and other machinery, preparing and spinning and weaving cotton on the different floors, with numerous girls attending them without any apparent labor or effort on their part.[2] It was at the close of working hours, and I was soon comfortably housed, and with a good supper prepared for a sound sleep and refreshing rest after my twenty-one miles' walk.

The next day was spent in the care of Anne, the daughter of about eighteen years, who showed me around town, taking in all the sights of rivers and steamboats, and glass and iron works, which at that time were not very extensive. I was greatly pleased and fully satisfied that I had learned everything worth knowing about the town and its wonders. On the following morning early I was ready for the return trip; and after a good breakfast Mrs. Dunford prepared me a lunch, with a half-pint flask of whiskey to keep up my spirits on the journey, as she expressed it. I mention this as an instance of the habits and opinions of that day. Whiskey or brandy of some kind was as usual in every household as tea or coffee is now—indeed more so, and no reproach attached to its use. The children were dosed every morning with bitters, whiskey and tansy or dock root. The men had their dram regularly before every meal. I cannot but regard it as a bad practice, and would not have it revived—it is dangerous to handle edged tools—and yet I must say that throughout the country among the farmers, nearly every one of whom had his own distillery, and in the towns too where liquor was plentiful and sold cheap, there was then less excessive drinking and actual drunkenness in proportion to the number of inhabitants than exists to-day. Public opinion frowned on excess in drink and drunkenness more then than it does now. In all our neighborhood there were but two men who would drink to become drunk, and then only when on a frolic, such as a house-raising, log-rolling, husking and the like. They were regarded derisively as weaklings who were unable to take their drink as other men without swilling it to excess. Their weakness so mortified their families that the sons would never attend a gathering where the fathers were, and despised liquor so much that they would not drink at all.

However, on my return trip I did not apply to my flask until about half way home, when I sat down by a cold spring at the side of the road, drank from it and ate some biscuits, and tasted my liquor without reducing the quantity much. Thus refreshed, I was home again before the middle of the afternoon with most of my liquor, and pocket money unspent; pretty well fatigued, but with a bright impression of the numerous wonders I had seen.

Chapter VI

— • • —

School Days

IN ALL THE STRESS of farm work and farm payments and family cares, my mother did not neglect my education. There was no school within reach during the first summer, but she drilled me pretty well at home in the spelling book. The following summer a school was opened about three miles distant, which I attended perhaps two months in all. Over two miles of the way was through dense woodland and across a branch of Turtle creek, which was frequently unsafe to cross by foot log after a heavy rain. My attendance at school was on these accounts much interrupted; but my mother still helped me on during that year also, and by the end of it I had committed to memory the first chapter of St. John, and could get through an easy reading lesson moderately well. During the first two years I could not contribute to household or farm labor to an extent sufficient to keep me from school, if one had been convenient; but after this my services at home were too important to permit attendance at school in the summer time, and my educational season was limited to the winter, seldom over four months. But the limitation in time was made up by closer application while the opportunity lasted.

The custom was for a teacher to go around in October soliciting scholars for a school; there would often be two or three of them rivals, each having an article of agreement with him, containing the time and terms and place of teaching. To this article those who would patronize him set their names with the number of scholars or pupils they intended to send, and were called subscribers. The school generally commenced about the first of November, and ended the first of March or April.

I had the benefit of attending one of these schools from three to four months every winter. We had no female teachers in those days; sometimes old men, sometimes men who had farms and worked them during the summer, devoting the winter to teaching as a more lucrative business. At one time we had a young man for a teacher named Wallace, who was a great favorite, and rapid progress was made on account of his better understanding of human nature, especially boyish nature. He sympathized with us, and joined in our sports as well as in directing our studies; and yet preserved a dignity commanding our respect and admiration. We had neither free schools nor trained teachers. It may be inferred that education among us was at a low ebb; and yet, when I remember my early schooling, I cannot but believe that the teaching was thorough and efficient as far as it went. It seldom aspired to more than the elementary arts of reading, writing and arithmetic; but the teachers were always competent for what they undertook, and the pupils, for the most part, eager and earnest to learn. The opportunity of schooling was regarded as a valuable privilege, and improved by most of them to the best of their ability.

A place to teach in had also to be secured in most instances; not many school houses, as such, existed. Often the school would be kept in some vacant log cabin. The cost of tuition was cheap at that day. Old men and cripples and others disqualified in any way for active pursuits, prepared themselves for teaching, and a good deal of rivalry existed between them. Some neighborhoods were much better than others for the maintenance of a school, and as among the schools of philosophy in ancient Greece, the most popular teachers obtained the most scholars. They were all pay schools. Free schools with their advantages to ambitious local politicians, and affording a wider but thinner spread of knowledge with the disadvantages of heavier expense to parents and taxpayers, were not yet introduced. Whilst the teachers were perfectly competent and gave thorough instruction in whatever branches they undertook to teach, the compensation which they demanded was remarkably moderate: much less than parents and guardians are now subjected to for extras and contingent expenses alone, under our present free school system. Some teachers' receipts for my schooling which I find among my father's old papers will illustrate this.

RECEIVED, August 22d, 1822, of Andrew Mellon, per son, fifty-six and one-fourth cents, for the quarter's schooling ending on the 25th day of last July, as per subscription.

WM. G. TORRANCE

RECEIVED of Andrew Mellon, two dollars and sixty-two and one-half cents, for four months of schooling of son and daughter, May 17th, 1827.

WM. MASTERS

GREENSBURG ACADEMY, April 1st, 1829.
Thos. Mellon dr. for tuition, to Wm. Will,
    From the 21st of November, 1828, to the 21st
of March, 1829, deducting two weeks for Christmas
vacation, to three months and two weeks $3.50
    To fuel   .25
                                                        —————
                                                        $3.75
                                    Received payment,
                                                WM. WILL

Whilst these rates may seem extremely low, it must be remembered that the value or purchasing power of money was greatly higher then than it is now. The reason of fractions of cents appearing so frequently in accounts of those days was, that Spanish coin was in use almost exclusively, in which the fractions of the dollar were halves, quarters, and twelve and one-half and six and one-fourth cent pieces. The two latter were commonly called elevenpenny and fi'-penny bits.

School hours were from nine to twelve; an hour for luncheon, and then from one to five, Saturdays included. The school books were the United States Spelling Book and Western Calculator, published by Patterson & Lambden of Pittsburgh; and the Bible and Testament for higher classes. The New England Primer, however, containing the picture and the poetry regarding the burning of John Rogers at the stake,[1] with the Shorter Catechism, was an indispensable class book; and drilling on the catechism was a daily exercise, and advanced scholars were expected to be able to repeat it from memory from beginning to end, without failure.

The most valued and exciting custom of the schools of those days was the "Barring Out." It much resembled the modern "strike" among workingmen. On such occasion, in pursuance of a preconcerted plan and secret conspiracy concocted by the larger boys of the school, the teacher, shortly before Christmas on the day appointed, would find the school house strongly barred and barricaded against his entrance. The scholars were all on hand long before the school hour in the morning, and utilized all available means to prevent the entrance of the teacher: and the boisterous hilarity of the youngsters on the inside at the crestfallen condition of their master in his unsuccessful efforts to gain admission, was unbounded. The master readily took in the situation and would meet the emergency according to his temper; some would become angry and indignant, and make loud threats of severe punishment for such a flagrant defiance of their authority, much to the terror of the younger children and the fun of the larger boys, if they felt secure in their fortification. Others of more discretion or greater experience would accept the inevitable with serene composure; and others again, mostly of the younger and more active class, would intentionally and good humoredly increase the excitement by trying to storm the citadel, in which they were not always unsuccessful. The occasion, however it might eventuate, was of absorbing interest and enjoyment to the scholars of all ages. Its success involved a holiday vacation and an ample treat of apples and cider, which was the penalty prescribed by custom for the master if he failed to take the fort. The event was inaugurated by a whisper being passed around the evening before that the barring out was to come next morning. This was enough to assure the presence of every youngster, large or small, at daybreak next day. But the secret sometimes leaked out; and if so, the teacher would be ahead of them and in possession, and perhaps a second and third attempt would have to be made. But once the port was closed and the enemy on the outside, the siege and the parleys between the opposing forces commenced. The terms of capitulation were carefully prepared in writing inside and handed out through some crevice to the teacher. These consisted of a specified number of days for holiday vacation, two or more bushels of good eating apples, and two or more gallons of cider, according to the size of the school.

In some instances the demands were agreed to at once; but in that case less of a good time and boisterous enjoyment was afforded the scholars. The result was that if the master forced an entrance he gained the victory, no matter if the larger boys were able to eject him—even that would not avail to change the situation; custom held them as conquered and the school had to furnish the treat to the master.

On one occasion our barring out continued day and night until the afternoon of the third day. William Masters, the teacher, a cranky little man, in high dudgeon called to his aid the trustees, and kept up the siege all that time without avail; only obtaining easier terms from us on the amount of apples and cider.

On another occasion we were fairly defeated, after the most vigorous resistance for a couple of days and nights, by Mr. Wallace, the young teacher already mentioned. He maintained a close siege of well directed force and strategy and finally succeeded; but his good natured bravery and energy made him more popular with the school than ever—he had before been a master but now he was a hero! He would grant no terms, more doubtless to afford fun and frolic than for anything else.

On this occasion a sufficient force of the larger boys had to be detailed to hold the fort during the night. This guard was relieved at daybreak by others. Wallace made numerous attacks every day, sometimes by trying to dislodge a window-sash, sometimes trying to make an opening in the lap-board roof; but we were well armed with hand spikes and sharp pointed sticks, and always baffled him. But on the third morning, before our guard was relieved or the fire well started in the wide fireplace, suddenly and to the amazement of those on duty Wallace dropped down the chimney, stepped up to the master's desk and called the school to order. He had climbed upon the roof and from there to the top of the chimney down which he descended. To accomplish this was not so difficult, as the chimney was not over ten or twelve feet high and about three feet square inside, constructed of sticks, plastered on the inside with mud, the fireplace wide and high for wood as fuel. The feat was less difficult or dangerous than sooty and unpleasant. This was the only occasion of the kind in my experience where the scholars were defeated. On these occasions all sizes and sexes joined, and aided to the best of their ability, the night watch being held by boys alone. It was usual for boys and girls to unite their strength, shoulder to shoulder, against the door to prevent an entrance in that direction; and in barricading the windows with wooden benches when an entrance was attempted through them. Ingress and egress were effected when the enemy was off his guard or out of sight. The barring out was always looked forward to and anxiously awaited as the great event of the school season. The treat, whether furnished by the teacher or the defeated school, was taken and consumed on the premises in general jubilation, on the first day of the vacation.

The practice of barring out was general throughout the country, and too popular to have been discontinued but for the greater authority and power which teachers acquired by the introduction of the public school system. There was an inconceivable amount of fun and enjoyment in it to the scholars. The teacher would not unfrequently bring a friend or two to assist him in the attempt to break in. In such attacks the scene would be exciting beyond description. Some thirty to forty boys and girls between the ages of five and eighteen, excitedly and earnestly barricading the doors and windows with benches and bars, prudently changing the greater force to the point of immediate attack; whilst occasionally some of the smaller ones would become frightened at the noise and disturbance and threats of the parties outside. Then cries of fright and alarm would mingle with mirth and laughter, and earnest shouts of orders given by the leaders: altogether worth a whole session's attendance to witness. I have heard a great deal about fox hunting and tournaments, but for downright fun and frolic give me back the Barring Out, and my schoolboy youth to enjoy it. It is noteworthy how indelibly every incident and circumstance of a barring out or similar enterprise fixes itself on the young memory. It proves the great advantage of cooperation between the emotional and mental part of our nature. When the heart and will are in the work the pleasure afforded makes an impression which lasts through life.

In those schools of children of plain, rugged farmers, in that remote district, there was more to be learned than mere reading, writing and arithmetic. The variety of human nature afforded lessons for use in after life. The various nationalities and degrees of mental and moral culture in the children exactly represented the parents, and cropped out in every thought and action: the children of each family in the school presenting the counterpart of the family at home—the oldest girl being the little mother and governess, carrying the lunch basket, and at noon distributing among her little brothers and sisters the slices of bread thickly spread with yellow butter overlaid with half an inch or so of dark brown apple butter, to give it a relish; and giving them well directed admonition, and sometimes a vigorous slap or two to regulate their behavior; and warning the reckless brothers of the way they would "catch it" at home for tearing their pants in climbing after nuts or chasing ground squirrels. The earnest care and tone of voice, or temper and spleen of the mother at home, would show out in every word and accent of the little daughter at school. Although dressed in homespun, home-made and without regard to fashion, these wild, vigorous little women were not unattractive to their schoolmates of the other sex. In a promiscuous school of the kind, such freedom and companionship cannot exist long without every boy over ten years seeing some one little girl which he thinks just a good deal nicer than any of the rest; and whom he will feel inclined to give his nicest apple to, not for any particular reason that he knows of, but just because he likes her. It was only recently I met in New Salem an old schoolmate of sixty years ago, who told me that the severest flogging she had ever received was when detected conveying to me a note of acknowledgment of a favor of the kind. I had entirely forgotten the circumstance, as such occasions were not infrequent, and corporal punishment at that time was very liberally administered in the schools.

I had progressed through one after another of these winter school sessions from 1822 till 1827, until reading, writing and arithmetic were made quite easy. Besides the Western Calculator then in common use, I had twice gone through the well preserved copy of our family standard arithmetic, "Gough," of Dublin, which had been my grandfather's and father's school book. Gough's methods were more varied, and his examples more difficult than those of the modern class books; but I have never seen clearer illustrations or plainer rules for a thorough study of the science in all its parts than those to be found in this ancient author. Besides arithmetic I had also gone beyond the curriculum of the schools in using for a time, in a class by myself, Murray's English Reader, a copy of which I found in a lot of miscellaneous books sent me by my uncle from Philadelphia. And I had gone so far as to adopt even a novel which I found in the same lot for some of my reading lessons, on account of the long words so difficult to pronounce or understand: much however to the annoyance of the teacher who was himself no great expert in the art of reading and defining. I had got on so far that when a new teacher presented himself at the usual time in the fall for commencing school, it had become necessary for me to find out, before entering as a scholar, whether he knew more than I did myself.

Nor was my education all this time confined to the regular routine of the winter session of school. I was making a broader and a better progress in another direction: this was in the variety of knowledge gained by employing all the spare time I had, at all seasons, in reading the various and curious miscellaneous literature furnished me from time to time by my kind uncle, who had an exalted idea of the advantage and importance to young people of acquiring general and useful knowledge.

It was in this condition my uncle Thomas found me, on his visit to us in the summer of 1828. He saw or supposed that I properly appreciated his views and was improving my opportunities: for he prevailed on my father to allow me the privilege of a session or so at some better school than our neighborhood afforded. He recommended Pittsburgh, and gave my father a letter of introduction to an old friend of his there, a Mr. Ekin, with whom he had become intimate in New Orleans. Accordingly when through with our farm work in the fall of 1828, my father and I visited the city with a wagon loaded with farm produce; and after our marketing was disposed of we called on Mr. Ekin, finding him a genial and clever old gentleman, who, according to the custom of the time, had a well stocked sideboard of fine liquors, to which his applications and invitations were numerous and pressing. I remember the splendor of his parlor was quite dazzling to my inexperienced eyes, and strongly impressed me with the advantages of wealth. He accompanied us to the school of young Walter H. Lowrie, kept in a little upstair room in a small frame house on the west side of the Diamond, behind the old Courthouse. This, as Mr. Ekin advised us, was the best select school in the town; and I suppose he was right, as its teacher, Mr. Lowrie, became in his day an eminent lawyer and distinguished judge, at one time Chief Justice of the Supreme Court of Pennsylvania.

After a conference with Mr. Lowrie however, and inquiry as to the cost of board and lodging in the city, the situation did not strike my father favorably: it was too expensive and too far from home. Accordingly, after our return a visit was made to the County Academy at Greensburg, which we found more pretentious of educational facilities, more moderate in expense, and much nearer home. Here I entered on a higher grade of studies, geometry, history, grammar and geography. Tytler's Ancient History, Murray's English Grammar, Woodbridge's School Geography, and Simpson's Euclid were my school books there. I

have them still preserved in good condition; and had the pleasure lately
of confronting Mrs. Murphy of Uniontown with a piece of sentimental
poetry which she had written on the fly leaf of my geography when a
girl at school, fifty-five years ago.

Thomas Will, the principal of the academy, a Scotchman, was a correct scholar and a first-class teacher. He spent a long life in teaching
and died only a short time since. My time there was but four months,
as I had to return home for farm work when the spring opened. Whilst
at Greensburg I boarded in a family whose talents were far above the
average for literary taste and culture. A class of society existed at that
day which has since become almost extinct. With them a higher estimate was placed upon refinement than wealth, and they constituted a
sort of aristocracy. Our county towns then contained many of this
class, dignified and stately in their manners, exclusive in their companionship, high toned in regard to honor and morality! As a rule they
were educated and well informed people; mostly belonging to the professions, but not at all dependent on wealth for prestige. The Williams
family, with whom I boarded, was of this class, although the father had
only been a justice of the peace of the borough. The mother, then a
widow, had managed to give her children a good education. Mrs. Murphy, above mentioned, was one of the daughters; and three of the sons
became eminent lawyers afterwards. Joseph and Robert successively
held judicial offices for many years at Des Moines, Iowa. Robert still
held the office of Probate Judge in that city at the time of his death, in
1873. The entire family was also endowed with fine musical talent and
literary taste. Other branches of the same stock were equally gifted. A
cousin of theirs, who at that time was a quiet, modest student of law,
the late well known Honorable Thomas Williams of Pittsburgh,
acquired much deserved distinction as a lawyer and statesman. He was
in Congress, and one of the impeachers of President Johnson. The
society of this family opened to me a new field of thought and ambition. It was well calculated to alienate me from the rude pursuits of
farm life and the low sentiments and purposes of our neighbors at
home, with whom I had, until that time, mostly associated. Its tendency, as my father very well divined, was to spoil me for a farmer.

After leaving the academy my heart was not in farm work, although
I continued to execute it with due diligence for two or three years, until
a final decision respecting my future course was arrived at. From the

time I was a very small boy, the question of future occupation was uppermost in my mind; and now this question pressed upon me with renewed force. I derived little pleasure from mingling with the young people around me at home: their tastes and pursuits were not congenial. My source of pleasure was reading, which I resorted to at every spare moment. And thus the time passed till an event occurred which forced me to decide.

Chapter VII

The Decision

I WAS OF AN EARNEST turn of mind, and the question of a calling was cogitated over and over again at every new phase which life presented. My father's uniform advice was decidedly, indeed almost peremptorily in favor of farming. In his eyes no other calling seemed so honest, reliable and respectable. He was reasonably prosperous in that line himself, and looked upon the vocation of a prosperous farmer as the safest and best that any sensible young man in my position could aspire to. His opinion on the subject was so well settled that I never could get him to discuss any other course with patience. Whenever my mind rebelled against farming as a pursuit it was my mother I appealed to for sympathy and advice. We could discuss the matter freely, as she was as undecided as I was myself. At times I would become reconciled to the farm, take an interest in the different kinds of crops and stock, and work on diligently and patiently; but the contrast of life on the farm with what I had seen it to be among the merchants, lawyers and clergymen of Greensburg when at school, would still recur to disturb my contentment and suggest that I was making a mistake in not aiming at something different. When at Greensburg I read with avidity "The Portfolio,"[1] a leading magazine of the day, taken by the family where I boarded; and afterwards had been reading everything in book shape which my uncle was in the habit of sending me from Philadelphia. This course tended no little to promote my discontent; but what acted most to unsettle me as to farming was reading Dr. Franklin's Autobiography. What he had done in the line of enduring hardships and deprivations and incessant labor to work himself up in the world, I could attempt—that kind of thing was just to my taste. Still I was undecided. I had no means of my own, and could expect none from my father in a pursuit so contrary to his wishes; and a regular college course of education, which was my greatest desire, required more time and money than was reasonable to expect under any circumstances. Merchandising was more available. Robert Graham, a Greensburg merchant and relative of ours by marriage, had proposed to me when at school there to enter his store, board in his family, be clothed, and receive one hundred dollars at the end of my term of three years to learn the business. This was at that time a liberal offer to a boy of my age. I would have accepted it at once, but my father objected. He needed me on the farm. After I did learn storekeeping, as he reasoned, I would have no capital to begin with; my wages as a clerk in a store would be no better than for farm work, and my habits of industry would be destroyed. If I remained at home industrious and contented, he might be able, when the time arrived for me to begin the world for myself, to assist me in part or in whole to procure a farm of my own, which would be better and surer than to become a hireling in other people's employment. This view of it excluded merchandising and limited the dilemma to farming or a profession. At last, after two or three years of this uncertain and unsettled state of mind, the crisis came when a decision must be made.

Originally the farm on which we lived comprised three hundred and sixty acres, settled upon and patented by John Hill. In his will Hill divided it, subject to certain charges, equally between his sons Peter and John. John had sold his share, the south half of the farm, to Mr. Shaeffer, from whom my father purchased, as already stated. Peter still resided on his half, which contained rather the better part of the land. Selling out to my father had often been talked of between them, but never seriously entertained on either side until my father conceived the idea that if he purchased Peter's farm and interested me in its payment under the assurance that I should own it afterwards, this would settle my mind and anchor me permanently to farming as a pursuit. This he supposed would extinguish my foolish hankerings, as he regarded them, after merchandising or a learned profession. And the project did exert considerable influence on me as offering a certainty in the line of well doing, whilst the outlook of the future afforded little encouragement in other directions. I at length consented, and the terms between my father and Peter were verbally agreed on. My consent was a prerequisite, in view of the fact that if I left home my father would be unable to manage so large a farm himself, and would have difficulty in meeting the deferred payments. The whole arrangement therefore depended on me. I was now seventeen years of age, and my service in the work and management of the farm important; and the contemplated purchase closed, I must settle down to farming for life. This decision would therefore determine my fate, but I could not see my way to anything better. So the day was fixed for Peter and my father to go to Greensburg to have the papers drawn and the bargain closed. They started about seven o'clock in the morning, and I went to my work as usual, cutting rail timber on top of the hill above our house. I remember the spot and its surroundings well, as it was the scene on that morning of an exceedingly violent mental agitation, the result of which changed the whole course of my subsequent life. I had worked on for an hour or so, more vigorously perhaps than usual on account of the excitement over my fate, which was to be sealed that day at Greensburg. From where I stood I could overlook the farm that I was to own when I became of age and it was paid for; and on which, if I should marry, I was to spend my lifetime making an honest, frugal living by hard labor, but little more. The die was cast, or so nearly so as to be almost past recall. All my air castles and bright fancies of acquiring knowledge and wealth or distinction were wrecked and ruined, and to be abandoned forever. Must this be? I suddenly realized the tremendous importance of the moment. The utter collapse of all my fond young hopes thus suddenly precipitated nearly crazed me. I could stand it no longer. I put on my coat, ran down past the house, flung the axe over the fence into the yard, and without stopping made the best possible time on foot for the town. My father had taken the only available saddle horse, but my feet were light under the circumstances. It was ten rather long miles over a hilly, rough and muddy road, in March. I noticed little by the way, for time was precious. The papers might be signed before I got there. As I gained the top of the hill above the town, I could see Peter and my father standing on Welty's corner on Main street, and soon joined them, so much exhausted that it was difficult to express myself sufficiently to allay their alarm, as they supposed something awful had happened at home. All I could say was that I had come to stop it, and it must be stopped so far as I was concerned. My father seemed bewildered at such determined self-assertion. Peter seemed rather amused than displeased. They had only had their horses put up after getting into town. They had not hastened as I had done, and were consulting what lawyer they should call on to prepare the deed. There was no discussion. My long walk and sudden appearance indicated such resolution as precluded argument. My father, although disappointed, offered no rebuke or remonstrance, and I was rejoiced that I had arrived in time, feeling as if I had escaped a great pending calamity; and our good natured neighbor, the other party interested, was most jubilant of all, saying he owed me a present for getting him out of the scrape, as he had wished ever so much to rue bargain but disliked to say so. After a comfortable dinner we all returned in good humor, Peter or my father walking some times to allow me to ride in view of my fatigue.

This decision was the turning point of my life. My career has been entirely different from what it would have been had those papers been signed; for then I would have settled down in good earnest to work and manage the farm, and would have abandoned all thoughts of any other pursuit. But now, after a lapse of over half a century since that day, and the results of that act have transpired and their effect been experienced, how is it? Have I enjoyed more happiness than I would otherwise have done? Perhaps not. Happiness is not confined to position or condition of life. But that act cast my lines in pleasanter places—pleasanter for me than they otherwise would have been, because better suited to my nature and disposition; and though with a different nature and disposition my choice might have been disastrous to my future welfare, yet I am satisfied now that it was wise and for the best. Success in life depends greatly on the occupation we permanently adopt at the outset; and that again depends so much on whether we are suited for the occupation selected, that the question should rather be the fitness of the individual for the occupation than the merits of the occupation itself.

> Honor and shame from no condition rise;
> Act well your part, there all the honor lies.[2]

But undoubtedly to act well your part in life it is necessary that your faculties and nature and disposition should be suited to the part chosen; otherwise it will be uphill work all the time. No one can be at ease and successful in his profession or calling who is unsuited for it. The great and momentous question, therefore, to every youth at the start is, what pursuit or calling he is best suited for. In the choice I made, under the decision referred to, I have realized all my hopes and succeeded in all my projects far beyond my utmost anticipations, and find myself in very different circumstances from what in all probability would be my condition now had those papers been signed. But still, am I happier in this condition than I would have been in that? There are compensations everywhere in life, under all conditions. Who can say! I acted on that occasion as I thought for the best, and I have never had cause to regret it. The position which nature has fitted us for is the one best suited to promote our happiness.

The decision thus suddenly precipitated rather discouraged my father's hopes of making a farmer of me, but did not reconcile him to my course nor incline him to aid in its accomplishment, and my farm labor was not slackened for the present. He regarded my aspirations for mercantile or professional life as the folly of youth; but after steady persistence in my purpose had satisfied him that my assistance on the farm could not be expected much longer, he began to contract his farm operations so as to enable him to manage it without me. He had before acquired two other farms in the neighborhood, as already mentioned. The M'Closky farm had buildings and could be let; the Moore farm was unimproved, and in order that it might be let, buildings had to be erected. In their construction I spent the winter of 1831–2. All through that winter there was unusually deep snow, and the cold was intense; but the weather had little or no effect on such vigorous health as I enjoyed. The work was entirely entrusted to myself, with the help of Samuel Walton, a rough carpenter of the neighborhood hired for the purpose. He, poor fellow, did not escape so well the severity of the weather, as according to his own opinion the exposure and hardships of that winter's work in the timber brought on the disease which a few years afterward caused his death. Some features of it, it is true, were pretty rough. As workingmen generally do, we carried our dinners along with us to the woodland where we chopped, and at dinner time would find our bread and meat and coffee thoroughly solidified and requiring to be thawed out by the fire. Though not very robust or able-bodied, I acquired the sleight of handling an axe during that winter to such an extent that I had no trouble *dubbing in* for the hewer: that is, standing on the log and chopping its side to the chalk line ahead of the man with the broad-axe. And in splitting and shaving shingles I found no difficulty to finish as many per day as my companion, although he was considered a good workman. It was the first job of which I had the management and control entirely to myself. Early in March, when we had the logs hewed and shingles prepared and foundations put in, the neighbors were invited to the raising. To attend such a gathering was a social duty which no one who valued his good name among the farmers in those days would ever neglect.

Whilst engaged in this work I boarded a good deal of the time with my good uncle Archy, whose farm was adjoining; and during the long winter evenings with him and my aunt, I had many gratifying consultations with regard to my future plans of life. With the exception of my mother, they sympathized with my views more than any other friends. Although I had decided against farming, no definite decision was yet arrived at as between merchandising and a professional life. Merchandising was the more immediate, practical and available; whilst the attainment of a profession was almost too remote, and attended with too many difficulties to be within my reach, although more to my desire. With my uncle's aid as a partner, merchandising was available. I was then in my nineteenth year, an age when an active life was more becoming than attending school. An education required time and money, but was what my heart most hankered after. With the glimpse I had already acquired by desultory reading, the fields of knowledge which lay beyond seemed a fairyland full of wonder and intellectual pleasures. But to devote six or seven years to preparation, at an age when I ought to be engaged in the serious business of life rather than the gratification of a fanciful desire, was in itself a discouraging thought; and still more discouraging was the fact that I was utterly impecunious, and without any reasonable prospect of material aid. Merchandising therefore seemed most advisable in our thoughts and plans. My uncle had no family, and his health was such as unfitted him for rugged farm work. He therefore seriously entertained the project of joining me in getting up and managing a country store. My father owned a suitable house for the purpose in the village of New Salem; and it was contemplated for one of us to attend the store whilst the other would drive a market wagon around the neighborhood peddling goods for farm products, such as butter, eggs and poultry. With these, and the like taken in at the store a weekly trip was to be made to Pittsburgh, when goods could be brought back to replenish the stock. The plan was a good one—many have succeeded in the same line since, and I have no doubt that with our joint sagacity and industry we would have succeeded to our utmost expectations, as our expectations were quite moderate. We did not make the attempt however: we hesitated too long. My uncle was timid regarding the risks we should run, and I was not sanguine on my part, as I still had a lingering hope of obtaining an education. It was finally given up by mutual consent, and probably for the best, as I might never have been content to have been excluded all my life from such a glimpse into the ark of knowledge as I expected from a college course. Had I not gotten such an education, I have no doubt I would always have greatly overrated my loss. It is well for every young man to see for himself how much less there is in it than he expected to find. Not by any means that mental training and useful knowledge are unimportant: they are, on the contrary, all important and must be acquired in some way sooner or later by any one who aspires to respectability in professional life. But he who has gone through a college course and has to elbow his way up afterward among those who have not had that advantage, but are self-taught, will more clearly realize the fact that he has gained no monopoly of knowledge by it; and also that he has spent much valuable time in acquiring certain kinds of knowledge which he will very soon lose again for want of any use or necessity for them.

After this project for merchandising was dropped and our other farms were let to tenants, nothing remained to disturb my aspirations for an education; but when I did obtain a partial release I had still to assist in harvesting, and in all other urgent farm work on the homestead farm for some two or three years longer. But education was uppermost in my mind all the time, and no opportunity however slight was ever neglected to further its object.

I had already acquired all the elements of a fair common English course. I had also acquired some considerable knowledge of physical geography and ancient history during my short term at the Greensburg Academy; and had, for a year or two after leaving the Greensburg school, availed myself as much as possible of every facility afforded for acquiring a knowledge of grammar, trigonometry, mensuration and surveying.

At that time in our county the public school system had not been introduced, and a better class of teachers prevailed than are now to be met with. They were not perhaps on the whole so thoroughly and accurately drilled regarding special methods; but their knowledge was chiefly self-acquired and thorough, and preferable to the product of educational machinery. What they knew or professed to teach they were apt to fully understand. They did not always transcend the prescribed curriculum of reading, writing and arithmetic; but teachers were not uncommon who taught Murray's English Grammar and the higher branches of mathematics. Besides such advanced information as I was able to pick up in the way mentioned, I lost no opportunity of inquiring all about the study of Latin and Greek, and the sciences taught at college. Any college student or clergyman whom I might meet with at this period must have thought me peculiarly inquisitive. By private study of the grammars of Murray and Kirkham I obtained a reasonable proficiency in English grammar; and knowing that the Latin had to be acquired chiefly through the use of its grammar, I procured a copy of Ross, and arranged with Dr. Sterrett of New Salem, the tenant in our house there, to take lessons. The doctor's stock in Latin was but slight, but then it served the purpose for a beginning; indeed, I found that progress could be fairly made in the grammar without the aid of any teacher, as it was easily understood and depended chiefly on memorizing: so that my lessons from the doctor were but few. In the periodical box of miscellaneous books and papers which my uncle was in the habit of sending me from Philadelphia, was a small copy of select fables of Æsop, Latin and English in parallel columns. The Latin of these was so plain and easy, and the grammatical construction so simple, that with my Ross' grammar I could make as much headway as respite from work would afford. Time for study was scant; occasional half-hours at meal time, evenings and Sundays before and after church—because any kind of study was resting from labor, according to my opinion of the fourth commandment. Want of time to study was a greater obstacle to progress than any difficulty in the subject. But progress was slow, and evidently must be so whilst I remained at home engaged in farm labor. But nevertheless it afforded some valuable preparation for the preparatory school.

Finally it was arranged in the spring of 1832, after I had assisted in putting in the corn and oats crops, that I should go to the preparatory school of the Rev. Jonathan Gill, a Covenanter minister residing near

Monroeville in Allegheny county, and board in his family during the week, returning home on Saturday evenings. I well remember my first interview with that worthy gentleman: it was not very auspicious or encouraging. I had set out from home early on a Monday morning, with my Latin grammar and a spare shirt and collar carefully folded with it, expecting to make a full week of study. I was inclined to apply myself as energetically to it as I had done to the work of building the farm houses already mentioned. It seemed to me then that energy and push was the proper thing in any line, and I am still of the same opinion.

When arrived at Mr. Gill's, about ten o'clock, I was informed by one of the students that he was trimming apple trees in the orchard. This was not as dignified an employment as I had expected to find him engaged in. I went in search however and found him; but he continued to devote more attention to his work than to me, and manifested a depressing coolness at my proposed course. His progress at work was exceedingly slow, and I felt provoked at his indifference and my own loss of time. I thought I should be immediately installed at my studies. But it was only two hours till noon, he said, when we could talk it over at dinner. He also remarked that he found a great many young men who commenced the study of Latin and Greek as I was about to do with great haste and ardor; but their resolution soon failed and in the course of a few months their ardor cooled, and then education was abandoned for other pursuits. Another remark he made as we passed by a row of new oak posts which he had set for a garden fence, was not very reassuring. I inquired why he did not use locust posts, of which I saw so many fine trees close by, as they would last for twenty years whilst the oak posts would rot off in five or six. This was the first remark of mine which seemed to really attract his attention. He stopped suddenly, and turning with a look of earnestness replied, "That is very true, Mr. Mellon, but the oak was more convenient, and will last longer than either posts or fences will be needed in this world." He saw this was beyond my comprehension, and explained that if the obvious meaning of Scripture was to be relied on, especially the books of Daniel and the Revelations, the end of the world and general conflagration would take place on a certain day in March, 1837; possibly, by reason of certain differences of calculation between Sidereal and Julian years, he allowed it might not take place till the year following, but that its certainty was assured about that time. This amazed me, and I re-marked if that was to be the case there was little use in my entry upon a course of study that would require several years. His unanswerable suggestion was that I might as well be engaged in that as anything else at the awful hour; but that such would be the result could not be doubted unless we denied the truth of the Holy Scriptures.

As I had no wish at the time to deny the truth of the Holy Scrip-tures, I waived any further discussion of the subject, but had some doubts of the entire sanity of my prospective tutor. I remained long enough acquainted with him however to find he was not at all insane, but like thousands of others, too confident in his Biblical interpreta-tions. And what was more to my purpose, I found him to be a pro-found scholar and a genial and polished gentleman, and he and his family were always afterwards among my best and most esteemed friends.

Chapter VIII

Academic Course

I FIND THE FOLLOWING memoranda in a note book which I kept at the time:

"Monday, April 16th, 1832.—Commenced the study of Latin grammar at Tranquil Retreat Academy, under the tuition of Rev. Jonathan Gill. Tuition to be $4.00 per quarter. Board in his family, $ .75 per week—that is, from Monday till Saturday of each week."

"June 30th, 1834.—Left the academy and paid Mr. Gill balance for tuition, $1.50; in all, $22.00 for 59 weeks or 5-½ quarters, exclusive of board."

The same note book shows I had been absent from time to time, in all 55 weeks, or nearly half time.[1] I ceased to board with Mr. Gill at the 1st of April, 1833. This was caused by our removal from Westmoreland to Allegheny county to a farm which my father had purchased near by Mr. Gill's place, and on which he afterwards resided till his death. Our new home was situate about a mile north of Monroeville in Plum now Patton township, and is since owned and occupied by the heirs of Samuel Beatty. Board at the academy seems remarkably low to us now, only one dollar for an entire week; but the price of living then was so cheap that board anywhere in the country could be obtained by students for one dollar, and in the city at from one dollar and a half to two dollars.

Although absent from the academy and engaged in farm work a great part of the time during my preparatory course, the absent time was not left unimproved. Whilst at home it was nearly as well utilized in educational progress as if spent at the academy. In June and July, and afterwards during the first summer, I perfected myself in Murray's

72

Latin Grammar, committing to memory the entire seventy-six rules of syntax, with the more important notes, so that I could repeat them from beginning to end without once referring to the book. I accomplished this by repeating the rules when following the plow; keeping the book in the crown of my hat, I resorted to it whilst the team was turning at the end of the furrow, until finally I mastered the whole so perfectly that I could dispense with the book altogether. And I found this thorough mastery of the rules of the greatest service throughout all my subsequent college course.

My note book shows: "May 7th, 1832, commenced reading 'Selectae Profanis.' November 5th, commenced Caesar's Commentaries. February 11th, 1833, commenced Ovid's Metamorphoses. April 22d, commenced Virgil." After the usual course in Virgil, six books, I was absent during November and December; and being unwell and mostly confined to the house, I read Virgil entirely through at home. This familiarized me so much with the Latin that I had no trouble with it afterwards. I also read Horace, and had made a good start in the Greek Grammar and Greek Testament before leaving Mr. Gill; and at college afterwards I found the remainder of the Latin course, Cicero and Livy, an easy task. During all my preparatory course I was off and at work on the farm over half the time, as is seen, but made up for it by private study; and in this way I was enabled to keep up with my class, and for thoroughness could always compare favorably with any who had their whole time for study without interruption. Custom had rendered farm work so nearly automatic that I could give my mind to memorizing whilst engaged in it; and the half hours of rest and leisure during the day and evening afforded the necessary opportunity to consult the books. This was pursuing a course of classical study under difficulties, it is true; but in all my experience, whether of study or business, I succeeded the best when hardest pushed to overcome difficulties. The greater the obstacle the stronger my desire grew to overcome it; and my power to succeed seemed to rise with the occasion for it. Energy, persistence and the contrivance of ways and means inspired by a strong will would always overcome the difficulty. "Where there is a will there is a way," contains a great truth. I was happy in the consciousness that I was achieving the object of my earliest ambition. The world was before me then, and showed a rosy outlook. But now, since I have passed through it all and experienced the reality of things, and can weigh the value of the education for which such a struggle was made, and have realized and weighed the value of the ulterior objects which were expected from it, I can see life and its objects and purposes in more sober colors. Whilst not what they seemed to me in pursuit, yet I am satisfied with what I have found them to be in possession; and I feel that all the extra exertion, labor and deprivation expended on the various objects and projects of my life have been amply repaid.

The world owes no one a living, but sooner or later rewards him fairly for his exertions in the proper direction.

It is a beautiful provision of nature to make life rosy at the beginning. It develops young hope and incites to action—renders work a pleasure and lures us on. As age approaches and strength declines, the enchantment is removed and we see things differently—I will not say in their true colors, because they may be as much disguised to us in age as in youth; as much underrated in the one case as overrated in the other. It is thus, however, we are brought gently to the point of departure. "Our little life," as Shakespeare has it, "is rounded with a sleep." And we are made to see or at least feel, with the wise man, that all is vanity. And so we are prepared to step out without regret!

My preparatory course was a struggle. My time and energy were severely taxed between study and help on the farm, and yet it is a period which I recall with pleasure. The society was most agreeable, and I formed friendships there which lasted throughout life. Mr. Gill was a fine classical scholar, and his family a model of all the virtues and graces necessary to a happy home. Then among the students were Sutton, Beatty, Kuhn, Aikin, M'Farland and others, several of whom rose to distinction in their respective professions in after life.

In life's journey we meet with pleasant companions and bright spots of sunshine here and there by the way, to which we like to go back and revel in their remembrance. Tranquil Retreat Academy and its characters still afford memories of this kind to me.

Chapter ix

College Course

IN THE SUMMER OF 1834, after leaving the preparatory school, the question which most agitated me was the college I should attend. The chief points regarding a choice were time, thoroughness and expense. The popular college in this section of the country at the time was Jefferson, located at Canonsburg.[1] My companion at the preparatory school, John I. Kuhn, afterwards a highly respected physician of McKeesport, for whom I had formed a warm attachment, had entered there, as also several others of my acquaintance. Accordingly I attended the September commencement in order to learn the course of procedure, with a view to entering. There was a hack between Pittsburgh and Canonsburg, charging a dollar for passage, but I preferred to walk. The distance was under twenty miles, and walking rather a recreation compared with my usual labor on the farm; and economy, wherever it could be brought to bear, had a commanding influence with me as I was forcing my education without any adequate means. The incidents of that bright day's journey, and my thoughts and anticipations by the way, remain very clear in memory yet, but are not of importance to relate.

There were some three or four hundred students at Jefferson then, and all seemed hilarious in anticipation of Commencement Day. They did not present the earnestness of purpose for knowledge and mental improvement which I had expected. Next day the students were formed in procession a short distance out of town, and headed by the faculty and trustees and preceded by a brass band, they marched through the town to the college. There assembled in the college hall or chapel which was crowded with spectators, the senior class, who were to receive diplomas, appeared on the platform; and after much parade of salutatory and valedictory and other addresses, the diplomas, profuse in sealing wax and blue ribbon, were delivered to the members of the class. The whole performance struck me rather as an advertisement to attract students and tickle the fancy of the shallow public; but what discouraged me still more was the prevailing frivolity. The spirit among the students was not of the nature which I expected: not at all in accord with the earnestness which the important purpose of training for life's serious work seemed to me to demand. Earnest educational purpose and enthusiasm for literary pursuits appeared at a discount; and how *not* to do it and yet get through it was the more popular sentiment. Those in downright earnest were regarded rather as bores. I found also that the rules of the institution were more stringent regarding the time or number of sessions for attendance than as to close attention to studies. This did not suit me, as I felt that by more labor more branches could be included in each session, and the time for graduation shortened. As the vacation intervened before actual study would begin, there was opportunity for further deliberation, and I walked home again, not at all as much elated with the prospect as on my way out; and on reaching the city I concluded to visit the Western University, which had long been in operation and well known, but not with the same degree of èclat and notoriety as Jefferson.

Here I found a very different state of affairs.[2] The numbers of students and professors were fewer, but what they lacked in numbers they appeared to make up in energy and earnestness. The purpose of all seemed to be work and progress, and accorded better with my own spirit and disposition on the subject. I found the conditions for a diploma were not fixed as to time, but only regarded the proficiency of the student in the studies of the curriculum; and a short time in the president's recitation room satisfied me that he was a man of extensive and accurate learning and great ability. It seemed to be just the place I had been searching for. The college edifice was a large and imposing stone building fronting on Third avenue, between Smithfield and Grant streets, afterwards destroyed in the great fire of 1845. It contained many vacant upstair rooms, some of which were easily obtained as students' domicils; and in a day or two I found several students as impecunious as myself and ready to join in a sumptuary club.

Accordingly, on the second Tuesday of October, 1834, with my trunk and table, bed and bedding and a few cooking utensils stowed upon a wagon loaded with farm products for market, my father and I made our way to the city, not however without experiencing the misfortune of a breakdown in Ferry's Hollow, as it was called—a deep ravine which crosses the Frankstown road a little west of Homewood. This difficult crossing has long since been overcome by proper grading. We finally arrived in the city in good condition, and the same evening I had my bed and furniture conveyed to the college rooms selected for the purpose; and the next day my companions of the club joined me with their furniture and bedding, and we soon had our rooms in snug and comfortable condition.

The arrangement was to procure the provisions at joint expense, and each to serve in rotation a week at a time, as cook. There were five of us, and the cooking was extremely simple. The labor was light and recurring only every fifth week. Our food was abundant but plain, and few dishes; but on that account it was best fitted for the condition of a sedentary student. And the cost of board on this plan at no time exceeded seventy-five cents per week to each.

A. W. Patterson, Wm. Canders, John and Jacob Fretly and myself composed the members of the club. Patterson was a tall, athletic young man from Freeport, Armstrong county, with fair talents but more addicted to writing doggerel poetry than to close study. Canders—I never learned where he was from—was possessed of a mathematical mind, but of little else. The Fretly brothers were from somewhere on the Susquehanna river, Pennsylvania Dutch; amiable in character, but possessing little else mentally than the faculty of memory. John, the elder, could readily commit a whole chapter of Scripture to memory in half an hour; and in his prayers and speeches—for he was exceedingly pious—could produce little more than Scripture quotations. Patterson aimed at becoming a medical doctor; Canders and the Fretlys intended the ministry, and I was undecided as between the ministry and law. My inclination was for the law, but I was uncertain whether I suited or could succeed in it; whilst I felt satisfied that in the ministry I should be provided for by the church in some way.

The first question which arose in our club had reference to prayers and graces. Piety in that direction had the majority of votes, but Patterson and I obtained a compromise by limiting the practice to Sundays. In all other respects we got along together quite agreeably, and our club continued in profitable operation for nearly two years. At times one or other would be absent, and we had a temporary member: William H. Sutton, afterwards Judge of the Probate Court at Little Rock, Arkansas, was with us at one time. Apart from meals and recitations our time was filled with constant study, with the exception of Dr. Patterson, who devoted some attention to poetry and the fine arts.

In Latin and Greek, mathematics and mental and moral philosophy Dr. Bruce, the president of the college, heard our recitations. He was one of a class of men rarely met with: modest and retiring of manner, shunning notoriety, and averse to anything having the appearance of ostentation. He was highly cultured in general literature, an extensive reader, liberal minded, and a most accurate scholar in the several branches he professed. He was not only learned, but extremely critical. He had all the philosophy of Bacon and Descartes, Hume, Reid and Dugald Stewart at command—he had himself been a student of Dugald Stewart; and his lectures on mental and moral philosophy were exceedingly interesting, profitable and practical. He had the learning of a great scholar and the ability of an apt teacher; and what was no less important to his position, his dignity of manner and kindness of heart secured the love and respect of the students; so much so that during my time, when the trustees made a change on one occasion interfering in some respect with his position and dignity as head of the college, the students actually rebelled—or in working men's language, we inaugurated a *strike* until the doctor's rights and privileges were restored.

An excellent literary society, "The Tilghman," possessed of a fair library, was attached to the college, and to its weekly exercises I feel that I owe nearly as much in the way of educational advantages as to my college studies.[3] This society, in its active and honorary members, comprised many at the time who became eminent afterwards in their respective professions; and among them I formed several lasting friendships which were valuable to me in after life.

My time at college was not continuous, my father often requiring my assistance on the farm; and not unfrequently in the summer time I would walk home from the city, eleven miles, between sundown and midnight, to be ready for work in the harvest field the next day.

On one occasion, on account of some rearrangement, we had a vacation extending over three months which I undertook to utilize to more advantage than in farm labor; and to that end I organized a pay school on the South Side, for a three months term. The common school system was in force then, but the school houses were vacant during the summer months, and privilege of one of them was easily obtained. Most of them in the suburbs contained but one room. The one which I selected was situate pretty well up on the side of Coal Hill, now Mount Washington, opposite the Point.[4] Tom Jones maintained and operated horse-power ferry boats directly across the Monongahela river to Penn street; and the coal mines were then in operation on the hill above, which, together with the glass factories of Frederick Lorenz still in operation near the southern terminus of the Suspension bridge, afforded a sufficient population for the school; and when I went around among them in the primitive way of obtaining subscribers I met with all the encouragement and success I could desire. The parents expressed themselves as not only willing to pay, but highly pleased to have the school in order to keep their children off the streets and out of mischief. Even Tom Jones of the ferry, who had no leaning towards literature judging from the rudeness of his expressions, when I informed him of my purpose showed his good will by wishing me success; and as an inducement to my perseverance declared that he would ferry me over free all the time, as it might keep the "little devils" off the boats and from falling into the river.

I was not long in obtaining all the scholars I could well accommodate, and was met on the morning of the opening with a full attendance of both sexes between five and fifteen; and it was not without some nervous trepidation that I entered on the work of organizing them into classes, as the organization and control of a school was a new enterprise to me. I succeeded however in a few days in having it reduced to order. And it is always with a pleased and gratified feeling that I recur to those three months of school keeping upon that hillside. The study of the thoughts and motives, the likings and antipathies of the miniature men and women whom I presided over, was neither unprofitable nor unpleasant. They were all children of work people, who at the end of the term paid me promptly, many of them warmly urging me to continue the school. The enterprise was a pecuniary success, netting me nearly one hundred and fifty dollars, which at that time was regarded as full compensation for the service; and to me it was an important amount.

The next enterprise for replenishing my funds was not so successful.

In the vacation of the year following I noticed a flattering prospectus and advertisement offering high profits in the book agency business. A firm of lawyers of Wellsburg, West Virginia, had taken it into their heads to make money by republishing books. A queer place it was for such an enterprise; but perhaps they were as inexperienced in that line of business as I was in the business of canvassing. They proposed the republication of Hallam's "History of the Middle Ages," a book but little known to the general public, although possessing merit to those who can appreciate it. This was the agency in which I concluded to spend a month or so in Ohio. I did not desire the field nearer home as I did not want the experiment known to my acquaintances; and I wished to know something of the manners and customs, thoughts and opinions of the outside world, as Ohio was regarded. So, armed with my commission and the prospectus and a few specimen chapters of the book, I set out for my field of labor.

I left home upon a young horse which my father wished to dispose of. I had never been from home beyond the city and its vicinity, and all lying west of it seemed a distant country for exploration. I spent my first night at Economy, with great interest and curiosity regarding that singular people.[5] From there I struck out south across the Ohio to the Steubenville turnpike at New Florence, taking in the Frankfort Springs on my way, all of which were interesting objects. Thence by way of Steubenville I went down the south side of the Ohio to Wellsburg, where I had an interview with my employers. Leaving Wellsburg my next station was Wheeling, where I disposed of my horse for a much better price than I had expected; and after seeing the sights of that city took stage on the National turnpike for Zanesville, Ohio, which was to be the first point of attack. After finding a boarding house and spending a day in examining the situation, I found the town had a public library of considerable magnitude and free to strangers. This became an object of much interest and occupied more of my time than was devoted to canvassing for the book during the few days of my stay. I soon found that book canvassing was not my *forte*. Although politely treated by the citizens I called on, the frequent refusals discouraged me. It was never in my nature to insist or "talk up" bargains of any kind. I had not sufficient assurance to press on any one to subscribe; and I found that leaving it to the unbiased choice of the party is not calculated to succeed in that line of business. Such was my experience; and after one day's canvass, and obtaining but three or four subscribers out of thirty or forty applications, I gave up the enterprise in disgust, and returned the papers to my employers. I have never heard since what became of them or their book.

But the sightseeing part of my enterprise was still ungratified; so I spent two or three days longer uninterruptedly in the public library and then struck out for Circleville afoot to see the remarkable prehistoric mounds and fortifications of that place. After examining those mounds I made my way to Chillicothe, where I arranged for a voyage by canal boat to Portsmouth on the Ohio. There were no passenger boats on that canal at the time, and the freight boat on which I embarked was poorly provided with provisions and accommodations. The crew consisted of an old man and his daughter and little boy: the old man acting as captain and steersman, the daughter as cook and the boy as driver. There was another passenger besides myself. Our beds consisted of a plank shelf fixed against the side of the boat, with a blanket and pillow; but the bed was more agreeable than the meals. We improved them greatly however by requisitions on neighboring cornfields as we passed along. The corn was not yet overripe for roasting ears. After a couple of days and nights of this voyage we reached Portsmouth. Here I took deck passage on a passenger steamboat, "The Argo," for Wheeling, the water being too low above that point. From Wheeling I made Washington, Pa., on foot in one day's journey, and the next day arrived home. Thus ended my first excursion to the outer world. It was a short trip, but replete with interest and incident on account of its novelty. Now I might travel to California and back in the same time, but with less of novelty and satisfaction. The world has grown older and more familiar to me since.

My college course wore on apace, prolonged on account of interruptions for farm work more than it otherwise would have been. But the end arrived at last; and on the appointed day in September, 1837, our class was assembled in the college hall for the customary valedictory of our president. It was one of the few really impressive addresses of the kind I have ever heard. Its sentiments have influenced my life and still abide in my memory. After the valedictory we received our diplomas, without the pomp and circumstance usual on such occasions at other places. I had worked hard for mine and anticipated much benefit from it as an endorsement of character and acquirements—far more than it ever afforded. In after life I did derive benefit from the studies I had pursued, or some of them; but from the circumstance of having a diploma I never derived any benefit whatever. In the professions and business management certificates of either ability or learning are value-less. In the battle of real life an exacting public will only estimate the ability and qualifications they see in actual practical use. Like California miners, they estimate the value of the mine by the amount of ore in sight. After obtaining the bauble which I had so eagerly sought for it was laid away as any other child's plaything, not again to be adverted to. I had supposed the fact of having a diploma for a regular college education would be a potent recommendation and essential to success in any profession; but in my forty years of subsequent experience in the legal profession it never occurred to any one among my numerous clients to inquire whether I had a diploma, or as to the kind of preliminary education I had received.

Chapter x

Study of Law

ONE PART OF MY CHIEF ambition, a college education, was now an accomplished fact. I had spent about five years for it at a valuable period of life, and about five hundred dollars in cash. The cash part may seem small, but it must be remembered that straitened circumstances compelled economy, and money went further then than it does now. It was a hard struggle all through. I got little help in it except from my mother. Once or twice I nearly gave up the effort, but pertinacity to a purpose has ever been part of my nature; and now when nearing the end of my journey and reviewing my past life, I find no instance where I had set my mind earnestly on an object that I did not succeed in devising ways and means to accomplish it.

Was the prize worth the cost of time, money and exertion required? To me I should say it was, but to many others it would have been waste. Educational advantages depend on their relevancy to the future occupation, and the aptitude of the individual for the occupation intended. Life is too short for proficiency in all branches. For the legal profession, which I afterwards adopted, considerable time and labor might have been saved without disadvantage, by omitting several of my college studies. The Latin has been of use in its superior grammatical science and by affording a valuable insight into the derivation and original meaning of English words. The Greek and Latin classics have also been of some value historically, as affording an insight to the manners, customs, thoughts and opinions of the people, and the state of civilization in past ages. The practical branches of mathematics have also been found useful; but the Greek as a language, or so much of it as I was able to acquire, and the higher branches of mathematics and the

French, and much else that consumed part of my time at college, were entirely useless. It is only what we shall have frequent occasion to call to mind and put in practice in after life, that we can retain in memory. The rapidity with which school-acquired knowledge, or indeed any other kind of knowledge fades from the mind unless frequently re-freshed or recalled for practical purposes, is a factor in education not sufficiently regarded; and to retain dead languages or any other such knowledge by frequent review and revival for their own sake as orna-mental accomplishments, is a practice more fanciful than sensible. But an essay on education is out of place here. Any of my descendants in-terested in that momentous question, the education of youth, will do well to consult Herbert Spencer's book on the subject.[1] I am aware of no other source of so much wise and practical advice.

Now that I had obtained an education, the more important ques-tion, what to do with it or how to live by it, was still unsolved. I was yet undecided as to a profession. I had made up my mind against the min-istry, but hesitated to venture on the law. Two insuperable objections existed to the ministry: I could not give up the hope of bettering my condition by the acquisition of wealth, nor could I submit to become a pliant tool of any church organization, or be subject to the unreason-able prejudices and whims of those who rule in congregations. And as to the legal profession, I had at that time an erroneous opinion of what was necessary to success in it. I only judged from what I saw in the courts—the performances of the lawyers on the trial of causes. The op-portunity for display and notoriety afforded the successful advocate was tempting enough; but these opportunities seemed too limited, and success in that line by one so nervous and diffident as I was, seemed too uncertain. I was not aware then that the money making part of the business lay in the back ground, and not in the line of speech making to any great extent; and that those growing rich in the profession were seldom seen in court. That many of those who did appear in the trial of causes only did so as incidental and necessary to the more profitable part of their business.

In this hesitating condition I was relieved from making a decision for the time being by a circumstance which occurred in the college which I had just left. Dr. Sproull, of the First Reformed Presbyterian Church of Allegheny, was Latin professor at the time, but fell sick dur-ing the vacation after I had graduated, and remained so at the beginning of the following session. In this emergency the faculty sent for me, as I had shown efficiency in the Latin, and invited me to take Dr. Sproull's place, if not permanently at least temporarily. The offer was flattering and the position agreeable, and so at the opening of the session I assumed the duties of Latin professor, and filled that position for several months, until I decided to enter upon the study of law.

Teaching is a sure way to thoroughness; and it may be from the fact of thoroughness that Latin has always benefited me more than any other of my college studies, although even in it I could not now read with any degree of ease, without constant reference to the Lexicon.

After I resigned the Latin professorship, I was duly entered as a student in the office and under the direction of the Hon. Charles Shaler, ex-judge of the Court of Common Pleas of Allegheny County; and thereupon entered with all my might on a course of legal study. I found it easier than almost anything else I had been engaged in; almost as easy as reading history, except for the discrimination required to distinguish between legal principles. Necessity for self support still attended me, and in the following March, 1838, a vacancy occurred in the prothonotary's office and the place was offered me which it was my good luck to accept.[2] Two clerks were all that were then required. James Logan, the prothonotary, had died shortly before, and Thomas Liggett, a highly respected old citizen, was appointed by the governor to fill his place. Thomas MacConnell, senior clerk, a nephew of the deceased officer, remained; and Robert Robb, Esq., the junior clerk, retiring to enter on the practice of his profession, left the vacancy which I obtained. Mr. Liggett's son William was my companion and friend in the Tilghman Society, and through his influence with his father I was appointed assistant deputy prothonotary, a position which I held under Mr. Liggett and his successor for over fifteen months. Until after I entered the prothonotary's office I was not aware of the great importance of that position in my legal studies. It opened up the whole field of legal practice to me. Here I saw the law and its principles in their actual application. Technical terms and rules were made clear which I had not before understood. All the details and formalities of procedure became familiar. My study of the text books with the work in the office united theory with practice—a condition essential to proficiency in any profession or calling. After my entrance into the prothonotary's office I studied the law subjectively; and whenever some new point was raised

in the courts or novelty in practice occurred, my reading was directed
to its elucidation. The text books in the law office and the documents
and legal proceedings in the prothonotary's office illustrated and explained each other.

Besides this, it was an advantage to learn the methods of the leading
lawyers; and the acquaintance formed with all the members of the bar
was in itself a valuable acquisition. And the position also necessarily
led to an extensive acquaintance with such citizens as had business in
the courts or county offices, from which I derived much advantage in
my subsequent professional life. But one of the best acquisitions was
the friendship I formed with Mr. MacConnell, my associate in the
office. The friendship of some men is valuable on account of their
good qualities, although not contributing to one's business or pecuniary interests. He and I had the management of the office to ourselves,
as Mr. Liggett paid but little attention to it. I had not before been personally acquainted with Mr. MacConnell, and had only known him by
reputation as a modest, quiet young school teacher, who had made
some progress in educating himself; and who had gone so far as to
have himself enrolled as a student of law under Mr. Shaler, my preceptor: which last step I regarded as rather presumptuous in one who had
received none of the advantages of an academic or collegiate course.
This feeling was rather aggravated at first by a habit he had of asking
me troublesome questions concerning the derivation of Greek and
Latin roots, or the bearing of problems in geometry. I regarded it as
pretentious on his part without a diploma to aspire to such scholarly
attainments. And what made it more annoying I found it very difficult
to answer some of his questions satisfactorily; and being a college
graduate I could not plead ignorance on any point of knowledge. I was
occasionally even put to the necessity of skirmishing for time to se-
cretly consult my books at home for an answer. Although he had neither been to an academy or college and I had a regular diploma, he
would not take it for granted that I knew everything, which I thought
courtesy at least demanded of him, but like the locksmith in Dickens,
he was continually "wanting to know." But it was not a great while until I discovered the unpleasant fact that he really did know far more
about the Greek at least, and algebra and some other branches of
mathematics than I did myself; and that his questions were only
prompted through an earnest and honest desire to be informed rather

than to display his own knowledge or chaff me. I was greatly surprised to find in him a really self-educated man, who could read both Latin and Greek with ease; and was equally familiar with all other branches of a classical education, and more accurate and critical in most of them than many of those who possessed diplomas. But I was still more surprised on being invited to his rooms to find there an excellent library, not only of the usual literary and historical works of the best authors, but also a law library containing the usual text books and the entire set of Pennsylvania Reports to that date. Out of office hours it was here he lived and moved and had his being. After we better understood each other and found our relative educational level, we became of mutual advantage and a lasting attachment grew up between us.

It will be readily perceived therefore that in him I had a valuable associate in the study of the law. We read separately at nights and other intervals, and compared notes at leisure moments in the office. In this way we achieved a pretty thorough understanding of the law in general; and particularly those branches of it more immediately applicable to our own state. Every new point of interest raised from day to day in the courts was noted and discussed: often with the benefit of the rulings of the court and the views of counsel concerned in the case. In these studies and exercises and the performance of the duties of the office, we progressed smoothly and agreeably for many months, until we deemed ourselves ready and prepared for examination and admission to the bar. This purpose was precipitated by a desire on his part to leave the prothonotary's office and join his friend and former office companion, Mr. Robb, in the practice of the profession.

Our preceptor, Judge Shaler, had taken little trouble with our legal education. He excused himself on the ground of press of business and because, as he alleged, we were progressing very well without his assistance. The most he did was occasionally to offer a word of advice. I remember at one time, before I entered the prothonotary's office, he suggested that I was confining myself too closely to study. It appeared to him I studied night and day without taking necessary exercise or recreation. I justified my course on the ground that I felt no injury or inconvenience from it; that my health was good, and the sooner I could be admitted to the bar the better. He allowed that was all well enough, but I should consider whether ten or more years at the end of professional life might not be of greater value than two or three at the beginning. He thought that by the course I was pursuing I might come to the bar a year or two sooner, but in doing so might injure my constitution in a way that would shorten my life very materially. I have often thought of this advice since; and to some other students it would probably apply with much force, but it was inapplicable to me. A sedentary condition and mental work, no matter how severe, never gave me any inconvenience or interfered with my health. I have been favored with a remarkably tough and enduring physical organization; and on the physical organism depends, in my opinion, the health of both body and mind.

The judge was excusable for the neglect of his students, as he was so closely pressed with professional business at the time that to hear recitations or attend to examinations was out of the question. He was learned and eloquent, as well as a pleasant, genial gentleman; witty, humorous and kind hearted. His outward appearance and manner misrepresented his true character: without a spark of pride or hauteur in his disposition, he would seem on the street to those unacquainted with him the embodiment of pride and self-sufficiency. In fact, there was an air of reserve and dignified superiority about all the lawyers of the old school in those days which has long since disappeared, and as I think, much to the injury of the profession. He was also a man of refined taste in art and literature, and a devout Episcopalian and great admirer of Bishop Hopkins. Hopkins and he had been intimate friends at the bar here before the former deserted the law and went into the ministry.

A fine oil painting was displayed in the judge's front office, the central figure of which was an English barrister in his professional robe, with a sturdy countryman on each side of him. The barrister was in the act of swallowing a large oyster from a fork in his hand, whilst the countrymen were each admiring the beauty of an oyster shell. The countrymen represented the parties to a lawsuit; and after its termination were considering the result, which they expressed in these words:

> A pearly shell for you and me;
> The oyster is the lawyer's fee.

I expressed some surprise at the display of such a picture in a law office, as clients might think it presented more truth than fiction; but the judge declared it gave them a hint which if they did not heed, still afforded much relief to his conscience.

The examining board at the time were not very punctual or attentive to their duties, though frequently exacting and critical when once in session; and it was only after several efforts and abortive attempts that MacConnell and I procured a meeting of a majority of the members at Mr. Lowrie's office—the same Lowrie to whom I had so nearly become a pupil when a boy, and who afterwards became a judge of the Supreme Court. Those of the board who attended were Mr. Lowrie, James Finley—son of ex-governor Finley, and then a prominent lawyer here, Thomas H. Baird, ex-judge of Fayette and Washington county courts, and James Dunlop, author of the "Digest;" all able and critical lawyers and rather jealous of each other's pretensions.

My companion and I experienced to its fullest extent that nervous trepidation natural to the pending ordeal, and would have felt relieved perhaps had the board for some unexpected reason disappointed us again. Our time had come however and the board with stern dignity signified its readiness to proceed; but as luck would have it, or because he was my senior in years as well as clerical position, a protracted bombardment was first opened on my alarmed companion. But he stood it well and was prepared with correct answers as readily as the tumult of his faculties would allow, though not to as much advantage as he would have done had the same questions been asked him under other circumstances, on some less important occasion. Luck still favored me; for when in an exhausted condition the gentlemen of the board turned their attention to me the first question was by Judge Baird: "Whether the consignor or consignee should bring suit against a common carrier in case of non-delivery of the goods." Although practically of common occurrence, the question had somehow escaped my attention in the books; but on that very day I had heard it discussed between Baird and Finley in a case on trial before Judge Grier, where they were opposing counsel. Discretion taught me to answer as I had heard the judge rule, to the effect that the suit should be brought by the consignee; and I did so without intimating the source of my knowledge, as I saw it might lead to a dispute. Baird at once pronounced my answer erroneous, but Finley as promptly pronounced it correct; and the two immediately went into an excited discussion on the same line of argument they had followed in court. This was soon joined in by the other members of the board and kept up till it was time to adjourn. So our fate, as we thought, was left undecided. We received a note however the next day from the chairman of the board, informing us that they were satisfied with our examination, but as the member had not been present who should have examined us on criminal law, we must submit ourselves to him for an examination on that branch before our certificates could be granted.

The member in question, W. W. Irwin, Esq., was deputy attorney general for this district at the time, and so busily engaged in the criminal court that an interview with him was very difficult to obtain during business hours; and being a gentleman of festive disposition, he did not like to have his evenings disturbed. But my companion and I understood what perseverance could accomplish; and after numerous attempts at last intercepted him in his office on a cold winter night whilst he was bestowing some forcible epithets on the absent office boy for letting his fire go out. He was not altogether in a patient or favorable mood for a protracted examination; but he had disappointed us so often that politeness compelled him to entertain our application for a hearing; and after succeeding in lighting a candle—it was before the days of gas or petroleum—without inviting us to be seated, and with poker in hand making threatening gestures at the empty grate whilst looking disagreeably askance at us, he demanded of me who was nearest him to define murder. I gave him the definition I had learned from Blackstone. He then demanded of my companion a definition of manslaughter, and was as promptly answered; whereupon, in an expression more forcible than polite, he declared himself satisfied that any student who could tell the difference between murder and manslaughter was competent to practice in the criminal courts. After this we obtained our certificates and admission to the bar in due course.

Doubtless our intimacy with all the members of the board, through the business of the prothonotary's office, had a good deal to do with the leniency of our examination. We were both sworn in and paid our dollar each to George Kinzer, chief tipstave of all the courts, on the same day, the 15th of December, 1838. And here I may as well explain how it was I should be admitted to the bar so soon after graduating at the University. It occurred in this way: whilst I had not decided in favor of the legal profession, I had a strong inclination that way; and knowing the rules of court required registration as a student for two years before admission, I had procured myself to be registered a considerable time before I graduated, feeling that if I decided in favor of the law I might be able to prepare for admission in a shorter time. The true time of my law studies therefore did not much exceed a year and a half, and for nine months of this the business hours were occupied in the duties of the prothonotary's office.

On admission to the bar Mr. MacConnell entered upon the practice of his profession at once; and I became the senior clerk and remained in the prothonotary's office for several months afterwards. I stuck to it for so long because I was doubtful of being able to sustain myself at the bar, and would not give up certainty for hope. My salary was but twenty dollars per month before Mr. MacConnell left, and twenty-five afterwards; a small income for board, clothing and incidental expenses, but I saved some of it nevertheless. Board was but two dollars per week, and with what I had saved from my salary as Latin professor and two hundred dollars which I obtained from my father, invested from time to time in little speculations in the purchase of small judgments, mechanic's liens and like securities wherever the holders were anxious to realize without the delay of awaiting their maturity, I had accumulated some seven hundred dollars, which I invested in a law library before I ventured to give up my situation for the uncertainty of professional practice. I hardly expected to make a living at the bar for a year or two, or to get enough to do to occupy much of my time; and in this view before leaving I arranged with the prothonotary for a share of copying work: exemplification of records and the like, such as I could do at my law office. But I had no occasion at any time afterwards to apply for work under that arrangement. On opening a law office in June, 1839, I was very agreeably surprised by a fair share of professional business—more than usual for a beginner; which I attributed as much to the knowledge which suitors in the courts had obtained of me whilst in the prothonotary's office as to any particular efficiency on my part in the law.

Chapter XI

———◆ ◆ ◆———

Bread Winning

WHAT I DID SO FAR was merely preparatory or incidental to the real business of life. I had procured an education and a profession—had learned my trade; and now I was to apply it and find out what could be accomplished by it. My hopes were far from sanguine. Apart from the casual acquaintance formed with the people attending the courts and the public offices, I was a stranger. I had no relatives or influential friends to introduce or recommend me; and I supposed, though erroneously, that it required both favor and friends to obtain business. But I felt I must try; and having already several offers of professional employment, which with such compensation as I might get from the prothonotary for copying records would afford support for some time, I ventured to try the experiment. Accordingly in June, 1839, in common parlance I hung out my shingle, as stated in the last chapter.

There was a long, low two-story frame house fronting on Fifth street now Fifth avenue, at the southeast corner of Market alley, which belonged to Mr. Drake. On the lower floor the room at the corner of the alley was without a tenant. This I obtained at a rent of six dollars per month. The adjoining room was occupied by Sands & Reineman, watchmakers, and the entire upper floor by the owner of the building and his family. Finer buildings now stand on the same spot. Fifth avenue was not then a business street, and mine was the first law office opened on it. The law offices were chiefly on the west side of the Diamond behind the Courthouse—some few on Fourth street, between Market and Wood. It was before the courts were removed to Grant's hill. That location on which the new Courthouse was afterwards built was yet a part of lawyer Ross' apple orchard, and rather out of town.

The old Courthouse stood where the Diamond market house on the west side of Market street now stands. It was an ancient looking, square brick structure with a cupola and bell on top, and a low one-story building on each side. That on the north side contained the office of the prothonotary and clerk of the Orphans' and Criminal Courts, all in one room, which was convenient enough, as those different official functions centered in one individual. The building on the south side contained the register's and recorder's office in one room, and with one individual officiating for both purposes. In the main building the sheriff's office was in front on the left, and the commissioner's office on the right. The residue of the lower floor was the court room, paved with brick, with a high bench on the west side for the judge and a circular railing around it, including the jury box and attorneys' tables. The grand jury and other jury rooms were on the second floor. Such was the arena of my first professional labors.

My office was of rather plain exterior and spare of costly furniture within; but nevertheless I was very soon agreeably surprised by clients and frequent accessions to their numbers. It was not long before I had business enough, with reading and preparation, to keep my time fully employed. The business and profits of that first year entirely exceeded my highest expectations. Before commencing, the most I had ventured to hope for as a result of the first five years was a living practice and accumulated surplus of fifteen hundred dollars or so; but I had fully secured this by the end of the first year. In fact, I had underrated my own business qualifications and legal abilities. I had not taken into consideration that I was then at an age to possess mature judgement; that I was of an earnest, cautious and painstaking disposition, had a good education and a rather extensive and accurate knowledge of the law, and had become favorably known to many of the business men; and what was of still more importance to litigants, I had already much experience in the methods and practice of the courts. To this I added, not eloquence so much as the faculty of persuasion on jury trials. And above all, I possessed a quality rather painful to myself but of much advantage to clients: which was that I espoused my client's cause as if my own. If I could not do this I did not engage in the case. I either believed at the outset or became convinced that my client was in the right; and under this feeling if I lost a case I felt the chagrin of being to blame for it. Indeed I have often found that the loss of a case annoyed me more than it did the client. I know that this is contrary to professional sentiment, which holds that the attorney should not identify himself with his client or mix up his own personal feelings in the case; but I was of so sanguine a temperament that I could not avoid this. It was not remarkable therefore that those having legal business or litigation on their hands should find it to their interest to retain me.

Two other traits of character also promoted my advancement: one was my industry in hastening a suit or other legal proceeding to a conclusion and having it closed and settled; the other was moderation in fees and charges. I never overrated the value of my services—in fact I rather underrated them; and in looking back over my professional career, if there is any one thing more than another in which I feel that I was to blame, it is for having done too much service for too little money. There is a medium course which is the best and safest in all things. If left to myself I hardly ever charged enough; whilst some other young lawyers, my contemporaries, on the other extreme would charge their clients so excessively as to drive them off ever afterward. There is no fee bill or schedule of rates and charges in the legal profession and no law regulating the subject; it is left to the lawyer himself and depends on his own discretion. If the charge is unreasonable the client is without remedy unless it is so flagrantly unreasonable and extortionate as to shock all sense of justice and propriety. The client may refuse to pay, and put the attorney to the trouble of a suit for his fees; but when the case comes to trial the influences are all unfavorable to the client. The attorney plaintiff is a witness himself to relate and magnify the importance and value of his own performance; and he can always find numerous members of the bar who prize legal services so highly as to be able to testify in his favor to the justice of his claim; and in addition, when the judge comes to charge the jury, he will most likely instruct them that services in the legal profession are of such a peculiar nature that no one can be so well aware of their extent or value as the attorney himself who has performed them.

My undue moderation in charges soon led me to discover that it was often my best policy to leave the amount of the fee to the client himself. On that line most of them would hand me over much more than I would have fixed had I been insisted on to make the charge. Another point I may mention here in regard to which young professional men are apt to be mistaken: the world mostly estimates professional merit pretty accurately; and those requiring such service almost invariably employ the man who will serve their purpose best. In my experience I found friends and favor go for little. Litigants will pass by friends and relatives and retain whoever will serve them to the best advantage. Caste or class and relationship have little influence. Although I was comparatively poor and obscure, yet I soon had a fair share of clients of wealth and position in society, even among those who had nephews or other relatives in the profession. Nor will sectarianism influence men in this respect: although I had several rivals at the bar of the Catholic denomination, I obtained as fair a proportion of Catholic clients as of any other sect. And whilst I am on the subject of professional qualifications I may as well say something here by way of advice to those who shall have occasion to employ a lawyer. Of course, the kind of service required will in the main indicate the kind of lawyer to be retained; and I cannot do better than repeat here some general suggestions contained in a pamphlet which I published at one time on legal remedies for certain grievances:

> Inasmuch as an attorney at law is necessary to the application of any legal remedy, a word here in regard to his choice may not be amiss. Nearly every business man has the acquaintance of an attorney whom he prefers, and to whom he applies whenever he has occasion for professional services; but to such as have not I would say in cases of this kind, avoid extremes. Go neither too high nor too low. In the one extreme you may meet with humbug or extortion, and in the other extreme trickery or incapacity. You want an earnest, energetic, reliable man of good character and sound common sense, with a clear head and respectable knowledge of the law and practice of the courts; one who will take the trouble to learn and comprehend all the facts and circumstances of your case, and who can in a clear and persuasive manner present the evidence and arguments in your favor to the court and jury. Such a man is more likely to bring you through safely and with a more satisfactory result when you come to settle up with him than either a lower or higher grade lawyer. I by no means underrate the value of high talent in the profession, but the employment of such talent is unnecessarily expensive, and its possessor is apt to be so full of business more congenial to him that he may give your

case far less attention than it requires. I have seen many mistakes made by men when in a difficulty of this kind, retaining a lawyer of great public celebrity. Flashing eloquence and the arts of oratory are not near so potent with the clear-minded courts and jurors of the present day as is often supposed. Dogged tenacity and earnest perseverance will accomplish more in all ordinary legal controversies.

From the first my business and profits rapidly increased, and at the end of three years, or about the beginning of 1843, when I made a rough estimate with a view to ascertain whether I might safely make a change in personal relations, I found my accumulations amounted to about twelve thousand dollars. This was not composed entirely of professional earnings, although chiefly so. It was unusually large in those days for a young lawyer so short a time at the bar. Economy in expenses and prudent investments had also a good deal to do with it. I might have earned all I did, but without them would have been worth no more at the end than at the beginning. My nature and early training protected me from the folly of earning money and throwing it away; and common sense and every day experience teach the lesson that wealth rightly acquired and wisely managed possesses a power and advantage never to be despised or disregarded. According to my observation those in our profession who pretend to disparage accumulation of wealth are the readiest to grab and extort when they have the chance, and the foremost to misuse it when obtained. In pursuance of the wise advice of a favorite poet, I was disposed

> To gather gear by every wile
> That's justified by honor.

I take it this is the pith of the whole matter and the true course supported by philosophy, morality and common sense. Accordingly when I obtained money I used it to the best advantage, in the safest and most profitable investments I could find; and thus by my earnings and investments and reinvestments, my accumulations have increased ever since.

For instance: before my first year in the profession expired I had obtained from my landlord, Drake, a favorable five years lease of the whole lower floor of the building by paying him a fixed sum for the entire term in advance. I saw that business even then was beginning to flow into Fifth street; and this lease in the end afforded me a net profit of over one thousand dollars. My next adventure in the real estate line was the purchase of a new unfinished building on Prospect street, on which I soon realized four hundred dollars profit by a resale; soon after that was the purchase of a house and lot on Penn street in the Fifth now Ninth ward, which I fitted up for a home and occupied with my parents for some two years before my marriage.

Within three years after I commenced, the courts and public offices were removed to the new Courthouse on the hill; and in 1842, in view of the prospective advantages of convenience to the courts and increasing value of the location, I purchased a lot for fifteen hundred dollars at the corner of Fifth and Wylie, on which some years afterwards I erected three buildings and had my office there until I finally quit the practice to go on the bench.

I mention these instances merely to show in what way my professional labors and private business were conducted; and it was when progressing in this manner in 1843, that the most important event of my life took place, which I shall relate in the next chapter.

Chapter XII

Courtship and Marriage

THIS CHAPTER INVOLVES the sentimental and emotional. From what has gone before the reader might infer that I had a hard time of it, that it was all work and no play: that my youth was one of effort and hardship with scarcely a glimpse of pleasure and enjoyment; and that I was either void of the emotions and the desire of recreation natural to youth, or that they had been dwarfed and extinguished in my struggles to rise in the world. Such inferences however would be wholly erroneous. Although my road was a pretty hard one to travel it was never without its compensations in pleasures which were keenly relished, though few and far between. Rest and recreation from work were limited, but what was lacking in extent and frequency was made up in intensity of appreciation. It is so with all pleasure: if limited, it is the more highly enjoyed; whilst too much only cloys the appetite and destroys its effect altogether. It is a poor and barren nature which cannot derive a fair share of enjoyment from any condition of life whatever. Poverty may be a misfortune to the weaklings who are without courage or ability to overcome it, but it is a blessing to young men of ordinary force of character: it protects them from excesses, withholds unwise pleasures and indulgences, teaches the value of time and of wealth, and the necessity of well doing to better their condition. It brings out their latent energies in a manner to train them thoroughly for the active duties of life. If I had been raised in the lap of wealth, my nature would have led me to greater indulgence in ease and luxury. I would have lived higher, spent more money, indulged more in company and recreation, would in short have taken it easier. But I do not believe I would have realized as much true happiness by such increased indulgences as I did without them. I certainly would not have made the same efforts to acquire an education or a profession, nor would have accomplished as much in life afterwards. It was from the struggles necessary to remove the obstacles in my way, and the satisfaction resulting from overcoming such as seemed insuperable that I derived the most enjoyment; and in my case the opportunities for pleasure in overcoming difficulties were abundant. Rigid economy was essential to success, but my pecuniary condition was never so straitened as to deprive me of adequate necessaries and comforts; and I am very sure that if I had been more plentiful of money I would have lived more freely and accomplished less; and that if I had had all the indulgence in youth which wealth could afford, and the enjoyment of pleasures to the event of my natural desires, I could feel neither happier nor better for it now when my course is nearly run. It would not have left me as much satisfaction as the results of my early struggles have done. It requires a higher nature than the average youth possesses to resist the temptations of wealth and ease. It is not impossible, but the instances are exceptional. My children have been able to resist its influences more successfully than I fear their father would have done. As a rule it is only the man who has passed through tribulation, and has had his energies aroused and his faculties strengthened by the necessity for great exertion, that accomplishes much in the battle of life.

But the exertion necessary to success does not dwarf the passions; and with me the tender passion and love of children and domestic life was always strong—even when a boy at school I would single out some one little girl I admired above any other. After I was smitten with the ambition for a professional life, prudence compelled me to suppress any leanings in that direction: in order to succeed when any great purpose is formed whatever would hinder it should be dispensed with, and complications of the kind would only have hindered and obstructed mine. Nevertheless throughout all my prolonged efforts the day dreams of the distant future still presented a happy home with loving wife and bright children as the ultimate consummation of my hopes: in fact I was by nature what the Germans aptly term a "family man." I take it to have been owing to this trait that although easily served and not hard to please with board or lodging, yet so long as I remained single I never felt settled or contented. I always experienced a feeling of solitary isolation or unrest without knowing the cause; no matter how pleasant or agreeable my associates and surroundings, it was not home.

After admission to the bar and I could afford the expense I tried different methods of living, at one time a boarding house, at another a hotel, and again a pleasant private family where I had all the comforts and privacy attending domestic life; but still the heart's desire was not satisfied. Supposing the longing would be gratified in the parental home which I had left, I induced my parents to leave their farm in the country and come to the city to live; and when once domiciled with them again in a house of our own I found it to be a great improvement and it succeeded very well for a time. But the spirit of unrest would not down: and early in 1843, after my father determined to return to the country, I began for the first time to think seriously of marriage. The prospect of returning to a boarding house or a hotel was discouraging, and marriage the only alternative. Marriage at some time or other had always been in contemplation, and I had now attained to a position which would justify its consummation. I was in my thirtieth year and now was the proper age, neither too soon nor too late; with experience and settled habits not fully attainable at an earlier age, and not yet subject to the fixed tastes and crusty disposition of a bachelor, and with the possibility of a long enough life still before me to care for and train a family of children, there was no reason why I should not enter the marriage relation. Thus it was when I set out in search of a wife.

It was an enterprise new to me, but as I had succeeded in others more difficult I undertook it without any apprehensions of failure. All the circumstances were not in my favor however. I was no society man, and my acquaintance with the fair sex was limited. I had been too close a student at first and was too much engaged in business afterwards to cultivate the graces popular with them. It is true I was acquainted in some few good families, two or three of them with marriageable daughters, where I had visited occasionally for rest and amusement when wearied with business cares and labors. Such visits being without serious purpose, I had always avoided pointed attentions such as would indicate affection or raise expectation. I never would trifle with female affections, nor excite groundless hopes. Honor and self respect made anything of the kind repugnant; and I always felt a contempt for those who acted otherwise to gratify selfish vanity. I had mingled little in society, seldom even attending the theatre or other places of public amusement. Reading and rest in the evenings in my own room was more agreeable.

Under these circumstances, when the resolution was taken to change my mode of life and I began to cast about in mind for a wife, I was not attracted towards any particular lady acquaintance, but compelled to extend my researches into new fields. With this view I obtained introductions to several new lady friends, but without results. Some were too gay and frivolous or self conceited; others too slovenly and ungainly, and others again too coarse or stupid. It was a rather more difficult task than I had expected, and I was impatient of spending much time upon it. Great beauty or accomplishments were not demanded. I wanted a wife for a helpmate, not for display; one who could bear up and help me in adversity should it overtake us, or share with me the satisfaction of success, as the case might be. I was not of an age to be easily led astray in my selection by premature emotional excitement or falling in love, and could therefore consider and decide impartially regarding favorable and unfavorable qualities with due deliberation. In this respect there is great advantage in mature age. There is a time for everything, and the right time for men to marry in my opinion is between twenty-five and thirty-five, and for women between twenty and thirty. The minds of both sexes at these ages are more likely to be clear of the fog arising from the *veally* condition of the emotions at an earlier date.

It was when feeling my way in this manner that the following circumstance shaped my destiny. Dr. R. C. Beatty, an old and warm friend, then a practising physician in East Liberty, informed me of his approaching marriage in a few months and of his wish to have me as his attendant on the occasion. This was interesting, as it was to my purpose to make new acquaintances. His glowing description of his intended bride did not interest me much, as I accounted for it by his feelings in her favor; but some reference which he made to her sister was more in point. He had at first a greater admiration for the sister, he said, who was a leader among the young ladies of their set; but she was rather too independent for him, had no elasticity in her composition, and did not seem to appreciate gentlemen's attentions. These traits excited my curiosity sufficiently to inquire of other parties more about her family connections and the society she moved in. I had known the family favorably by reputation long before, but not sufficiently to judge whether so intimate a connection with it was desirable; and could not rely much on my friend the doctor's views under the circumstances. I happened to have other acquaintances in the neighborhood however, from whom I gathered enough without betraying my purpose to satisfy me that she deserved attention. Accordingly at the next interview with the doctor I suggested the propriety of giving me a previous introduction to his lady, if he intended me to be his groomsman. To this he readily assented, but appointed no time; and I had at the next interview to suggest it to him again, when he manifested a willingness to comply but still proposed no method for its accomplishment, at which I felt rather disappointed. Whatever was the cause—whether the danger of rivalry or not in his own affair—I could not surmise, but he showed no alacrity towards giving me an introduction. This incited me to seek one without his assistance, and I soon devised a way.

In a few days was my birthday, for which I planned a sleigh ride to the country to visit the family of my old friend and employer, Mr. Thomas Liggett. I was acquainted with his daughter Sarah, afterwards Mrs. Hitchcock, herself the right type of womanhood for a wife, and of a good family and very wealthy; but I feared hereditary consumption. Her brother William, my friend and college mate already mentioned, had died of it, and her own appearance indicated a tendency that way. And although I was mistaken in this, because she is still living and well now after more than forty years, yet she would still have disappointed my ideal of domestic happiness as she is childless. But it was not on her own account I called, only to invite her to take a sleigh ride with me, to which she readily consented. I knew she was intimate with the young ladies in question, and we were soon driving in that direction; and on their name being mentioned I expressed a wish to make their acquaintance, mentioning the circumstance of my friend's engagement to one of them, and that I felt a desire to see her. She expressed much pleasure at the opportunity of obliging me by an introduction, and very soon we were in the spacious parlor of the old Negley mansion, where I found myself for the first time in the presence of her who was afterwards to become my wife. I took her in at a glance; and now, after over forty years, can well remember how she looked then, even to the fashion of her hair and every minute particular of her dress. I see her now in the mind's eye, as she stood there in the sunlight which was struggling through the window curtains giving me a full view of her appearance—quiet, pleasant and self-possessed. I remember thinking to myself, in person she would do if all right otherwise. I remember also of its flitting across my mind, whether this might be the one of destiny!

After a short but pleasant interview we left; but the interview created a good impression, and the way was now open for further effort in that direction. The surroundings were favorable, neither too coarse nor too fine: country life and reality blended with the refinements of wealth and education. In a few weeks I called again, this time in company with my friend the doctor, and did not call afterwards until his wedding, when more time and opportunity was afforded for observation.

It was an old-fashioned wedding at the house of the bride's mother, with an *infare* the next day. The *infare* consisted in the bride and bridegroom with their company visiting the home of the groom or his parents, and there having another day of fun and feasting. In this instance it was a long and rather unpleasant ride of some twelve miles into the country over bad roads, in the month of March. But as I was interested in gaining a fuller knowledge of the sister, who by right of custom was my companion on the way, the discomforts of the weather and roads did not disturb me. After that however I did not renew my visits for several weeks. Whilst the impression was favorable, I was yet undecided. Not knowing enough to stimulate pursuit, and as yet uninfluenced by passion, I wished to scrutinize closely and proceed cautiously.

Marriage is by all odds the most momentous event of our lives. Character, temper, disposition, taste, sentiment and inclination should all be ascertained with certainty and considered carefully. Besides this, family, ancestry, health and position should be allowed their due weight and carefully considered. I fully realized all this at the time and was disposed to hasten slowly; and after obtaining as much insight and information as I could from other sources, then if I should think it advisable to go further I supposed I could do so and try to gain a fuller knowledge of herself. Such was my plan; and after gaining all the knowledge I could from other sources I did feel inclined to go further. But when I began to visit oftener and tried to study herself, I found my plan completely blocked in that direction.

Hitherto nothing had transpired beyond the courtesies of ordinary acquaintance. After this preliminary stage was passed my visits were more frequent, but progress was slow—entirely too slow to be satisfactory. What further light I obtained in this way on manner and habit, sentiment and taste, temper and disposition were favorable enough; but what the doctor had said of her seemed too true. She did not seem at all susceptible of tender emotions, or to appreciate my attentions, which it must be admitted were not very pointed as I met with no encouragement in that direction. She was pleasant, cheerful and polite, with ready conversation on general subjects, but without affording the slightest opening towards intimacy or suggestions of personal application. She evinced the dexterity of a special pleader in evading all approaches to any discussion of the real business I had in hand; and this was the more provoking as it seemed to be entirely artless and unintentional. It was no little annoying that after leading the conversation to the very verge of some tender sentiment or serious discussion of personal relationship, she would break the thread of the discourse by a remark or suggestion foreign to my purpose, and in that manner lead off to some irrelevant subject. I was not there to take lessons in flora culture or botany, or to learn the history of birds, fishes or butterflies. I did not want to spend evening after evening in admiring pictures in her album, or in having items read to me from her scrap book. But to her credit I must say that she never inflicted any music upon me, as she professed no special efficiency in that accomplishment. In this line visit after visit was made to no purpose, till at last the procrastination became provoking.

A radical reform is needed in the art of courtship. As its object is so important, I would have it conducted in an open, candid, earnest, truthful and practical spirit. Instead of the shy, coy, evasive methods in use it should be first settled between the parties that both are candidates for matrimony; second, whether each is acceptable to the other *prima facie,* subject to rejection on further acquaintance; third, no love to be excited or admitted on either side until each party is fully satisfied with the nature, disposition and character of the other; and fourth, each to be bound to the other by honor and etiquette, in case the relation is declined on either side, to entertain no ill feeling in consequence, and never to divulge any information whatever obtained during such preliminary stage. The utmost candor should be observed; nothing whatever should be concealed which it would be relevant to know, and no restraint put upon inquiry. In this way each other's views could be had regarding married life and its duties, sentiments and expectations in the future, style of living and ability to support a family; as also natural tastes and appetites, and everything else of importance to be known. The faculties, abilities and proclivities of every human being are in some respect more or less different from all others; and if this plan was adopted the suitability of each to the other for such a union might with far greater certainty be ascertained beforehand, and much misery, dissatisfaction and necessity for divorces avoided. This would be the rational course, and after it was gone through it would be time enough to begin love making. The best interest of each would be subserved by divulging all and concealing nothing which might mislead the other; and after the freest communication and consultation through out this preliminary stage, if the result was found satisfactory to both, abiding love and affection would soon grow to leaven and ratify the proceedings.

It may be objected that timid, shy girls and backward young men could never be brought to conduct courtship in such a practical, business-like manner, but we are not sure of this; it need only to be made fashionable to become the approved style. Those too young might lose their heads and shut their eyes too soon in the performance; but those who are too young ought not to enter on the business at all. In my own case both were of a proper age and could have managed the matter after this fashion if we had been so disposed, and such a method of proceeding would have been much more to my taste; but owing to the tyranny of custom and etiquette we had to proceed in the old way.

Just here also it may be in place to introduce the scientific view of the subject; and I shall do so by an extract from the work of an eminent author:

> One notable peculiarity in the character of the woman is that she is capricious and coy and has less straightforwardness than the man. * * * * The drama of courtship, with its prolonged strivings and doubtful success, would be cut quite short, and the race would degenerate through the absence of that sexual selection for which the protracted preliminaries of love making give opportunity. The willy-nilly disposition of the female in matters of love is as apparent in the butterfly as in the woman, and must have been continuously favored from the earliest stage of animal evolution down to the present time. It is the factor in the great theory of sexual selection that corresponds to the insistence and directness of the male.

Coyness and caprice have in consequence become a heritage of the sex, together with a cohort of allied weaknesses and petty deceits that men have come to think venial and even amiable in women, but which they would not tolerate among themselves.

The argument is that nature herself provides for a season of courtship through the character implanted in the female. Her emotions prompt to union, but timidity, distrust and aversion hold her back till time and familiarity smooth the way, thus affording opportunity for observation, discrimination and choice in the selection of a mate. This distinguishing quality between the male and female belongs to the lower animals in proportion to their intelligence, as well as to man. It is readily perceived in the lively excitement it produces among the birds at their pairing time in the spring season. Among the lower animals however the chief qualities of advantage for sexual selection are strength and energy; consequently less time is required for courtship. But in man, where the characters and qualities are so numerous and different, more time is required for a proper choice. Nature distinguishes the finest bird in the flock and the finest animal in the herd by their superior form and dress, and sexual selection among them is thus made easy. The dress of the female is never padded, nor the adornments of either sex artificial; but still they are allowed their season of courtship in order to promote sexual selection for the betterment of their species.

The greater importance and the greater necessity for the exercise of this function in the human race can only be fully appreciated by a knowledge of the sure propagation of character and qualities from parents to children, and from one generation to another. The fact is, each individual is a mosaic work of his ancestry. His character and qualities are made up of shreds of this one and patches of that, among his progenitors.

The sciences of biology and psychology are but in their infancy, and yet they disclose wonders in this direction. The facts and data are yet meager—derived only from records of the inmates and their progenitors found in prisons, hospitals and poorhouses; from which it is discovered beyond question that both physical and moral qualities and characteristics run in the blood and are transmitted for many generations. Consumption, scrofula and other organic diseases have been long known to be transmissible, and also any other physical peculiarities of the individual, whether of health or disease. But moral and in-tellectual character and peculiarities have also been traced with great certainty. Thus the records of the New York City prisons show the same traits of criminality to have been propagated from one individual through six generations, until the descendants have increased to nearly five hundred, whose domicile in the main has been the prison or poor-house. So too with the appetites and desires and passions, whether lawful or unlawful. Even the peculiarities of energy, sociability, truth-fulness, lying, thoughtfulness, refinement and the like are all more or less transmissible and crop out in the offspring sooner or later. How important then the principle of sexual selection, and how kind it is of nature to encourage its exercise, as on it depends the improvement of the species in man and animal. When the instinct of the brute observes it, how much more should the reason of man prompt him to comply with its demands. In view of its importance, candidates for matrimony should be encouraged by all social customs, and enjoined by moral and religious duty to the most careful examination and consideration of each other and of each other's past history before entering into this most serious and important of all relations.

But returning to my narrative: the inconsequential procedure of company keeping without courtship, referred to above, had gone on for several weeks without any visible result, when I became impatient. I had an earnest ulterior purpose besides amusement and conventional chit-chat on general subjects, and she did not seem the least disposed to promote that purpose. To all appearance I had made no impression. It was becoming monotonous. I had now been in search of a wife for nearly six months and had spent much valuable time, somewhat to the prejudice of my professional business. I could not divine the cause of her imperviousness. If wholly indifferent to my attentions, why did she not dismiss me or give me some slight indication that I was not wanted? Just then I would have taken an intimation to that effect as a favor; but she showed no sign whatever which a word or glance of the eye could have so easily afforded. I was always pleasantly received and entertained, mostly in the presence of some lady friend, and always without the slightest opportunity of approach to personalities; and never could tell whether my presence or absence afforded her most pleasure. Perhaps she might be void of all tender emotions, and if an icicle I did not want her for a wife. In this impatient condition of mind

I felt half inclined to drop the suit, and began to cast about for another object.

It was long since I had experienced the sweet, soft sadness and tender longings of calf-love, which for once attacks every young man; but that early fire had left a spark in me which could have been very easily rekindled, and I began to regret that I could not have married at a period when neither party takes the trouble to look ahead, but unites with the other blindly as if by instinct. One of my early loves, the last one, had long continued to haunt my imagination and was fresh in memory yet. Such kind of early love keeps best if the object of it is out of sight. It is too delicate for every day wear, and to keep must like canned fruit be preserved from the common atmosphere. This early love of mine had the good fortune to be preserved after that fashion. I had neither seen nor communicated with the object of it for upwards of seventeen years; but I knew that she still lived single with her widowed mother in an obscure corner of Westmoreland county.

Mary Young was a nice little girl whom I had met at school when life was new and fresh; the daughter of the teacher who taught one winter in our neighborhood. She was about my age, perhaps a year or two my senior, a quiet, modest, pretty little girl. I had admired her very much, but never let her know it past a furtive glance or slyly transferred trinket. Afterwards throughout all my tedious years of study and bachelor life, Mary would occasionally appear to my fancy in all her early beauty. When we read poetry or fiction of any kind, we are apt to apply the qualities of the hero or heroine to some one in real life within our knowledge. In this line Mary had all along served me as a model to which I had been attaching the charms and virtues of the different heroines I had met with in fiction. Thus she had become my ideal of feminine beauty and perfection.

In my present dilemma and impatience it was natural for Mary's image to reappear, and natural also to wish to see her before going any further in this unprofitable pursuit. She might not appear on sight as lovely as pictured in my fancy; but it would be well enough to see and ascertain the fact. She was poor and obscure, but what of that: I was now free to act independently of these considerations. She might not possess the social graces of refined society, but they were unessential or could be acquired. She did not have much education, but might have informed her mind and developed her intellectual faculties in the meantime by reading. All this could be readily settled by a visit, and in this spirit one warm day in June I turned my horse's head toward Westmoreland county instead of the Negley mansion. I had relatives to visit in that county, which afforded me an excuse; and I could take in Mary's home without going greatly out of the way. She lived in a rather unfrequented locality of Beaver Run Valley. Of course I had read the story of the lovely young Lavinia in Thomson's Seasons, and why might not Mary be the counterpart of Lavinia, who "once had friends," but "fortune smiled deceitful on her birth?" For like Lavinia,

> In her helpless years deprived of all,
> Of every stay, save Innocence and Heaven,
> She, with her widowed mother, feeble, old
> And poor, lived in a cottage far retired,
> Among the windings of a woody vale.

And this was exactly the kind of a place where Mary and her mother lived now, as I was informed. The coincidence was striking and propitious. I could not expect to see her decked out in fine dress or artificial adornments; but the same author informs us that loveliness when unadorned is adorned the most.

Such were the agreeable reflections and anticipations which occupied me on that pleasant journey of thirty miles; and in this high mood and well on in the afternoon of the same day I approached the home of my charmer. As if to afford an excuse for the abrupt visit, the elements favored me. A thunder storm had been looming up for some time, and culminated just as I neared the house. I had hardly time to tie my horse in the cow shed near by when the big round drops began to come down heavily and I made for the house on a run. It ought to have been, as I had fancied it, a cozy little cottage hidden with honeysuckles and sweetbrier, and surrounded by flower beds displaying Mary's taste in selection. But even on the run a glance at the situation dispelled this vision. It was no cottage, but a desolate looking, dilapidated old log cabin with not a tree, shrub or flower about it; not even a tuft of grass or an enclosure about the house, but the bare earth trampled hard about the door by the cow and pigs, and everything movable lying around loose in disorder.

As the rain was coming in a manner to excuse ceremony, I entered the open door without announcement. Just inside a dazed looking old woman with a pipe in her mouth was seated on a rickety chair without any back to it, which she relinquished and pushed towards me and shifted herself to something else for a seat, and commenced "shooing" at a hen with a flock of young chickens parading over the floor. But the noise only excited the hen and frightened the chickens, and at last the attempt to expel them was given up; when the hen, emboldened and indignant came forward, throwing her head to one side with an angry glance towards me, as much as to say, you are the cause of this racket. The place was rather dark, there being but one door and a small window, and I had not yet observed all the objects in the apartment; but an exclamation of the old woman directed to a distant corner beyond the cooking stove, attracted my attention to that point: "Mary, you must learn this hen to stay out after this." The tall, lank, ungainly looking object in the corner thus addressed made no reply. Was this my Mary? It was. Well, I did not rush to embrace her, did not utter a single exclamation, but felt rather inclined, in common phrase, to freeze to my seat in astonishment. She had lost every feature of the beauty she possessed when I had last seen her at school; and now all the fictitious charms which I had accorded her were dispelled as she stood there in the dim light of the squalid cabin which, without a feature of the romantic cottage, seemed only a fit setting for the picture presented by "my Mary" with her untidy, faded, soiled and slovenly looking garments and frowzy hair. Although she could not be much older in fact than I was myself, yet she looked so very much older than I expected that it was some time before I was assured of her identity; and her voice, in the few words exchanged between her and her mother, was void of any harmony. In some, youthful beauty soon fades; and Mary was a striking example. To cap the climax she settled herself down on a stool behind the cooking stove and taking a crockery pipe from a shelf beside her, commenced smoking like her mother. She did not recognize me, and I was glad of it; and as soon as the shower was over I resumed the even tenor of my way a wiser but not a sadder man, for the result of my visit showed I had lost nothing by neglect.

My vision of youthful beauty had vanished quicker than the summer shower. Men and women are but matter-of-fact creatures at best, and subject to speedy changes both in person and feelings. Love is but a passion like the other passions, and is excited or allayed as the object of it attracts or repels: just as the other passions rise and subside. Permanent affection, like friendship, depends on esteem and regard for a worthy object. Beauty alone may excite love, but it does so by subsidizing the imagination to supply other good qualities; and as stern reality soon discloses the mistake, love resting on beauty only must necessarily be short lived.

This journey to my imaginary Amarilla and its results clipped the wings of fancy and she fell flat. What was next best to be done? Very little would have decided me just then to abandon the pursuit of a wife in disgust. I knew no one but Miss Negley who would suit, or whom, all things considered, I could risk entering into so close a relationship with; the only obstacle was her manifest indifference, which wounded my self esteem to a degree that repelled me. But whilst not encouraging my attentions, I could remember no instance wherein she discouraged them. Whilst provokingly difficult to discover the condition of her feelings, I had no valid reason to abandon the attempt. It was a problem requiring effort, but not impossible of solution. There was nothing for it therefore but a return to her. If the reformed system of courtship which I advocate had been in order, I could on my return have made a clean breast of it and sought her opinion on the situation. We could then have had an interesting exchange of views and opinions leading very naturally to what we both wanted most of all to get at. But under the prevailing system of suppressing everything worth knowing, I kept it to myself, more especially my late adventure; and we proceeded on in the usual way of "how not to do it." And so there was no better progress after the Westmoreland episode than before. The opportunities for love making seemed more hampered than ever. Acquaintance and familiarity so far had produced no effect. If my attentions were not acceptable I thought it would be so easy to let me know it that I felt provoked at being kept in suspense. Whatever she might think I knew that her family understood the object of my visits, because her brothers had been making very pointed inquiry into my private character and habits; with which I found no fault, knowing this to be a duty of parents and friends seldom performed sufficiently. I had now learned enough of her character and qualities to determine me in her favor. All in all, I saw no one that pleased me better, or that I thought would wear better roughing it through life; but the hitch was to find out what she thought about it. To propose without some previous show of love making would seem rather abrupt; but no opportunity for the purpose was ever afforded. The conversation could never be turned from general topics, nor polite attentions allowed to drift into tender personalities. Her demeanor was inexplicable. She allowed not the slightest opening for flattery or any expression of affection—no place for the "soft flood of loving argument" suitable on such occasions; and yet I could see evidently enough that it was not through coquetry or any insincerity or dissimulation, but I was made to feel that to talk love would be out of place and might subject me to ridicule. Time after time I visited with a firm resolution to break the ice and make love to her whether or no, but was as often baffled, not by any set purpose on her part that I could see, but by some unaccountable influence which seemed to surround her; and cooler reflection convinced me her procrastination was not unreasonable. I had been paying her pointed attentions for but little over three months, which I would have to admit was a rather short time for the preliminary acquaintance to a life partnership.

But when my own mind was made up I wanted the suspense ended. I no longer possessed the amiable mood of a wooer; impatience and baffled expectation annoyed me, and at each successive visit I usually left in a temper entirely unbecoming a lover and unsuited for expression in her presence. Finally impatience and disappointment gave way to curiosity, and a disposition to persevere and see how it would end. At last I thought I discovered enough to show that she felt some interest in me; still there was no apparent yielding, but after that I resolved to embrace the very first opportunity to break through all conventionalities and find out the result.

Fortune soon favored my purpose. At the very next interview, in the dusk of evening when the clear moonlight was streaming through the curtains, we happened to be left alone for a minute or so—an unusual circumstance. Feeling that now was the time I drew my chair up closer to her than I had ever ventured before and remarked that I supposed she was aware I had not been paying attention to her so long without an object, and that I had some time ago made up my own mind and now wished to know hers, as I was satisfied if she was, to risk the future together. She neither spoke nor gave any sign. I drew her to me and took a kiss unresisted and said that would do, I was satisfied; and left her abruptly, feeling unnerved for conversation.

The die was cast—I had crossed the Rubicon. And that night, as I turned the head of my trusty grey up the lane now Negley avenue, and passed the old quarry on the hillside, queer thoughts flitted across my mind of the time I had rested there when a boy on my first journey to the city, when I first contemplated the great meadow and mansion and imagined how proud and happy must be the family which possessed them. The whirligig of time produces strange results. But even on that night I did not anticipate what was yet to come. Still closer relationship to that hillside was in the future for me. It so transpired that that hillside and meadow has been my happy home for more than forty years, surrounded at a later date with equally happy homes of my married children.

At my next weekly visit we met on closer terms and more cordial feelings; the wall of separation was removed and I applied to her mother for her consent, and received a ready and satisfactory answer to the effect that as we had agreed she knew of no objection. I then applied to my affianced to set the day, suggesting a week or ten days as sufficient interval. This she opposed with some surprise, and insisted on six weeks. We finally compromised on a month, and accordingly the transaction was consummated on the 22d of August, 1843. The details of the wedding are uninteresting; all such ceremonies are pretty much alike. Her distant and independent attitude, so well maintained during our preliminary acquaintance, had made me sometimes fear a cold and unsympathetic disposition; but I found her nature quite the contrary, her feelings warm and abiding, but undemonstrative.

I have somewhere seen a division of marriages into two sorts: the one by spontaneity of love beforehand, leaving judgment and discretion to approve or disapprove afterwards; and the other requiring the approval of judgment and discretion in the first place, leaving love to follow. One author expresses it thus: "Marriage to be of value, presupposes one of two things—the love which creates its own title to respect, or the respect which by time ripens into love;" and the chances of a happy married life are held to be largely in favor of the latter sort. With this I agree, for my marriage was undoubtedly of the latter sort, and I have found it to be a happy one. There was no love making and little or no love beforehand so far as I was concerned: nothing but a good opinion of worthy qualities, and esteem and respect. When I proposed if I had been rejected I would have left neither sad nor depressed nor greatly disappointed, only annoyed at loss of time. Married as we were however, without any appreciable excitement of the tender passion on my part, I did not continue so, but as the goodness of her heart and mind developed more and more to my comprehension, love did take root and grow, and that steadily to ripe maturity. It was a marriage of judgment and discretion in the first place, ripening into love after-wards, and for over forty years has been a happy one.

Thomas was born in this cottage at Camp Hill, near Omagh in County Tyrone, Ireland. It is possible that this is one of the photos mentioned in chapter 20 that was obtained by Thomas's son James in 1874. Thomas Mellon and His Times, *orig. ed.*

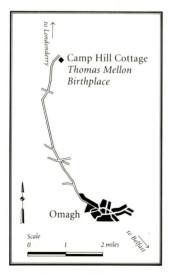

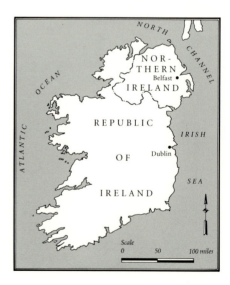

Maps by Christopher H. Marston

Thomas helped to build a six-room log farmhouse on Duff's Hill outside Pittsburgh in Westmoreland County, and he lived there as an adolescent. This photo of the house in the 1880s shows later renovations. Westmoreland County Historical Society

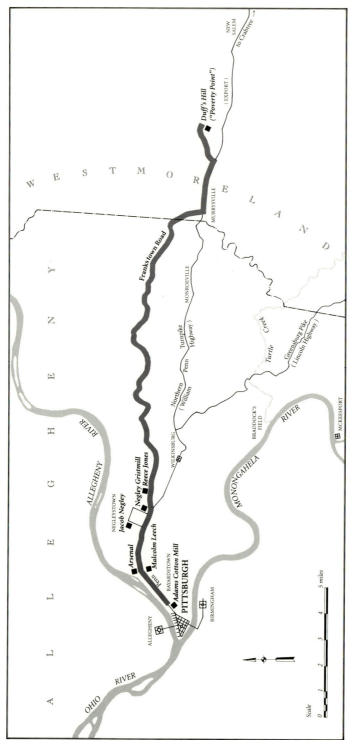

At the age of ten, Thomas Mellon walked twenty-one miles to Pittsburgh from his father's small farm on Duff's Hill in Westmoreland County. Describing the trip years later, he wrote of the "numerous wonders" he had seen. In Negleystown (present-day East Liberty), the home of Reece Jones, the Negley gristmill, store, and "mansion house" caught his imagination. On the way to Bayardstown (the Strip District), where he spent the night, Thomas passed the country seat of Malcolm Leech who, like Jacob Negley, "had also accumulated much wealth" (see chapter 5). Map by Christopher H. Marston

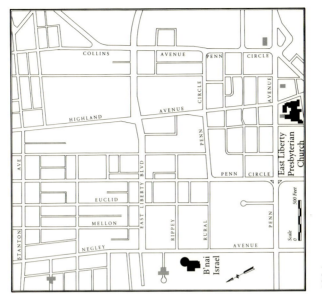

1994

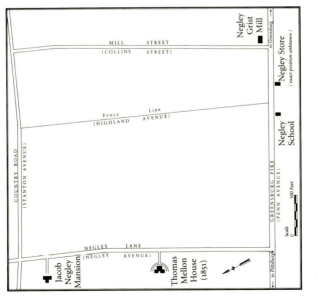

1823

Maps by Christopher H. Marston

The home of Jacob Negley impressed ten-year-old Thomas on his first visit to Pittsburgh. Here it is visualized in a 1950s painting by Pittsburgh artist Susan Tucker. Mr. and Mrs. Robert G. Runnette

In 1817, the year before Thomas emigrated from Ireland, Pittsburgh was a village.
Historical Society of Western Pennsylvania

By the end of the nineteenth century, Pittsburgh was a major industrial center.
Historical Society of Western Pennsylvania

As a student at the Western University of Pennsylvania, later the University of Pittsburgh, Thomas lived on an upper floor in this main building in downtown Pittsburgh with other students who, he wrote, were "as impecunious as myself."
Historical Society of Western Pennsylvania

The Great Fire of 1845 destroyed fifty-six acres in downtown Pittsburgh and left twelve thousand people homeless. Watching from the roof of the courthouse, Thomas saw it "surging like a vast flood, devouring dwellings, warehouses and churches." Richard King Mellon Foundation

Thomas included this coat of arms in his memoir, although he found the tradition that linked it to his own family "too shadowy to be relied on." He translated the motto as: "Virtue is the safest defense." Thomas Mellon and His Times, *orig. ed.*

Andrew Mellon (1785–1856), Thomas's father. "A man of sound common sense and temperate habits . . . pleasant and agreeable in his manners . . . [who was] popular with his neighbors and acquaintances." Thomas M. Schmidt

His mother, Rebecca Wauchob Mellon (1789–1868). "Her strong common sense made her a valuable adviser even in the most important affairs. . . . She shunned extremes and approved the middle course in life." Thomas M. Schmidt

At the age of thirty-five, Thomas was a promising young attorney. James
R. Mellon II

Thomas at seventy-two. This portrait was the frontispiece of the original edition of Thomas Mellon and His Times.

When Thomas Mellon and His Times *was printed in 1885, Thomas wrote that* "the dark shadows of the evening of life are extending towards me." *He was to live twenty-three years longer.* Richard M. Scaife

Thomas built what he called "my country home" in 1850–51, less than a half mile from Jacob Negley's home. He and Sarah Jane lived here at 401 Negley Avenue for fifty-seven years. Thomas Mellon and His Times, *orig. ed.*

Reading Benjamin Franklin's autobiography was the "turning point of my life,"
Thomas wrote. He placed a statue of Franklin above the front door of his bank.
Mellon Bank

GROWTH OF MELLON BANK IN DOWNTOWN PITTSBURGH

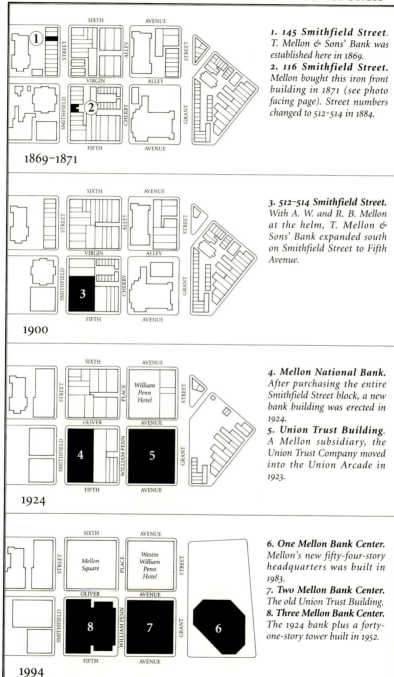

1869–1871

1. 145 Smithfield Street. T. Mellon & Sons' Bank was established here in 1869.
2. 116 Smithfield Street. Mellon bought this iron front building in 1871 (see photo facing page). Street numbers changed to 512-514 in 1884.

1900

3. 512–514 Smithfield Street. With A. W. and R. B. Mellon at the helm, T. Mellon & Sons' Bank expanded south on Smithfield Street to Fifth Avenue.

1924

4. Mellon National Bank. After purchasing the entire Smithfield Street block, a new bank building was erected in 1924.
5. Union Trust Building. A Mellon subsidiary, the Union Trust Company moved into the Union Arcade in 1923.

1994

6. One Mellon Bank Center. Mellon's new fifty-four-story headquarters was built in 1983.
7. Two Mellon Bank Center. The old Union Trust Building.
8. Three Mellon Bank Center. The 1924 bank plus a forty-one-story tower built in 1952.

Maps by Christopher H. Marston

Thomas called his marriage to Sarah Jane Negley "the luckiest event of my life." In this photo from the original edition of his book, she is thirty-one. Thomas Mellon and His Times, *orig. ed.*

Thomas Alexander Mellon (1844–1899). He was in charge of the development of the Ligonier Valley Railroad. Thomas M. Schmidt

Samuel Selwyn Mellon (1853–1862). Of the death of his nine-year-old son, Thomas wrote years later: "Time has brought me consolation in all other deaths but this: for Selwyn I cannot be comforted." James Ross Mellon, Letters

James Ross Mellon (1846–1934), head of Mellon Brothers, which dealt in lumber, building supplies, and real estate. James Ross Mellon, Letters

Andrew William Mellon (1855–1937) at the age of seventeen. He became Secretary of the Treasury, 1921–1932, under Presidents Harding, Coolidge, and Hoover. *James R. Mellon II*

Richard Beatty Mellon (1858–1933), who became president of Mellon Bank, with his son, Richard King Mellon (1899–1970), who was a major force behind the post-World War II Renaissance of Pittsburgh. Photo ca. 1902.

George Negley Mellon (1860–1887) was plagued by poor health and died at twenty-seven. *Thomas M. Schmidt*

The Mellons pose for a family photo, apparently with little enthusiasm, at 401 Negley Avenue. Behind Sarah Jane and Thomas are, left to right: James R., Andrew W., Richard B., and Thomas A. Photo ca. 1895. James R. Mellon II

Thomas and Sarah Jane in their last years. From at least early middle age to the end of his life, he wore the same style of clothing. James R. Mellon II

Before the fireplace at 401 Negley Avenue. The photo of Thomas on the left side of the mantel was used as the frontispiece for the original edition of Thomas Mellon and His Times. James R. Mellon II

1813

1817

Birthday Greeting
from
Thomas and Sarah Negley Mellon
February third, nineteen hundred and eight

Thomas and Sarah Jane planned to celebrate their birthdays jointly on February 3, 1908. On that day, his ninety-fifth birthday, Thomas did not wake up. Sarah Jane died eleven months later, on January 19, 1909, at the age of ninety-one.
Richard King Mellon Foundation

The gravestones of Sarah Jane and Thomas Mellon in Allegheny Cemetery, Pittsburgh. Clyde Hare

Chapter XIII

Wedding Tour and Housekeeping

NEITHER OF US HAD traveled much. She had been to Louisville on a boat excursion with some friends, and I had been to Zanesville and Portsmouth, as already related. This was the extent of our travels. So we concluded to conform to the custom not then very common, of taking a wedding trip; and we extended it considerably farther than was usual, in order to see a little more of the world before settling down to domestic life and business duties.

A recital of the journey will show the difference between modes of travel then and now.

Leaving Pittsburgh on the 24th of August, 1843, we reached Erie after two whole days and one entire night spent in jolting over rough roads in an old-fashioned stage coach; and after resting there a day and night we took boat early one fine morning for Buffalo, which we reached after a pleasant day on the lake. Here we spent another day to see the town, and again took boat for the Falls and had an enjoyable voyage down the Niagara river, landing on the Canada side about two miles above the Falls. From there to the Clifton House on the Canada heights, since burned down, was our first experience of railroad travel. From the great elevation of the Clifton House the first impression of the Falls was disappointing: they appeared diminutive. But the point of view may not have been entirely accountable for this. I have noticed that an excited imagination always transcends the reality so far as to cause disappointment when the occasion for a comparison between them arises. It was only when we got down to the water's edge and had time to take in the whole scene that we began to apprehend its grandeur. A right conception of the magnitude and sublimity of Niagara must have time to grow—it cannot develop in an hour or even a day. After two days we were still loth to leave it.

Our next movement was crossing Ontario to Oswego, which included a night voyage, and a rather tedious one as our boat broke a shaft some time in the night to the great consternation of such of the passengers as were awake. We were not disturbed however, and awoke in the morning to find her flopping along with one side wheel in motion, like a lame duck. At Oswego, after seeing the fort and other sights of the town, we took passage on a canal boat for Albany. This was a more tedious voyage than any before, occupying several days. The boat cabin served for parlor, dining room and sleeping room, and was quite contracted in space at that. Sleeping was done on shelves of about eighteen inches in width attached to the sides, having a curtain suspended in front from the ceiling. But we had some very agreeable company on board and fine weather, and spent most of the daylight on deck. At a point near Albany we abandoned the boat and proceeded by rail. The change from the speed of the snail to that of the race horse was cheering; and just before reaching Albany the car was let down an inclined plane to the city level by ropes and machinery. This method of overcoming grades was common in railroad engineering at that time.

At Albany we found nothing to see of special interest except some hieroglyphic signatures of Indian chiefs in the State House. This was their method of signing treaties. These aboriginal proprietors of the soil, for themselves and the members of their respective tribes, had made the sign or ink picture upon these treaty documents, ceding forever their lands to the white man. The mark or picture character designating the particular chief was invariably in the form of some natural object, animal or tree; and in it lies the origin of the practice which elsewhere has resulted in the coat-of-arms so highly esteemed by the nobility of Europe in our day. Man everywhere in the same environments and conditions presents the same aspect, practices the same customs, and entertains the same opinions. The language may be different, the forms may vary, but the ideas and sentiments are always and everywhere found to be the same: the same religious sentiments although the gods are named differently, the same political ideas under different forms of government, and the same practices in conducting their affairs. At a period when less than one in a thousand among our European ancestry could read or write, and reading and writing was considered too low and venial a practice for gentlemen and only fit for clerks or priests, the seal was used to establish and evidence a covenant or contract of any kind. Each man carried a seal with a device peculiar to himself, to distinguish him from all others. The device on the seal, like this Indian hieroglyphic, usually represented a natural object; but in time, when the art of writing became more general and was admitted to be respectable among gentlemen, seals with particular designs for personal identification fell into disuse, and the designs were transferred to the panels of coaches and furniture. Unfortunately for these poor Indians whose hieroglyphic characters are attached to ancient treaties at Albany and elsewhere, they did not hold their own or rise in the world's regard, but have gone down under the rule which accords success only to those who are fittest to secure it. Stupidity and ignorance always suffer. If they had retained some portion of the vast estates which these documents describe, and the civilization which overwhelmed them had been less democratic, their descendants might to-day be displaying their armorial bearings with these eagles and owls and deer and buffalo as their coats-of-arms, with all the pomp and consequence of European aristocrats. It is curious too, how pertinaciously the skeletons of manners and customs will cling to society for ages after their life and usefulness are entirely gone. Thus neither the seal nor its successor, the coat-of-arms, has any longer a use or meaning, and yet both are retained to some extent. The seal or its sign at the end of a signature converts a simple contract into a specialty under the legal distinction still retained in law between specialties and other written contracts; although the reason why a name with a curl of the pen or sign of a seal after it makes the transaction more certain or obligatory has long since ceased. The signature itself, and the witnesses to the paper are what is relied on at the present day to establish its authenticity, not the seal mark. And as to the design or form transferred from its original use as a seal to the owner's carriage or harness, it is hard to see what honor or dignity it can confer, or how it can flatter his vanity to advertise to the public in this way that his ancestors at one time could neither read nor write. The lowest as well as the highest are equally descended from savage ancestors, if that is anything to boast of.

We remained but a short time at Albany, and took the train from Troy to Boston. This railroad was new and the longest out of Boston westward at the time, and a ride over it was regarded as quite a novelty.

Our trip on it was pleasant. The poor and stony quality of the land and the dwarfed timber through which we passed much of the way was a surprise on account of its difference from our own country. Boston and its bay afforded us wider scope for sightseeing than we had yet met with, and we spent some days there quite enjoyably, when we returned by rail and boat to New York, and crossing the sound had a sight of the sea and some sensations of its heavings. After exposure to the raw cold air in the early morning in order to see the bay of New York, we found a warm breakfast at the Astor House—then the most fashionable ho-tel—unusually gratifying.

New York occupied our attention some three days. I remember a walk on the Croton water reservoir, which was then one of the great wonders of the city; and all the country beyond it was a waste of poor land covered with boulders, without buildings or other improvements. Now that rough country, excepting the Central Park, is all closely cov-ered with the finest buildings of the city. Finally we arrived in Philadel-phia where we were taken in charge by my kind uncle Thomas, and spent a week with him in the pleasant society of his family. I had never been in Philadelphia or any other such city before; and for a pleasant place to live, and pleasant society, and the gratification of literary taste, it appeared to me to have the lead.

From Philadelphia to Pittsburgh the Pennsylvania canal had super-seded the stage coach and was quite an improvement so far as ease and comfort was concerned, and even had some little advantage in time, as the passenger boats were dragged through with pretty fair speed; and the Portage railroad over the mountains, with its inclined plane at either end making connections with the canal, expedited passenger transportation considerably. After we took leave of our Philadelphia friends and their happy home and boarded the westbound canal packet, no incident worth notice occurred till we reached the Juniata river above Harrisburg. The method of crossing it was by the horses passing over a bridge and dragging the boat after them in the stream below until both horses and boat reached the other shore. The cable connecting the horses and boat had to be of considerable length. The river was high and rough, and poured over a dam a short distance be-low. Such of the passengers as understood the danger had left the boat and followed the horses on the bridge. We and others who did not take that precaution saw the danger when it was too late. After we were fairly launched on the river and saw the difficulty with the horses to hold the boat, and heard the shouts of the captain and crew mingled with the roar of the river pouring over the dam just below us, we would have given a good deal for the privilege of the safety of the bridge instead of the ease and danger of the boat. But commonly people do not see danger till too late, and then they see it too clearly. But we were in for it and alarm was useless, although some of our fellow passengers were rather demonstrative of their apprehensions. In this crisis I first noticed my wife's entire command of her feelings in the suppression of every sign of fear or alarm.

We passed the river in safety however, and no further incident of note occurred till the following morning, when on waking we found the boat motionless in the mud, without any water whatever in the canal. A great rain storm had occurred in the night, west of where we had stuck fast, and it had washed out large openings in the canal embankment. These breaks were too extensive to be repaired shortly; so after a detention of two nights and a day at Millerstown, farm wagons were procured on which we were all mounted and jolted over the rocky road some twenty-five miles to Lewistown. It was a rough ride, but entirely preferable to the monotony of enforced delay at such a sleepy little place as Millerstown. From Lewistown we had a pleasant journey over the mountains and inclined planes. Occasionally leaving the boat at a bend in the canal and taking the near cut on foot, we would get a mile or so ahead and wait till it would catch up. Finally we arrived home again after a little more than a month's absence.

The mode of travel then and for some years before was a vast improvement over what it had been in the old stage coach on the turnpike road, and was looked upon as a pleasurable enjoyment. And yet when I recollect the contracted space and the delay and uncertainties of the journey, and compare it with the speed and luxury of the palatial parlor, dining room and sleeping cars of to-day, the difference is as great between that time and now as between that time and the stage coach period.

On our return I found my business a good deal in arrear and clients anxiously waiting, as the session of the Supreme Court was about to commence; and for a week or so I had a busy time of it. For a while we made our home with my motherinlaw. A horseback ride morning and evening was healthful, and for comfort and agreeable companions my motherinlaw and her family were all that could be desired. As acquaintance ripened into familiarity I found her not only agreeable and pleasant, but a kind mother possessed of superior qualities and sound, practical good sense—one whose ruling passion was the welfare of her children; and the other members of the family, Catherine and Alexander, my wife's elder sister and youngest brother, feeling cordially towards me as a brother. Our stay at her mother's home was everything that could be wished to make us happy; but my ambition was for housekeeping and a home entirely my own.

So before the first of December, 1843, I had procured a lease from Alexander McClurg of a suitable house on Fifth avenue, next door west of the present *Dispatch* building. It comprised a nice basement dining room and kitchen, with convenient stone steps in front to the hall, from which opened the parlor and sitting room on the first or street floor; and two good chambers on the second floor, with a finished garret for the servant. I soon had the front room or parlor converted into an office; and the house was about as near the right thing as was available at the time for a young couple in our circumstances to begin with. By the first of December we were ready to move in, and engaged a girl for general housework. On the day we took possession I was busy in court and had to attend an arbitration immediately after court adjourned, which lasted till after dark; and on returning home I found my wife in full possession and master of the situation, not the least discouraged though without any company or help, the girl having disappointed us. All that was needed was pepper and salt and other little items necessary to getting up a meal; and after I had taken my first lesson with a market basket to the nearest grocery we soon had a nice supper, as my wife was herself a good cook and not in the least averse to work. And we enjoyed it all the more on account of the novelty of having it all to ourselves. It was our first meal in the line of home and housekeeping, and without waiter or guest. We were alone for that night and the next day, but none the less happy, as we were all in all to each other. Such was the beginning of my married home life.

Chapter XIV

Professional Life

MY PROFESSIONAL LIFE of twenty years commenced in 1839 and ended in 1859. I went on the bench on the first Monday of December of the latter year; and after leaving the bench at the end of my term ten years afterwards I did not resume the practice of law, but only tried or assisted in trying an occasional case where myself or some company or corporation in which I was interested was a party. Very few such suits have arisen however, considering the extensive business enterprises which I have been engaged in at one time or other during my life; but such as have arisen were rather memorable, and a narrative of them will be given in some future chapter, if space permits.

By the time of my marriage I had obtained a fair and profitable business—unusually large, indeed, for so short a time at the bar, and the more gratifying because not acquired through any adventitious circumstances or extra efforts to attract clients, nor through any special display of eloquence or sharp tactics in the courts. My success was due simply to the exercise of practical common sense, a competent knowledge of the law, and persistent care and industry to promote the best interests of my clients. I practiced very little in the criminal court, avoiding it as much as possible. It was only at the instance of some client for whom I had profitable business in the civil courts that I entered it at all.

And now since marriage, the last important event of my life was consummated, and nothing left to distract my attention from business, I could feel that I was fairly settled and could work with a will without further interruption; and I did so with gratifying results. My business, which was good before marriage, continued to improve afterwards, not only in extent but in quality and profit. But the practice of the law, although apparently exciting and varied and fruitful of striking incidents, is yet so monotonous to the practitioner that now, at the distance of twenty-five years from the time my professional career ended, it appears almost a blank as I look back over it. It is not for the want of excitement and variety in each particular case that this obliviousness of the past arises; but whilst each case has its different prominent features of vital interest, they are so much in the same general line they become blended together and their distinctive individuality is lost. One case with its peculiarities succeeds another as one man with his peculiar features succeeds another in a passing procession, until in the distance they all look alike, and not one in a hundred is remembered. The incidents and hardships of each case are indelibly impressed on the minds of the parties to it because they have no other cases to distract their attention; but to the lawyer or judge they succeed each other too rapidly to be kept separate and remembered.

Personal and family affairs and outside business matters and investments of importance transpiring during this time appear distinctly enough in memory, because in them I was individually interested; but the routine of my law business has almost entirely faded out. I am often accosted by some old client and special reference made to an important suit or other proceeding in which he was a party deeply interested, and the incidents of which are still fresh in his memory; and he is greatly surprised when he finds I have forgotten all about it. So too of the period of my judicial life. Of all the numerous cases, civil and criminal, which were tried before me and which of course were of paramount importance to the parties concerned, few of them are recollected. Nor is this the result of age or lapse of time, but on account of the sameness of the feelings and faculties involved in trying causes at the bar or hearing and deciding them on the bench.

In regard to the bar: when I entered the profession the leading lawyers or those having most practice were Burke (Robert), Metcalf, Loomis, Biddle, Bradford, Forward, Lowrie, Shaler, Simpson, Hampton, Millar, Dunlop, Eyster, McCandless, McClure, Mahan, Darragh, Irwin and Thomas Hamilton. Of these Hampton, Forward, Lowrie, Shaler, McCandless and McClure became judges afterwards. Besides there were a number of younger men in fair practice, some of them of superior talent: as for instance, George P. Hamilton, Samuel W. Black, my friend Thomas MacConnell and Robert Woods. There were others also of fair mediocrity, and then still a lower grade as usual, whom nature never intended for the profession, who were unqualified either in mind or morals—guerillas—a kind of floating class who eke out a living by pettifogging until something occurs to slough them off. Others too of fair morals and intellect who had mistaken their calling and who might have done well in another vocation, but for want of some essential qualification were unfitted for success in this. I have seen good men fail utterly because of the egregious mistake of following a profession for which they were unsuited. But I cannot enter into a description of the natural and acquired qualifications necessary for a lawyer. I may say however, that no one but a gentleman can be a good lawyer, and not then unless nature has fitted him for it. Natural qualities show themselves in this more than in any other profession, because it calls into activity before the public all the qualities and faculties of mind and heart, whilst other professions leave much of them undeveloped. Thus the medical doctor exercises his faculties of memory and observation on the kinds and qualities of medicines, and their effect on different diseases. So too the minister has his memory filled with the doctrines of his sect and texts of Scripture and pious ideas and quotations to facilitate and beautify his discourse. Each has his specialized line of thought in which he can become proficient and even eminent, without knowing much else; but the lawyer's profession embraces the whole field of human nature and the entire scope of human knowledge. He must be intimate with the objects and feelings which actuate the busy world in every department of life. Hence the more comprehensive and clearer his perceptions the better he is calculated to succeed if he possesses the necessary energy to propel him.

It has been well observed by writers on class peculiarities that lawyers are the only class, with the exception perhaps of newspaper editors, who in manners and conduct display no trade mark. You can distinguish a medical doctor or a minister anywhere by their distinctive professional air and appearance. But not so with the lawyer: there is nothing to distinguish him by except his natural qualities. He is necessarily a man of the world, mingling with all classes and acquainted with all interests; hence his profession leads to the exercise of all his faculties, and is never confined to one set so as to keep him in one rut of thought or habit long enough to create a common professional cast of manner or appearance. A successful medical doctor or minister can be made out of a man possessing not half the qualifications needed for a lawyer, provided those qualifications are of a kind suited to his particular profession. Nature must make the lawyer. Education is only necessary to inform and polish him off and produce the easy action of his natural abilities. It is on this account we see such great variety and obvious differences among members of the legal profession. Every shade of the natural character is brought out in strong relief: thus in the two brothers, Robert and Andrew Burke, who were at the bar when I was admitted, both were about equal in talents, but differing in their quality. Robert had the propelling energy which Andrew lacked, and Andrew had the easy flow of eloquence which Robert lacked; consequently Robert accumulated considerable estate although he was in practice comparatively a short time when he died, whilst Andrew remained at the bar for nearly forty years, with more education and acquired accomplishments than his brother, and died in poverty. Robert was an energetic business man and industrious; Andrew had no business tact whatever and was indolent. Robert practiced the law as an active tradesman would his work, whilst Andrew spent his time preparing polished addresses in the few cases in which he was retained. Andrew's adversary would usually gain the case, leaving him but the empty honor of a fine speech.

So too with the brothers Fetterman, who were also in practice when I was admitted. W. W. practiced here, whilst N. P. practiced in Beaver for a short time and afterwards removed here. W. W. practiced but a few years till he died. He had fair average business abilities and a pretty thorough education, but he was full of energy and concentrated his mind on his business and profession, and in the ten years or so that he practiced he accumulated a fine estate which is in his family yet; whilst his brother N. P. spent a life of about three times the extent in the practice and died, not poor, but comparatively so. It could not be said that much difference existed between them in the knowledge of the law, and indeed N. P. was the more eloquent of the two; but W. W. monopolized the energy and industry. So too with Metcalf and Forward, who were long time partners. Forward was indolent and eloquent, Metcalf was active, argumentative and practical; and the difference told in greater benefits to Metcalf's clients, and consequently increased profits to himself. Judge Shaler, who was twice on the bench at different intervals of a long lifetime, but spent the greater part of his time at the bar, was active, industrious and eloquent, but lacked all the qualifications necessary to accumulation. If his clients paid him, well and good; if not he never took the time or trouble to collect his fees, and what money he did get was handed over as fast as it came to family or friends, as needed or asked for. Of course he died poor. Richard Biddle was a man of splendid talent, a Philadelphian, possessed of wealth which rendered him rather independent of professional emoluments, and would only engage in select cases with some junior counsel employed to do the drudgery. He finally went to Congress for a term, where politics disgusted him so much that he declined a re-election. He declared to me that if necessary he would prefer to practice law for a living in aldermen's offices rather than go back to Congress. He was somewhat exclusive and unsocial in his manners, disliked to be bored, but was genial to those who secured his confidence.

George P. Hamilton was admitted shortly before me; was a close student and a hard worker, and attained to a deservedly high reputation as a sound lawyer and logical reasoner. He acquired considerable estate, but broke down in health after being at the bar about thirty years, and became suddenly insane—it was hereditary in his family. After remaining at Kirkbride's Institution in Philadelphia for about six years he returned fully recovered and recommenced with his son just then admitted to practice. His narrative of his condition and sufferings whilst in the insane asylum was very remarkable. He told me that during all those weary years of insanity he suffered the most fearful agonies, none the less so for being only imaginary. The awful feelings of a horrid nightmare were nothing to it, he said: the pain of terror, apprehension and despair, as if falling from a precipice or being crushed to death by rocks, or precipitated into the deep sea; some terrible calamity always imminent, with impossibility of escape. What was the strangest part of it, he said, was that he had all the time a glimmering consciousness that he was insane and mistaken; but the threatening objects were so real as to enforce belief and torture him all the same. He would remember but for a moment that it was all a dream or fantasy and hallucination; but this consciousness of insanity was too weak or short lived to overcome the sense of danger or mitigate his sufferings in the least degree. His was a curious case of an educated insane man conscious of his condition. After his recovery he continued to practice a few years cautiously to avoid excitement or anything tending to bring on a relapse. It returned upon him nevertheless worse than before, and when a few more years at the asylum he died.

I have already described my relations with Thomas MacConnell; and Robert Woods was also one of my particular friends at the bar throughout his whole life. He was admitted to practice a short time before me, attained to an equally profitable law business and held it undiminished till he died, which was but a few years ago. He was the most constant and indefatigable worker I ever knew. A good lawyer of unblemished moral character and of great influence with the jury; devoted to his profession, looking neither to the right nor to the left, neither to politics nor to speculation, he pursued the even tenor of his way with an eye single to the interests of his clients and his own emolument. But it would take too much space to notice all of my contemporaries at the bar. The bar has so increased of late years and so many new faces appear that I now feel myself a stranger among them. One after another my old friends have dropped out till but a very few remain; and I find myself the oldest survivor of the date of my admission. The besetting sin which more than anything else destroys the health and prospects of the lawyer is the habit of strong drink. He is exposed to this temptation more than men of other professions. The excitement and worry of trying causes produces a corresponding depression of spirits which the lawyer is liable to try to counteract by drink; and they are thrown together so much as to foster habits of conviviality. I can run my mind back over hundreds of young men of bright promise who before getting fairly into practice acquired this habit which grew until at last it rendered them sots and imbeciles. Many others, temperate drinkers, carry the habit often past middle life; but of course the keen edge of the intellect becomes blunted, energy weakened and life finally shortened.

My own course in the practice of the profession was one of active exertion. My object in every case was success in preference to display. I never cared to prepare or deliver a set speech to gain applause: that required too much waste of time, for in professional life, especially this profession, time is actually money. We only possess a limited amount of mental power, and the result or product therefrom depends on how it is expended. If unexerted and it remains idle, nothing whatever is accomplished; or if exerted in useless ornamentation and display or other frivolity, a proportionate loss accrues to the clients in the management of their business and to the attorney in the amount of his income. If the acquisition of money is the object, it must be exerted in the line that will most profit the client, and this will profit the attorney also by increased business. To that end he must thoroughly understand the law, learn all the particulars of his client's case, devote incessant attention to it, and neglect nothing calculated to bring it to a speedy and successful conclusion. The labor and care therefore, with a hundred or more important cases on hand at the same time, can readily be understood to be onerous.

Of course men have different aims in the practice of a profession. There may be a phenomenal lawyer who would practice law for the love of it, but in my forty years about the bar I did not meet with him, and have set him down to be a mythical character like the Wandering Jew. There may be medical doctors who would follow their profession for the mere love of the healing art and benevolence to the human race, but I have not become acquainted with them; and there are some fanatical preachers—or were some in former days (the race is now perhaps extinct)—who would preach without pay and live on faith and hope, and what they might pick up as mendicants! Such phenomenal beings are rare, but there are exceptions to all rules; the rule itself however, in all pursuits of life, is the acquisition of means to the attainment of some ultimate personal end. The ends may differ, but in nineteen twentieths of all the cases which have come under my observation, that end is the acquisition of means for a livelihood and ultimate independence. The attorney's best course to this end is to look for and secure a proper equivalent for his services, but to avoid extortion. I have seen much arrogant pretense and nonsense on this point. I have seen exorbitant fees charged for pretentious ability and fictitious services; and I have heard a great deal from men of this kind about the necessity of large fees to maintain the dignity of the profession and high toned views regarding it. There is no greater danger a client can encounter than to fall into the hands of one of these supercilious pretenders; he is sure to be fleeced unmercifully, regardless of any professional benefits conferred. Wise business men avoid such stiltstalking professional gentry. They may be able to squeeze a client and grab an unjustifiable fee occasionally; but where the fee is obtained without an equivalent in benefits conferred, the goose is killed that laid the golden egg: for the goose that once pays such fee is not likely to pay another to the same attorney, and is apt to warn off the rest of the flock. There are men occasionally whose chief end and aim in the practice is ambition and notoriety; but such vanity is mostly accompanied by innate weakness to a degree which defeats its object. The sensible and best aim of the professional man therefore is what I have indicated: the acquisition of means for a livelihood and ultimate independence through fair and honorable professional industry. In this respect the natural principles of human affairs invariably result in rewarding each according to his merits; and the acquisition of wealth is really therefore a badge of merit and ability. It is true men may earn and obtain money to an extent which would make them wealthy, but through some flaw or imperfection of judgment they let it slip through their fingers without benefit to themselves or others, which shows disability to retain and is as bad as want of ability to acquire.

In my course I have known many who pretended to a disregard of money and exhibited contempt at its accumulation; and yet I have invariably found this class to be so inconsistent and wanting in principle that, whenever they could, they would make the most extortionate bargain or exact the most unconscionable fees possible. Consistently with their contempt for accumulation they might spend money carelessly, but always showed themselves the most inexorable money hawks when they had it in their power. In the regulation of professional conduct under all circumstances, a good name and the respect and esteem of our fellow men is to be highly prized, but need not be made the leading object. It is best secured when there is a legitimate pursuit vigorously followed on account of its substantial results, in an independent spirit of conscious rectitude. Name and fame are incidental to well doing, not ends in themselves.

If asked by a student entering the profession what should be his chief object and best course to pursue in order to obtain remunerative business and ultimate independence, I would, after all the experience I have had in what may be regarded a successful career of sixty years at the bar, on the bench and in the affairs of private life, say to him to devote his labor and energy to the establishment of the truth in regard to both law and facts. This is the policy of honesty and I advise it not any more on the ground of moral duty than for self-interest: because in this respect they coincide. The greatest difficulty to be overcome and which requires the highest talent of the lawyer, is to establish the facts of his case; to draw them out of the stupid or confused and often unwilling and prejudiced witnesses. Even the fair and intelligent witness needs time and opportunity in the examination, in order to tell what he knows effectively. Not only is the lawyer's tact and ability required in getting out all the witness knows, but in getting it out in such manner and clearness as will impress it on the minds of court and jury; and no talent will suffice to accomplish this unless the lawyer has first made himself acquainted with all the facts and details of the case, even to the minutest circumstance, before venturing on the important business of examining the witnesses on the trial. If the material facts are well established the task of applying the law to them is not difficult, but still deserves close attention so as not to confuse or mislead. The lawyer must remember that, whilst he may be fully acquainted with the facts of the case from frequent discussions with his client and conversations with his witnesses, it is all new to the court and jury. They hear of it for the first time, and their opportunity to master the details must be brief at best: hence the necessity of clear and forcible presentation of the testimony in natural order, so as to make a good and abiding impression. It requires no mysterious or occult talent to examine a witness properly: nothing more than the common sense natural method of interrogation concerning the facts and circumstances necessary to get out all he knows about it. What I have said applies in equity cases where the hearing is before the court or a master, as well as those at law before a jury. The great point is to open up the minds of those who are to decide to a clear understanding of the truths of the case; and this cannot be done even by a multitude of witnesses, unless deliberately handled and clearly presented.

You may think it is a lawyer's duty, and that his ability is shown in concealing the facts and suppressing the truth against his client as well as in establishing the truth in his favor. I would say, No! Such a course is not to the lawyer's best interest in the long run. He need not volunteer to bring out facts favorable to the other side, but leave that to his adversary; and after all the investigation he has been able to make beforehand, he may find he has not discovered the whole truth even on his own side till after full examination of the witnesses on both sides on the trial. But, whether before or after the trial, so soon as he discovers the facts or law to be against him, his best course for his own and his client's interests is to advise a settlement or compromise, or abandon the case if his client is unreasonable. It will pay best in the end. Before dismissing the subject of lawyers, I may advert to another feature of the profession which unduly attracts the attention of spectators in the courts: quarrels and disputes between them. Mostly such broils and wrangles are but slight outbreaks of temper from sudden irritation, or are pretended for effect, and are seldom carried out of court or into private life. It not unfrequently happens however that they strike in and take the shape of deep personal animosity. Nearly every attorney in full practice with much sensitiveness or aggressive temper about him, has always one or more of these quarrels on hand; but men of even temper and wise discretion avoid them as much as possible. Display of temper on the trial of a case indicates weakness and should be carefully avoided. If found necessary to contradict an unwarranted assertion or to resort to repartee, it should be done without any show of temper whatever. The attorney with such control over his feelings possesses a valuable power; but after all, occasions may arise in the course of a varied practice and contact with attorneys of all shades of character, where substantial disputes will necessarily occur and involve personal enmity. I managed to have but two serious disputes of this kind in all my professional life, and it may not be uninteresting to relate them.

Samuel W. Black figured more prominently than any other in my early intercourse with the profession. He was at one time my bitterest enemy and afterwards my most devoted friend. Eloquent, impulsive and passionate, he was kind and generous at heart. His ambition and desire for display often led him to be aggressive and offensive to the opposite counsel; and as I was opposed to him more frequently than any other and disposed to retaliate in kind, the frequency of such altercations between us resulted at last in personal animosity of unusual bitterness. He was the son of the Rev. John Black, an eminent scholar and professor of languages in the Western University for many years. The family was one of the most respected and influential of the city. Samuel was educated at the University and a member of the literary society to which I belonged. He was admitted to the bar about the same time as myself, and we became rivals in the profession as we had been at the University. He was neither so studious or industrious as I, but was eloquent and ambitious; and his discriminative powers both as

to law and fact were admirable. His ambition was not so much for increase of business or emoluments as for victory and fame; and on this
account he soon acquired an extensive practice in the criminal and
civil courts, and the rivalry between us grew so strong that it finally degenerated into personality. His powerful eloquence was of a nature to
captivate and mislead the jury: which I could not submit to, as I always
felt that I had the right side of the case and if I failed to gain it that it
was my own fault. My most efficient weapon against his eloquence was
to turn him and it into ridicule by pointing out its absurdities and
nonsense. This would irritate him so much that it led to frequent outbreaks of temper and broils in open court: and Benjamin Patton, Judge
of the Common Pleas where we most frequently appeared, was too
weak a man to maintain dignity and good order on such occasions. It
culminated at last in threats of violence on his part; and in strength of
muscle he was much more powerful than I was, and was regarded as an
athlete among the young members of the bar at the time. On the occasion of his final burst of passion he declared he would deal with me
personally out of court the first time we met. Not to be outdone in the
same line of foolish bravado—for I was impetuous also—I replied that
I had no fear of anything of the kind; but if he attacked me I would be
ready for him and would repel brute force as it deserved, being no
pugilist myself. I knew from the glance of his eye that he meant mischief; and he knew from the coolness of my reply that I meant all I
said.

A collision was expected by our friends, but it did not occur. I prepared myself to meet it, and certainly would have killed him had he attacked me and it became necessary. I am aware of no duty, either legal,
moral or religious, which requires one man to submit to personal violence at the hands of another. The fault lies in giving provocation; but
no matter what the provocation, a man is not bound to submit unre-
sistingly. Every man's person is sacred to him; and the right of self defense is consequently sacred also. Although the assault may not be
likely to kill, yet the assailed party is not bound to take that risk: he is
not bound to suffer the infliction of personal indignity and injury of
any kind. Every one's manhood resents that; and every man has a right
to resort to the most efficient means within his power to defeat the
purpose of the assailant. If the physical power of the assailant is the
greater, the assailed is under no moral or legal obligation to interpose

his lesser physical power against him, but may resort to the most convenient weapon of defense within his reach. The law of self defense in all countries rests on this principle. Our moral duty to ourselves and society justifies it. The spirit of violence is not to be fostered and encouraged by abject submission to it. Nor does religion require such submission: passages of Scripture to the contrary are either interpolations or erroneously interpreted. The nature which God has implanted in us contradicts them; and the uniform practice of the Christian world for over eighteen hundred years contradicts them. I have given this supposed Christian doctrine very considerable attention, and made what research was possible regarding it in history contemporary with the origin of Christianity; and I find it, as also the doctrine of community of goods, was derived from a sect of Jewish ascetics then rather extensive, called "Essenes," and by some "Essenians," to which the family of Jesus belonged. And I have discovered also that historians of those times, and until a much later date, were in the habit of putting sentiments and words and speeches in the mouths of their chief characters which they supposed they would or ought to have used under the circumstances. How this may have been in regard to the doctrines referred to is uncertain. The church has from time to time eliminated many things in the Old Testament and some in the New as apocrypha; and it may be that some things still remain to be expurgated. Sentiments repugnant to the best regulated minds, contrary to common sense and the nature which God has implanted in his creatures, as well as contrary to the interests of society, may fairly be regarded as apocrypha, and part of the old leaven of the Essenians which has crept into some of the manuscript copies of the Scriptures of the early church.

The proposition that we should encourage wickedness and violence by extending safety and immunity to its perpetrators: as by exposing one side of the face to blows because we have been beaten on the other; or encouraging idleness and indolence by dividing all we have among the poor and consequently adding ourselves to their number; or giving away our clothing even to the coat off our back to any tramp who may ask for it, is too great an absurdity in the line of religious teaching to be imputed to Christ. Besides it is in conflict with the reasonableness of his instructions elsewhere; as for instance the declaration that he who provides not for those of his own household is worse than an infidel. If a man should follow the practice of giving all he hath to the poor, and even the coat off his back to the first who asks for it, it is not possible he could make provision for those of his own household. No, these extremes of non-resistance and charity cannot be sound doctrines; but if apocrypha, that circumstance does not impugn the authority of the Scriptures in other respects. Good temper and gentle and peaceable habits are Christian, and liberal charity according to our means to the deserving poor as taught in our Christian churches is a Christian virtue. But that is very different from the degrading communistic principle of having all goods in common and of non-resistance to every insult and indignity that is offered us. Neither Christian charity nor Christian forbearance can be carried to extremes any more than human laws, in regard to which one of the oldest and best founded maxims is, that "needle points of law are not law."

But to return to my narrative: I took no precaution to avoid Mr. Black, and met him frequently in the pursuit of my business about the Courthouse; but perhaps on cooler reflection his better judgment prevailed, for he showed no disposition to attack me; and so the matter passed off without further results than to make each more respectful to the other and more guarded in his language when we met in the trial of causes. For several years we remained in this attitude towards each other, without reconciliation but avoiding as much as possible any show of rancor when we met professionally; and this continued till the breaking out of the Mexican war. He had high military ambition, and volunteered in the United States service and was assigned the command of a regiment. The day arrived when he and his regiment were to embark for Vera Cruz. The occasion was one of much public excitement, and people were turning out to see the soldiers off. Whilst standing in my office door at the corner of Wylie street, I noticed my former college mate and present enemy in full uniform, coming down on the other side. I felt kindly towards him in view of the risk he was running from the chances of war as well as the dangers of climate; and to my surprise, when opposite, he turned and came directly across the street towards me, and holding out his hand said: "Mellon, let us make it up! I may never see you again and would like we should become friends before I go." Tears were standing in his eyes. This was too much; I had never entertained any ill will towards him. It was only rash expressions on both sides in the heat of passion which had produced the difficulty, and for which we were equally to blame. He left and served throughout that war with much honor and distinction. It was a kind of life that suited him. He was warm hearted and affectionate, and after his return we soon became faster friends than we had been bitter enemies before, and this friendship continued till his death. After the close of the Mexican war he remained chiefly in the government service; was for some time governor of Nebraska, and was engaged in other important public duties. But when at home he would participate in important trials in the criminal courts here, as he still entertained a fancy for the arena of his early forensic battles. He never did things by halves; he was either a bitter enemy or an ardent friend. When governor of Nebraska he saw my name mentioned as a candidate for the judgeship and wrote to encourage me to accept the nomination, reminding me of the strong literary proclivities I had shown at the University, and the excellent opportunities which the judicial office would afford for their exercise. He not only showed his friendly regard in this way, but actually came on from Nebraska to stir up his friends to aid me in the canvass.

The result of this quarrel shows we should never persist too far in fostering animosity and ill will. We can never know what is in the heart; and bitter feuds are often kept alive because the parties do not fully understand each other. It was only a year or so after my election when the war of the Rebellion broke out, and Colonel Black was among the first to take the field. With his popularity as a man and a soldier, a regiment of volunteers was easily raised. A day or two before his departure I had my last interview with him. He was brave but possessed of a very tender heart, and was much depressed at our parting. He told me that this time he had a strong foreboding he should never return, or see his wife and children or his friends again. And so it turned out, for after serving in several engagements with great bravery and distinction, he was instantly killed by a bullet through the head, whilst leading his regiment in the hottest part of the fight at the battle of Gaines' Mill.[1] And with him fell one of the truest personal friends I ever had.

My other unpleasantness occurred at a more recent date with an attorney of an entirely different type, one with whom no reconciliation is desirable; a kind of man whose likes and dislikes we feel indifferent about; who is neither valuable as a friend nor dangerous as a foe, but whom we shun when we can as we would anything else disagreeable.

He presents a fair exterior, and makes high pretensions to religion and professional etiquette; and as people are much influenced by a man's pretensions and the character he claims for himself, he manages to hold a fair standing among his fellow members of the bar; full of self-conceit and excitable in temper, never able to conduct professional business in a gentlemanly way, but when thwarted or defeated always turning the matter into a personal wrangle, and ready to vent his spite and animosity against his opponent; without any generous or honorable sentiment in his nature, a kind of hybrid between the Oily Gammon and Pecksniff breeds, with more of the Pecksniff: such was the hero of my second quarrel. I bear him no ill will and would say nothing to his disparagement if writing for the public eye. His impotent malice only injured himself so far as I was concerned; and I exposed his true character in a matter where he attempted to gratify his spite against me, but which resulted to the serious detriment of his client. What was the ulterior cause of the spite I have never discovered or cared.

The immediate occasion of our dispute was his bad advice and evil counsel to a foolish, misguided young man, a client of his and relative of mine, who had involved himself inextricably in debt. He advised him to repudiate a considerable sum which he owed me on his notes and the rents of certain property; and forced me to sue, when he hatched up an unconscionable defense and imbued his client with the idea that he could defeat my claim. In his abortive efforts to maintain this sham defense and after its utter overthrow, he manifested a degree of personal vindictiveness and malice so entirely unprofessional and uncalled for as to suspend all amicable intercourse between us. Not content with this, he tried by false representations to poison his client's mind against me; manifesting a disposition the most dastardly that can well be imagined.

But bad as was his defeat in the young man's case, he fared still worse in an equity case in which we were opposed to each other. On the argument in court his animosity in the latter case got the better of his discretion, and he asserted that the contents of a certain paper not then before the court were different from what I had stated them to be, and then proceeded to give his own version; whereon I interrupted him with the assurance that the contents of the paper were precisely as I had stated. This excited him and he declared he knew what he was saying and there was no mistake about it, and that my statements regarding the allegations in the paper were knowingly untrue. The matter was plain and unquestionable. I asked him to withdraw his assertions until the paper could be procured and referred to; but he declined, became excited and reiterated his assertions to be true in every particular. This was more than I could submit to. I had been at the bar or on the bench for over thirty years, and had not before been accused of falsehood. I called the court's attention to the circumstance and that I did not propose to allow it to rest there. Accordingly after the argument was over I procured a certified statement of his language and a certified copy of the paper to which he had referred, showing as it did that his statements to the court were entirely false. I then prepared a formal charge of willful lying in the practice of his profession; and with the documentary proofs attached, presented and read it in open court to a full bench on the following Saturday. This is one of the most serious charges that can be presented against an attorney, as it involves his oath of office; and one which it behooves any responsible party to be cautious in making unless he has clear and positive proof to sustain it. He could make no reply, but hung his head in confusion. I stated to the court that I took the course I did in no spirit of vindictiveness against him, but as a duty to myself and the proper administration of justice; and I now made the charge in legal form and should leave the matter in the hands of the judges to take such action as they deemed proper, considering my duty in connection with it ended. And thereupon I placed the charge and documents attached to it in the hands of the court, and the matter was held over for the time being to give him an opportunity to answer it or explain. It turned out as I knew it must, that he could give no explanation, and the charge remained against him and still remains against him in full force. One of the judges with whom he had studied law, and to whom he was useful in various ways, took an interest in shielding him from further exposure. Some sympathy was felt on account of his family relations also, and the matter was allowed to lie over for some time, when application was made to me through my counsel to withdraw the charge. I declined, stating that whilst I had no disposition to persecute him I would not do so, but leave the matter entirely with the court. Some time after that the president judge of the court spoke to me to the same effect in a private interview, and I made him the same reply. He and his

connections had and still have a following and some influence politically, and judges are always reluctant to punish a member of the bar of
their own motion where the matter is not pushed by a prosecutor; and
as my purpose in vindicating myself was accomplished, I had no vindictive feelings to gratify in pursuing him further. If he could afford to
lie under the charge of willful lying, I had nothing to complain of.

In such a long and active professional career, I regard it to my credit
to have been able to conduct myself in a way to produce so few personal difficulties with my brother members of the bar, and yet at all
times to maintain a firm and straightforward course. I have tried several important suits where large amounts were at stake, and where I
was myself the party interested. Such a position is apt to give rise to
personal feeling; but in not one of these, excepting with the party mentioned, did there ever occur the slightest unpleasantness or any disagreeable personal feeling between me and the opposing counsel. I
never could see any ground for dissatisfaction with the counsel opposed to me, even where I was a party to the suit, no matter how pow-
erfully he exerted himself to defeat me, so long as he confined himself
to the weapons of legitimate warfare. It is only where the counsel pur-
sues unwarranted methods, and goes outside of the facts and evidence
to covertly cast undeserved odium upon his opponent that proper
cause of offense can arise. To conduct himself through the trial of
a cause without excitement or irritability and without giving just
grounds of offense to the court or opposite counsel, in other words to
deport himself as a gentleman, is one of the most difficult and important duties a lawyer has to observe, and requires both experience and
ability. If he allows his feelings to get the better of him he is sure to lose
his head and render himself ridiculous; and if he conducts himself or
uses language to give personal offense to the court or opposing counsel, he becomes contemptible and is sure to prejudice his case. He must
preserve a cool, collected, dignified and gentlemanly demeanor and a
perfect mastery of himself, and use gentlemanly language under all circumstances. Occasion may occur in the course of a trial to cause a temporary expression of indignation; but such feeling should be sup-
pressed as speedily as possible. Any man with sufficient ability for a
lawyer, if he is naturally a gentleman and possessed of good breeding,
will seldom give occasion for offense. He can make the sharpest thrusts
and repartees without what lawyers call ugliness; and they will be all

the more effective on that account. There are always vulgar or weak
and irritable men enough at the bar, like the party mentioned, to
wrangle and make themselves personally offensive, but they belong to
the inferior class.

A most interesting consideration to the lawyer is the character and
qualifications of the judge before whom he practices. In my career at
the bar, Grier and Dallas were the judges under whom I commenced. It
was not long till Dallas died. He is buried in the northeastern corner of
Trinity churchyard. A modest little square shaft about eight feet high,
standing solitary and alone near the Sixth avenue wall, marks his resting place. I was a contributor to its erection in his memory, and it is
the only monument I have ever known to be erected by the members
of the bar to the memory of a deceased judge; although resolutions to
that end on the death of a judge are seldom wanting at bar meetings,
yet they are just as seldom carried into effect. Dallas was an amiable
young man of polished manners and fine education, with pretty fair legal attainments and of a distinguished Philadelphia family.

Benjamin Patton, of a Lewistown family, succeeded him, and with
poor health and moderate ability, continued to worry through the
business of the court for many years. Judge Grier of the District Court,
in which most of my practice lay, was a learned and able judge; so
much so that I depended frequently on him to instruct the jury on the
law of the case without taking the trouble to argue the question or cite
authorities. He was arbitrary however in his rulings and proceedings,
as able judges generally are. They are apt to feel such confidence in
their legal knowledge and ability to see the true state of the case, that
they become impatient. But when Judge Grier made a mistake in the
progress of a trial, which he often did, no judge was more liberal or
ready in acknowledging it and taking the necessary steps to correct his
error. Shaler, my preceptor, who afterwards became associated with
Grier, was also a keen sighted, clear headed judge, and exceedingly
kind and affable to the attorneys. After Grier's removal to the United
States Supreme Court we had Lowrie and Hepburn, both able men and
excellent judges. To Patton succeeded McClure on the Common Pleas
bench; and Hampton and Williams succeeded Lowrie and Hepburn in
the District Court, and were on the bench of these different courts
when I left the bar in 1859.

It would naturally be supposed that with able judges on the bench and careful, keen sighted lawyers on either side of a case on trial, justice would be administered with great certainty and exactness. Such supposition is a mistake however. Generally justice is fairly administered; but under the varied circumstances of different cases, conflicting legal principles arise continually, which after the fullest discussion and investigation by court and counsel, remain uncertain and without any satisfactory conclusion. Many instances of the kind occur in every lawyer's practice, where he can neither satisfy his own mind as to what the law is or guess what the court will decide it to be; and can only exercise his best judgment as to what it ought to be. I may mention one among the many notable instances of this kind which occurred in my own practice.

It was the case of Lee *vs.* Lee, reported in the Supreme Court Reports [9th Barr, 169].[2] It presented little difficulty as to the facts, and the law applicable to it was supposed to be well settled; and yet the result shows the uncertainty of litigation. Richard Biddle, one of the very ablest lawyers of his day, turned it over to me as a hopeless case when he went to Congress. He represented it very truly as one of great hardship to his client, a widow with a family of small children: the merits in her favor, but the law against her. She was in the possession of a good farm which her husband, who had died recently, supposed he owned, but after his death his father claimed it; and the suit was an action of ejectment to turn the widow and children out of possession. Mr. Biddle had been employed by the widow to defend her, and his plan was to baffle the plaintiff and keep her in possession, and afford her the benefit of the crops and profits as long as possible, but without any hope of a final decision in her favor. The deceased husband had previously owned a small piece of land in the neighborhood, but after his marriage it was found insufficient to maintain a family; and his father, who owned a large and well improved farm near by which he did not occupy, proposed to exchange it with the son for the small farm, the son to pay to two of his sisters two hundred dollars each after the father's death. Thus the small farm and four hundred dollars and what the father regarded as the son's prospective share in his estate, was to be an equivalent and sufficient consideration for the larger farm. No written contract was executed; the arrangement was entirely verbal, but under it and in entire confidence of its efficacy, the son had removed to the larger farm, and shortly after made a deed to his father for the smaller farm, which the father afterwards sold and conveyed to a third party. Three or four years after this the son died, and by some undue influence the father's mind became prejudiced against the widow and children. Hence this suit to eject them: it being well settled law that a verbal contract for the sale or exchange of land is entirely void and of no effect unless reduced to writing and signed by the parties; consequently it was supposed on all sides the widow and children had no hold on the land. The case was forced on after some delay, and was tried by Messrs. Burke and McCandless for the plaintiff and by me for the widow. I proved the verbal contract and other circumstances of the case on which I relied as a defense, to the satisfaction of the jury, and insisted on two exceptions to the general rule of law regarding verbal contracts: the one is, that where the party has taken possession and makes permanent and valuable improvements the cost of which cannot be easily estimated, in such case the bargain will hold, though not in writing, as the party seeking to rescind the contract must do what is equitable by refunding the expense of costly permanent improvements on the land, and where the expenditures are of a class difficult to be estimated, the contract will be enforced as if in writing. The other exception which I contended for was, that where an exchange of different pieces of property is made verbally and possession taken in pursuance of the agreement, and one of the parties afterwards seeks to rescind the contract because not in writing, he must restore the property he got in exchange, so as to put the other party in the same condition as before the exchange was made.

In regard to the first of these exceptions my testimony was clearly inadequate: the improvements which the son had made in his lifetime were no more than the ordinary repairs necessary to keep the place in good order and condition, and which are supposed to be compensated for by the use of the land. But the more I considered it the stronger my faith grew in the other exception. Although the small piece of land which the father had got in exchange was insignificant in value compared with the large farm, yet I contended that no matter how small in comparative value the father could not recover, having disposed of it, and having become unable to restore it as he should have done before bringing suit. But Judge Grier charged the jury to the effect that however harsh and unfeeling it might seem to them to turn out the widow and children under the circumstances, the law was decidedly against them; that only one exception to the law applicable to the case existed, and that was where the purchaser had taken possession under the contract and made expensive and important improvements on it, the value of which could not well be ascertained and refunded; and under the evidence in this case all the improvements made, he held, were such as were fully compensated for by the use of the land. And as to the small farm the widow and heirs could sue the father for the value of it, and recover the amount with damages. But notwithstanding this explicit instruction the jury rendered a verdict in favor of the widow and heirs, which was equivalent to at least a year's extension of time of possession, as the case could not come up again in a shorter period. The judge, as is usual where a verdict is rendered contrary to the law as laid down by the court, granted a new trial. He left the bench before it was tried again, and the new trial came on before his successor, Judge Hepburn, who ruled in every respect as did his predecessor, and with like result; for, after several days trial, the jury again rendered a verdict in favor of the defendant, against the charge of the court. This verdict was also set aside for the same reason as the first, which gave us another year of the farm. The next trial came on before Judge Lowrie, who ruled as did his predecessors, that the defendant showed no legal defense; and with like result, as the verdict was again in favor of the defendant and against the charge of the court, and was at once indignantly set aside by the judge.

This afforded us another year's possession. But I was now so filled with my own theory of the case, and had such strong faith in the exception which I contended for regarding the principle of exchange of lands, that I persisted in my efforts for final victory. The fourth trial also came on before Lowrie, who was determined this time that I should not get a verdict. He regarded the former verdicts as against the law and charge of the court, and as due to my unwarranted appeals to the sympathies of the jury for the widow and orphans. And it did seem so presumptuous to contend against the opinion of all the judges and most of the lawyers, that I advised the widow to obtain assistant counsel to share the responsibility with me on this fourth trial. Accordingly she retained Judge Shaler, who was again at the bar. But when the trial came on and the plaintiff had given his testimony and documents in evidence, and we proceeded to introduce ours as we had done before, the judge refused to permit us to do so, declaring that all the evidence we proposed was insufficient, if the jury believed every word of it. We objected to this of course, and at the close proposed to address the jury on the evidence produced by the plaintiff alone, which the judge refused to allow us to do, declaring that nothing we could say would justify the jury in disregarding the plaintiff's legal title. Thus we were shut off both as to testimony and speeches; and as Judge Shaler and Judge Lowrie were both excitable and irritable, a good deal of feeling was manifested between them. Judge Lowrie told the jury that he would take the responsibility of having the verdict recorded in their presence in favor of the plaintiff; and did so, declaring at the same time that it was their duty to render such a verdict under the law, the plaintiff having made out a *prima facie* case, and the defendant having presented no adequate evidence to rebut it there was nothing for the jury to deliberate upon.

To this verdict so recorded against our protest, we took a writ of error to the Supreme Court, where it was vigorously contested and the decision rendered conclusively in our favor, Judge Coulter of the Supreme Court delivering a rather caustic opinion, severely criticising the course of Judge Lowrie of the lower court. He declared that by constitutional right every citizen was entitled to be heard in a court of justice either by himself or his counsel, and that the course of the judge below was arbitrary and unprecedented. Some of the expressions in the opinion were so severe on Judge Lowrie that at his instance and with our consent, Judge Coulter expunged them before the case was reported in the books. But this was not the best part of our victory: the decision of the court below was not only reversed as to the procedure on the trial, but my position as to the necessity of a reconveyance of the small farm before bringing suit, was fully sustained and established as a legal principle. The result disconcerted the plaintiff and his counsel so much that they never again renewed the suit, and the widow and heirs remain in possession until this day, some thirty-five years. The discomfiture was so complete that the plaintiff never proceeded further, not even to collect the four hundred dollars which was properly chargeable on the farm. So the result has been better for the widow and children than if no litigation had been instituted against them. The only injustice done has been to the sisters who were to receive the four hundred dollars, and to myself. I never received any adequate compensation for my services. It was all the widow could do to make a living for her family, and pay her witnesses at the several trials and meet other incidental expenses. I never received exceeding one hundred dollars on my part for the whole business, when I ought to have received five hundred at least. I was able to wait, and did so on account of the widow's straitened circumstances, till my claim became too stale to insist on. This I have done too often in other cases as well. A professional man should never make an exorbitant charge but should be vigilant to obtain his just dues.

Another case which I recollect was attended with peculiarities which distinguished it from the common run: the case of Brunot against Peterson. Hilary Brunot, the father of Felix R. and Hilary of the present day, had become a client of mine in some ordinary law business, and made frequent mention of the great loss he had sustained several years before by Lewis Peterson, who had at one time been the proprietor of a cotton factory, and extensively engaged in business. Brunot was honest, pious and unassuming, but not very bright; and had acquired considerable property by close industry in the manufacture of white lead, but unfortunately had placed too much confidence in his friend Peterson, indorsing for him to the extent of about twelve thousand dollars. Peterson failed and took the benefit of the Bankrupt Law of 1842; and Brunot had to pay the notes as is usual with accommodation indorsers, getting extensions from the banks and otherwise as best he could. It nearly broke him up, and was a constant theme of lamentation with him. One part of his statement attracted my attention: the injustice of the Bankrupt Law, as he considered it. Peterson had paid nothing, he alleged, and still retained all his property. This was no unusual circumstance, but I thought it worth while looking into, and I found it substantially true. Peterson was still in possession of all the property he ever owned, and had been treating and using it as he had done before his bankruptcy, six or seven years previously. It consisted of two very valuable coal farms and salt works near Tarentum, and several good properties in Allegheny City. As to some of it, I found that the title never had been in him, but in an old bachelor uncle in Maryland who had not been here within the memory of any one; and such of it for which there was record title in himself he had before bankruptcy conveyed to a relative. For many years before he had held all this property as his own, but had not returned it in his schedule for the benefit of his creditors; and if his own, this was a fraud on the Bankrupt Law, which rendered it inoperative for his protection. But the trouble was to prove the property really belonged to him, and not to the uncle or relative.

I found that Brunot, however loud his complaints, was utterly incompetent to ferret out the facts. He was very anxious that something should be done, but was helpless to render any assistance himself. I saw that if it was a fraud it was a big one and the amount worth fighting for, and I employed a detective to make himself acquainted with the Peterson family, and with all Peterson's previous history and business; and in this way soon found circumstantial evidence sufficient to justify the bringing of a suit, leaving it to good luck in future developments to obtain facts enough to sustain it. But whilst I had no doubt of the fraud, evidence to prove it came in slowly; and when the case was reached Peterson, backed by a strong array of able counsel, urged on the trial. I went into it with all the evidence I had been able so far to gather. It was all circumstantial, and the difficulty was to make out such a connected chain of circumstances, indicating fraud in the concealment of property, as would justify the court in submitting the question to the jury. I felt if I could succeed in that I would be safe, as I saw the jury comprehended it; but Judge Williams, who happened to be on the bench, was very rigid and particular regarding the admission of testimony. He would admit no circumstances unless their immediate relevancy to the question of fraud was clearly obvious. And as the relevancy of any particular circumstance among a great variety of others which taken together tend to establish a fact, can seldom be shown without all the circumstances connected with it being presented; and as only one circumstance can be proved at a time, I found it very difficult to get in my evidence at all under the judge's proclivity to rule everything out which did not on its face show its relevancy.

I worked along for a couple of days however as best I could, till at last he excluded the evidence of two important matters without which the case might be jeopardized. Without them I disliked to risk it with the jury or with the Supreme Court on the rulings of the judge excluding them, and took a nonsuit, deeming it best to act on the Hudibrastic principle that

> He who fights and runs away
> May live to fight some other day.[3]

And the costs of a nonsuit were not as heavy then as now. This apparent defeat greatly depressed and discouraged my client, who feared it was all up with him, as he expressed it. But I soon brought another suit and had nearly another year to mature my plans and obtain more corroborative facts and circumstances; and when it came on the second time I was better prepared than before, and luck was on our side in having Judge Hampton on the bench when it was called. He was a more liberal minded man and had a better perception of the nature and relevancy of evidence, and I had less difficulty in getting all my testimony admitted and fully considered. But the peculiar circumstance which more than anything else impressed the case on my memory, has reference to the mind and disposition of my client. After two days spent in presenting all the testimony and evidence in our possession to the court and jury on the second trial he still seemed as despondent and hopeless of success as ever, in view of the strong opposition made to it by defendant's counsel. But on the third morning, when he appeared at my office before the court opened, he was brightened up and elated and seemed every way different. I was surprised at the change, and asked him what had turned up. A great deal, he said; he was now confident and sure I would win the case. I was elated too, supposing he had made a discovery of new evidence, and asked him what it was. He said that before retiring to bed on the previous evening he had done what no good Christian should ever dare to do unless in the last extremity: he had gone into his closet and prayed fervently to the Holy Ghost for success in the case, although he knew it was a great sin to pray to the Holy Ghost unless in such an emergency as left no alternative, and prayer to the other persons of the Godhead might be inadequate. But he knew that if he lost this case it would be his ruin, and on that account he ventured on this awful course. And in the fervency of his prayer it was clearly revealed to him that we would succeed, and he had now no misgivings whatever. This revelation surprised and disappointed me. One credible witness in the flesh would have been more to the purpose than any number of revelations from the spirit land. But we gained the case and recovered back all the money he had ever paid for Peterson with interest; yet to the day of his death my client gave more of the credit of gaining the suit to the Holy Ghost than to me.

I relate these two cases as well to show the uncertainties of law as the peculiarities of clients. When a lawyer has justice on his side and can invoke some reasonable principle of law or equity to sustain him, he need not be discouraged because such principle had not been applied in former cases. New cases invoke new applications of old principles, and the principles of equity and justice are as old as society itself. Another qualification indispensable to success in the legal profession is first class business talent; but if pecuniary success is the object first class business talent can mostly be utilized to better advantage in other pursuits: especially is this the case if the party has any capital of his own to operate with. It is in view of this fact that I have never encouraged one of my own sons to enter the legal profession. They are all endowed with first class business talent, and by its application to the capital under their control can do far better than in the practice of a profession of any kind. Attention to other people's business is a waste of time when we have profitable business of our own to attend to. In my own professional life I never neglected my private affairs however, excepting in the matter of collecting fees; and as my private affairs increased through the accumulation of money and property, I had necessarily to diminish my professional work, until in the long run I had to give up both legal and judicial business altogether: however gratifying to get into a good practice and achieve success, professional life, as I have said before, is not followed for the love of it; and from the outset I had husbanded my means with a view to independence and ultimate retirement from it.

During nearly all the time rates of interest on the street were from ten to fifteen per cent., and securities of the best kinds could be purchased at good profit. The Loomis boys, sons of attorney Loomis, were my brokers; Benjamin McClain also acted in that capacity for a long time, and others as well, investing and reinvesting for me in first class paper. Hence my means, aided by a good professional income, accumulated rapidly. Besides this I invested a good deal in the construction of buildings after the Great Fire of 1845.[4] That catastrophe was of historical interest. It occurred on the 10th of April, a clear but rather windy day; and I was busy between watching my cases on the trial list in court and superintending the building of a dwelling at the corner of Wylie and Fifth avenues close by the Courthouse. Soon after twelve o'-clock the fire bells commenced ringing, but I paid no attention to them for an hour or two until people in an excited condition began hurrying up and down the street declaring the town was on fire. I then went to a position in the Courthouse from which I could see the lower part of the city, and found the fire was becoming really serious and might eventually reach the boarding house of Miss Jane McLain on Third, between Wood and Smithfield, where we had been boarding during the rough winter weather. I thought it safer to remove our furniture from there to the finished part of the new building. My wife and child were on a visit at the time to our friends in the country. I ordered the carts which I had at work to the boarding house; and so rapid was the progress of the fire that it had already spread all over the district between Ferry and Wood streets, and was crossing Wood street before we had the carts loaded.

As I came up Third to Smithfield people were running in all directions wild with excitement, and cinders and burning shingles were falling everywhere, setting fire to everything combustible. I saw people on Smithfield street actually throwing china and crockery ware out of the upper windows, and carrying beds and bedding down stairs. I unloaded the goods at our new house on the hill, where they were perfectly safe, as there was no other building in the neighborhood except the Courthouse. It was brick yards on one side and open lots on the other all around. I then went upon the roof of the Courthouse, from which the sight was grand and appalling. It was about four o'clock, and the fire had progressed from Ferry street consuming everything between Fourth street and the river, and was now in its utmost fury approaching Smithfield, surging like a vast flood, devouring dwellings, warehouses and churches, and our great old stone university building with all the contents. In a few minutes it approached the Monongahela House; the flames soon shot into the sky from the entire area of the building, and directly the wooden covered Monongahela bridge was on fire, one span speedily falling into the river after another, like a straw rope on fire, until in about twenty minutes the fire reached the South Side and the structure disappeared. The wind was high and its direction up the river, and the fire swept the entire district between Fourth street and the river, on through what was called Pipetown, as far as there was anything combustible to burn. The whole district, comprising about a quarter part of the then city, was soon reduced to a mass of smouldering coals and ruined walls; and singularly enough the only building which it respected and avoided in all the district was a large and very old frame structure yet standing at the southeast corner of Fourth and Ross. The entire destruction was completed by five o'clock.

Of course little or no goods of any kind were saved. It was as much as the occupants of stores and dwellings and factories could do to escape with their lives. Some half a dozen or more were lost, among them Samuel Kingston, an old and active lawyer. He rushed into his office to secure his papers and was overcome before he could escape. The confusion and excitement was great, and business was suspended for several days. I remember when on the Courthouse viewing the scene of disaster and contemplating the vast amount of wealth destroyed, that I regarded it at the time as a great calamity to the city and likely to produce a depression in business and hard times; but the result proved I was mistaken in this. Instead of depression it gave an impetus to every kind of business, especially everything in the building line. Mechanics of all kinds flocked in from other places, and all obtained ready employment at better wages than formerly; and new life and increased value was infused into real estate, and rents were higher for several years. In 1845 I built at the corner of Wylie and Fifth dwellings and offices. In 1846 I built some eighteen small dwellings which brought me an income of about ten per cent. on the investment, until I sold them at a profit afterwards in 1860. Taxes were not so exorbitant then.

After some two years in my new dwelling I discovered that city life was not so congenial to my wife's health and spirits as country life; that every time she returned from her mother's at the East End she was brightened up by the purer air and agreeable surroundings; and by 1848 our two little boys were in a condition to require more outdoor privileges and exercise than they could obtain in the back yard or on the front pavement of a city house, and I concluded to try the experiment of country life. I greatly feared the loss of time going out and in and the effect it might have on my business, and on that account made no permanent arrangements until I would see how the experiment would operate. Accordingly in April, 1848, I took the cottage on my motherinlaw's place, now belonging to Mr. Holmes, near my present residence. After establishing my family there I went into the city regularly at six o'clock every morning on horseback, and returned in the same manner at six in the evening, and was agreeably surprised to find that it had no injurious effect on my business whatever. In fact, the morning and evening ride only brightened me up and enabled me to accomplish more work. The fresh air and exercise going and coming, and the opportunity for reflection and rest afforded by the repose and exemption from the continuous annoyance of clients, gave me more vigor and enabled me to work harder and more systematically during the business hours of the day.

We remained in this cottage, one of the most cozy and delightful spots I ever occupied, until the spring of 1853, when we removed to our new house near by which I had built the year previously, and where we have remained ever since. I continued to go out and in on horseback for some years in all seasons and in all kinds of weather, after which I resorted to a Jersey wagon in order to have with me more constantly my young man, Mr. Shields, as a clerk or private secretary.

After some thirteen years of active practice and accumulation my investments had increased to a considerable extent; and a good many of them being in mortgages, I was compelled, as might be expected, from time to time to become the owner of some of the mortgaged properties by foreclosure; and it was in this way I first became interested in the coal business, by becoming the owner in 1849 of a piece of coal land, about sixty acres on the *berm* bank of the Pennsylvania Canal, near Tarentum, this county. The *berm* bank of a canal is the opposite bank to the towing path. The land had been procured by Robert Hezlep for salt works purposes. He had built several dwellings suitable for workingmen and bored for a salt well without success, and proposed to sell—in fact was forced to sell; and as the coal in this land cropped out along the bank of the canal and looked very fine, and canal transportation to Pittsburgh was a mere trifle, the temptation was great to go into the business of producing coal for the Allegheny City market.[5] All the coal used in Allegheny City and Pittsburgh at that time was brought down the Monongahela river in flats, or hauled by wagons from country pits. None was brought by canal; and in view of the certainty, convenience and small cost of transportation, the profits of coal delivered from the canal appeared much larger than by any other method. Accordingly I proposed to Benjamin Patterson, an active young carpenter and client of mine, that if he would furnish the energy and industry to operate the business and carry it on in his own name, I would become a silent partner with him and furnish the money necessary. He was delighted with the proposal, and a dozen handcarts were ordered to begin with—handcarts were the kind used by miners at the time—and a couple of flat boats, and four stout horses for towing purposes were procured and formed our equipment, not very costly or extensive. I proceeded cautiously to first find the outcome before investing too much money in it. Everything seemed to promise well; but obstacles more or less formidable present themselves in all kinds of business. In running the main entry or tunnel, sufficient coal was obtained for the first cargo, and sent down to a cotton factory on the bank of the canal in Allegheny City, and quite a flattering report received from it; but when the second cargo was sent down the report was not so good: it was to the effect that the coal was equal in all respects to the Monongahela or Pittsburgh coal for heat and production of steam, but after it was taken out of the flats and exposed to the atmosphere for three or four days, it gradually broke up and dissolved into nut coal and finally into slack. This was not so insuperable an objection; the coal might be different in other parts of the mine, and at the worst it could only affect its competition with Pittsburgh coal in the market, which could be overcome by a slight difference in price. But the serious difficulty, and the one which defeated us, was the variableness of the coal seam in thickness. After my partner had run his entry some seventy-five yards into the hill he reported to me that for some time the coal seam had been diminishing in thickness, or the bottom and roof were approaching each other. I advised a continuance to see what the result might be; but he soon reported only eighteen inches of coal, which was gradually getting less and would soon be cut off altogether, and that he had had to blast the rock of the roof in order to follow it so far. This caused a suspension of operations; and after an investigation into the geological coal formations of the district, through the experience of farmers and salt works operators of the neighborhood, I found this irregularity of common occurrence in this particular coal seam. Mr. Karns, the proprietor of a neighboring salt works, was compelled to abandon his mine on this account, and open a new one on the other side of the hill. These rolls or swells, as they were called, generally cut off the coal seam almost entirely for two or three hundred yards or more, and then would gradually open out again to the usual size. I concluded the business would not support an uncertain expense of this kind, and abandoned the project altogether. We sold our horses and flats and carts at very little loss; and in a few years I sold the property itself, at a gain, to the Pennsylvania Salt Manufacturing Company, which had located its works close by.

This coal vein crops out about Tarentum and has since been worked extensively by P. Y. Hite & Co., and sinks south until at Pittsburgh it is several hundred feet below the regular Pittsburgh seam. It has been recently shafted for in Allegheny City by the Messrs. Watson, and found there at a depth of a few hundred feet, and the coal is now produced by them at a fair profit. But the same uncertainty from irregularity of thickness still accompanies it. In some places where the vein is not gradually diminished, the coal is found to be abruptly removed as if washed out by water, and its place supplied by drift and boulders. After this unsuccessful experiment I had no more to do with the coal business until 1859, when I became a silent partner with another young man in a similar enterprise, but which did not result so pleasantly in the long run as that with Patterson had done. In this latter enterprise I furnished the money for the purchase of the Sandy Creek and other works; and about the same time became a silent partner in the firm of J. B. Corey & Co., with David Shaw, J. B. Corey, and my brotherinlaw, George M. Bowman, as active partners in another coal business.

In 1856 I was in like manner under the necessity of taking a furnace property of some seventeen hundred acres of a defaulting mortgagor in West Virginia. The furnace was in full blast, with a good deal of stock of ore and charcoal on hand, and other inducements to continue it in operation. I visited the place to examine the situation and the facilities for ore and cost of transportation and the like, and after a close investigation of nearly a week, I saw the impolicy of continuing the business. I studied the nature and character of iron production in its different phases and the future prospects of the trade, and arrived at the conclusion that the best course was to run out the stock and material then on hand and close up. This I accomplished in due time; and the result proved the wisdom of the course, because in a year or two it was discovered to be more profitable to obtain ore from the lakes and elsewhere westward than to prospect for and obtain it in small quantities along the western slope of the mountains, as had been the practice up to this time. This change of the source of ores changed the furnace business west of the mountains ever since. In my early days our iron was all produced along the western slope: Ligonier Valley alone containing some fourteen blast furnaces, was a lively place then. This West Virginia furnace business however, brought me into closer acquaintance than formerly with the iron and coal trade. I mention these outside enterprises merely to show how increase of means leads away from professional pursuits.

Between 1850 and 1860 my private as well as my professional business increased so rapidly that it became difficult to do justice to either, and as my own affairs were the more important and profitable, I attempted to make up for the time devoted to them by taking partners in my law business. My first partner was William B. Negley, my wife's nephew, who had studied with me. He was a sound lawyer of good judgment, pure morals, and an efficient practitioner. We remained together seven years, until after his marriage; when he formed a law partnership with his brotherinlaw, D. D. Bruce, Esq., in which connection he has remained ever since, and has been successful.

My second partner was Nathaniel Nelson. I had been acquainted with him from boyhood; he was a good scholar and had taught school in Allegheny City and county for upwards of twenty years before entering the profession of the law. As a teacher he was quite a success: that indeed was what nature had fitted him for. After studying law for sometime in Pittsburgh he went to our mutual friend Judge Sutton, then Probate Judge at Little Rock, Arkansas, where he finished his law studies and was admitted to the bar; after which he practiced in the State of Missouri until he exhausted what means he had accumulated in his former profession as a teacher, and in 1856 returned to Pittsburgh in an impecunious condition. He at once applied to me as an old friend, not for aid, but advice as to whether he should continue in the law or return to his former vocation. I knew his ability as a penman and accountant and that he was honest and honorable, and extensively acquainted and favorably known throughout the city and county. As to his legal acquirements I knew nothing at that time; but as his expectations of profit and emolument were extremely limited, I supposed I could utilize his talents, at least to the extent of the value he placed on them. Accordingly I stipulated to give him a share in certain departments of our law business, which I knew would far exceed his utmost expectations in the way of profits. I found him of much use in the office, and a safe counsellor to clients where no difficult law questions were involved. And he was useful otherwise, because nearly every new client had been a pupil of his, and had the utmost confidence in his advice; and his plain, neat, uniform handwriting was admirable in the preparation of deeds and documents of all kinds: the only drawback in that line was that I had myself to dictate or sketch out for him every-thing new or difficult. And as to the business in the courts he could render but little assistance there. He was so diffident he could hardly make a motion in court; and was inefficient at devising proceedings where any intricate questions were involved. I still needed some one who could try causes, or at least assume some part of that labor and re-sponsibility. And just at this time, early in 1858, a new man came here from Fayette county, R. P. Flenniken, Esq., a gentleman of imposing presence and pretensions. He had been minister to Denmark, and was well spoken of as a man of honor and gentlemanly qualities. He pro-fessed to be able to conduct equity proceedings and try causes in court, without assistance from any one; and with this view I gave him an in-terest also as a partner. But after several months of trial I found that whilst all that was said of him as a gentleman of honor and integrity was true enough, yet his tact and legal ability in the conduct of pro-ceedings or trials in court was so deficient as to gain me the blame and reproach of nearly every client whose business I entrusted to his care.

I soon found that such superadded partners afforded me little relief under the undue burden of labor which I had assumed. The legal pro-fession is peculiar in this respect. Where there are partners in a law firm each client looks to some one of the firm as his particular adviser, and relies on him to manage and conduct his case; and I found it im-possible to transfer clients who relied on me to my partners, without losing them altogether. Indeed, as a general rule there is no benefit in law partnerships. The confidential relation of attorney and client is of a personal character, and the attorney who has sufficient ability to at-tract clients can accomplish as much by competent clerks as by part-ners.

My private affairs had increased to such an extent as to demand much personal attention. Besides this I had also been appointed, from time to time, to several important trusts involving the management of some large estates; and as a man's own affairs and trust property under his care are of more importance than the contentions of litigants, it was natural I should devote more time and attention to them than to ordinary law business. But when the contemplated relief by introduc-ing partners failed I found myself in a rather unsatisfactory predica-ment, and owing to the worriment and extra labor cast on me my health was severely taxed to bear the strain. I could not have the legal department of my business as well conducted as when I attended to it myself; and I could not give it my whole attention now without neglecting more important affairs. The condition was calculated to produce dyspepsia and was having that effect on me, when one morning in April, 1859, soon after I entered my private office, and before any clients appeared, three of my particular friends of the bar, Thomas M. Marshall, A. M. Watson and Stephen H. Geyer called, and announced themselves as a delegation to procure my consent to become a candidate for the office of assistant law judge of the Court of Common Pleas. An act of Assembly had just been passed for the election of an additional judge in that court, giving him equal power and salary with the president judge, and authorizing them to hold court separately or jointly in all other cases except for murder, in which they were required to sit jointly. One cause for the creation of the office was the peculiarity of temperament and opinion of Judge McClure, then president of the court. He was a man of excellent qualities, but regarded as a little erratic in his rulings, and especially in his sentences in criminal cases.

I regarded the proposition rather in the light of a practical joke. I had never entertained the slightest desire for office of any kind, or given a thought to seeking popularity, or indeed taken any share in party politics, and accordingly scouted the idea. But they returned again and again to persuade me of its advisability. I was overwhelmed and oppressed with business at the time, and in a mood to get rid of my law business and last law partners together if I could; and they finally persuaded me that this was the way to do it, and an honorable way of retiring from the profession. I knew nothing about party maneuvering and electioneering, but they proposed that if I consented they would attend to all the electioneering that might be required. Nothing was needed but a nomination, they said, and they professed to be able to procure that; and I was aware that no other three men in the city or county possessed more political influence in the republican party at that time. These assurances and considerations inclined me to accept. To take such an office was the best thing I could do under the circumstances. My trusts could be settled up and discharged and my money permanently invested in real estate, requiring but little attention afterwards to my private affairs, as I supposed. I had never failed in anything on which I had set my mind so far, and why might I not succeed in this also? But whilst I stood reasonably well as a lawyer and private citizen, I was so little known in party politics that my friends had to obtain a certificate of some of the leading local politicians of the day to show that I had always been an old line whig and consequently a republican. I gave my consent in May to stand as a candidate, and there was but a month between the time when I gave my consent and the nominating convention, scarcely time for my old clients and friends in the country districts to become aware of my candidacy.

My competitors were James I. Kuhn and Edwin H. Stowe, who were already in the field and their friends exceedingly active. Kuhn was a man of high legal ability, and had a large following of friends and relatives in several of the country districts of the county. Stowe was a much younger man, little known in the country districts, but popular in the city, and had many warm and influential political friends. The canvass soon became much more lively and exciting than I had anticipated. Mr. Kuhn traveled and electioneered a good deal, and Mr. Stowe to a lesser extent. I did not go out at all or appear in public, leaving electioneering in that line to my friends, confining my own exertions to writing notes to such of my intimate friends and acquaintances as I could rely on to exert themselves in my favor; and in regard to them I was not disappointed—they worked for me faithfully. There were few incidents of the campaign of much interest; I may mention two of them, however.

Penn township was a stronghold of Mr. Kuhn, the home of his ancestry, and all the local politicians there were related to him in one way or another. To obtain delegates in my favor from that township was out of the question, as was supposed. To attempt it would only stir up a bitter fight in which we were pretty sure to be worsted. My city friends therefore abandoned the idea of obtaining delegates for me in that township, as I would at any rate be preferred to Stowe by the Kuhn delegates if he could not be nominated, and therefore better not irritate them. But David Collins, a popular man and warm friend of mine in that township, called to see me to know why no exertions were being made in my behalf; and when I informed him the reasons he took in the situation, but a mischievous twinkle of his eye showed he had something in his mind. He did not divulge what it was, but acquiesced in our plan; said it was just right; that to make a fight in his township for delegates if unsuccessful would be injurious. Accordingly when he returned home and reported what my friends had told him of their intention of making no exertion for delegates in his township it relieved the minds of Mr. Kuhn's friends of all apprehension, so they made less exertion. But on the evening of the primary, when the election was proceeding quietly and but an occasional voter appearing at intervals and casting his vote for the Kuhn delegates, the only ones in the field, a procession of hay wagons appeared in the distance carrying thirty to forty voters who when they arrived voted solid for David Collins and another of my friends as delegates in my behalf; and they were elected by a large majority. I was not aware of this strategic movement till after it was over, but was nevertheless gratified at its success, as he and my other friend from his township were active and influential workers in the convention.

In Wilkins township Mr. Stowe was deservedly popular. He had taught in an academy at Wilkinsburg at one time and had gained many warm friends there, chief among them James Kelly, the great land owner of that locality, and an active and influential local politician: so much so that he was regarded as carrying Wilkins township in his pocket politically, and he seemed to take it for granted that the township must send delegates in favor of Mr. Stowe. I disliked this because it lay in the district where I considered myself popular, and I was intimately acquainted with Kelly whom I had expected to act for me. Two or three days before the primary election was to come off I met him at the Union Depot and concluded to let him know what I thought about it. So I informed him that his opposition was unexpected and I did not like it. He apologized on the ground of pre-engagement to Mr. Stowe before I became a candidate, and declared it unfortunate that two of his friends were running for the same office at the same time. I knew there was no use to attempt changing his mind as he was noted for obstinacy; but I was aware that he was neither an active nor effective worker at the polls, and asked if it would offend him for me to see his son on the subject and try to enlist his influence in my favor, as I wished if possible to have the delegates from that township. He replied I was welcome to see his son, but that his son had little influence. I knew differently, that character and standing went for nothing, and often the greater rowdy was the more efficient local politician; and as the Wall's accommodation[6] was moving out I stepped on it, and contrary to my policy of avoiding personal interviews in my own behalf, landed in a few minutes in Wilkinsburg where, not far from the station, I met the son. He had become intemperate and neglectful of all business, and was to be found mostly in the saloon or on the street. He was an abrupt customer, and I treated him accordingly; said to him that I had just seen his father at the depot and was surprised to find that he was in favor of Stowe, but he had consented that I might see his son who, however, he said had no influence. And now, said I, you have my errand; influence or no influence, you can help me; I don't want to lose the delegates from a township so near my old home; and it is hardly the right thing for you, an old citizen, to treat another old citizen so and give a comparative stranger the preference. He hesitated on the ground of the campaign having progressed so far before I was announced. He had made no promises, he said, but on his father's account he supposed he was expected to work for Mr. Stowe's delegates, although he did not care a d__n for Mr. Stowe, nor very much for any one else. But he admitted that if his father was not in the way he would do all he could for me. I told him his father had given me permission to apply to him, allowing he might do as he pleased, and he would not feel sore about it if I did get the delegates. He admitted it was hardly the fair thing to prefer a stranger over me. I told him I knew he could do the business if he would: the matter was entirely in his hands. As the train was coming I was about leaving him and asked him to pronounce the word, yes or no. He hesitated, but when I was part way to the station he called after me that I might rely on it my delegates would be sent in. This was the full extent of direct electioneering on my part. And sure enough, to the surprise of my opponents, two of the best delegates in the convention were sent in for me from Wilkins.

On the day of the convention my friends estimated that I had two-thirds of the delegates and would be nominated on the first ballot; but numerous candidates for other offices were to be nominated by the same convention, and so much log-rolling and trading took place before the judicial office was reached that I was nominated only by a respectable majority. My friend Kuhn never succeeded in getting a nomination afterwards; but the office of second assistant law judge being created before the end of my term, Stowe was elected to it and was on the bench with me for some years before I left it. And he has been elected and re-elected and remained on the bench ever since.

In those days the nomination was everything in the republican party; after it no more electioneering was required. The democratic party only made nominations, as the leaders expressed it, to keep up their organization. George F. Gillmore was the democratic nominee. He was a lawyer of some prominence at one time, and was popularly known to his party by having been for a long while editor and proprietor of the *Post,* the only democratic paper of the city. On the second Tuesday of October I was elected with rather more than the usual republican majority; this was on account of getting a good many democratic votes. Between the nomination in June and the election in October I was busied in arranging my private affairs in a manner to require as little time and attention to them as possible when I should go on the bench. I invested all my loose means in coal lands which turned out very profitably afterwards; and entertained a vain hope that I could lay all my private business on the shelf to remain there in a manner undisturbed. But I soon found that no man's private estate, if of any extent, can be left to take care of itself. Frequent attention to securities and their safety and to reinvestments cannot be dispensed with. My candidacy and political experience was rather a pleasant one—without contention or excitement or much expense. Candidates were not assessed then as they are now by the party leaders under the pretext of funds needed for campaign purposes. Mr. William B. Herron was the chairman of the republican county committee and attended to the procuring and distributing tickets and other incidental expenses, and assessed the amounts on the candidates proportionately to the importance of the office. My share was one hundred and fifty dollars, and no money was required for anything else.

So it transpired that on the first Monday of December, 1859, my commission was read in open court, and being sworn in I took my seat on the bench. And thus ended my professional practice at the bar; because after leaving the bench at the end of my term ten years afterwards, I never attended to any law business except such as I was personally interested in myself.

Chapter xv

Judicial Life

THUS I ASSUMED THE duties of the judicial office, as before mentioned. The Hon. Wm. B. McClure, my colleague on the bench, was a high toned gentleman of the old school, pure and honorable, and of fine literary attainments, and reasonable ability in the law; but was subject to a slight mental obliquity regarding criminals in general, and homicides in particular. He was determined to let no guilty party escape; but his prejudice against the class was so great as not always to discriminate between the guilty and the innocent. Whilst giving to the accused the nominal advantage of the maxim that every one is to be presumed innocent until his guilt is proved, he acted rather on the principle that the accused was guilty until his innocence was proved. This rendered him severe on the accused during trial, and sometimes rather cruel in the sentence, if convicted. A silent and strong opposition to this course grew up among the lawyers in the criminal courts; but to oppose his re-election on that ground would have been utterly futile. It was the quality which most of all made him popular with the people. Severity to criminals is always a popular quality in a judge. And as the civil business of the court had increased to such an extent as to justify the appointment of an additional judge, that plan was adopted with the double purpose of bringing up the civil business and mollifying in some degree the punishment of criminals. With this view the office was created which I was to fill for the first time. We were to have equal salaries and equal powers in all respects as judges, and might hold court separately or together as we pleased, only in capital cases, where, in order to secure the defendant a fair trial and reasonable sentence, we were to sit together.

The usual business of the court had greatly accumulated—too much for one judge to dispatch satisfactorily. It had jurisdiction not only of ordinary civil suits but also exclusive jurisdiction of all criminal cases, and all Orphans' Court business. A separate Orphans' Court had not yet been established, and the District Court, which has been superseded by the Court of Common Pleas No. 2, had jurisdiction only in civil suits.[1]

Such association under such circumstances might seem calculated to produce disagreements and unpleasant relations between us, but this was not the case. Judge McClure was a genial and agreeable companion, with no arrogance or aggressiveness of disposition. We had been intimate from our first acquaintance, which commenced when I entered the prothonotary's office as a clerk, in 1838. He was then quite a young man and had been admitted to the bar but a few years before. But he and his brotherinlaw, Wilson McCandless, afterwards judge of the United States District Court, had already succeeded to an extensive practice; and McClure being the junior partner attended to all their business in the prothonotary's office, and this threw us frequently together. He found great difficulty then in observing the forms and rules of practice, and would resort to me when a new form of procedure was to be devised, or any difficulty was to be overcome in his pleadings or papers. One day at the dinner hour when, as usual, I was alone in the office, he appeared with an elegantly bound copy of Shakespeare and presented it to me as a memento for my kind attention in keeping him right, as he expressed it; a memento which I have carefully preserved and still highly prize. He declared it to be a singular intellectual feature of his, that whilst he could not recollect a rule of practice or the provisions of an act of Assembly from one day to another, it was impossible for him to forget any interesting passage in Shakespeare even if he tried. We were on the bench together for three years, when he died of heart disease: and in all that time our relations were of the most agreeable character. I do not remember of a single unpleasant feeling between us. We of course differed on legal points sometimes, but in regard to the conduct of criminal cases we had no difficulty at all. In ruling on points of evidence he usually deferred to me, and in regard to sentences we were always able to agree upon some satisfactory mean neither too lenient nor too severe. His disposition to wit and humor was so strong that, unless in very serious cases, he had much difficulty to restrain it; and where he clearly discerned the merits of the case, woe to the party who was in the wrong, and to the attorney who should attempt to make the worse appear the better reason: for the satire and irony of his charge to the jury was like the keen edge of a dissecting knife.

A few months after I was on the bench with him he asked me what I thought of it. I said I felt quite comfortable in the situation so far; and that what surprised me most was the ease with which we could discover the right and the wrong side of a case. This was the difficulty I had most apprehended, as it was in this I had greatest difficulty at the bar; cases in which I was certain of having the right side frequently turned out the other way on hearing the testimony at the trial. So far on the bench I had met with no serious difficulty of the kind. He remarked that the same thing occurred to him before going on the bench and with the same result afterwards. It might be accounted for, he thought, by the different standpoints of the lawyer and judge. The lawyer saw but one side of the case till it was tried. His mind was prejudiced to begin with, and was full of apprehension of the tricks and misrepresentations of his adversary. He could only liken the position of the lawyers to that of two dogs, he said, barking at each other furiously under great apprehension on opposite sides of a close fence, through which neither could see the size or appearance of the other. But the judge sat in safety and indifference on top of the fence where he could see the dog on each side and quietly make up his mind in regard to the contention between them. However true this explanation, there is no doubt of the fact that the merits of a case are more easily discerned from the standpoint of the judge than from that of the counsel or attorney.

Some others of my preconceived views were destined to undergo a change also: for instance the duty of the judge regarding jury trials. Whilst at the bar I had entertained an exalted opinion of the importance of the jury, and the necessity for non-interference with its functions by the judge. This was not far wrong in the abstract, but was found not to work well in practice. Non-interference with the province of the jury according to the common notion too much respected by many of our judges, especially the juniors on the bench, goes to the extreme that the judge should give no intimation whatever as to his opinion of the weight of the evidence, or how he would find if in their place; that the facts should be left exclusively to them without any intimation from him on the subject. I commenced upon this theory, and continued to apply it for a few months, until I found it was calculated to work injustice in a large proportion of the cases tried. It is a theory popular among the members of the bar, especially among those who pride themselves upon ability to humbug the jury and obtain verdicts by clap-trap; but it leads to giving the party in the wrong an undue advantage. Jurors are not accustomed to analyze testimony and accord to its different elements their due weight and effect. They have but little apprehension of the legal and philosophical rules and principles established in the law of evidence for the discovery of truth. These rules and principles can only be applied by experienced minds trained to such work. They are established by law because sanctioned by our mental and moral faculties and uniform experience. To weigh and accord to the different parts of conflicting testimony their relative values, taking into account all the attendant circumstances, is the most difficult and important task of the legal or judicial mind, and requires a degree of training which jurors know nothing about. This artificial training, if too much depended on however, may lead to error almost as readily as the want of it. It is from the due interposition of the trained mind of the judge in directing the untrained minds of the jurors called from the common vocations of everyday life, that the best results are obtained; but this can only be accomplished when the judge discharges his full duty to the jury by carefully giving them thorough instructions on the weight and relevancy of the testimony on both sides, and its effect in solving the questions involved. This is the oil which renders the mental operations of the jurors smooth and easy. The judge should explain clearly to their comprehension the issue or essential points in controversy and discriminate and arrange the different parts of the testimony, and point out the relevancy and weight of the documentary evidence if any in the case, and the corroborative or detractive circumstances, and the reasons on which his instructions rest. He may even go so far as to tell the jury how on the whole the weight of evidence strikes him: indeed it is his duty in most cases to do so. The law allows it, and he does not transcend his sphere or trespass on the province of the jury, so long as he gives them no peremptory instructions to find the one way or the other. He may tell them how he would find if in their place so long as he does not bind them to do as he would, but leaves it open to the exercise of their own judgment. Such directions regarding the evidence, coupled with clear instructions on the points and principles of law and equity involved, will enable the jury in most cases to arrive at a correct conclusion without much difficulty. This constitutes that union of trained skill and experience of the judge, with the familiarity with common everyday affairs and motives of action ascribed to the jury which the law contemplates for the determination of controversies; and if a judge performs his duty fully and correctly, he is by no means liable to the charge of partiality or prejudice, although his application of the proper rules to the testimony may make it very apparent which side is in the right and which in the wrong. Such a result grows out of the nature of the case, not from the judge's analysis of it; and can no more be attributed to the prejudice or partiality of the judge than the discovery of a counterfeit coin, and loss of value to its owner, can be attributed to the party applying the crucial test.

It is not to be expected that both sides will be pleased with the decision and result in any case.

> No rogue e'er felt the halter draw
> With good opinion of the law,

nor indeed with its administrators; and as one side must be disappointed it ought to be the wrong side, even if it should be to its dismay. It is perhaps a misfortune to society that the good old judicial quality does not continue which rendered the judge "a terror to evil doers and a praise to those who do well."

After going on the bench I followed this preconceived erroneous theory of judicial impartiality already adverted to, for a short time, but so many wrong verdicts were rendered, making it necessary to grant new trials to prevent injustice, that I was compelled to change my course. By wrong verdict I mean one which shocks the conscience of the judge, and which he plainly sees to have been rendered under some misapprehension or mistake on the part of the jury. The jurors seldom disregard the law of the case as laid down by the judge, but are liable to misapprehend the testimony and its application to the law. Any one acquainted with the vagaries of the jury room will see the necessity for the supervision of a fair minded, wise, careful and painstaking judge. With some among the jurors the confusion of ideas is often amazing.

The testimony, the speeches of counsel and charge of the court are all in scraps indiscriminately mixed up in their minds. Others are entirely indifferent, exercising little or no thought on the subject, but going with the majority, or with some leader to whom they defer; and it often happens that right conclusions are arrived at from wrong reasons, or the contrary. It would often astonish both judge and counsel to know the absurd reasons and futile circumstances relied on to justify a verdict founded on favor, ignorance, or prejudice. I remember one case tried before me, illustrative of this proclivity.

It was an action for the machinery of a steamboat. There was a specific contract for the work; but in a few hours after the boat left port an important part of the machinery broke down through defective castings, and she had to be towed back to the wharf, where a delay of some weeks occurred before the broken machinery was replaced. In the action, no claim was made for replacing the machinery. The iron was so clearly defective that a claim on that score could not have been sustained; but an extensive bill for extra work was claimed, none of which was proved on the trial, except such as the contract included; and after the items on which no proof was given, and those included in the contract, were ascertained and eliminated from the bill, it left nothing but the balance of the contract price in controversy. But as usual, the plaintiff's counsel made a pathetic appeal to the jury on the loss of his client by reason of happening to use defective iron; and his generosity in replacing it without charge; and the ingratitude of the boat owners in refusing to allow the extras, under the technical objection of their being covered by the contract, and want of proof and the like. It was not a case involving much difficulty; and, after plain directions regarding the unproved extras and what were not extras, the jury retired, and remained out nearly all day, returning a verdict for the plaintiff in an amount which indicated they had included either the unproved extras, or the cost of replacing the machinery. And as they apprehended their verdict might be criticised by the court on this account, they accompanied it with a note addressed to the judge, in which they informed me they had strictly complied with my instructions in excluding the extras; but, as the plaintiff had replaced the broken machinery without claiming for it, whilst it was his misfortune rather than his fault to have used defective iron in the first place, they had concluded to allow him as much for it as he lost by extra work.

Thus a claim not made was allowed, to compensate for a claim made but not proved. Such are the subterfuges often resorted to by juries to satisfy their own whims. For the judge to sustain or overlook such findings would neither be administering justice judicially nor according to law or fact, and would be trifling with the legal rights of the parties. When rules and laws are enacted by the Commonwealth, every individual is entitled to their application and enforcement for the protection of his person and property; and in courts of justice, the judge is the public officer on whom rests the responsibility of having this duty performed correctly, as I have intimated before.

The best jury judge I have ever known was James P. Sterrett, who succeeded Judge McClure, and was on the bench with me till the end of my term, and is now on the bench of the Supreme Court of the State. Under his rule not only judicial but natural justice also was maintained and protected. He was keen sighted in human character and motives of action, and would explain and re-explain to the jury, in a conversational way and mild manner, the whole nature of the case, and the character and effect of the evidence on both sides regarding it; and would do this so thoroughly, that the stupidest juror could not be mistaken as to how to find. There was nothing arbitrary or dictatorial in his manner calculated to create opposition in the jury box, a quality which in some very good judges weakens the effect of their instructions. Under one of his charges a new trial was seldom necessary, except for some misdirection in the law, and even that was infrequent. He was ponderous and slow, mentally and physically, but progressed through a case with a steady momentum which accomplished more in the long run than is usual where more nervous mental activity is displayed. Quiet, dignified but pleasant, he saved time by talking little during trials or arguments,—no more than to ask a question or suggest a difficulty needing explanation. His merits as a judge were so highly appreciated that in time he was nominated and elected to the Supreme bench over Chief Justice Agnew, himself an eminent judge and a candidate for re-election.

Before the end of my ten years' term the business of the court had increased so much that a third judge was added, and Mr. Stowe, the rival candidate at the time of my own nomination, was now nominated and elected: so that for some years before my time expired he was on the bench with me. Judge Stowe was a contrast to Sterrett in some respects. After his term expired he was re-elected, and is now president judge of the same court. He was perhaps fully equal to Sterrett in knowledge of the law, but different in his methods, and less careful at times to superintend the duties of the jury, or to lead them gently by full explanation of the testimony to a correct conclusion. His manner was more abrupt. Although of a congenial and kindly disposition, he was sometimes liable to hurt the feelings of young practitioners who did not understand his ways. He would often blurt out something to the discomfiture of the attorney, and on seeing that it touched the feelings would relent and try to make up for it by subsequent kindness. After an escapade of this kind he has more than once whispered to me on the bench with him, "See now, I have put my foot in it again, and touched that man's sensitiveness." But perhaps very soon, when another case would come on, and some other attorney would present an absurd proposition, forgetting himself, he would take him down in the same abrupt way, thus keeping up a running fire to the end of the argument, which his own remarks would often unduly prolong. This would occur on the argument list, and was not so prejudicial as when he might neglect to lead and control the jury to a true result. Although impartial and possessed of a strong desire to promote justice, he would not always see the necessity of controlling the jury. In many cases where his attention was aroused he would perform this duty effectually; but I speak of his general habit, induced perhaps by the too common belief that the judge is not responsible for the finding of the jury. With his present advanced knowledge of the law, he would suit better for a seat in the Supreme Court than a court where the chief business is that of jury trials. I have known one case where injustice was done through neglect in the respect mentioned. It occurred some years after I left the bench. I was well acquainted with the parties and the facts of the case. The circumstances were somewhat complicated and conflicting testimony on some points calculated to mislead the jury; but really eighteen hundred dollars was due the plaintiff, which to be seen and understood needed but slight attention and analysis of the testimony. But it was plain the jury had a very confused idea of the matters in dispute, and this confusion was much augmented by the clap-trap speech of defendant's counsel. The judge was most of the time engaged in side bar interviews, and when he came to charge the jury, after giving them a very full and correct synopsis of the law, he told them that, as to the facts and testimony, he had nothing to say; that it was their province to decide what was proved or disproved, and they should find accordingly. This was sound as far as it went, and to an inattentive spectator of the trial would appear a fair and impartial charge; but to such as knew the facts beforehand, or attended to and understood the evidence, it fell entirely short of meeting the exigencies of the case. The jury was left in a state of uncertainty, and as a consequence, guessed at a verdict for the defendant. It was a plain mistake, and the remedy by a new trial to prevent injustice still remained, and was relied on by plaintiff's counsel. But on the argument of the motion, still adhering to his abstract principle, he declared that although it might be a mistake, yet if it was such, the jury, not he, was responsible for it: it was within its constitutional province, and he would not interfere with its act. Consequently the plaintiff, who was not well able to bear it, lost his money. Justice was judicially administered, it is true—the case was put through the judicial mill in a regular way, and the controversy ended, but actual justice was defeated. Such results may be lightly regarded by a judge, and he may shift the responsibility on the jury; but it is a serious matter to the party who loses his hard earnings by that course.

This was the only instance in all my experience, either at the bar or on the bench, where to my own knowledge a serious loss occurred and injustice was inflicted through a mistrial. Results of the kind in Judge Stowe's hands are not of common occurrence: not so common indeed as with some others. He is in many respects an excellent judge of superior ability, and by his bluff but kindly manner has made himself deservedly popular with the bar. I have not mentioned the above instance by way of disparagement of his many good qualities, but to illustrate the importance of judicial supervision of the jury. I have been more particular on this subject because a wrong impression prevails very generally regarding the duties of a judge in this respect. It is mostly supposed his office in the trial of a cause is but to rule the law correctly, and that he has nothing to do with the facts, or any responsibility as to how they are found.

In regard to our jury system, if there is any truth in human progress, and that all systems have to be adjusted and readjusted to suit the changed conditions of society, it is high time some important changes were made in the selection of jurors, and some discrimination and restriction in the cases to which they are applicable. It is many centuries since the present jury system was adopted in England and gained abiding fame as a bulwark of popular liberty against the encroachments of the crown and persecution from government officials. But no occasion arises for the protection of the people by a jury against the government where the people have the power peaceably to make and unmake or change the government to suit themselves. If it is a government by the people, the people need no such protection against themselves; and if they did, the jury would be ineffectual. It would be divided according to the party principles of its members. We see this again and again occur in the courts and other judicial tribunals of the different states, from the highest to the lowest, where a higher degree of intelligence might be expected to prevail than in the jury box.

An erroneous opinion also prevails to some extent regarding the distinction between natural justice and justice judicially administered. It makes too great a difference between them, to hold that justice rendered through a trial in court may be quite a different thing from natural or exact justice. Whilst too true that it often results so, yet such is not the fault of the law or the purpose of the judicial system, which is intended to do exact justice between the parties, or natural justice, as it is commonly called. There is no such thing as artificial justice. It is true that society must have fixed general rules of law for the conduct of affairs between its members. It is to the benefit of all concerned that such rules be established and adhered to, so that every one may know how to shape his conduct; and it may and often does happen that by neglect of one or other of those rules some one gets himself into trouble, and his punishment or loss in consequence of his ignorance or neglect may seem harsh or unjust, but it is not so. Wise and general rules for the conduct of affairs cannot be set aside or disregarded to screen every one who breaks them either intentionally or through negligence. In that case the law would be a dead letter, as these rules of action comprise the law. Therefore where a man disregards the law, he and not the public should bear the consequences, even if it does give his adversary an undue advantage. To illustrate: suppose a man enters into a contract with a minor or married woman, and advances money or other valuable consideration on the faith of such contract; he does so in disregard of the rule of law that the contracts of minors and married women are not binding, and has only himself to blame for his recklessness. The law in this regard is useful and necessary for the protection of minors and married women and must be maintained, although its enforcement will sometimes work a hardship. So too with the statute of limitations. It is a wise rule in order to suppress stale claims, and produce repose in the transaction of business after a certain period has elapsed; yet its enforcement may sometimes work apparent injustice. Hence those who disregard or neglect the established rules rightfully suffer the consequences; and hence also a hardship occurring through a correct application of the law in judicial proceedings, although producing a seeming injustice by justice judicially administered, as it is called, is but natural justice all the while.

It not unfrequently happens however, that justice is artificially administered and injustice done by misconstruction of a particular rule of law itself, or the true effect and influence of different rules of law on each other, when it happens that different rules are involved in the case. The relation between a case and the rules of law bearing on it is like that between a moving body and the forces bearing on it. The course it takes is not in the direction of any of them, but a modified result of the whole; and the judge who has sufficient comprehension and full enough knowledge of the different rules of law and equity which apply to the facts and circumstances, will find that the course usually tends towards natural justice. It is to the end that natural justice may be administered that courts are established; and where general rules of law for the protection of society are violated or neglected under circumstances which do not admit of the interposition of other rules and principles to afford relief, it is still natural justice which is the result, although the party in fault may suffer great hardship in the particular case. The distinction between justice as judicially administered and natural justice should never be made a scapegoat to bear the blunders and shortcomings of either judge or jury.

I had not been long on the bench until I began to realize the hoped for improvement in health. I found the labors of my new position exceedingly light compared with those I had left at the bar. The labors of the judge are in no wise so severe or wearing on the constitution as those of the lawyer in extensive practice. The confinement and strain of attention of the judge is required to be nearly as close, but is stripped of the care and worriment devolving on the lawyer. He takes his seat at a comparatively late hour each day, and in our courts now sits only till three o'clock.

This is an innovation on the old practice however. Up to the time that Hon. Moses Hampton was elected president judge of the District Court, all the courts of the city opened at nine in the morning and sat till twelve; then adjourned till one for dinner and sat again from one till four, sometimes till five, in order to finish a case on trial. Shortly after Judge Hampton went on the bench he introduced the practice in his court of sitting from nine A. M. till three P. M., with but a recess of fifteen minutes at twelve o'clock. The hours have since been further reduced from half past nine or ten till three. The shortened hours lessens the labor of the judges, and suits the convenience of the attorneys, who have more time left to prepare their cases in the afternoon; but it is attended with loss of time and seriously increased expense to suitors and the public. I was myself the last judge of our courts to give up the old practice, and continued to the end of my term to hold daily sessions from nine till four, excepting the noon recess mentioned. In the neighboring counties, and other country districts which I am acquainted with, the daily session of the courts is from nine to five, and some of them still longer. In Westmoreland county, one of the largest counties if not altogether the largest in the state, with a very numerous farming and manufacturing population and much litigation, my friend Judge Hunter holds court from half past eight A. M. till about six P. M., with but the usual recess of an hour at noon. The greater labor of judges in rural districts results in a measure from the greater intelligence and jealousy of farmers and property holders and other direct taxpayers of their rights, and of the services performed by public servants for their salaries. A judge who would shorten the daily sessions of his court in a country district from ten till three o'clock would excite an immediate storm of indignation; whilst in the city no attention is paid to the matter. A large majority of the inhabitants of a city feel no interest or concern in economical management of public affairs. Whether the session is long or short however, he hears the cases brought before him in the manner presented, and considers and decides them according to his best judgment at the time; and when he leaves the bench in the afternoon his cares and responsibility for the business of the day are over. He knows that if he has erred in the law his error can be corrected in the Supreme Court, and if he has erred in presenting the facts to the jury, his attention will be called to it by the losing party, when it can be corrected by granting a new trial; and when off the bench he has abundant leisure to look up the law regarding reserved questions and points of uncertainty.

There are occasions, it is true, of heavy responsibility and severe mental strain. These are mostly in trials where the consequences of the verdict are momentous and the facts uncertain; oftenest in criminal cases. In civil cases an occasion seldom arises for much strain or anxiety of mind on the part of the judge; he has only to exercise care and attention to do his duty, and its due performance leaves no regrets as it may do in criminal cases, attended with the serious consequences of conviction and imprisonment, or the infliction of the death penalty. Especially does it become a serious matter to decide where the facts are doubtful and the accused is poor and obscure. The result may involve long years of suffering and disgrace; or perhaps an ignominious death on the gallows; and in all cases, but in such as these particularly, does it devolve on the judge, and every one connected with the trial in its different stages, to proceed with the greatest care and circumspection. But it is doubtful cases only which can give trouble to the judge. The fear of convicting and punishing an innocent party is distressing; where innocence or guilt is made clear however, the responsibility is light. It may seem a hard task to condemn fellow creatures to long years of confinement in a prison, or "to be hanged by the neck until dead;" but it is not so hard if they clearly deserve it. The community or commonwealth is a family or society which has established laws and regulations for the conduct and protection of its different members, and each member is under the highest social and moral obligation to abide by and respect these laws and regulations; and when a member becomes a rebel to the community and regardless of law and order and fatally bent on mischief, he renders himself an outcast and enemy to the society to which he belongs, and assumes the consequences. If these consequences are the loss of liberty or life it is his own act: he knows the penalty and ought to be content to pay the forfeit. It is an unpleasant and painful duty for the judge to pronounce sentence of death in such cases,—a duty which devolved on me on several occasions in regard to both males and females during my term; but where it is the result of their own wicked doings, and the protection of society requires it, there need be no regrets. In fact, on the part of the unthinking multitude there is entirely too much sympathy and consideration for criminals, and too much time wasted and expense incurred by the public on their behalf; and unfortunately this unreasoning sympathy increases with the enormity of the crime. The trial should proceed speedily after the arrest in every case, and the infliction of the allotted punishment immediately after the conviction where guilt is established. Such is public policy and the intention of the law, and if put in practice would have a most salutary effect.

The manly criminal whose guilt is clear, can have no valid objection to a speedy infliction of the penalty of his crime. If he did not hesitate or exercise either pity or delay in depriving another fellow being of his life or property, why should he ask greater indulgence himself than he extended to his victim? It is this spirit perhaps to some extent which of late produces a growing tendency to self destruction on the part of criminals, and it is a course not to be discouraged. Criminals of this type are doubtless such as are stricken with repentance and remorse, or those whose distress of mind and unfitness for life's duties had predetermined them on self destruction before committing the crime; and others whose rashness and uncontrollable passions drive them unthinkingly to commit crimes for which returning reason plunges them into insupportable despair. Such criminals manfully rid the world of their presence, and society of the expense and trouble of their trial and punishment. It is only the mean spirited and cowardly, for the most part, who occupy the time and attention of our courts through long trials under trumped up pleas of insanity and other excuses, and invoke public sympathy to screen them from their just deserts. The most frequent and notable examples of this sort of criminals at the present time are afforded by the trials in England of Irish assassins, who in unblushing effrontery lift their bloodstained hands in whining appeals for sympathy and impunity, and consume the time of the courts of their country in hearing fictitious pleas in their behalf; and when convicted under the clearest evidence of guilt, take occasion to spurt their malicious invective in all directions against the government and judges and other public officers, for vindicating the violated law. Of course these remarks do not apply to doubtful cases, or where the guilt or innocence is uncertain, but only to such criminals whose guilt is obvious and unquestionable.

Other business of the court in either civil or criminal cases is mostly routine practice, requiring little effort; and the few hours of the day in which courts sit in our cities, and the alternation of the judges on the bench where there are more than one in the same court, and the frequent vacations, render the judicial office a very easy position compared with the labor and worriment of a lawyer in full practice,—such at least was my experience. I pity the condition of the lawyer with perhaps two or three cases on the same day's list in each of several courts. His attention is divided and distracted with clients waiting and impatient of delay. Whilst his whole mind is absorbed in the trial of one case, he is given no opportunity to study or prepare for the next that may come up; yet each of his clients expects him to be ready, and to know every circumstance regarding it, and to be familiar with what each witness is expected to say, and to have them called in their proper order. Not only this, but he is generally expected also to give particular directions as to the witnesses to be subpoenaed, and the time for their attendance. It is this kind of annoying irritation that strikes in and affects health, and drags the lawyer down, especially if he is of an earnest, painstaking temperament, and anxious to do his full duty to every client. It was to escape this condition that I had sought the judicial office, and found in it all the relief I had expected.

The outbreak of the Rebellion took place in the first years of my term. Litigation was paralyzed for a while in consequence and there was little or no demand for money. Excitement prevailed everywhere, and it was two years or so after the war commenced before business began to revive. But after that a general and steadily increasing activity prevailed in every direction. Business pursuits of all kinds were multiplied, and became so profitable that people did not spare time for litigation, and our court was not much pressed with work, although under an extension of jurisdiction a large portion of the business of the District Court had found its way to us. The office whilst in this condition seemed to me rather in the nature of a sinecure, with just enough labor to make it interesting. Under these circumstances I found an opportunity for general reading which I had not enjoyed since leaving college. From the time I was admitted to the bar till the time I went on the bench I was kept too busy to keep up my reading in literature, history or science; but now I had the pleasure of going back to the classics: translations of them of course, as I was now too much rusted in Latin and Greek to read the originals in either of them with convenience.

It is wonderful how soon the memory loses such knowledge as we do not keep in constant use; and this hint from nature's law should teach us not to waste our precious time in youth laying up treasures to be lost. After the classics, I took an excursion through ancient and modern history, and then settled down to the new philosophy of our day. In this I was greatly assisted by the suggestions of my early friend, Thomas MacConnell, who had read everything published on the subject. No matter how alert in procuring the latest publications, I could never get a valuable book which he had not read already and could give me all its merits and defects. He was the most indefatigable reader I ever knew. And not only did he read, but thoroughly digest the subject matter of the author. Our conversations in this new field of thought, as we traveled to and from our homes at the East End, and on other occasions, were most agreeable. The only other great reader on the same subject at the time was Dr. Jacobus, of the Western Theological Seminary.

I had taken a great interest in the English and Scotch philosophy when at college. Bacon, Descartes, Berkeley, Locke, Hume, Reid, Stewart and Brown were familiar names in the lectures of Dr. Bruce to our class, and I read those authors at that time with much interest. But in the few years which had elapsed, a new set had superseded the old favorites: the new system had come in and measurably supplanted the old. Darwin, Spencer, Wallace, Huxley, Tyndall, Buckel, Argyle and others were the deities now installed in the temples of philosophy. According to the old system the mind was an entity—indeed it was nearly everything, the body being considered of little account. The one was immortal, the other but a vile worm of the dust. A duality was acknowledged between them it is true, but in which the body played only an ignominious part. On the other hand, according to the new system which I was now reading up, mind is only incidental to the body, and the body not a material substance as our senses regard it, but a conglomeration of forces; atoms held in place by magnetic attraction and repulsion, and these atoms again composed of smaller atoms held in their place in like manner, downward beyond microscopic ken *ad infinitum*—force alone being the essence of what we regard as material, and all the phenomena of the material universe but force under different conditions; and what we call mind and mental faculties but other forms of the same force, resulting from the organism to which life belongs. And life itself one of those inexplicable mysteries beyond our finite comprehension.

In this new school, mind is the result of bodily organism, a manifestation of chemical and electric forces, the body, the musical instrument; mental action, the music given off, which ends when the vital forces are exhausted—the light which disappears when the oil in the lamp is consumed. Mental action in man and animal is the same in kind, only differing in degree; the phenomenon of being, both animate and inanimate, an enigma little understood. All we know of it is as results from mediate and immediate causes, the great First Cause of all remaining unknown and unknowable. This great First Cause, working through secondary causes in producing the phenomena of nature, governs our moral and physical being, by universal and unvarying laws which it is man's chief end to learn and obey. If however these universal and unvarying laws are regarded as the laws of nature, they are none the less the laws of God. Such is the doctrine of evolution now rapidly supplanting all other philosophical theories: not in the common and vulgar sense of deriving the man from the monkey, but in the general sense of causation, which derives everything from a pre-existing cause. Every thing and every institution, every doctrine, habit or custom is evolved from some previously existing object, creed, doctrine, habit, or custom. Modification after modification takes place, to meet other modifications in the environments. Everything in the realm of matter or mind is the child of what has gone before and retains more or less of the nature of its parentage.

Nor can this philosophy, it is held, be regarded as irreligious or undevout. It claims to teach a still better religion than now exists or has gone before; to be another step in advance, as Judaism was in advance of paganism, and Christianity in advance of Judaism. The chief feature of this new religion is that it would supersede government through special providences, by government through God's unvarying law, implanted in his works of nature. And this is a most important feature, as it destroys the hope of the fool who declares in his heart, "There is no God," and infers from such hope that he may enjoy ungoverned license in his evil ways; because science establishes the fact that no infraction of any moral or physical law can escape the penalty, sure and certain, which is invariably attached to it. This is a religion which regards God as a spirit, infinite and unchangeable, creating, pervading and operating all things. A Providence unvarying and unknowable to our finite comprehension, except as presented in the phenomena of his works and ways.

It is claimed for this new view that it magnifies the Deity beyond all former conception of him. It makes him the All-seeing Eye—the Spirit Infinite, in whom we live and move and have our being; everywhere with us, discerning the innermost thoughts of our hearts; and presents him as the unknown cause of all causes.

If this new religion, or rather philosophy of religion, is founded in truth, it will succeed in due time. Truth is in accordance with the will of God, and always will succeed eventually, and can only produce good effects; but its truth can hardly yet be regarded as fully established. It is very rapidly permeating the mind of the general public however, rather too rapidly I think for the public good. It has thrown religious thought into a transition state, and is loosening its fastenings from the old faith before people are fully prepared for the new. If a personal devil and local hell is a myth, the inference of the ignorant and unthinking is that they may do as they please with impunity. They are unable as yet to comprehend that under the religion of the new philosophy there is no escape whatever allowed from the punishment of sin or evil doing. They do not realize that under the new religion the consequences of every act, good or bad, go on and on to all eternity; and that the laws of God are impressed on all his works, and apply to and govern all his creatures, animate or inanimate, as well as all thoughts and actions, moral or immoral, good or bad; that the infraction of any of these laws carries with it in the infraction itself and its consequences, the punishment foreordained for it from all eternity. And that no one can escape the fixed effect, according to the degree of the sin or "want of conformity unto or transgression of the law of God," but must pay the penalty, either in this life or that which is to come, in the future of himself or his offspring. It does not, like the old faith, leave a loophole for the wicked to escape at the end of their evil career by turning state's evidence as it were, and obtaining a free pass to the realms of bliss. If the moral and intellectual faculties of the people could be educated to a living realization that honesty is the best policy under all circumstances, and that in the very nature of things the ways of righteousness are the only ways to happiness now or hereafter, and that the evil ways necessarily and unavoidably lead to pain and misery, they might be in a condition to be benefited by this new philosophy.

But returning to my narrative, the period of the intensest excitement of the war was during the first years of my term of office. I was fortunate in the position I held, as it retired me measurably from the trouble and turmoil of the occasion in both public and private affairs; and yet before military operations progressed very far I found I had enough of interests at stake in money and property to afford me much anxiety for their safety. Forced levies of money and taxation for war purposes were heavy, and no telling whether they might become heavier, or how long they might continue. The waste and extravagance indulged in by the state and local authorities in military affairs was amazing. Besides this our homes and property were at one time in actual danger of destruction by the rebels. The firm of J. B. Corey & Co., in which I was the capitalist and chief owner, had over thirty thousand dollars worth of coal afloat on the Monongahela river below McKeesport, when the rebels raided the country to the state line near Morgantown; and no military force whatever in the district to prevent them from extending their raids and destruction of property between that point and Pittsburgh. Another fleet of our coal of equal or greater value had rather an eventful history. Shortly after the Rebellion broke out, and before it was apprehended that it would assume such wide proportions, my partners had shipped a fleet of boats to New Orleans, not suspecting the navigation of the river would be interfered with. But not long after they had passed Vicksburg the rebels took possession of that city and cut off all communication with parts below it. For two years or more we had no news whatever of the fate of our boats or the crews accompanying them. The supposition was that the rebels had confiscated or destroyed them, and conscripted the men or held them as prisoners. But when General Butler got possession of New Orleans, and postal relations were reestablished with that city by sea, we received a letter from John Peterson, our supercargo, that the boats were safe, laid up in a nook of the river a short distance above the city. He was clever and prudent, and made friends with all he met, joining in their meetings and parades and contributing small sums to their projects. In this way he and his men made themselves popular with their neighbors and were allowed to tend their boats without molestation from the rebel authorities. When Butler took possession and drove out the rebels, and Peterson found it safe to do so, he dropped his boats down to the city where he found almost a coal famine to prevail among the transports and merchant ships and steamboats which had followed Farragut and Butler up the river.[2] But as the highest price and surest pay was offered by the captains of Butler's ships Peterson sold out to them, and soon had his entire cargo delivered, and vouchers from the different captains for the quantity delivered to each; so that according to the price to be received, the result was apparently much better than if no obstruction or delay had occurred. But here was where the trouble arose. Butler's brother was the commissary and treasurer of the expedition, and when Peterson called on him with the vouchers he at first had no apprehension of any difficulty in getting his money; but he was delayed and soon began to receive evasive answers, till at length it became serious. And whenever he called on Butler himself he was curtly referred to the brother. Finally he was confidentially informed, in professed friendship, by a gentleman of the staff, that the matter could easily be settled and he could have his money if he would respect the usual custom of a clever bonus to the chief of the department. Peterson seeing that he could not get his money without complying with this fraudulent extortion, wrote to me to advise him what to do. I advised him not to submit to it, but to bring his vouchers home, and we would apply at Washington. But when he asked for a return of his vouchers he was foiled there again. The clerks in Butler's commissary department understood the trick and pretended they had mislaid them. After repeated promises to search for them, he was assured they were lost and compelled to abandon farther pursuit in that direction. I next advised him to procure duplicates from the captains of the different ships, and bring them home. He did so and on his return I accompanied him to Washington. It was in the time of the greatest excitement and heat of the war, when Washington itself was threatened; and the war department at Washington was crowded every day with officers on urgent and important business. But I relied on my intimacy with Stanton, the secretary of war, for a hearing: we had long practiced at the same bar here before I went on the bench. And I was not disappointed, for he received me cordially and telegraphed to Butler to report immediately why the Corey & Co. coal claim was not paid. To our great surprise he received for an answer that this claim had been rejected on the ground that the coal belonged to the rebels. This

of course involved a question of fact which I could not expect the secretary of war to decide against the assertion of one of the United States
generals without investigation. In fact he could not; and he gave us a
very favorable letter of introduction to General Meigs, the commissary
general of the United States, to whose department such matters belonged. On presenting our itemized claim to that general, with the
vouchers properly authenticated, and an explanation of the circumstances, he was not backward in expressing his indignation at Butler's
course. "If Butler remains much longer at New Orleans," he said, "he
will bankrupt us. Every day claims like this of yours are presented for
supplies, when we had supplied his fleet with all the coal and other
supplies he could possibly need for twice the length of time before it
left for New Orleans; and how he could have consumed them so soon
is a mystery." He mentioned similar other coal claims of well known
Pittsburgh coal merchants—the Watsons and others. He then turned
to me saying, "What can I do in the face of this telegram from Butler
himself? From what Mr. Stanton says, I suppose your claim is correct;
but it would be contrary to official etiquette and propriety to disregard
Butler's report." I replied I was aware of that, and only wished to present our claim to the proper department, that it might be disposed of
in due course. He gave me some useful information in regard to the
practice in the Court of Claims; and before leaving Washington I
placed the matter in the hands of a Pittsburgh lawyer then practicing
in Washington, Mr. John A. Wills, an old acquaintance of mine. He
brought suit and obtained judgment eventually, and we got our
money, about forty thousand dollars, without interest however, as the
government pays no interest on claims of the kind. The interest and
delay and other expenses about equaled the bonus which we might
have had to pay to Butler's brother to have obtained the cash at first;
but we had the satisfaction to disappoint the thieving propensity of
those gentlemen.

On leaving General Meigs, and surprised at the feeling he expressed
against the enormous expense of Butler's expedition, I asked Peterson
how it came about they had run out of coal. Peterson understood it
perfectly well. He said that when Butler's fleet and transport ships
came in, it opened up navigation and a large number of steam vessels
followed them, and there was little or no coal to be had and Butler's
men sold out their coal to them at enormous prices, and then had to

purchase other coal like ours to replace it. He had no doubt that Butler's fleet had all the coal they needed had they kept it.

This is a little bit of unwritten history in the career of one of the
greatest demagogues of the age. The war made him a man of immense
wealth, spending his surplus revenue since then in building palatial
residences at Washington: and yet, whilst I am writing this, he poses
before the world as the poor man's candidate for the presidency, and
the workingman's defender against the encroachments of capital and
monopoly.

Returning to our narrative: the scare of the Morgantown raid, before adverted to, called out every able bodied man or boy, and rifle pits
were dug on every hill about the city; but these, if filled with the
promiscuous population and inadequate weapons at hand, would have
afforded little or no protection.[3] The regular militia were all in the
South, and just then it was all they could do to protect themselves
there. Military skill and experience had not yet been developed to render them effective. But as time passed on, and larger and better organized forces were placed in the field under better generals, aggression
on the part of the Southern forces was repelled and the rebels kept better in check. And whilst this was being accomplished, local trade and
manufactures at home received such an impulse that prices of all products began to rise; business became active and money in demand: a
state of affairs which continued to increase rapidly, not only to the end
of the war, but for many years afterwards. The momentum imparted to
it by the war continued to inflate values and increase the volume of
business until the great collapse of 1873. General business became so
active that such opportunities for making money had never before existed in all my former experience; and for some two years before the
end of my term, although the judicial office was entirely to my taste, I
discovered that in holding it I was making too great a pecuniary sacrifice, and my salary afforded no adequate compensation for the loss
sustained by declining passing opportunities for making money.

It was not my habit to neglect the duties of any position I was ever
in, either at the bar or on the bench; and hence the duties of my office
left little or no time for attention to private affairs or business transactions. In the first half of my term there was little private business requiring attention. Capital was idle and useless; but for the last half, after the war was fully under way and caused activity in the production

of military supplies, an impulse was given to dealings in real estate and coal and other property, and to productive industry generally, which demanded too great a sacrifice to neglect. And above all this I had two bright boys just out of school, the idols of my heart, merging on manhood, and with fine business capacities, whom I was eager to launch on this flood tide of business prosperity, and to pilot them in the channel for some part of their way.

For these reasons I came to the conclusion some time before to leave the bench at the end of my term, and not become a candidate for reelection, and so informed my friends; and when the time for my release came, I was even more elated at the prospect of freedom from the restraints of official life than I had been at the beginning of it at escaping from the onerous labors of the bar. At length after continuous session of over six weeks in the criminal court, I delivered my last charge to the jury and took my last verdict; and on the first Monday of December, 1869, stepped down and out and was again a free man. The term of my official life was ended. Its experiences were altogether pleasing and satisfactory to myself, and their retrospect leaves nothing to regret. And so far as I could tell at the time or afterwards, my administration was entirely satisfactory to the public. On my retirement the bar extended me the courtesy of a banquet, a distinction unusual to Common Pleas judges, and not over frequent to judges of the Supreme Court.

Their kind appreciation was gratifying, and the request of course complied with; and at the Monongahela House, on the evening designated, my relation to the bar as a judge was concluded in one of the most agreeable festivities of my life, constituting one of those bright spots by the way which afford pleasant memories to revert to.

Chapter XVI

Vexatious Litigation

LITIGATION AFFECTS THE lawyer, the judge, and the party involved in it quite differently.[1] The lawyer is animated by the spirit of mastery natural to combatants; the judge regards it with cool indifference, only desirous to discover the truth; but the party involved in it is steeped in anxiety. He has more at stake than either of the others. Ambition to win, pecuniary loss, and pride of character are all involved: but, whether much or little is involved, he can not avoid anxiety. And the intensity of feeling is greatly augmented if the litigation happens to be vexatious, unjust, or unfounded, and is persisted in by a designing adversary who thinks he has or can obtain an advantage by it. No one in a long and extensive business career can hope to entirely escape some unpleasant experiences of the kind, and mine may be worth relating. Those who have had similar experiences will appreciate the difficulties and dangers they involve; and to those who have not, a knowledge of what they may be called on to contend with may be of use. The chief peculiarity of my experiences in this line was their baseless character. They will serve to illustrate the facility with which litigation and contention can be created out of nothing, and will admonish against undue confidence in those we deal with; and will serve to show also that neither knowledge of the law nor business ability will protect you against troubles of the kind. But the benefit of previous admonition can be but slight, as such troubles usually come from unexpected sources, and must be met by judgment and discretion equal to the emergency. Instead of naming my adversaries I shall represent them by the letters of the alphabet A, B, C.

To understand "A's" case in all its bearings I must state it fully.[2] The litigation under it commenced in 1876 and ended in 1880, but its roots reached as far back as 1859, when I first entered into business relations with "A." Before that time and long afterwards the coal trade was good, and I was in the habit of investing money in coal lands, and having them developed by taking an interest with others who would attend to the actual management and operate the works. When I became acquainted with "A" he was a young man, smart and full of energy, and seemed to possess the ability and push so necessary to success in active business. He had just left an extensive coal firm composed chiefly of his own relatives, and explained his leaving as voluntary on his part, but towards the end of my connection with him I found out it had been compulsory.

The railroad coal trade was then in its infancy, and his great desire and ambition was to re-enter the trade as a rival to the firm he had left. He seemed to me remarkably well qualified for the business, and I had means to spare, but, on account of my candidacy for the judgeship, with almost a certainty of election, I could not engage in any business requiring my personal attention. My capital was idle, but if I met with a reliable and efficient party to manage such a business himself and in his own name exclusively, for mutual benefit, the money could be usefully and profitably employed. I never was a very good judge of private character at best, and after repeated interviews and glowing representations from him of what he could accomplish, I concluded he was just the man for the place.

The result was I entered into a contract of partnership with him in September, 1859, by which he was to manage the business in his own name, and I was to be a silent partner: such partnership is legal and customary. He was to receive a salary of twelve hundred per annum out of the profits for his services; and I to furnish capital for the purchase of the necessary coal property, rolling stock and other appliances of the business, he paying interest on his half until he could refund it. The profits, after deducting his salary and other expenses, were to be divided equally between us; the partnership to continue until terminated by mutual consent. The arrangement exactly suited both our conditions. His ambition was active, open business control; and to have it managed without participation in its details was what suited me best.

According to our arrangement I furnished the money to purchase a valuable coal works at Braddocks. The business promised fairly at first, so much so that I furnished additional money to enlarge it by purchase of another extensive coal works at Sandy Creek, on the Allegheny Valley railroad. After this we continued to do a moderate business for upwards of two years; but as soon as the war commenced it began to improve rapidly. A drawback to our prosperity soon appeared, however, which I had not anticipated. Whilst overflowing with push and energy I found his judgment and discretion seriously defective. Besides this, he was fickle of purpose. But at this time and for long afterward, I had no misgivings as to his honesty; indeed so great was my confidence in him that during all the time our partnership lasted I never once examined the books or accounts or took any note of the business.

In 1862, in face of the growing price and demand for coal under the war influence, he perpetrated a mistake which, in its consequences, might have ruined both of us. Without consulting me he entered into five year contracts in writing with Shoenberger & Co., of the fifth ward, and with Dalzell & Co., of Sharpsburg, to furnish all the coal necessary for their respective iron mills, the one at four and three-quarters, the other at five cents per bushel. These contracts required a delivery of about five thousand bushels daily; and it was but a month or so after he made them till mining advanced one cent and a half over former rates, and with other expenses went on steadily advancing until 1864–5, when coal delivered to mills and factories commanded eight and nine cents per bushel. As soon as he informed me of these contracts I saw my danger. He had nothing to lose, but I had. To fill them for a period of five years would have been ruinous, and at first I saw no possible way out of them; but fortune favored us eventually. It was the first time I had ever been in such a predicament, and it opened my eyes to the impolicy of entrusting another with power to act for and bind you. I felt that we were in a desperately bad box, and was ready to relinquish the extraordinary profits which the impulse of the war was contributing to the business. However, "A" was about as expert at devising means and ways to get out of a difficulty as he was rash and reckless in getting into one. The plan he took in regard to the Shoenberger contract was to annoy Mr. Shoenberger, who was of an irritable temper, by furnishing coal of inferior quality and measure, and irregular delivery; and he succeeded in this course so well that at last Mr. Shoenberger inadvertently wrote him a note to the effect that his manner of fulfilling his contract could not be submitted to, and, unless he commenced at once to fulfill it properly, he could consider himself discharged and the contract cancelled. This was intended only as a threat, but "A," by my advice, wrote him a note forthwith accepting the proposition. This ended a complication which might have cost me a very large amount of money. The price of coal had not advanced greatly at the time, or perhaps Shoenberger would not so easily have fallen into the trap. As to the Sharpsburg mills he was not so fortunate; his ability for strategy did not succeed regarding them, for they held on to their advantage.

But it was not long until he caught the military fever and declared his intention to abandon the business altogether. This was still worse, unless some practical plan could be devised to dispose of the property, and get out of the business without loss by procuring others to assume the unfortunate Sharpsburg contract. I insisted he should do this before giving up the business or going into the military service. If this was possible I was rather favorable to anything that would relieve me from the risk of such a partner, although the prospect of large profits was tempting; but, however profitable, I saw that his reckless and unwise course of dealing might at any time precipitate us into some disastrous enterprise that would swamp the whole concern and my private estate with it. And, besides the risk of his making improvident contracts, he was constantly annoying me with the numerous petty lawsuits and contentions which he stirred up in conducting the business: for, whilst he showed himself perfectly fair towards me down to the last, when he could use me no longer and declared open hostility, I found afterwards that he was notorious for crookedness in his dealings with others. I was on the bench, and could give no personal attention to it and knew of no one to whom I could entrust its management. If I had known then what I discovered afterwards regarding the capacity of my son Thomas for such business, I could have taken the partnership property and business off his hands at a fair valuation; and had I done so would have realized a handsome fortune by it in a short time, because in all my experience I never knew any trade so profitable as the coal business continued to be for several years afterwards. But he was too young, as I supposed, to manage such an extensive business: and it was not until after the opportunity was gone, I found that even then he could have managed it far more safely and profitably than "A." There was no alternative left but to sell out, settle up, divide assets and dissolve. We had little time to do it, as he was busy in raising a company of cavalry and urgent to leave. But I insisted on a settlement, dissolution of the partnership, and disposition of the property before he should do so. The firm's business could not go on in his absence; and he might never return, as I supposed. It was not hard at the time to dispose of such profitable coal works if offered at a sacrifice; and to dispose of them in some shape was inevitable. He soon found a purchaser for the Sandy Creek works at first cost, but less than half their fair market value: but the condition that the purchaser would assume our Sharpsburg contract was a powerful inducement with me, so I consented to it. The same purchaser disposed of them on the same condition, however, within two years afterwards, at over double the amount paid for them. He next let the Braddocks works on a five years lease to a retail coal firm at one cent per bushel for the coal as taken out. This was better than the Sandy Creek transaction, and relieved us of the business; and then we had nothing more to do than to settle up as between ourselves, and divide the remaining property and assets of the firm.

Accordingly I allowed him to make an inventory, setting his own valuation on the Braddocks works with its lease and other real estate which we had acquired, and to divide the property and assets into two shares in order to a division. He did this, but made the shares very unequal, placing the Braddocks works and other real estate on one side at a valuation of about $150,000, and the deferred payments on the Sandy Creek works, amounting to about $66,000, on the other side. I saw that he desired me to take the property part and allow him the cash accruing from the sale of the Sandy Creek works as his share; and I agreed to this, as it suited him best to have available funds, and I was able to take the property, although the larger share: as his share of the capital invested in the business, which I had advanced for him and he still owed, equalized the cash portion which he was now to receive with the property which I would take. After this was agreed on, we met to settle and divide, and settled in the manner stated according to the schedules and valuations he had prepared; and thereupon we had a document drawn up, dissolving the partnership, settling each partner's accounts with the firm, and specifically awarding and transferring the real estate and Braddocks lease to me, and the cash and deferred payments of the

Sandy Creek works to him; providing also that the outstanding accounts of the firm should be collected by him or his clerk in his absence, and after paying any floating debts that might remain, the balance to be equally divided from time to time between us. Duplicate copies were made of this paper, which were duly acknowledged before an alderman. There was not sufficient time in his great haste to get away to have regular deeds executed, and I took these precautions to have everything clearly arranged lest he might not return: I was not then aware that patriotism so suddenly aroused would as suddenly subside. Thus in July, 1864, our partnership ended by mutual consent, as provided for in the partnership contract.

He had his company already organized and was mustered into the service immediately, receiving instructions to proceed to the frontier along the West Virginia line to guard Fayette and Greene counties from anticipated rebel incursions; but after he and his men had loitered about in that region for a couple of months, his patriotism and military ardor would seem to have subsided, for he and they procured their discharge and came home, where he remained quietly without further effort to save the country. His sole occupation for a year or more afterward was the collection of outstanding accounts of the firm, as had been arranged; but this part of the assets I never got any account of, always being put off with the assurance that it had taken it all to pay outstanding debts against us: and at that time I had so much confidence in his honesty that I believed him, and never knew that he was deceiving me all the while until it was disclosed in the suit I am about to relate. After this source of income was exhausted he began to look about him for something to do. He still held most of the deferred payments on the Sandy Creek works, but they were inadequate to the purchase and development of a coal property of his own, as prices were then greatly inflated; and I had in the meantime developed a new coal works on the Pan Handle railroad, known as the Camp Hill works. He was anxious to take hold of it, and urged a renewal of the former partnership: he had fared better in that partnership than I was then aware of. His proposition was that I should put in the Pan Handle works at a valuation, and he would operate it; but I had had enough of partnership with him, and positively refused. He then proposed to lease the works from me, to which I consented; and in 1866 I leased it to him for two years at half a cent per bushel.

But this turned out to be a losing transaction on my part, as he always had bills to present for alleged necessary improvements sufficient to offset the rent, and I got very small returns from him for coal mined; and after his lease expired, when the interior of the mine was surveyed, I discovered that a serious discrepancy existed between the coal which he had reported from time to time, and accounted for, and the quantity which on actual survey was found to have been taken. I had settled up all transactions under the lease, however, before I discovered this, and his excuses were so plausible that I disliked to make any trouble about it. The coal trade was yet quite profitable; and he had in the meantime purchased other coal works on the Pan Handle road, a farm on the old Washington turnpike in Union township, and some other properties. After his lease of my works expired, he continued to run coal rather extensively for six or seven years. Though he led me to believe he was making money, he was all this latter period a persistent borrower, to maintain his business and make payments on his different speculations. I was then in the banking business, and he was one of my most persistent applicants for loans, though undesirable, as his haphazard methods rendered it almost impossible to prevent him from keeping his bank account overdrawn: which, when the balance against him would amount to from ten to twenty thousand dollars, he would importune me to fund into a mortgage on one piece or other of his property. As his banker, and furnishing him money in his speculations and otherwise, he constantly manifested the highest friendship and regard for me, and was careful to assure me continually that he considered me his benefactor. He had that peculiar tact, which some men have of ingratiating themselves into your good will by manifesting friendship and dependence. They will constitute you their friend whether or no. He made strong pretensions to honor and honesty, and was always ready with a plausible excuse for anything that looked otherwise than correct. Besides, he had secured such remarkable good bargains in some of the properties he had acquired through my advancements of money to him for the purpose, and I had helped him out of pecuniary difficulties so often, that he was the last man of all my business friends or customers whom I should have suspected of turning traitor to me. But I was not thrown off my guard entirely, for I had discovered he was tricky with others and might be so with me; and I took care to have all my business with him clearly understood and evidenced in writing. My cashier, Mr. Senft, was instrumental in impressing on me the necessity of this course. He suspected him of sinister designs all the time, and frequently so expressed himself. But I had not yet discovered the depth of his cunning, and supposed him sincere in his manifestations of regard; and so far as at all safe to do so I was inclined to help him in emergencies, sometimes even beyond what was prudent or profitable. He was a free purchaser of property on his own account—much beyond his ability to pay, as results proved; and from the time of his leasing the Camp Hill coal works from me, for upwards of ten years, until the disruption of our business relations in 1876, he professed to show his gratitude for my favors by pointing out for my benefit such good bargains in coal properties in his neighborhood as were beyond his means to appropriate to himself. In this way through him I acquired several tracts, and disposed of some of them afterwards quite profitably, but others are on my hands yet and may have to be disposed of at a loss. Thus in some respects favors were reciprocal; and as he had a constant itching to negotiate purchases either on his own or other people's account, and always assured me that if I were known as the purchaser my wealth would prevent me from getting the property at as low a price as he could obtain it for: I allowed him in most instances where I was concerned to purchase and have the deed made to himself, taking care, however, when I advanced him the purchase money in such cases, to take a receipt for it, expressing the fact that the purchase was made for me, and the title to be held in trust for me until transferred. And in due time he did transfer to me the title of the properties so purchased by regular deeds. But dealing to any extent with a bad man is sure to result in trouble sooner or later, no matter how you try to protect yourself. I knew he was very shrewd and cunning, and had great ability in scheming and contriving, but I had not yet discovered the full extent of his ability at concocting schemes of so dangerous a nature as the one he finally developed in this case. Several of my friends had warned me during the long continuance of our dealings, that he would assuredly give me trouble in the end. But he had become a protege of mine, and I attributed their bad opinion of him to prejudice, and could see no room for any trouble to arise where everything was done on the square, and all accounts clearly presented on the books, and every business transaction fully stated in writing. He finally showed me how egregiously I was mistaken in this latter opinion. With men like him, papers and vouchers and correct accounts are inadequate to prevent trouble and litigation, and are of use only to defeat litigation after the trouble and expense of it are incurred. Vicious, unprincipled men of sharp and narrow intellect will not weigh and consider such obstacles, but dash into litigation haphazard whenever their career is checked or their schemes counteracted, and depend on their strong desire and power of invention to gain their end.

He and his wife had, soon after his return from the army, conveyed to me the Braddocks Fields coal works and other real estate, according to the contract of dissolution and settlement previously made, and also all the different properties he had afterwards bought in trust for me; and there was no ground for dispute or misunderstanding on any point. I was particular in keeping everything straight between us, not so much in distrust of his honesty as in pursuance of my general habit, which was invariably to have the proper accounts, documents, and vouchers in every business transaction; and as my dealings with him were long continued, and often extensive and complicated, I relied not only on the customary vouchers and accounts in each separate transaction, but, at certain intervals during the seventeen years of our business relations, I had procured full settlement statements to be made out and signed, showing the exact balance outstanding from all sources. These were in duplicate, a copy held by each, and were found of great advantage to me in the litigation which occurred, as simplifying and explaining the different transactions, and showing the true nature of the business between us. It is often useful to retain a copy or duplicate of the document or voucher you give to the other party; because, in the vexatious cases in question I discovered the futility of the law compelling the production in evidence of receipts or vouchers in possession of an adverse party to a suit. All such party need do to evade the law, if he will, is to deny that he received or has, or knows of the existence of the papers demanded; and my experience with such parties is that they will do this with great facility.

One of the transactions, among others in which I involved myself for his benefit, was the endorsement of his notes for the purchase of a coal tract appurtenant to the coal works he owned on the Pan Handle railroad. He represented there was sixty acres of coal still remaining in this tract, for which the owner would accept thirty thousand dollars on long time notes if satisfactorily endorsed, but would not take a mortgage as security, because the coal might be taken out and the security lost before the notes fell due. He figured that at three-quarters of a cent per bushel, the rate of rent which he was paying under a lease for it, the purchase would be a saving to him of ten thousand dollars; and assured me that the net profits in his business were twenty-five hundred dollars per month, and that half the coal would not be taken out before the notes would be due and paid. But I found out when too late, that the true motive in the purchase was to get rid of payment of his rent to the owner of the coal. It was against my rule to endorse for any one, and as the result proved, this was one of the unwisest transactions of my life. It is well my endorsements and guaranties were few, because I remember of no instance of endorsing or going bail for others, that I did not get trouble or lose by it in the end. But the advantage to him was represented to be so great that I consented and endorsed the notes, taking an indemnity mortgage, however, on the coal and his works adjoining it, to secure me as far as such security would reach, in case of his failure to pay them.

Under similar assurances of rapid profits, he had before this induced me to join him and his soninlaw in the purchase of a large tract of coal, some three hundred acres in the rear of the same works, for sixty thousand dollars, each to have a third interest as tenants in common; and for fifty thousand dollars, the deferred payments of this, I joined them in a bond and mortgage, which, of course, rendered me liable for the whole in case they defaulted, which both did afterwards. Only one deferred payment on this last mentioned coal tract, and but one of the notes endorsed for the first mentioned coal, were paid when the panic of 1873 set in, and I had to pay the whole as the obligations fell due. Although he showed no signs of weakness as yet, I thought it prudent to have another settlement with him, which resulted in an undisputed balance in my favor of nearly sixty thousand dollars, exclusive of the above mentioned transactions. This comprised various overdue notes discounted for his benefit, and notes of another party which he had endorsed and procured me to discount, and which were under protest for non-payment; and also an overdrawn bank account of some sixteen thousand dollars at the time. Yet whilst in great need of money to keep my bank open as long as possible, as the panic was upon us, I found that he and more than half a dozen others whom I had been carrying along for many years in the same way, were utterly unable to pay anything on the emergency. Under these circumstances, and his lack of effort to pay, I proposed that he should secure me; and here he first began to show obstinacy. The cause of this, as I discovered afterwards, was that he supposed that he was at the end of his string in drawing more money out of me; and a mortgage encumbrance for such an amount on his remaining property would put it out of his power to borrow from others. I had to insist with some rigor: and here, for the first time in fourteen years, a shadow of dissatisfaction arose. I had to importune and insist for several weeks, and finally to tell him plainly that he would have to choose between three courses in twenty-four hours: either to pay, give security, or be sued. This brought him to consent. All the security he could give me was a mortgage on his Union township farm—already subject to two mortgages, and a separate piece of about thirty-five acres of coal land, and an eight thousand dollar purchase money mortgage which he held for some land he had sold: but under the depressed condition of affairs at the time I could not have realized half of my claim from all of it. Finally, on the first day of October, 1873, he reluctantly executed a mortgage on these properties, and assigned me the eight thousand dollar purchase money mortgage according to the settlement and extension of time of payment we had agreed on; but, at the same time, earnestly entreated me not to record this new mortgage against him of upwards of sixty thousand dollars for some time yet, as under the excitement of the panic its appearance on the record would have a bad effect on his credit: pledging his honor, and assuring me positively, that he would in no event whatever make a mortgage or give a judgment to any one else, or allow a judgment to be taken against him without first acquainting me of it in time to record my mortgage as a prior lien. Upon this assurance, made to me in the presence of my cashier and clerks, I instructed my Courthouse clerk not to have it entered of record until he or I should order it.

Thus transactions between us were closed for the time, and remained satisfactorily so for a few weeks, until one morning my clerk informed me that he noticed a ten thousand dollar mortgage recorded the day before, against my friend "A" on the thirty-five acre coal tract included in my mortgage. Ten thousand was about the value of tract. This astonished me, and I was incredulous of it at first, but on examining the records found it true. I then recorded my mortgage forthwith, but of course was too late for the thirty-five acre tract. As his reluctance shown to giving me a mortgage at all to secure me was the first cloud on our business relations, this was the first overt act of downright bad faith. I sent for him, and, as he never was at a loss for a plausible excuse, he actually deceived me a second time by the positive assurance that the money he had thus borrowed on the recent thirty-five acre mortgage he had applied in payment and satisfaction of the other mortgages before mine on the Union township farm, and therefore, that my security was not diminished in the slightest degree; that the parties holding the prior mortgages had insisted on payment, and he had the receipts at home and would have the satisfaction entered in a few days. This looked plausible, but it was a breach of his plighted faith nevertheless; and I found out afterwards that it was a sheer fabrication to serve the purpose of the moment. He had applied no part of the money to the prior mortgages, and never did. After this I declined all further transactions with him, but did not press him for payment on any of my claims, as that could only be done by judicial proceedings and sheriff's sales of his property, which I wished to avoid. I thought, as he still professed to be making money in his business, he might eventually be able to get through and pay me, or at least reduce the indebtedness without a resort to legal process. I indulged this hope for over two years, till it became obvious his condition was growing worse instead of better. He and his soninlaw had defaulted on their shares of their payments of our bond and mortgage for the purchase money of the three hundred acre coal tract, and as I was jointly liable with them I had to pay the whole; and I had also to take up my endorsements given on his purchase of the coal lease tract already mentioned.

I then began to urge him for payment of part at least of one or other of these different claims, or to give additional security for them. He had some twenty thousand dollars worth of railroad cars and other personal property in his possession; but on investigation I found he owed about sixteen thousand dollars in floating debts, and suits were beginning to be brought against him. I saw now it was time for me to secure myself as far as I could by obtaining a judgment, and a lien on his personal property by the issue and levy of an execution. I sent for him and he consented to this; and he and my clerk examined a statement of my claims and adjusted the interest on the different items. He expressed himself favorable to this course, inasmuch as it might bring his other creditors to terms, as he said, when they saw they could accomplish nothing by coercive measures against his personal property. He only stipulated that I should not file a statement on the amount of my claim in the prothonotary's office until the day arrived for taking judgment, as he had in contemplation a plan, and negotiations were in progress which might lift him out of his present difficulties: and a sixty thousand dollar claim appearing to be filed of record against him might affect his prospects in this direction. This was his excuse for not confessing judgment to me at once. It looked plausible, and I entered my suit in the prothonotary's office accordingly. It was for my own direct claims alone; but I was liable for the mortgage on the three hundred acre coal tract, and had to pay and have it assigned to me. This secured me on the shares of him and his soninlaw for what I had to pay for them on that property; and the indemnity mortgage for the endorsements on the purchase of the leasehold tract secured me to some extent for them, although all the coal was mined out, except six or eight acres, before I obtained possession. All the securities I held at the time, according to the depressed values prevailing then and for several years afterwards, would not have realized me one-half what he owed me, and what I had to pay out for him to others to clear the different properties of prior encumbrances.

Such was the condition of affairs between us at the time when he concocted his remarkable scheme to defeat all my claims, and now to be related. When my clerk visited the prothonotary's office to file the statement of claim, on the day when the case was ripe for judgment, as had been agreed upon, he returned with the report that "A" had filed a voluminous affidavit of defense. This surprised me, as well it might. How could he make a defense where there was no dispute, and where he had consented to be sued and to have a judgment entered against him, only stipulating for the amount of the claim to be withheld till the time arrived for taking judgment? I soon found, however, that the plan and negotiations which he had on hand was a scheme to cover up his property by a transfer of his coal works, railroad cars, and other personal property to his son, on long time notes without any security, although the son was wholly irresponsible; and thereupon, his property being securely placed in his son's possession, and nothing left that his creditors could touch except the son's long time notes given to legalize the transfer, he placed these notes also out of the power of his immediate creditors by making a general voluntary assignment to a cousin of his wife. All this had been done in the ten days between the time I had brought suit and the day for taking judgment.

But the scope and extent of his scheme was not limited to this, as subsequent developments showed. It included the design of not only annulling my mortgages and other securities, but also of rendering me personally liable for all his own debts to other parties besides a very large sum to himself. The scheme was concocted with most remarkable ability and cunning, and enabled him and his son to go on with his coal business without interruption and as if he owed no one anything. And as to the son's long time notes, amounting to twenty thousand dollars, when they fell due the son alleged and set up as a defense against them, a claim of equal amount on his part against his father for services rendered before the notes were given; and on the trial, both father and son testifying in support of this claim, the notes were cancelled and the creditors got nothing whatever out of them. But the still more audacious part of the scheme was that which related to me, embracing as it did a well planned conspiracy to defeat my mortgage claims and securities altogether, and make me liable for his general debts and a large amount besides. In scope and subtlety it was the boldest piece of iniquitous invention I ever witnessed in all my experience at the bar or on the bench, or since. Our long continued and extensive transactions had in every instance been conducted regularly, the accounts and vouchers in legal form; and repeated settlements made and duly witnessed, the details for the most part having been arranged between him and my clerks. An attempt to avoid and set aside the facts and documents of such a course of dealing covering seventeen years might seem preposterous to a man of ordinary mental resources. Yet this was what he proposed to do; and fabricated a somewhat plausible theory for its accomplishment. He had nothing to lose, but everything to gain, and throwing off the mask worn so long, he came out in his true character. His peculiar defense made to my suit, and the tedious litigation resulting from it, produced the most formidable legal complication of my life, to a full understanding of which the foregoing prolonged statement is but introductory.

If my astonishment was great at the announcement of a defense at all, it was still greater when I learned its nature. It alleged that he had a good and sufficient set-off against the whole amount of my claims, and

that I owed him at least one hundred and fifty thousand dollars besides; that he and I had entered into a partnership in the coal business
as long ago as 1859, in proof of which he exhibited a copy of our former
partnership contract, and alleged that this partnership had continued
ever since, and had never been dissolved; that a division of partnership
property and assets, and partial settlements it was true had been made
from time to time, and a provisional dissolution agreed to, and in consequence a temporary suspension of the business had occurred while
he was in the army, but that the partnership was revived by verbal
agreement a short time after his return, and the Braddocks Fields
works restored again to the firm; and that he had gone on purchasing
coal property and doing business for the firm in his own name, as provided for in the partnership articles, ever since; and that my claim in
this suit, and other claims for which I held mortgages, were all advancements on my part to the firm, but kept in the shape of personal
obligations against him by my advice for some purpose of my own;
and that on the whole I had realized at least one hundred and fifty
thousand dollars from the firm over my advancements, out of rents
from the Braddocks lease and sales of other partnership properties,
whilst he had realized nothing but a bare livelihood.

When any one is sued he generally has an inkling of what the suit is
about; and when any one sues and a defense is made, the party suing
generally has an inkling of what the defense consists in before he sees
it. But it was not the case in this instance—I never could have imagined such a defense. He had never intimated a partnership or joint interest of any kind with me in the business he was doing, or the purchase and sales of coal lands which each had been concerned in from
time to time since our dissolution consummated in July, 1864. Not only
so, but when he leased my Camp Hill coal works, as before mentioned,
and also when he purchased the other coal works on the Pan Handle
road, which was now transferred to his son, he had urgently impor-
tuned me for a renewal of our former partnership, which, on both occasions, I had positively declined. There could therefore be no mistake
on his part in regard to the existence or non-existence of a partnership
between us. On reading his defense, and for some time, I could not divine how it was he made me a partner in all his business and everything he was concerned in, even in the Union township farm and his
homestead, as well as in all my own separate coal properties which he

had negotiated for and deeded to me; but omitted the coal works which he had transferred to his son, and cars and appliances belonging to it, which was the only property bearing a semblance of partnership through my having endorsed the notes relating to the purchase of part of the coal belonging to it, and becoming a part owner in the three hundred acre coal tract intended to be mined and run through the same works. But after I discovered that he had transferred these works and cars to his son, and barricaded them against his creditors by a general voluntary assignment to his wife's cousin, the reason was both apparent and transparent why they were excluded. This was his most profitable investment, and he had secured it to himself and did not care to share it with a partner. A continuous partnership throughout our transactions was the corner stone of his defense: if he established this, everything else that he claimed would follow, of course. Instead of his owing me sixty thousand dollars I would owe him one hundred and fifty thousand or more. I had been handling the Braddocks works skillfully for twelve years, ever since they were transferred to me. When the coal originally belonging to them was mined out I had purchased other adjoining coal at a cheap rate, and kept them running steadily at a profitable rent, as they were in a desirable position, my income from them averaging over ten thousand dollars a year; and most of the coal properties in Union township which I had purchased through him as above mentioned, I had sold again at good profit. Whilst on the other hand, what he had purchased on speculation for himself he still held, encumbered, and badly depreciated by the panic.

He had sunk the deferred payments of the Sandy Creek works transferred to him, and, as it then appeared, had been losing all the time in his coal business and other transactions; all of which losses and depreciations I would, of course, have to sustain one-half if made out to be a partner, besides becoming liable to his other creditors for the full amount of their claims, over sixteen thousand dollars. The whole scheme to involve me and share my profits and make me share his losses after turning his own property over to his son, was a stupendous one and skillfully contrived, doubtless with legal assistance; and the consequences to me would have been disastrous had it succeeded. To one unskilled in legal devices such a defense, without a shadow of foundation in truth or fact to rest it on, might seem preposterous, especially so in the face of all our separate and distinct dealings and settlements, and the execution of deeds and exchange of receipts and vouchers of every kind upon a basis of individuality the reverse of a partnership. He was equal to the occasion of all this formidable mass of evidence against him, however, and evaded its effect by another piece of strategy known in law as an *averment of fraud:* to the effect that he was not learned in law, but I was, and that he had all along placed the utmost confidence in me and invariably followed my advice in the method of transacting the partnership business between us; and had always executed whatever deeds or papers, receipts or vouchers I requested without question, in whatever shape I presented them; but that he had now discovered that all this was done by design on my part, to deceive and defraud him. And that whenever he hesitated to execute any papers or give a voucher apparently inconsistent with part-nership relations, I had always assured him that it was the proper method and necessary for our mutual safety, and that nothing of the kind should have any prejudicial effect on his rights in any future or fi-nal settlement of our partnership affairs. This broad suggestion of fraud, if established by sufficient evidence or testimony, would have the effect to set aside every deed or document of a character interfering with the partnership theory. So that, as the defense was presented, there was no documentary evidence of any kind which could avail to prevent a trial of the question of partnership or no partnership, or ex-clude verbal testimony to overthrow the documentary evidence. He knew or had been advised that fraud, if proved, would avoid docu-ments or writings of every kind, and had shaped his defense accord-ingly.

It evolved a more formidable controversy, therefore, than at first sight might appear. A false claim or defense skillfully devised is vastly more dangerous than an erroneous claim or defense honestly enter-tained through a misunderstanding. The party who claims or defends through a misunderstanding or wrong information, may be conscien-tious enough not to assert or try to prove what he knows to be untrue; but the party who fabricates a claim or defense out of the whole cloth never hesitates to supply all the incidental facts and circumstances nec-essary to sustain it. Thus, since the law has been changed to allow the parties to a suit and all others interested to testify, a party placed in the situation I was necessarily runs very serious risks. My unscrupulous adversary was remarkably skillful for a layman in legal quirks and catches, and no one could relate a more plausible or circumstantial and better connected story. Besides, with a man who will adopt such a course, there is no telling how far he may influence members of his family or others to corroborate him; and the trial of such a case by a jury is not very reassuring. Twelve common men indiscriminately picked up, unacquainted perhaps with the character of either the parties or the witnesses, and inexperienced in business affairs—for such men to comprehend all the numerous and various transactions covering a period of seventeen years, and to understand the significance and legal effect of the different actings and doings of the parties during all that time, with the meagre opportunities and limited time of a jury trial, was nearly impossible. The jury would listen indifferently to the complicated details of the case, without comprehending them in the hurry of the trial, and would jump at the conclusion first suggested by one or more of their number after going to their room.

The plot was well laid, and it required thought and care to defeat it. I had consolidated all my matured claims of every kind against him in this suit, not anticipating any objection, as they had all been submitted to and approved by him in our last settlement, and again on the day before the suit was brought. Now, if the case went to trial as it stood, and the verdict was adverse to me, it would cancel the whole; but it could do no more, as the suit was not of that kind which would settle the question of partnership. But such a defense, if sustained by the jury, might defeat a claim made by one partner against the other for advancements to the firm. I therefore modified the claim, withdrawing most of it and leaving only such parts as had least connection with anything which could be distorted into a partnership. If a defeat ensued it would not preclude other suits for the parts withdrawn.

This movement worked to my advantage in a way different from what I had expected. The defendant and his attorneys took it as a sign of weakening on my part, and it encouraged them to resort to a method which, if successful, would not only defeat all my claims against him, but would establish the partnership, and a decree against me in his favor for one hundred and fifty thousand dollars and upwards. Under this impression they assumed the aggressive, and filed a bill in equity, alleging what he had stated in his defense, crediting me with the items of my claim as advancements to the firm, and charging me with all the assets I had received under our division in 1864, and the profits arising therefrom ever since, together with all profits I had made under resales of the properties which he had been instrumental in purchasing for me; also crediting himself with a continuous salary for managing the business, and all the losses he had sustained in the mismanagement of his own affairs, as if partnership business, and bad bargains in property since 1864; and leaving to the firm the different properties he had still on hand, purchased at high prices and yet encumbered with purchase money mortgages, and now unsalable—all except the works which he had transferred to his son, as already mentioned.

This, though apparently a formidable equity bill, afforded me the first gleam of light and hope of a safe exit out of the labyrinth he had constructed. It transferred the trial and decision of the main question from an ignorant jury to an intelligent tribunal. The incapacity of a jury to cope with such an extensive and complicated series of business transactions covering such a length of time, and to comprehend the mixed questions of law and fact arising out of them, was what had alarmed me most. But here was to be a trial by judges instead of a jury; and that was just what suited me. Truth and right was on my side; all I needed was the opportunity to show it, and capacity in those appointed to decide to comprehend it. The difference between trial by jury and trial by judges is contained in a nut shell as expressed by a writer of great experience. "If I were guilty," he says, "I would desire to be tried by a jury; if innocent, then give me a trial by judges."

Whilst the trial of an equity suit under our practice is not held, as it should be, directly before the judges—that is, the trial so far as the hearing of testimony is concerned—yet as the master who is appointed by the court to take the testimony and report the facts and recommend a decree is always a member of the bar and mostly of equal ability and capacity with an average judge, his report and finding, and the consideration and decision of the court thereon, is equivalent to a trial by judges. Besides so much greater certainty of a correct decision, this equity suit would settle his entire defense; and when settled, there would be nothing further to do than take judgment for my different claims, and foreclose the mortgages which I held for their security. I therefore filed my answer to his bill with alacrity, and succeeded in having a highly respectable and competent member of the bar appointed as master. The hearing before him was of course a protracted one, and made more so than was necessary by what transpired during its progress, extending from first to last over a period of three years. The testimony on his side was multifarious and voluminous. It transpired that he had been collecting material for a controversy of some kind from the very beginning of our business relations in 1859. During the existence of the partnership between 1859 and 1864 the notes passing between us were almost daily, as we had no telephone then, and I was under the necessity of giving him constant direction regarding the business and the numerous petty suits he was always involving himself in. These notes were mostly written by me in pencil, hurriedly and carelessly, in court or on the cars, on scraps of paper sometimes without date: none of them of any importance, and none of those received by me from him ever preserved. But on the hearing before the master, every scrap of mine with the slightest allusion to our partnership, or any partnership business, was presented either without date or with the date torn off, and verbally testified to as of a date posterior to the dissolution. This was with a view to prove a continuance of the partnership. But one of these notes, written long after the dissolution, was inadvertently by him presented to the master with the others. He had not read its contents fully, nor discovered that part of it was a reply of mine to a previous letter of his proposing a renewal of our partnership relations, which this reply of mine directly declined, giving the reasons why I would not entertain the proposition on any conditions. This piece of testimony, produced by himself, had a damaging effect, but nothing to daunt him. The taking of his own testimony covered many months, and that of his wife and son and soninlaw as many more, although they were never in a position to know anything about it except through him. Of course he had no documentary evidence to present other than the distorted letters and fragments of letters mentioned, and which had no relevancy to the question at issue except by force of his own verbal testimony.

The testimony of his family had little effect: they could relate no facts, but simply express opinions or beliefs. But a thousand people testifying to their belief is inadequate to prove anything. Legitimate testimony consists in such facts as are calculated to produce belief; and whether they are of weight to produce belief is for the tribunal and not for the witnesses themselves to decide. It is in its liability to go wrong in performing this discriminative function that an ignorant jury is dangerous to the cause of justice.

When he ended his own testimony, I had the pleasure of applying to him a cross-examination, covering more time and paper than his examination in chief; for I never met with a witness who could parry questions so adroitly or give more plausible excuses of matters incapable of explanation. It required a rigid and protracted cross-examination therefore to break down his testimony. I have always felt sure that if a witness goes wrong to any great extent, and the party cross-examining him fully understands the subject matter, he can be confuted out of his own mouth, provided the cross-examiner has time and skill enough to follow up his questions. And in this case, before I was through, I had succeeded in making the unreliable and improbable nature of his story so conspicuous that his attorneys abandoned the case. They were of too high a grade of professional character to follow up a case of the kind after they saw its rottenness. But its abandonment by his attorneys was no alleviation, but rather a calamity to both myself and the master; for he then undertook to try the case himself, as he had a legal right to do, and continued to consume time with all manner of preposterous testimony and senseless objections to testimony on my part, introducing himself and members of his family as witnesses again and again as often as he got in a pinch. Every transaction of the old partnership, and the different separate transactions between us or in any wise connected with the business of either for the past seventeen years were canvassed, and irrelevant testimony of witnesses taken which had no connection with the question at issue. He grew desperate and malicious as he became more and more conscious of approaching defeat, and having neither money nor character at stake, nor legal knowledge to control his course within the bounds of discretion, he branched out into all manner of vagaries of argument and assertion, to no other end than to prolong the contention. In the course of the investigation, however, I made a discovery which would have been important to me if made some twelve or thirteen years before. If it had not secured me some eight or ten thousand dollars, it would at least have ended all business relations between us, and have saved me the present trouble. It was this. On examination of the old partnership books which were brought into requisition—I had never looked into them during the time of the partnership existence or afterwards, until now—we discovered that wrong entries and alterations had been made to my prejudice to the extent of nearly ten thousand dollars; and it showed on the whole that a large amount of what I was entitled to had never been accounted for or paid to me. After my testimony was given, with papers and documents showing the true nature of every transaction between us from first to last, and the testimony of my clerks and other witnesses showing the sayings and doings of both parties to be uniformly inconsistent with any partnership relation after the dissolution of July, 1864, the master had no difficulty in finding against every fact and allegation which he had set up in his bill, and reported to the court a recommendation that the bill be dismissed at his cost, concluding his report with these remarks: "The master cannot refrain from saying that the plaintiff's allegations and insinuations are utterly without justification or the least shadow of foundation in fact." The court of course approved and confirmed the report, and dismissed the case at his costs, which have never been paid to this day. The circumstance that any worthless, impecunious party of a crooked disposition can at will institute the most serious and unwarranted litigation, and carry it through to a final termination, and then beat his adversary and the officers of the court and county out of the costs he has occasioned, is one of the grossest defects of our judicial system. This case, for instance, covered a period of three years, during which we had one hundred and seventeen sessions before the master of half a day each, incurring also considerable expense for a stenographer whom each party was to pay for the testimony taken on his own side, and whom he beat out of his share by giving a check on a bank where he had no funds. The testimony, when written out, comprised over thirteen hundred pages of foolscap besides the papers and documents connected with it. The master's fees alone amounted to fifteen hundred dollars, of which he got nothing except five hundred which I afterwards paid him voluntarily, as I disliked to see his time and services go entirely for nothing, although I was under no legal obligation to pay it. And apart from the anxiety of mind which it occasioned me, my time and services, acting as my own attorney in the case, were worth at least twenty-five hundred dollars according to ordinary professional charges.

Thus it was that an investigation of business relations covering a pe-

riod of seventeen years was rendered necessary, although every transaction was plain and certain, and evidenced by receipts and vouchers
unequivocal and indisputable. After the case was decided against him I
obtained judgment on my claims, foreclosed my mortgages and perfected my titles to the different mortgaged premises, realizing eventually about all he owed me. Such was by far the most vexatious and important litigation of all my experience throughout my whole lifetime,
either personally or as attorney for others.

The next personal litigation of the kind which I had was with "B," a
fledgling lawyer, who, on admission to the bar, married a wife of a
good family, and acquired a valuable estate with her, which relieved
him from the necessity of earning a living by practicing his profession.
He had turned his attention to dividing his wife's property into building lots, and dealing in them and other real estate which he purchased
on credit; and after I commenced banking in the city in 1870 he became a customer and depositor, and frequently brought me purchase
money mortgages for property he had sold, for discount. Such mortgages were regarded as the best security to be had; but, after taking a
number of them in the course of a year or so, I discovered that two
were fraudulent, one for four thousand and the other for six thousand.

This produced an investigation of his financial standing, which I
found to be unsound. He had now no real estate, either of his own or
his wife's, clear of encumbrance; and very little on which there was adequate margin to afford additional security beyond the encumbrances
already on it. I found, however, that one farm at MacDonald Station,
in Washington county, had considerable margin left; enough, as I supposed, to secure from ten to twenty thousand dollars in addition to
what was already against it. I informed him that he must secure me for
the irregular mortgage transactions already mentioned, or a criminal
prosecution would be instituted against him. Besides these there were
some other matters to be made good regarding which he had made
false representations. Finally he proposed to give me an indemnity
mortgage on the Washington county farm, provided I would advance
him a few hundred dollars, not exceeding ten or twelve, to help him
out of some present difficulties. To close the matter without litigation and exposure I agreed to this, and a mortgage was drawn up accordingly, specifying its purposes to be in the first place as collateral security or indemnity against loss on the two questionable mortgages

and the other questionable transactions referred to; and in the second place for repayment of any further advances I should choose to make him.

The fraud in the questionable mortgages referred to was perpetrated in this manner: deeds were made to pretended purchasers expressing considerations much higher than the value of the property described in them, and mortgages taken in lesser amounts for the deferred payments. The difference between the consideration expressed in the deed and the amount in the mortgage showed, if true, that the purchaser had paid him a fair amount of hand-money, as he represented to be the fact. The deeds and mortgages were placed on record, and showed a fair transaction on their face. One was for six thousand dollars and the other for four thousand. These mortgages he had brought to me for sale; and, according to custom, I had directed my cashier to see the parties who had given the mortgages and procure a "no defense" paper from each, or ascertain the fact whether there was any defense against payment of the mortgage when due. One of the mortgagors reported it all right, that he had made a deal with "B," who was a good customer in his store; and the other reported that his mortgage was all right also, that the twelve lots of ground mentioned in it formed a beautiful location for a dwelling which he intended to erect for himself in a short time. This was satisfactory, and I purchased the mortgages and had them assigned to me. But when the first payments fell due a year afterwards the mortgagors had quite a different story to tell when they were called on for payment: which was to the effect that their part in the transaction was fictitious and merely for "B's" accommodation. They had each taken a bond of indemnity from "B" and his wife, stipulating that "B" would himself make the payments and save them harmless from all liability.

Such transactions constitute unlawful conspiracy to defraud; and, to make it worse, the panic had destroyed values in real estate to such an extent that the mortgage premises in either case would not have brought at public sale a third of the money expressed in the mortgage. Had the mortgagors been utter strangers to me I might have been more guarded at the outset; but the one in the six thousand dollar mortgage was city treasurer at the time, and the other was a wholesale dry goods merchant on Smithfield street, and both were apparently men of character and means. In order to secure myself when I discovered the spurious nature of the transactions, I brought suits on the bonds accompanying the mortgages to obtain a general lien on the mortgagors' other property. This opened their eyes to the serious nature of their position, as they knew "B" was worthless, and their attorney informed them that Mrs. "B's" signature to their indemnity bonds was worthless also, she being a married woman. But they had the effrontery to present their indemnity bond and the nature of their connection with the transaction, as a defense to my suits; this, however, did not hold, as the court entered judgements against them on the insufficiency of their defense as presented. This secured payment of the Smithfield street merchant's mortgage, as he was worth the money, and he and "B" turned over other securities to me to satisfy the judgment. But as to the city official's mortgage, it was different. It turned out that he had no personal property, and that the real estate which stood in his name was encumbered to more than its value. These and some other crooked transactions of "B's," in other mortgages which he had assigned to me, exposed him to a criminal prosecution for obtaining money on false pretenses, and hence the indemnity mortgage was given on the Washington county farm in order to save himself, as already mentioned; and on his doing so I advanced him sixteen hundred dollars, which was beyond the amount stipulated for in the first place. As it resulted that I obtained nothing from the city official mortgagor except the mortgaged premises, which were worth only a few hundred instead of six thousand dollars, I had to resort in time to the indemnity mortgage on the Washington county farm, and sold it at sheriff's sale, becoming the purchaser myself. This deprived "B" of his last resource for income, as he had squandered all the rest of his wife's property; and, together with his intemperate habits, rendered him desperate and reckless. As his real estate dealings and the construction of buildings which he had commenced on his wife's property were thus suspended, he alleged as an excuse to his creditors, regardless of truth, that it all came of my refusal to fulfill the understanding he had with me when he gave me the Washington county farm mortgage: that I had then promised to advance him twenty-five thousand dollars, but after advancing a mere trifle of it had refused the residue. Of course, this statement was entirely false. The mortgage showed on its face what it was given for and to what extent I was to advance; but it served the purpose as an excuse. Not only so, but to make it appear more plausible, and as he could tell the same story as a witness in court, he brought suit against me, claiming half a million dollars for alleged consequential damages which he pretended he had sustained in loss of property through sheriff's sales and the want of money to finish his buildings, by reason of my refusal to advance him the entire amount which he alleged was stipulated for. This too, in plain contradiction of the statement in the mortgage, that any money to be advanced under it was to be optional on my part. But his allegations, though in direct conflict with the mortgage itself, would not in law prevent him from setting up a separate, distinct agreement or understanding, nor from alleging that part of the agreement was left out by mistake. Hence such a case, however groundless, cannot be thrown out of court summarily, but must be heard and determined in due course.

This half million claim afforded him a sensational lawsuit, a luxury which he greatly delighted in; as well as a show of excuse for not paying his debts. He followed it up in court through the aid of his brother-in-law, a much better lawyer, but scarcely less unscrupulous than himself, giving quite a plausible narrative of all the facts and circumstances needed for his purpose, without any restraint or respect for truth; and if his poor deluded wife, whom he dragged upon the witness stand, had been like-minded and disposed to corroborate him, it might have made it more difficult for my defense. But she rather established my side of the case, giving a fair statement of the transaction as it occurred. All the rest was what her husband had told her after he raised the trouble. The cashier and clerks in my bank, with whom he had arranged the details of the mortgage before its execution, made it plain by their testimony also that his story was a sheer fabrication, and a verdict was rendered in my favor without any difficulty. The costs, however, still remain unpaid.

"B" was bright and smart, and knew just enough of law to render him dangerous to himself and others, but not enough to enable him to see the futility of such practices; and intemperance had contributed its part to render him vicious.

The last case of the kind I was involved in was with "C"; and what made it the more unpleasant for me, he was my first client as an attorney, and had continued to be my client for many years, and I had adhered to and helped him as a friend for more than twenty years after that relation had ceased between us. It was exceedingly unpleasant to have litigation in the end with one for whom I had done so much: he was indeed the man of all others for whom I had done the most. But to have business relations with some men to any great extent is sure to bring trouble in the end, especially so if they become debased by intemperance. The more you help and the further you carry them along, the worse it is for your prospect of getting off in peace or without loss. The trouble which "C" gave me arose entirely from undue indulgence on my part, and was remarkable for its unconscionable nature on his part. When I left the prothonotary's office in 1840 he was a vigorous young stonecutter, and was working on the new Courthouse then in course of erection on Grant's hill, the same which was recently burned down. He soon commenced to take jobs for himself, and to have mechanics' liens to file and claims to collect, in which he retained me as his attorney about the time I commenced practice. In business he was reasonably successful at first, but had little capital, and was very needy of money, as many of his jobs were not paid for a length of time after they were done. I became enlisted in his welfare, and advanced him small sums from time to time, which at first he repaid me with fair punctuality. But as he expanded his business more rapidly than the returns for it came in, and purchased and improved four lots on Wylie street, which absorbed his working capital, he became more and more urgent for loans, and his punctuality in repayment decreased.

In this way he had gotten into my debt by the year 1853 over two thousand dollars, which he was unable to repay without crippling his business; and he needed still more means. I had at the time purchased two acres of ground on Webster and Roberts streets, and laid it out in lots which were selling pretty freely to his acquaintances. Seeing this, he proposed that if I would give him six of those lots at their selling prices, and allow him time for payment, he would give me a mortgage on his Wylie street property, to secure payment of the purchase money as well as the amount he already owed me. He was confident that he could readily dispose of them to men in his employ and retain the price, or at least part of it, out of their wages: thus affording him the means of carrying on his business to more advantage and relieving him from the constant pressure for money.

This seemed reasonable and calculated to suit both our purposes: my purpose was to sell the lots and put their price on interest; his was to get money or its equivalent to carry on his business. Accordingly we made a full settlement in April, 1853. The price of the six lots was two thousand dollars, and his previous indebtedness to me exceeded two thousand; so I took a mortgage for four thousand, and a due bill for the surplus, and made him a deed for the six lots clear of encumbrance, so he could effect their sale. This was the first step of importance in our transactions.

Hitherto he had been sober, industrious, and attentive to his business, but addicted rather much to local politics for a well doing man in his position. From this time forward I ceased to act as his attorney, giving him as a reason that I considered the relation of both creditor and attorney as incompatible, or at least calculated to lead to misunderstandings; and as he was gradually getting more and more into my debt, it depended on how he managed his business whether he could pay me without compulsion. He always professed to regard me as his friend, and would insist on confiding all his troubles to me, whether of a domestic or business nature; because, as drink would sometimes get the better of his discretion, it caused trouble in the family. But he seemed actively engaged in business, and with ordinary success, as I supposed, and I had a liking to him and desired to help him on; and as the value of his Wylie street property was increasing, I was in the habit of cashing notes and liens which he received in payment of work, his credit being such that he could not obtain bank accommodations. But all this while, as I afterwards discovered, his intemperate habits were increasing and his pecuniary condition growing worse instead of better; and along in 1857 he began to be sued occasionally, and to have judgments entered against him. By his importunity I paid several of these judgments, and had them assigned to secure me for their repayment. His Wylie street property had increased so much in value that I considered myself safe in doing so; and he still professed the utmost confidence in ultimately getting through with all his difficulties.

In this way his entire indebtedness to me grew to more than double the amount of his mortgage, some of it secured by judgments as mentioned, but more in the form of unsecured notes which I had taken up for his accommodation when he was threatened with suit on them. Affairs progressed in this way from 1853 to 1857, when a judgment of eleven thousand dollars was entered against him as bail of a delinquent tax collector. This closed the door against the possibility of getting security for my notes; and when I investigated his affairs I found him

hopelessly involved through reckless mismanagement and neglect of
his business. His debts, secured and unsecured, exceeded twenty-five
thousand dollars, being three times greater than the value of all his
property; and he admitted his insolvency. It was not long till executions were issued and his property eventually sold by the sheriff. Just
before the sheriff's sale he applied to me to buy in the property for his
benefit, and as soon as he could he would raise the money and repay
me. I knew the futility of such promises, especially of a man wholly demoralized in health and character by intemperance; and even if it had
been otherwise it was entirely contrary to my business habits to become involved in a secret trust of the kind, or in an arrangement which
would carry the semblance of screening a debtor's property from his
creditors. I never knew such a transaction not to result in trouble. And
besides there was no reason for it in this instance, where the highest
value of the property at the time would fall short several thousand dollars of the amount of my own claims. I accordingly peremptorily declined his request, and told him that if I became the purchaser at the
sale it would be to save myself, and he must expect no future benefit
from it; that he had involved me in what would probably result in a
loss. Lest there should be any misunderstanding between us, I was
careful to tell him distinctly that I would make no such arrangement:
that whether I would have to pay much or little for the property could
make no difference to him, as he owed me more than it was worth in
any event; and that as I would have to take the risk of its depreciation I
was entitled to the benefit of any increase of value; that if he wished to
have the property bid in for him he would have to procure some one
else to do it, as I would be an adverse bidder and bid the property up
to what I thought it was worth on my own account. On the day of the
sale, in January, 1858, he told me he had applied to several other parties
to purchase the property for his benefit, but was unsuccessful, and
would make no further effort; and as I had always been his friend he
would rather see me get a bargain than a stranger, if it should turn out
to be a bargain.

When the sale came off I became the purchaser at the price of three
thousand one hundred and eighty dollars. This was equivalent to more
than eight thousand dollars, as it was sold subject to my first mortgage,
with its accrued interest, and was just about what the property was
fairly worth at that time. After becoming the purchaser I pitied his wife

and family of small children, and took no proceedings to turn them out, but gave him a lease of the house he lived in for a year at a low rent, feeling the amount was a matter of indifference, as none of it was likely to be paid. I wished to deal as leniently with the family as circumstances would admit of. The house he occupied was superior to all other improvements on the property. The other lots were covered with frame shanties from which very little rent could be realized, as he had let them run down to an untenantable condition. I had them reconstructed, however, and provided with new roofs and floors, but had not realized the cost of repairs out of them in rent at the time I sold them in March, 1863. And I not only received no rent for the house they occupied, but I had to put a new roof on it and make other repairs to preserve it; and I had invariably to pay the taxes, as all the money he received for the little work he did went for drink. Besides this indulgence to them, they got into such a wretched state of destitution and want that I had to advance them small sums from time to time to provide food for the children. His wife was high spirited and would starve before complaining to strangers, and he contributed nothing. Not only so, but the additional burden of supporting him was imposed on the helpless wife. I was encouraged to be liberal because the property was beginning to improve in value.

The preparations for war were producing a stimulus, and in March, 1863, I was able to sell the three lots with the shanties for nine thousand dollars. This, after paying brokers' commissions, left me eighty-five hundred dollars, which repaid all his indebtedness, excepting about three thousand dollars of unsecured notes and other claims which I held; and as the remaining property which he lived in was now become worth nearly double this amount I felt that I could afford to continue my liberality. During the five years since I had purchased the property, I had not only allowed them to live rent free, but had been advancing his wife ten dollars per month to help support them. The children were not yet grown to enable them to earn anything, and but for the help I extended to them they would have had to go to the poorhouse or starve. I had then no suspicion of bad faith on his part, nor had he any thought of a claim upon me or of any remaining interest in the property; but knowing the effect of intemperance and bad habits on a man's natural disposition, and how readily they will gratify their selfish purposes in disregard of truth and honor—especially if they fall into the hands of bad advisers, I took the precaution in January, 1864, to have him and his wife sign a declaration that they had no claim to nor expected any benefit from the property; that their occupancy of the house without payment of rent, and my monthly advancements theretofore, were entirely voluntary on my part, and without any right on their part to demand it; and that I held no property or other valuables in trust or otherwise for his or her benefit. This declaration, as it was the truth, was cheerfully made and duly signed by them before subscribing witnesses.

After this I continued the monthly advancements of ten dollars as before for upwards of four years longer, until the winter of 1869, when he seemed to have reformed considerably, and had been doing some small jobs of masonry, and claimed that he had relinquished his habit of drink; and in January, 1870, he applied to me for help to make a fresh start in the world. He declared he had seen the folly of his course, and had been getting along pretty well ever since he reformed. He had during the summer been employed on some public work in Tennessee, but had saved little out of his wages, and had been sober, as he pretended, since his return; and, if he had a small amount to pay his hands regularly whilst his jobs were progressing, he had no fear of want of success. He represented further that his family were now grown up and did not need the monthly advancements I was making them, and that if he could start right again it would be more advantage to both him and them than the ten dollars a month, which I could discontinue, and advance him the two hundred dollars he wanted to carry on his business with. He urged this repeatedly as a final act of generosity on my part, and also on the ground of my having obtained a good bargain in the property, the remainder of which was now worth some six or seven thousand dollars.

After some time I concluded this might help him and relieve me of all further annoyance, or any claims on my generosity. Besides, he assured me if I would grant him this last favor he would pay his rent promptly in the future, until he got a cheaper place, or moved to the country as he intended. He had in the twelve years previous paid no rent at all; and I finally consented that if he would put those statements down in writing, showing that I had treated him well and that I had his good will of the property, and stipulate never to make any further claims on my liberality, but begin to pay rent regularly as long as I continued his lease and leave peaceably at the end of any term on request, I would advance him the amount he asked. He was pleased at this and expressed himself so, and had my cashier take it all down in writing, and signed his declarations on the subject. I then gave him two hundred and fifty dollars, which was fifty dollars more than he had asked for, and after receipting for it on the back of the document he departed, warmly expressing his gratitude.

This ended the monthly advancements; but when the time arrived for paying rent there was none forthcoming, nothing but fair promises. However, in June of the year following, he had occasion to complain of an adjoining lady neighbor for creating a nuisance by allowing her sewerage to flood the cellar of the house; and brought suit against her in court, stating in his affidavit of claim truthfully, that I was the owner of the property, and that he held it by lease as tenant under me, and that the damage was suffered by himself and family in their possession of it as my tenants. This case was tried a year or so afterwards, and he testified to the same facts on the trial, and recovered a verdict of three hundred dollars, one hundred of which he assigned to his attorneys, and the residue to me, stating in the assignment that he was to be credited with it on the rent. At the same time he entered into a new lease on different terms from that which preceded it.

This two hundred dollars was the first proceeds received from the property he occupied since I had purchased it in 1858, a period of eighteen years; although I had been paying for taxes and insurance over one hundred dollars annually, besides having spent five or six hundred dollars during that time for repairs. Besides this I had paid out about fourteen hundred dollars to the family in advancements as stated, and two hundred and fifty dollars to himself; and yet was getting no income, and not likely to get any, as his habits had become as bad as ever. I urged him from time to time to leave the property and take a smaller or cheaper place; and he still promised he would do so, and assured me he was preparing to go to a farm in the country, where he would be removed from temptation and turn a new leaf. But he never accomplished this purpose: and I saw it was sorely against his wife's feelings to leave the house, as with the help of her daughters they were living respectably and in some degree of style. Her daughters were marriageable, and two of them already married, and they disliked to take a smaller house. I could not prevail on them to leave, although they set up no claim to stay; and the thought was repugnant to be compelled to put them out by force after all I had done for them. But at last I found there was to be no other way of it. I had indulged them so long, and so often desisted from threatened action, that they presumed on a continuance of the same leniency. I had allowed them to live so long on the property undisturbed, that they began to feel as if it was their own, and I must act or give it up altogether, as matters were growing worse. I was still paying taxes and insurance, and keeping up repairs; and whilst I could have sold the property for seven thousand dollars before the panic, I could not at this period get five thousand for it, although I offered it for that sum.

With the balance of my claim and the advancements I had made them, and the expense of the property to me from 1858 to the time referred to, 1876, I would still be out of pocket a thousand or two if I sold the property at its highest value; and as the family was now no object of charity—two able-bodied sons, and three or four active and intelligent daughters grown up—it was high time to take active measures to get them out. But still I neglected the unpleasant task until the first of April, 1879, when I found that nothing else would do but a resort to coercive measures. His repeated promises to get his family out were of no account: they paid no attention to him; and after due notice I instituted proceedings before an alderman to dispossess them. Under such a state of facts, and the relation between us so well established and fully understood, it was hardly to be expected that any serious opposition would be interposed to proceedings for possession. But not so: contrary to all expectation, my friend with an attorney appeared before the alderman to make defense, and through the ability of his attorney to contrive, and the ability of himself and his family to give testimony, such a formidable defense was eventually concocted as required over two years of litigation to settle. He positively alleged the very contrary of what had occurred, averring that I had bought the property in for him at the sheriff's sale under a previous verbal agreement to do so; that it was under this agreement that he had remained in possession of the property ever since; that I had been long ago repaid all he ever owed me by the sale of part of the property and otherwise; and that he had often requested me to make him a deed, but I had so far delayed to do so. He showed that he had been well posted in all the elements necessary to constitute a secret trust, and that he was equal to the occasion in brazenry to assert them. I did not expect this, but should have expected it from a character debased as his had become; and it was well that my caution was such that, notwithstanding his professions of gratitude so strongly expressed all along for the favors shown him, I had from time to time taken such documents and vouchers in writing as fully exhibited the true relations between us; so that when I presented my papers the alderman necessarily rendered judgment in my favor. From this, however, the defendant appealed to the court, thus prolonging his possession; but when it was tried by a jury the verdict was of course again in my favor, without any difficulty. But that was merely the beginning of the litigation.

In September, 1879, he filed a bill in equity, stuffed with all the offensive allegations which malice could suggest, or a cunning lawyer twist into legal shape. And thus, however preposterous and baseless his allegations, all the tedious delay and expense of an equity case had to be gone through with. In the face of all his sayings and doings during the twenty years I had already held title to the property; and the written leases he had signed; and the solemn declaration in writing, made on two different occasions, that he had no claim on the property; and his own sworn testimony in court in the nuisance case above mentioned, to the effect that he was in possession but as my tenant: in the face of all this, he set up in his bill that I had purchased the property in for him in secret trust at sheriff's sale, and had continued to hold it in trust ever since, and had been repaid my claims in full and a surplus over, whereby he was entitled now to a reconveyance and an account for surplus rents.

I felt perfectly safe when the case assumed the shape of a bill in equity. But the great drawback to equity proceedings lies in the opportunity afforded to either party to procrastinate the proceedings almost at will: and as he had imbued his two sonsinlaw with faith in his story, and his attorney had led them to believe he would succeed—as they were the source from which the fees were derived, which came so slowly that the lawyer found it to his interest to procrastinate—it was three years before the case was fully ended. And it was only in consequence of the total exhaustion or refusal of the sonsinlaw to advance fees that it was ended even then. I had possession of the property, however, in the meantime, after the verdict of the jury in my favor. Of course his equity suit was decided against him, both in the lower court and supreme court; but as usual with such characters in such cases, not one cent of costs has ever been paid by him. The fees drawn by his attorney from his sonsinlaw fed the flame of litigation and kept the case alive till they either became exhausted or disgusted, and it died a natural death. But neither I nor the county, nor the officers of the law, got any of the costs which the law allows us. Such is the advantage possessed by an impecunious and unconscionable litigant.

The foregoing cases comprise all the litigation of much importance in which I have been personally involved during my life. I may remark concerning them, in the first place, that they very clearly illustrate the wisdom of the old English common law rule of evidence, which excluded parties to suits or others interested from being witnesses. The rule was wonderfully effective in preventing a multiplicity of sensational and unconscionable litigation. It was abolished in this state in 1869, and since then all parties interested are allowed to testify, and litigation has increased remarkably. The expense of jury trials is becoming burdensome to the public; and additional courts have had to be established, and additional judges appointed, from time to time, in the courts already established, in order to breast the rising tide of litigation. When the rule of law excluding interested witnesses was abolished, the oath might as well have been abolished with it. Good and true men who respect their oath would tell the truth equally well without it; and it gives a degree of sanction to the lies of the false witness which they ought not to receive. A large proportion of witnesses of all shades of moral character regard the oath as but a matter of form and relic of ancient superstition; and there is no opportunity given the jury to discriminate. Under such circumstances the oath had better be abolished than have the jury misled by its solemnity to believe all true that is said under it. To accept a statement as true, or to give it weight, merely because it is sworn to, is about as rational as the old method of trial by battle, when the title to property or any other fact in controversy, was ascertained by finding out which party had the strongest muscle. Logically it is a *non sequitur*.

Under the old rule it will be observed that not one of the foregoing cases could have gotten into court; or if it did, it could have proceeded no further than the discovery that no other witnesses than the parties themselves existed to support the claim on the one side, or the defense on the other. The new rule is also detrimental to justice in this: that the party to a suit who can tell the most plausible story is the most likely to win; and the greatest scamp is generally the one who can tell the most plausible tale, and is under the least restraint in giving his testimony. The experience of all our judges, and others accustomed to court proceedings, confirms the fact that self interest, and passion and prejudice are in most instances too powerful for scruples of conscience to resist.

I have given the facts and circumstances of each of the foregoing cases at considerable length because I think they will afford some useful practical lessons. To be made a party to a baseless suit of the kind, where you are fully aware that your adversary knows what he is about, and intends to use fraud and falsehood without stint to gain his object, is a perilous position to be placed in: indeed exceedingly dangerous to one who is not a lawyer himself, or should happen to have an incompetent lawyer, without tact or ability to manage his case. If any of my readers should ever be placed in such a position he will find it may tax all his energy and ability to defend himself successfully. These cases show that you cannot have dealings to any great extent with evil disposed, crooked or narrow-minded men, without incurring trouble; and that no degree of precaution in having your dealings clearly specified and understood, and evidenced by regular vouchers and written documents, can always protect you. The most they can do is to protect you from ultimate defeat and loss when the trouble comes. And as you never can fully know the true inward character of the parties you deal with, because that is never fully developed until put to the test of strong temptation, the true policy is to deal on the square with all men without complications and with short settlements; and to have every transaction or settlement regularly and properly evidenced by the ordinary written documents. Such was my regular course of business, and in the above cases it was all that saved me. Indeed it is the best policy to avoid low, tricky, dishonest and trifling people as much as possible in your dealings. You will always deal more safely and profitably with the better class. It may be impossible in every instance to observe this rule in transient matters, but I have reference to extended or protracted business relations, such as partnerships, joint enterprises, successive loans of money, and the like. In short, I would advise you to keep the best company you can get into, in your business life as well as in social life. If your business connections are among the low, cunning and tricky, or the pinched and needy or reckless, you can hardly expect to prosper or escape trouble. It is for this reason a large city is preferable to a small town for a man of business ability. He is afforded more scope and variety of character and condition to choose from in business relations. Where there is little money and small trade it is difficult to rise above the common level of those you deal with.

These cases will also show the impolicy of helping men who cannot help themselves, of trying to keep them on their feet contrary to the law of their natural gravity. You may carry such men along for a time in the vain hope of holding them up, but they are sure to sink to their proper level whenever let go; and whenever you have to abandon them and try to save yourself, it matters not how much you have done in the past, you will certainly gain their lasting ill will for discontinuing your support. It has been one of my failings to sympathize with and extend assistance to lame ducks of this kind, and from that source alone has come all the enmity and detraction I have ever encountered. I was too easily persuaded of their ability to succeed. I could see very well how easily I could succeed myself if in their place, and would make the mistake of supposing success by them equally easy. The mistake was in not taking into account the difference between different capacities. In such cases you must not take the man's own plausible theory of what he can accomplish, or how he can accomplish it. You must look at what he has accomplished already, and determine your line of dealing with him accordingly. My experience has invariably been that the more I did for incompetent men, the greater their ill will when I had to refuse them further favors, or enforce compliance with their past obligations. The parties mentioned in the three described cases were the chief of that class of men it was my misfortune to encounter. And in case of loans I have discovered it to be exceedingly injudicious to take the party's word for his ability to pay. The security he offers may be good enough and he may be honest in his representations, but is apt to overrate his prospects; and if you do not want to be put to the trouble to compel payment by judicial process, you must scrutinize and determine for yourself his ability to pay at the time stipulated. Besides this, never take security on real estate or other property without leaving sufficient marginal value after your lien to make it the interest of the creditors who obtain liens after you to take the property, or protect it and pay you in order to save themselves in case of the owner's ultimate failure; or such margin as will fully compensate you for the trouble and possible loss occasioned, if you have to take it.

After all your precautions, however, you need not expect to escape losses and disappointments altogether if your business transactions are extensive. Apart from the "real hardened wicked" class you must bear in mind that your fellow men for the most part have in them a taint of insanity, or mental or moral obliquity, and you may as well regard them accordingly. You will meet with the harmless imbecile, rendered so by nature or bad habits, who is willing to deal with you on almost any terms, so he may accomplish his immediate ends; but if you are indiscreet enough to accept his liberal offers you will find your mistake whenever you insist on the fulfillment of his promises. He is too weak or narrow-minded to comprehend or regard his position; and if he does not make contention he leaves you the unpleasant duty of a resort to compulsory process. Then you have the smart, cunning idiot to contend with who is always overreaching himself by his own shrewdness, either involving himself beyond his depth or engaging in questionable enterprises and trying to draw others in with him. But when things do not turn out as expected, he will cast the blame on every one except himself. Then you have the hair brained, visionary speculator to encounter. He is himself utterly impecunious, but always full of plausible schemes with millions in them, and ready to take you in on the ground floor. He has nothing to lose; and if you go in with him the more you invest the better are his chances, as he shares your gains but none of your losses.

I speak of these classes as idiotic, or tainted with mental or emotional insanity. Every mental or moral obliquity is regarded in medical science as an abnormal condition—imbecility or insanity in a degree. All who do not pursue the right course are so affected, because the right course is the true way of life and the best way to success in all conditions. But the right way is exceedingly narrow and difficult, judging from the small number who succeed in following it. The best of us are always deviating to one side or the other. A well balanced mind, properly regulated passions and emotions, and sound judgment are rare qualities in the same person; and all which that implies even will not insure the possessor against mistakes and shortcomings. Of course there is an extensive variety of erratic conditions between such a clear-headed, truthful, conscientious, prudent man, and the man whose mental or moral faculties are so far blunted or deranged as to render him irresponsible for his actions and *non compos mentis* in law: and you are to remember that it is in this wide field of capacity, varying by slight gradations from utter legal incapacity upwards, that the bulk of your business transactions has to be conducted. In a community of crooks, cranks, imbeciles, and weaklings of all degrees, the stream of human affairs cannot be expected to flow smoothly all the time without obstruction and conflict. Instead therefore of crimination and resentment, or vain regrets at your troubles, or disappointments, or losses, my advice in every case is to blame yourself in the first place: you will be surprised at the benefit derived from this habit of introspection. No wonder that the wise men of old made self-examination a Christian duty. Whenever you find yourself worsted in a bargain, deceived or disappointed by some one in the fulfillment of his obligations, or when you become involved in litigation, do not waste your time in fault finding against the other parties concerned. Instead of this, attribute it to the evils inherent in their nature. What right have you to blame them for their weaknesses, or for obeying their nature, if you have contributed to the injury by dealing with or putting yourself in their power, or by your own defective judgment regarding the securities or enterprise they offered? Rather blame yourself. Inquire into your own past course in the matter: how you allowed yourself to be imposed on, why you were off your guard, what sources of information you neglected; what facts appear now which you could have known beforehand by a proper degree of vigilance, and which, if known, would have saved you the loss or trouble in question. Trace what elements of your own conduct contributed to or made possible the difficulty or mistake.

Thus, by way of illustration, let me point out some of my own failings and shortcomings which contributed more or less to the above troublesome cases.

Unavoidable accidents are few. But I was not so blameless in "A's" case. In it there was contributory negligence on my part. I should have known him sufficiently, from the four years' partnership experience I had with him at the outset, to have dropped him entirely, and have had no further business transactions with him afterwards. I should not have leased him another coal works; and when he did not return me true accounts under that lease, I was still more to blame for making him loans and advancements of money after that. But when I did make such advancements, I was further to blame for extending him such indulgence on their payment, and for allowing him to negotiate purchases of coal land and other property for me. I was to blame also for disregarding the warnings of my friends as to his tricky and troublesome disposition; and for allowing such a man to insinuate himself so thoroughly into my good graces as to blind me to his true character and lead me to assume the position of a friend and protector, and be used this way until I could go no further without palpable loss, when, as is natural with his class, he threw off the cloak of deception and tried to defraud and defeat me. A prudent discretion should have convinced me that extensive business transactions could not be conducted with a man of his character for any great length of time without incurring trouble. I should not have flattered myself into the belief that whatever others might think of him he would never betray me; or have the effrontery to make positive allegations in direct conflict with the well known and established facts of our business relations.

I was not so much to blame in "B's" case. I could hardly be expected to discover the fraudulent character of his mortgages when the makers of the mortgages themselves, well known citizens, declared them to be correct and made in good faith, and that they would pay them as they fell due. I was neglectful, however, in relying on the ability of the mortgagors to pay, and not scrutinizing more closely the true value of the property included in the mortgages.

In "C's" case I was more to blame, for allowing my feelings to be enlisted in any man's favor to such a degree as to cause me to support and maintain him and his family for so many years after it was evident that intemperate habits had utterly destroyed his prospects for well doing in any line; and for still continuing out of sympathy to indulge him, after these habits had destroyed the last remaining shreds of truth or honesty in his nature. It was not business. It was not business in either "A's" case or his, to carry them along so far through feelings of friendship. Feeling and favor mingled with business never do well together. To indulge a debtor with delays upon delays, and renewals of securities involving complications, on the ground of friendly feelings towards him, is always more likely to result in trouble or loss in the end than otherwise. When I purchased "C's" property at sheriff's sale to save my own debt I should have dispossessed him at once, and indulged my friendship for him afterwards to whatever extent I desired as a mere gratuity to his family. My whole business experience teaches me that whenever a creditor sees that coercive measures are clearly necessary to secure his claims or obtain payment from his debtor, speedy and decisive action is the best for both debtor and creditor.

I could see very well after the trouble was over how, in each case, by more prompt action and decisive measures when the debts fell due and the party was unable to accomplish anything to save himself, I might have averted the trouble or have removed some of the causes contributing to it. But that weakness in my nature which always led me to feel a deep interest in a client or a customer, and inclined me to listen favorably to his importunities and plausible representations, led me to depart from strict business principles in these as well as many other instances where, however, my kindness was not abused.

I may remark here also that, whilst "A," "B," and "C" were chief among my proteges, and I did more for them and indulged them longer than any others, they comprise but a small portion of those whom I have assisted more or less with means to tide them over difficulties. And it is gratifying to know that all men are not ingrates: for many have shown much gratitude for favors of the kind; and singularly enough, they have invariably been those who least needed it, well doing men, capable of managing their affairs successfully, but who had got into straits and needed limited assistance to help them out. I can number many such, some of them millionaires now, to whom I extended a helping hand when they were comparatively poor and struggling upwards, and who have shown themselves my warmest friends ever since on that account. It requires much discrimination, however, to mingle friendship with business. Pecuniary aid is more likely to destroy than increase friendly relations. If you extend such favors to the wrong party you are apt not only to lose his friendship by it, but when you insist on your own afterwards, he will, like other narrow-minded and spiteful men of his class, become your enemy, whether you have litigation with him or not, and repay you for what you have done for him with calumny and detraction, against which you have no protection.

These litigious troubles came on me late in life and near the same time, after the panic which had forced liquidation on all parties seriously indebted. I had escaped personal litigation during my long professional career: and, had the panic not taken place, precipitating the failures of "A" and "B" and had "C" been allowed to live rent free, and free of paying taxes or making repairs, none of these troubles might have occurred in my lifetime; but they would have been a bad legacy to leave to my heirs, as the trouble would have come, sooner or later, whenever my securities and legal rights were sought to be enforced.

And now there remains but one of my old proteges to be dealt with—my old friend McClowry's family. The father was one of my favorites long ago, and always resorted to me for help when in a pinch. This resulted in his giving me a mortgage on his little property for $1,700 about eighteen years ago, which in his lifetime he was unable to do anything towards liquidating; and since his decease his family have scarcely been able to subsist—an aged widow, a careworn daughter, and a helpless lawyer son. They were so worthy and deserving that I never had the heart to eject them from their home in the old lady's lifetime, although the mortgage with its accumulated interest has grown to exceed double the value of the property. In this last case, however, there has arisen no resistance or ill will. I have regarded the parties concerned as of a higher grade of humanity, and was not mistaken. The old lady died a few months ago, and I have just received a letter from the heirs thanking me cordially for past kindness, and informing me that they were about to vacate and wished to surrender the property to me. It is reassuring to know that our fellow men are "na' villains a';" but in a long life and multiplicity of affairs, there is much to increase our distrust and improve our worldly wisdom.

Chapter XVII

Private Life

IN THE PRECEDING chapters I have given some glimpses of my professional and judicial life; but there is another side from that which is exposed to the public, and to the individual himself this is by far the most important side. In it lies the main channel of his being, wherein his hopes and fears, joys and sorrows drift on and on to the end. All through those busy years of professional and judicial labors my heart was in my home; it was there I was happy, and there my feelings centered. When married and settled, the outlines of my destiny were fixed and nothing more to project regarding them: it was now only left to carry out the programme, to work and await developments. The fondest of my early dreams were now becoming a reality as fortune smiled and children were born, and their young minds and affections began to open like buds in early spring time. Infancy however, beyond the natural affection it excites, was never very attractive to me. It is only after the child begins to look about it and wonder at what it sees, and ask those curious questions which philosophy cannot answer, and to give its own fresh views and opinions on subjects which puzzle older heads, that it becomes intensely interesting, and the tendrils of the young vine take hold on the parental heart. It comes as a helpless stranger, wide awake but relying with confiding trust on parental affection, and returning double measure for the kindness it receives; weak and helpless and apparently destitute of everything, to our surprise as the recesses of the young heart and mind are opened up we find them stored with richest gems.

But the thread of my narrative requires me to go back to where I left off in chapter xiii, after going to housekeeping in the McClurg house on Fifth avenue then Fifth street. We remained there only from December till April. The contracted space and sulphurous atmosphere produced by the coal smoke of the lower part of the city seemed to me to have a depressing effect on my wife's health and spirits, and in the following spring we gave up housekeeping for a time and returned to my motherinlaw, whose place was one of the finest in fruit, flowers and shrubbery which the suburbs of the city afforded. During that summer, 1844, I built myself an office at the Courthouse, in the forks of Fifth avenue and Wylie street; and in the same summer, June 26th, my son Thomas was born, inaugurating the fond anxiety of parentage. In the following January we returned to the city and boarded with Miss McLain till the occurrence of the great fire described in a former chapter, when we returned again to my motherinlaw and remained there until I had finished the two dwelling houses fronting on Wylie street, in the rear of my office, one of which I intended as a permanent residence, and moved into it in the following October. I had this dwelling provided with every convenience, and as a compact and comfortable city home I have never seen anything to surpass it. A spacious basement nearly level with the street afforded two convenient office rooms; on the main floor were our front and back parlors, with ample bed rooms on the second story, and with very convenient apartments for kitchen, wash house and so forth, in the back building. I found myself so well fixed in this home that I fully expected to make it permanent. It was here our second boy James, was born, January 14th, 1846, and also our dear little girl, Emma, December 26th, 1847. But the experience of nearly three years here began to tell on my wife's health again as I thought; at least she did not always manifest the same brightness and buoyancy as after a visit of a week or two at her mother's home in the country. And besides this, it was becoming evident that my little boys required more scope for play grounds. These circumstances began to shake my resolution towards a permanent residence in the crowded part of the city; and in May, 1848, we removed to the cottage on my motherinlaw's farm at the East End, which stood on the same spot where Mr. Holmes has lately rebuilt, as already stated. It was situate in a retired nook of woodland overlooking the village of East Liberty; and when I had it put in order it afforded a delightful home nestled in the midst of a plot of shrubbery and fruit trees.

But I was of a disposition which could only be contented in a home absolutely my own. An elegant fifteen acre lot of my wife's property lay in front of us on the east side of what is now Negley avenue, and I concluded to build on it, but, on sinking a well, did not find the water satisfactory; and the rising ground immediately opposite on the west side of the avenue, near the cottage in which I lived, was more eligible. I had long admired it as a choice place for a residence. It was sheltered from the north and west winds by the steep hill rising immediately in its rear in the form of a semi-circle; and there, at the instance of my motherinlaw, I selected nearly three acres and in 1850 commenced erecting the dwelling where I have resided ever since May, 1851.[1]

It was whilst living in the cottage that our little girl Emma died, December 3d, 1850.[2] During her short existence the poor child suffered the pains of death perhaps more than a hundred times. Afflicted with heart disease from her birth she was every now and then shaken with a paroxysm of excruciating pain, mostly ending in a swoon from which she would gradually recover in a weakened condition. It was not epileptic, or affecting the mind, but resulting from sudden obstruction in the passage of the blood through the heart. The spells occurred as often as once a month or six weeks, and medical aid afforded no relief. It is wonderful how affliction in a child endears it to parental affection. She was a bright little thing, and although not quite three years of age when she died, seemed prematurely wise and thoughtful: I suppose much suffering brightened the faculties. Though intensely earnest, no child could be more sweet and lively in her brief intervals of health and ease.

Finally on the Sunday evening of her death her painful swoon occurred for the last time. It did not seem more severe than the others which she had so often survived. It was a fine evening, and I had just been showing her over our new house then nearly finished. She was in fine spirits and had expressed keen interest and delight at the expectation of occupying her new room—an expectation soon to end. I held her in my arms, waiting to see her recover consciousness as usual; but no recovery came, and at length the painful truth was forced upon us that she was gone. All the difference between this and the numerous similar and equally painful spells which had gone before was, that from the others she came to life again but from this one never. She had suffered many deaths but was now at rest. Such are among the pains and penalties of parentage. It increases the measure of our sorrows as well as our enjoyments. Wherever happiness dwells, pain is a near neighbor. This was our first taste of sorrow and sadness.

> A quiet, sick and suffering child,
> Sweet, patient little girl,

The tendrils of affection had so entwined themselves about her that the separation was severely felt.

After this the putting in order of our new home for a time occupied all my leisure hours that could be spared from professional business. Besides providing the buildings and outbuildings with every manner of conveniences I set out fine orchards of the choicest fruits. There is a great deal in having a home with pleasant surroundings. I have always thought that besides contributing to our own comfort it helps to refine the young and incline to domestic habits. My improvements were constructed in this view, modest in style, without any ostentation in architectural adornments: planned for comfort and convenience, but harmonious to the eye and in conformity with the fundamental principles of good taste. Apart from the egregious folly of wasting large amounts of money on costly buildings of pretentious appearance in a country where the style and surroundings of buildings change so frequently, often leaving them in a position undesirable for their purpose—especially so in the suburbs of a city: I have always thought it unwise and in bad taste to make an ostentatious display of wealth in this way. It requires ability to accumulate wealth, but a still higher degree of ability to use it so as not to show the spirit of shoddyocracy common among those grown suddenly rich.

In 1852, August 8th, our hearts were again wrung by the death of our second little daughter, Rebecca.[3] She was in all respects a healthy child; but an attack of dysentery soon overcame her, and the opening bud drooped and closed, having seen the light of life for but eighteen months. Death of children brings keen sorrow which time alone can comfort. When I advert now to our sadness of heart on those occasions, I can derive comfort from the reflection that it is well. How much better may it not have been for these gentle beings to have died young: may they not have escaped a world of hardships and trouble! Females may be brought up in all the comfort and enjoyment which tender care and wealth can confer, to be launched on a hard and unfeeling world. Whilst celibacy is the safest, it has its drawbacks; and marriage is a fearful risk. Apart from the pains and anxious cares of maternity, the chances are so great of obtaining a husband who may turn out to be heartless and cruel, or a drunkard and spendthrift, and the consequences so tremendous, that daughters who die young need not be greatly lamented: at least such is the kind of consolation which after years brings to the bereaved parent, but never suffices to allay the pain when the wound is fresh.

But whilst subjected to these afflictions we were not left without other sources of happiness. I was engaged in what was to me the most interesting of all enjoyments: the study of the opening minds and characters of my two little boys. Reading new books of able authors had always afforded me keen delight; but here I had two new books to peruse of absorbing interest in their relation to me and all my future prospects. Their study was continually affording new developments of the most delightful kind—developments of thoughts, feelings and purposes congenial to my own. It is only a parent who can realize the felicity which the discovery of one good trait after another afforded me. It was with the deepest interest and pleasure that in evenings at home, and in our Sunday walks and talks in the fields and woodlands, I would explore and forecast from the views and sentiments expressed in their free and joyous utterances the manner of men they were to become; and thus it was with all my children, as they appeared on the scene between the years 1844 and 1860. If asked the sources from which I derived most happiness I would name but two: the free interchange of thought and implicit trust and confidence between me and my children in their youth, and unity of sentiment and opinion between us after they grew up; there was a deep satisfaction derived from it exceeding that from the closest friendship in any other relation of life. This was my chief source of happiness; and the next to it was the achievement of success in my plans and enterprises, and prosperity in my affairs.

The aptitude of my little boys at comprehending the surroundings and in understanding my plans and motives greatly exceeded my expectation. I secured free admission to their confidence from the first, and participated in all their plans; and in return secured their willing co-operation in my purposes for their benefit. What appeared to me at the time very remarkable was that we never seriously disagreed, but seemed to see everything pretty much alike. This was what I never had met with in my former experience and had not expected in them. Between my only brother and me when boys, whilst the warmest affection existed, we could seldom agree cordially in any plan or pursuit whatever; nor had I met among my friends any who so fully appreciated my views. Congeniality of sentiment and desires is not so common between parent and child—too often indeed they are antagonistic. Nor was it through constraint or deference to authority that such concurrence arose on their part; very little restraint on my part was exercised. Their inclination seemed to concur with mine spontaneously. It was my care to learn their bent and inclination in order to lead it in the right direction. In this way before they were sixteen years of age I had fully discovered what pursuits or calling they were fitted for. It mattered little whether handicraft, business or a profession, so it might be what nature had prepared them for; and I soon discovered they were out and out business men. But preparatory education was the matter in hand first to be attended to, and in this I had their concurrence and effort as fully as in boys of their age could be expected.

But the proclivity to active employment so natural to boys sometimes outstripped the sense of duty toward their books. Thus at one time, whilst attending the village school, they became fascinated with the performances of the blacksmith who worked in a shop near by, and as in our conversations we had often been over the subject of the occupation they might follow when grown up, they concluded after full deliberation to become blacksmiths, and to go to learn the trade at once and confine their studies to the evenings. They admired the power and skill which enabled the blacksmith to convert the glowing iron into all manner of articles at will; and decided to work all day as apprentices and study their lessons at night. I readily concurred in this plan with slight modifications, merely transposing the blacksmithing to the evenings after school hours, and having the trade carried on at home instead of the shop in the village; thus leaving the school hours uninterrupted and dispensing with the interposition of the blacksmith as a boss. They readily perceived that it was the bellows and tools which were most necessary, and soon conceived full confidence in their own ability to manipulate the iron without the intervention of a boss. It was easy to improvise a blacksmith shop of our own behind the house, a shanty and set of old bellows and tools cost little and were soon in place: and for a long while the hammer and anvil afforded constant recreation, with no other inconvenience than blackened hands and faces. Thus the gratification of a whim was easily converted to the improvement of bone and muscle, and by concession and encouragement on my part, and bright and tractable dispositions on theirs, we went on in mutual satisfaction from childhood to boyhood, and from boyhood to manhood. And when I regard them now, with children of their own older than they were then, occupying elegant homes beside me—the fruits of their industry and ability, and conducting profitable business wisely and well, it may be imagined the gratification I enjoy in wandering back in memory over the incidents of their lives, from that early time of anxiety and hope for their future down until the present.

The schooling of my children was kept as much as possible under my own supervision, in private schools mostly, seldom the public school. The chief objection to the latter was the associations there met with—too many of that misgoverned or neglected class of children, outcasts as it were from the parental and moral influences of a happy home, whose parents govern them in a manner calculated to produce defiance and disregard. Frequently coarse and low by nature, this class of schoolboy rejoices in vulgarity, disobedience, and contempt for study. Such associates are injurious to those of gentle and higher nature. I had not forgotten the truth inculcated by the line of the Greek poet, Neander, quoted by St. Paul, that "Evil communications corrupt good manners," literally good morals: and on this account I did not patronize the public schools of the day to any great extent. I found the private, or select schools as they are called, somewhat liable to the same objection, and to possess another defect not chargeable to public schools: that is, a want of independence on the part of the teacher or principal. The principal of the private school depends on the patronage of parents and guardians, and this again depends too much on the good will of the pupils themselves. Few parents can brook the punishment of their children by the teacher, and with most tempers punishment or restraint of some kind is necessary to preserve order and enforce attention to study. But where the principal of a school depends for support on private patronage, and fears the displeasure of a patron if his child is punished or restrained, this wholesome exercise of authority is apt to be withheld to the child's disadvantage. I found that from this cause progress and improvement among the pupils of some private schools was nearly impossible, the principal being too dependent and timid to maintain the necessary subordination; and insubordination produces a spirit among the pupils rendering study and improvement unpopular and impracticable.

And another defect, common to both public and private schools, was that the children were not made to understand what they learned. Definitions and rules were committed and exercises performed without any adequate insight into the principles on which they were based. Under these objections to any school within my reach at the time I built a schoolhouse on my place and employed a private teacher, sometimes admitting a few other pupils of proper character in order to lessen the expense. Here the branches taught and methods of teaching were under my own control. The studies were such as would be most necessary and useful in the subsequent business of life; and the method was to train the pupil in the way best calculated to produce thoroughness in whatever was studied. In arithmetic, for instance, I required the pupil to depend on the rules which had gone before for the solution of what was presently to be resolved. When at fault I would not have the teacher to assist otherwise than by referring to and requiring him to repeat and explain the preceding rules, thus leading the mind of the pupil up to a solution of the difficulty; never to permit him to proceed a single step without a thorough understanding and mastery of what had gone before.

In this way, under the drill of a private teacher, leading the pupil to think and find out for himself, more progress was made and clearer ideas and conceptions obtained in one year than in three at any ordinary school. One reason for it is the greater amount of time and attention afforded to the pupil. This system was alternated however with private school and college, as better opportunities offered from first to last, until all my children had obtained such a degree of education in the arts and sciences as fitted them fairly for the pursuits they were to follow. For business men it is unnecessary to waste much time on the classics and special sciences, as such knowledge thus acquired soon fades from the memory. Proficiency in these belong to professional men and scientists. Historical reading and economic and social science, and popular science generally, is useful to every class of men, but can be best acquired as the mind opens and the desire arises for it.

Such reading and acquisition may begin in school, but is little worth if it does not go on afterwards through life.

Thomas and James being foremost in age had most personal attention on my part. Like most parents we at first placed undue importance on personal training. I had a high opinion of the strict exercise of parental authority. I had heard so much about the necessity of coercion and chastisement in the proper training of children, when necessary for their future good, and my desire was so strong to bring them up in the right way, that at the outset I was in danger of overdoing the business in that line; but before long I found out my mistake, and that parental government must be tempered to suit the nature of the child. With wise, confiding and gentle natures severity is injurious. A child keenly perceives and resents injustice, and this resentment destroys parental influence for good. There are many no doubt whose evil desires or wayward proclivities must be subdued, and who require to be governed by a strong hand, and on whom kindness is ineffectual. It is one of the most delicate and important duties of the parent to determine, and firmly but kindly pursue the course best adapted to the disposition. There is a great deal in proper training no doubt, but we should not expect too much from it.

The foundation for good or evil is laid in the child's nature. If that is low, gross and sensual, with appetites or passions of any kind disproportionately strong, or the intellect weak and stupid, very little modification or improvement can be produced by either training or example. The want of wise parental influence and training may destroy what would otherwise become a good and useful character; but the best training never can supply the want of natural qualities and good disposition. With all my care and anxiety I am very sure that no efforts on my part could have secured such happy results in my own children, had the foundation for it not existed in their nature. Precept and example go but a little way with a weak or perverse or evil temper. I could read much of my own nature in them, but improved in many respects; and much in their natural dispositions was attributable to their mother. The ancients were wiser than the moderns in crediting to the mothers the best qualities of the offspring. I may seem partial and unduly prejudiced in their favor, but I think I have said nothing regarding my children but the sober truth, as experienced in the development of one after another from childhood into bright intelligent youth, and thence into manhood, with all the qualifications of good citizens, and entirely free from folly or evil propensities or other bad habits which blemish the character.

This period of happy home rule wore on, till Thomas and James were through with their education and ready and eager for the earnest work of life. They had not yet attained their majority, but were ambitious to be accomplishing some useful purpose. I was awake to the importance of two principles applicable to the employment of young men setting out in the world: first, that the employment should have respect to their inclination, and be within the scope of their abilities; second, that they should have the stimulus of self interest to encourage them. Work is oppressive where nature, inclination or education withholds the necessary qualifications, and in time becomes irksome where no other motive but duty exists for its performance. I made it a rule therefore, even in their childhood, to give them a pecuniary interest in the performance of whatever work they chose to engage in. In this way the earning of pocket money was made a pleasure; and the labor of earning it afforded them an idea of its value and a disposition to economize its expenditure. I have never seen young men converted into hardy, durable business men by the forcing process. They flourish so long as you supply them with capital, but wilt like plants in a hothouse when the artificial stimulus is withdrawn. They must in self reliance travel the rugged road of experience, and learn to surmount the natural difficulties on the way to success. Acquisitions to be permanent must be the genuine product of their own thought and labor. In the making of a young business man too much capital at the start renders his task too easy, and is oftener injurious than otherwise. What he has hard work to get will stick to him longest.

When boys, Thomas and James appropriated a small piece of our homestead grounds to the purposes of an amateur nursery of shrubs and flowers. When at home from school they found both exercise and recreation in its cultivation, as well as profit in the sale of its products. This gave Thomas a taste for such employment, and when about eighteen and through with school, General James S. Negley, who for some years had maintained the most extensive nursery farm in the neighborhood, well stocked with young fruit and ornamental trees and shrubbery and flowers of all varieties, proposed to sell out to him at a tempting figure. The general had gone into the military service shortly before, and found his absence injurious to his business at home. To purchase and manage this stock, and sell it out together with his own at retail was my son's first enterprise, as he did not intend to make a permanent business of it. It seemed to me too much for one of so little business experience to undertake; but not caring to discourage laudable ambition in the right direction I advanced him three thousand dollars to pay the general. He labored at it vigorously, and, with that kind of judicious management which always insures success, he was able in a short time to refund what I had advanced him with interest; and in less than two years wound up the whole business with a net profit of several thousand dollars. I considered it quite a promising beginning.

The year 1862 was a sad and memorable one to us. Besides the anxiety on my son Thomas' account, who had volunteered and joined a regiment of emergency men called to defend the Maryland frontier, where he was then in front of the enemy and an attack imminent at any time; and the suspense regarding the near future which threatened the destruction of our homes, we were now to suffer a still greater though unexpected calamity—the loss of our darling Selwyn.[4] He was discovered to be unwell about the 14th of September, but not in a degree to excite any alarm as it did not prevent me from taking James and my nephew, Mellon Stottler, to Jefferson College at Canonsburg. When I returned the next day however, I found him worse, and the family physician being called in pronounced it diphtheria, a disease which I have dreaded more than anything else ever since. He lingered on for eight days afterwards, growing gradually worse till the evening of the 24th of September, when death closed the scene. He was in his ninth year. This was the hardest blow we had suffered yet. Whilst the death of Emma was sudden and distressing enough, yet in her hopelessly ailing condition there was a gleam of consolation in feeling that her sufferings were ended; but this was quite different. For his manly qualities he was a favorite with us all. Vigorous and healthy, thus cut down in the early morning of life! Time has brought me consolation in all other deaths but this: for Selwyn I cannot be comforted. The recollection of every little unkindness I subjected him to affects me with remorse. When I review in memory his short life in sickness or in health, I discover nothing to justify the slightest harshness of treatment. His ear-

nest and beseeching look of entreaty rejecting the medicine I was trying to force on him from time to time in the vain hope of saving his
life, still accuses me of cruelty. But our efforts were all in vain; the
dread disease had seized on his vitals. A remarkably strong affection
had existed between him and his brother Thomas; but neither he nor
James got home till after his death, and both felt the loss severely. An
inexplicable circumstance in relation to it was that Thomas, without
any knowledge of his illness whatever, had an irresistible impression
that a terrible calamity was happening at home, and obtained leave of
absence to solve the mystery, a day too late to see him alive. It was the
best he could do as there was no telegraphic communication to that
part of Maryland where his regiment lay.

Selwyn resembled Dick[5] more than any other brother, and had he
been spared would have become such a man I suppose. In my memorandum book of 24th September, 1862, I find the following entry:

> DAY OF SORROW. At half past ten o'clock this evening one of our loved
> ones, Selwyn, passed away in the morning of life. It is hard, but it may be,
> after all, the merciful hand of a kind providence, to shield him from the
> heat and burden of midday and the penalties of age. But, Oh God, thy will
> be done. The parting is hard, very hard.

James had been for a time at Jefferson College, but his health
seemed to fail, and under the advice of his physician, on November
27th, 1863, I sent him to St. Paul, Minnesota.[6] When he reached Milwaukee however, the roads were snowed up between that place and St.
Paul, and not being able to get further, he entered the office of Messrs.
Finches, Lynd & Miller, leading attorneys of Milwaukee, as their clerk.
Although without any previous experience in bookkeeping or the work
of a lawyer's clerk, he soon rendered himself very efficient and useful to
his employers. They procured him the appointment of Notary Public
for the convenience of their own and neighbors' business. The climate
was so favorable to his health that after remaining with them upwards
of eighteen months he returned strong, robust and hardy. The remu-
neration for his services had sufficed for his maintenance; besides he
had acquired a valuable amount of practical knowledge in the business
of conveyancing. In his absence he had not been without thought of
the future, but had been casting about with a view to the choice of a

pursuit. The question, what shall I do when I grow up, is of course uppermost in the mind of every thoughtful youth, and it is always the
most difficult of decision and most important in results.

In our correspondence we consulted freely on the subject, and he
seemed to have taken a liking to the foundry business. He had some
acquaintances at Milwaukee who were quite successful in it, and it
seemed as good at the time as anything else. The war was still in
progress and every business was prospering exceedingly. This was the
germ from which sprung our foundry and machine shops at Braddock.
With the aid of an old friend and practical foundryman, Thomas
McVey, I had the establishment constructed for James' benefit, expecting he would go into it as a regular employment when he came home;
but whether or not he should do so, I believed it a good investment in
that locality. But shortly before his return I had purchased the Osceola
Coal Works from David Steen. They were in full operation, with coal
yard and office on Ross street in the city. The object in the purchase of
the works at the time was to resell them at a profit, or let them out on
lease. But James, on his return, preferred to lease them and go into the
coal business instead of the foundry. He was yet in his boyhood, without business experience, and I hesitated very much to allow him to undertake such a task, or assume the care, labor and responsibility of a
business so extensive, complicated and troublesome as running a coal
works and retailing its product.[7] But he professed himself equal to the
requirements and insisted on trying it.

There could not be a much more difficult business imagined for an
inexperienced youth to take hold of. The management of coal mines
with a hundred or more miners and employees, and the railroad transportation and disposal of the product by retail in the city, with the
difficulty of collections and probability of many bad debts, was rather
more of a task than I thought he ought to undertake. But thinking it
best not to discourage him, I rented the works to him with a good deal
of misgiving as to what might be the upshot. It was his first adventure
in business and I thought it best to let him experience its difficulties
and responsibilities; so I gave him a regular lease on the usual terms,
fixing the rent at fifty cents per hundred bushels or about twelve and
one-half cents per ton, with a full understanding that the rent was to
be paid promptly. I think it advisable always to have young men depend solely on their own exertions at the start; to afford them the op-

portunity but not render it too easy for them to make money. He had returned from Milwaukee in August, 1864, and in January, 1865, when all was ready, Steen vacated and James took his place; and to my surprise, inexperienced as he was, he managed the business from the start with more tact and ability than Steen had done. He made considerable improvements in the city coal yard and paid his rent promptly—much more so than the parties who had other coal works rented from me at the same time. His business prospered remarkably well for a couple of years until a general depression in the local coal trade took place, after which it was found scarcely to pay expenses; and this depression continued until he deemed it best to sell out his lease to another party, C. Schad & Co. After settling all matters he came out with over five thousand dollars net profit; and had managed his retail sales so carefully that his aggregate losses did not exceed fifty dollars.

After this, neither of them cared for the foundry business. Other departments of the iron business I always regarded as too fluctuating, and requiring too much capital and constant attention to be safe or desirable. And with a view to its advantages for business purposes, I had purchased a piece of ground at the corner of the Pennsylvania railroad and Station street, about an acre and a quarter. It was then part of an orchard, but in good position for a railroad siding and retail coal trade. Here, as soon as a coal and lumber yard was constructed, Thomas, having previously closed out his horticultural enterprise, engaged in the business of coal and lumber and building materials, in which a thriving and profitable trade was soon established; and when James sold out his coal business in the city as already mentioned, he joined his brother in the same business, where they have been prosperous for now over twenty years. After selling such parts of the lot on Frankstown avenue as could be spared I leased the residue to them, at first on a full rent and afterwards, when they were well established and prosperous, at an easier rate. This was pretty much all the pecuniary benefit I ever extended them, as they always paid interest for and returned promptly any money they borrowed from me in their business. Youth and the vigor of manhood is the period when nature supplies men with energy, hope and courage to surmount difficulties and achieve fortune; and at this period of life they ought to succeed, if at all capable, without assistance. Indeed the most I have done for any of my boys was to point the way and direct them in it. Had they needed help at any time I would of course have gone to their rescue, but none of them ever needed it; and Thomas and James, by the time they were twenty-one years of age, had accumulated between them over one hundred thousand dollars. The gratification to me from the uniform good judgment, good habits, industry and aptitude manifested, and the congeniality of feeling between themselves which produced such results at so early an age, can only be fully understood by a parent whose life and hope is centered in his children. Most of my enterprise and exertion has been with a view to their benefit rather than my own. I had already done enough and accumulated enough for my own ends. I never had any ambition to achieve fame or notoriety or great wealth or prominent public position; but always preferred rather to go on in a quiet and unostentatious way, and having no expensive tastes to gratify it required but little to afford me a competence and independence.

I do not wish it understood, however, that the remarkable success of those two boys at such an early age was due to great talent or extraordinary abilities. It was simply the result of good judgment and persevering industry, and the tact to improve their opportunities during a remarkably favorable period for making money. It was such a period as seldom occurs, and hardly ever more than once in any one's lifetime. The period between 1863 and 1873 was one in which it was easy to grow rich. There was a steady increase in the value of property and commodities, and an active market all the time. One had only to buy anything and wait, to sell at a profit: sometimes, as in real estate for instance, at a very large profit in a short time. Taking advantage of this state of affairs I advanced money to them from time to time to purchase land in suitable localities about the city, which after dividing into building lots they would sell at enormous profits, always refunding me the money advanced with interest, and in some instances a share of the profits also. In this way too they extended the demand for their lumber and building materials and enabled men of small means to obtain homes of their own: as at Homewood, where sixteen acres were purchased for less than twenty-five thousand dollars, and upwards of one hundred and fifty thousand realized out of it eventually.

But in this chapter I do not intend going beyond the time I left the bench. The time of training and of anticipation, and of hopes and fears for the outcome of my children preceded that date. All of them, including George, the youngest, were now of an age giving assurance of

what they were to be. Whilst I had led them readily in the way I
thought they should go in all ordinary affairs, yet there were some
temptations from which it was more difficult to guard them. The general excitement and demand for recruits during the war was a powerful
and dangerous temptation to those approaching manhood. Strong inducements were brought to bear on James while at Milwaukee to enlist, which but for the influence I had acquired over him could not
have been resisted.[8] He was impulsive and had a strong desire to enlist,
if but in the one hundred day service, as it was called. But I was aware
that if once in the South the men of such regiments had little opportunity to return at the end of their term, and would have to remain; and I
succeeded in dissuading him from enlisting on any condition. Thomas
also at one time was taken with the war fever to such a degree that had
it not been for my influence over him he would have enlisted in the
service generally. Sometimes it is wiser to indulge rather than entirely
deny such impulses of youth; otherwise they may go to the extreme of
disregarding parental control altogether. With this view I consented to
his joining a regiment of emergency men raised for a special purpose
and limited time. I was acquainted with the colonel of the regiment, an
honorable, reliable and wealthy business man of the city, William Frew,
of the firm of Lockhart & Frew, and could trust in his care and prudence. They were to be transported to Maryland, and to be absent for
but a month or so; and, as I expected, the experiences of even this
short campaign allayed his military ardor. It was in October and the
nights were painfully cold, and without tents or shelter they suffered
severely. This, together with the humbuggery, imbecility and petty
tyranny of upstart subordinate officers, with other hardships to which
they were exposed, disgusted him with soldier life. They arrived at
Antietam a few days after the battle, but still in time to see enough of
its horrors to disclose the folly and wickedness of a policy leading to
war and such results. It was to prevent further incursion of the enemy
northward that the emergency men had been called out; but happily
their assistance was not required.

There may be occasions justifying war and making it the duty of
every citizen to engage in it, but in the present state of civilization such
occasions can seldom occur; and there is always a disproportionately
large class of men fitted by nature for a service which requires so little
brain work as that of the common soldier, and who are more valuable

to their country and themselves as soldiers at such a time than in any other capacity. It is a mistake to suppose it the duty of every man to enlist when his country needs soldiers. It should be remembered that in all ordinary emergencies of war a number is needed at home proportionate to that in the field. It is therefore egregious folly for men of superior talent and ability, whose services are valuable in private affairs and home duties, to go into military service as common soldiers or in any other position short of high rank; and even there it should be remembered that fame is but an empty bauble. My friend, Col. Black, is an illustration of this. Brave and ambitious and deserving the fame obtained for the time being, he is already forgotten. If a man is wise, and can perform the duties of private life with credit to himself and improve his condition at home, he will avoid the folly of soldiering. I do not insist on this view on account of the risks of battle so much as the almost certain loss of health from fatigue, exposure, irregularity of living and change of climate; and the danger of contracting idle, indolent or immoral habits. If a soldier returns after a year or two of service it is usually with impaired health, low habits and a distaste for the ordinary employments of private life. He is educated to idleness, indolence and the indulgence of the sensual appetites. It is a silly thing for a man of ordinarily fair ability in any industrial pursuit or business to give it up for military life. With men of low grade qualities who can do no better, the bounty money and pay and prospect of pensions is a fair consideration and a reasonable inducement, and deserves attention; but whilst the world is so prolific of this class, men of better qualities should have the good sense to avoid it. There are many, it is true, who are moved by ambition and the desire for notoriety, and to such it is excusable when a high office is in their offer; but to the common soldier, or any officer lower than a general, a man whose life is of much value to himself or his family should stay at home. On this account the parents and friends of young men of promise should use all their influence to guard them from the temptations brought to bear on them in times of military excitement. If allowed to follow the impulse of youth for the time being, experience may come too late to show them their folly.

Although this period of my life was in the main happy and prosperous, it had its share of anxiety and sadness. The society and mental development of my children afforded delight. My private affairs were prosperous and my public duties were light and pleasant; but there was the fear and anxiety consequent on the breaking out and continuance of the war. Then there was a time when it was uncertain how it might affect our lives and property in the North. But it was from a different source our real and saddest grievances came—the successive deaths of our two dear little girls and darling boy as related before. Loss of property or business disasters do not strike in like the death of dear ones. Pecuniary loss brings regret and disappointment, but death brings grief and pain. These were the real woes or heart-aches of an otherwise happy life.

In private life I lived in a quiet and unostentatious way, employing one male and two female domestics, and having twenty-five acres of land under my control. My modest home had all necessary comforts and conveniences without undue expense. It afforded the necessary quiet and repose for myself, with scope for healthy exercise and recreation to the children.

It was now that a new feature of my domestic life was developed: the tendency of one of my boys towards matrimony. When my son James was ready to return from his stay at Milwaukee as already related, I directed him to come home by way of Leavenworth, Kansas, in order that he might attend to some property interest which I had at that place; and whilst there he became acquainted with and subsequently formed an attachment for the lady who afterwards became his wife, Miss Rachel H. Larimer.[9] None of my children ever withheld from me any important matter which concerned them: the mutual interest and free confidence between us made secrecy unnecessary. Hence I was soon made aware of the state of his affections. My first impulse was to forbid the marriage: both were entirely too young to entertain thoughts of marriage, he being only in his twentieth year and she but seventeen. It had better be broken off at once, so I thought. But on due consideration and reflection I found the matter had taken deep root and had to be treated seriously. I felt that he would respect my commands even to the laceration of his own feelings; and on that account I must deal tenderly. He was of an ardent and impulsive disposition, and to prevail on him to break it off might do violence to his nature, and he might not make so good a choice again. It was a delicate matter to decide the best course to pursue. In every other respect than the age of both parties the union would be a suitable one. The lady was one of good stock, her grandfather, John McMasters of Turtle Creek, one of the wealthiest men in the city or county in his day, had been my client from the time I was admitted to the bar until his death, and had entrusted many important affairs to my management. His son John, her uncle, had been my companion, and my groomsman when I was married myself; and her father, General William Larimer, had been particularly my friend and confidential adviser from the time I first came to the city to attend college until he removed to Kansas in 1856, and then had left the settlement of his business affairs in my hands. But I feared the fickleness of early passion as well as the unwisdom of too early marriage. In any event time was needed to test the permanency of the affection which their letters plainly disclosed to be strong enough at present. So I concluded that to gain time was the best thing to be done under the circumstances, and agreed that if the matter was postponed for a year without any promises, as no engagement between them had yet been made, and they should find themselves fully of the same mind at the end of the year, I would then consent. This was agreed to, and after the year had transpired there was no change but a more settled purpose than ever. This was what I had wanted to ascertain and I consented; and a few months later, on the 3d of June, 1867, they were married, and he has in her a most excellent wife, and the union has been in every way a happy one on both sides.

The marriage of James led in a few years to the marriage of his brother Thomas likewise. Through Rachel, his sisterinlaw, he made the acquaintance of Miss Mary C. Caldwell, also of Leavenworth. She and Rachel had been schoolmates and always intimate companions, and the latter's good opinion of her had its influence. In family and character also she was every way acceptable. Her brother, Alexander Caldwell, is still one of the leading men of Leavenworth, with whom we have had close business relations ever since. In this instance there was less to object to on the ground of age than in the case of James and Rachel, and affection seemed to be mutual between them at first sight. They were married on the 10th of March, 1870, and the union has been equally fortunate and happy. No two could be more suitable to each other in every respect. These daughtersinlaw have in great measure supplied the place of daughters to us, they and our grandchildren contributing largely to our happiness and content at the present time.

Besides these changes in their domestic affairs, Thomas and James were branching out in business with much success, and I was anxious to throw off the restraints of official life and join them in private pursuits. It was a time for active business enterprise. With the exercise of ordinary discretion none could fail. I had now hearty and reliable coadjutors to execute with judgment, prudence and alacrity whatever I should plan. This was a condition I had never enjoyed before. Hitherto I had devised many well-planned enterprises which failed through the inefficiency of those entrusted to execute them. In professional and judicial life I could not give them personal attention, but had to depend on their execution through partnerships and agencies which never seemed to be able to fully accomplish what I projected. Now it was different: I could entrust such affairs to those who had comprehension to understand and will to execute.

Whilst engaged in plans and projects for the future of Thomas and James I had also the satisfaction of watching over the development of my younger boys, Andrew, born March 24th, 1855, Dick, March 19th, 1858, and George, June 30th, 1860.[10] I was not as strict with them as I had been with their older brothers. Whatever might be the case with other children it was evident that severity was not the better course with mine. They would any of them listen cheerfully to reason and conform to its dictates. Kind treatment and enlightenment was all which was needed to lead them in the right direction; and the death of our dear Selwyn had softened me so much toward those who remained that a harsh word or action to any of them went against the grain. The education of these three was provided for mostly at home in the manner mentioned before. Before the end of my official term their brothers were successfully launched in business, and the education of Andrew and Dick at least, was approaching completion; and I was anxious to join them all without being trammeled by official duties, as I have already related.

Chapter XVIII

Before the Panic

WHEN AT LIBERTY, after my judicial term expired, I began to cast about for a new vocation. It is always better to adopt some regular business to which we are accredited, and I did not care to return to the legal profession as I had now too many pecuniary and other interests of my own to make it profitable to attend to the affairs of other people; and in view of the condition of the times, and the position it might afford for some of my younger sons, I concluded to open a banking house. Accordingly I procured a suitable location on Smithfield street, and had it fitted up and ready to commence business at the first of January, 1870, a month after I had left the bench. Samuel McClurken was my first cashier. He was young and without experience, but he did very well for the small amount of business to begin with.

My sons Thomas and James had some time before organized a joint stock savings bank at East Liberty, which was obtaining a liberal share of deposits, and its management interfered but little with their other business. The banking business was unusually active at the time, and continued more and more so until the collapse of 1873. New banking organizations were forming numerously all over the city, and new buildings were in course of erection for their accommodation in almost every ward. Money was seemingly plentiful, special rates of interest in private banks from eight to twelve per cent., and fair lines of deposit. But money performed a small share in the vast volume of business transactions. Speculation was rife. My credit was good and attracted depositors to both our banks. Business had been prosperous so long, and money in the banks so abundant, it never occurred to any one that an occasion might arise suddenly when all the deposits loaned out on mortgages would be demanded by depositors at once, or as speedily as their deposit certificates would admit of. The reason for money being so plentiful was that credit had usurped its place, and people had become accustomed to purchase property and do business chiefly on credit. This inflated the sphere of speculation in all directions to a most unwise and unwarranted extent. Every one saw that his neighbor was growing rich by buying on credit and selling again on credit at a profit; but very few had any conception of the extent of debts and liabilities which underlaid this apparent wealth, and was liable to explode at the first spark of distrust. Business activity and inflation had received such an impetus during the war that it went on increasing by its own momentum afterwards.

At an early age I had seen the disasters produced by the great collapse of 1819, which followed the war of 1812; and expected a similar collapse after the late war, but had forgotten the fact that the collapse of 1819 was delayed so long after the war of 1812; and, in the present instance, the time of prosperity was so remarkably prolonged that I began to doubt my apprehensions, and to think it possible that some special virtue in our new greenback currency and national banking system had averted a collapse altogether. For a couple of years or so after the end of the Rebellion I had expected such a collapse and was fully prepared for it, and lost some fine opportunities by over cautiousness; but instead of a collapse business went on increasing and prices advancing. Such an excellent and reliable financial and banking system had never before existed in the country, and we were led to attribute the apparent prosperity and continued stability of affairs to it. This threw us off our guard, and as much better rates of interest could be obtained on long loans, and mortgage securities were much safer than common promissory notes, especially accommodation notes which were most common, we allowed a large proportion of our own bank capital and deposits of both banks to be invested in mortgages and similar securities.

Our business in the purchase and sale of real estate also was extensive and profitable. The price by the acre at this time, where it was suited for dividing into building lots, ranged from four to eight thousand dollars cash; and when divided into lots sold at prices, according to locality, ranging from six to eight hundred each, and at not less than twelve lots to the acre, usually more than doubled the investment in a very short time. In ordinary times the sales would have been too slow to be encouraging; but a mania existed in all classes for dealing in lots and other real estate, not alone for actual use but speculation. Every workingman and mechanic who had saved up any money invested in a lot, even if they could pay but a small portion of the purchase money, securing the balance on deferred payments. Even professional men and merchants joined the throng of purchasers. Our business in that line was conducted by private sales to individual applicants. But public sales was the general custom with others, who advertised extensively, and by means of brass bands and excursion trains, and the distribution of refreshments, would gather a crowd on the premises from time to time and dispose of large numbers of lots at auction. At the same time that this excitement in lots and real estate sales was raging, new rail-roads were under course of construction in all directions, and railroad bonds, and stocks bearing high rates of interest were pressing for pur-chasers at temptingly low prices. Such was the condition of affairs when I left the bench, and until the general collapse of 1873.

After I had our banking house in the city put in order and the books opened, and business fairly started, I made an interesting trip to New Orleans, my son James superintending the city bank in my absence. It was at the end of January, 1870, and I accompanied Captain William Ward, who had a business transaction in that city requiring some legal attention. I had never been further south myself than to Cincinnati, and thought I could spare the time now better than after my new busi-ness should assume larger dimensions; and Captain Ward was an agreeable traveling companion.

We went by rail to Cincinnati, and by boat from there to Louisville on an unusually high river, landing at Louisville in the early morning, and breakfasting at the Galt House,—famous for a good table, and it did not disappoint our expectations. We spent that day with Mr. Ward's daughter and soninlaw, Mr. and Mrs. Hodkinson, who showed us over the city in their carriage. In the evening we took the cars for New Orleans by way of Nashville, Mrs. Hodkinson providing us, be-fore starting, with a capacious lunch basket, which with its well se-lected contents and some bottles of her home-made currant wine, sup-plied us with excellent provisions to the end of our trip. We did not appreciate the value of this attention fully till on our return, when we were compelled either to fast or accept the unpalatable stuff provided at the railroad eating houses. The contrast between North and South was more remarkable in these establishments than in almost anything else.

The trip however, entirely upset my ideas regarding the South in other respects. I had always imagined it as exceedingly wealthy, and presenting great stretches of fertile lands under a high state of cultivation, with fine cities and the homes of the planters on their large plantations resembling rather palatial establishments of European aristocrats than the houses of ordinary farmers. Instead of this, I found the soil mostly poor and thin. This was easily seen in the character of the timber—the oaks of insignificant size, scattered far apart, showed quite a contrast to the tall, strong, closely set timber of Pennsylvania. It was also evidenced in the railroad cuts we passed through, mere sand banks for the most part, with a thin coating of six or eight inches of surface mold, which, when disturbed with the plow for a few seasons, disappears in the sand, and leaves the elevations over the country barren and unproductive. In most cases this had taken place already. The uplands were uncultivated and with little growth of anything on them; and irregular strips of corn or cotton cultivation were confined to the bottoms or lowlands. Of course there were exceptions, some places presenting the appearance of pretty good land; but thin or barren land was the general rule. The towns and country residences were still more disappointing. Nearly every town we passed, though a city in name, was hardly a village in fact. When approaching a city with increased expectation from having seen its familiar name in the newspapers during the war, imagine our disappointment on finding the entire place to comprise but a few poor looking, unpainted, two story frame houses, and as a general rule with brick chimneys at each end, built entirely on the outside; seldom two or more houses together, but each in a large lot of an acre or two by itself. This was the character of most of the cities and towns through which we passed on our route. As to imposing edifices of proud planters, we saw nothing deserving such a character.

As to the climate and appearance of the landscape, little difference was observed until the last day before reaching New Orleans. On that morning we experienced a marked change of temperature. All effects of the frost and snow in which we had set out a few days before had disappeared; now we had a bright sun and balmy air. The southern vegetation was beginning to show. The holly, with its broad, glossy green leaves protected with jaggers at the corners, and other kinds of evergreens, gave the woodlands a more cheerful appearance; and here and there, along the railroad, patches of the fan palm, resembling fence posts, with a great bunch of broad green palm leaves on the top of each; also occasional stretches of cane-brake thickly set with those tall slender canes used in the North for fishing poles. All this was entirely new to us. Among these, negro huts were frequent, surrounded with patches of cultivation, and turbaned negro women busy with the hoe, planting corn and beans and other vegetables. The day was warm and pleasant, and gnats and flies buzzing about as on a fine May day at home. Then little flower girls began to board the train at every station, with bouquets of sweet scented violets for sale, which they had gathered in the fields and along the roadsides. About noon we were at the end of our journey, and soon comfortably settled at the St. Charles Hotel, a quite imposing edifice, the only first class hotel then in New Orleans.

After being rested and refreshed we walked down to see the great river and celebrated levee, and were greatly surprised to find the river running in a direction contrary to what we had expected. I had been accustomed to regard it as running south into the Gulf of Mexico. But here it was, in all its majesty, running directly eastward past the city, and at quite a rapid rate for so flat a country. The sun was just going down, and seemed sinking into the river as it flowed directly toward us from the west. We spent two or three days there, and were much impressed with the beauty of the city. We found business of all kinds sadly depressed, owing to the wretched state of public affairs. The government of both state and city was in the hands of the carpetbaggers, as they were called. These were greedy and unprincipled adventurers, in the interest and under the protection of northern politicians, sent out by the general government to rule the seceded states, before the privilege of reconstructing governments of their own, and readmission to the Union was restored. These men manipulated elections to suit their own purposes, and were governing in the manner of the rapacious praetors and governors of Roman history, to whom the taxes of provinces were farmed out; and, like their ancient prototypes, had for their main object the plunder of the provinces, using the negroes as cats paws for the purpose. They elected their legislatures from among the grossly ignorant freedmen, with a sprinkling of unprincipled white men, just sufficient to manage the proceedings and direct the negroes how to vote. We attended one or two meetings of that august assembly, the legislature of Louisiana; and it was suggestive to see a presumably dignified body comprised of stolid, stupid, rude and awkward field negroes, lolling on the seats or crunching peanuts, except when the white leaders would by sign or signal arouse them to what was going on at the point where their votes were wanted: these white members among them standing in with the governor and other carpet-bag parasites in promoting all manner of corrupt schemes to rob the property owners and taxpayers. It was a sight depressing to the hope of popular self government; and the same danger to popular institutions still exists: now as I write, fifteen years afterward, this want of popular intelligence is the pressing evil both North and South.

Whilst we remained there as spectators bill after bill was put through, without any discussion or opposition whatever, voting heavy subsidies in state bonds to the aid of railroads and other projects which had no bona fide existence; and no other intention existing on the part of the projectors than to procure formal legalization of bonds to be sold for their private benefit in the Eastern market. State bonds were being voted for by the million, for the benefit of cliques and syndicates, in the proceeds of which the carpetbaggers of the state, as well as their confederates at Washington and New York, would participate. No wonder that many United States senators, and other notabilities of those times, accumulated immense fortunes; their numerous palatial residences in and about Washington City and elsewhere are evidence of it: the wealth of so many who went into the senate and other departments of the government poor and came out millionaires a few years afterwards, can be accounted for in no other way. One evening we attended a citizens' public meeting in Lafayette square. It was an immense affair, comprising most of the business men and property owners of the city. Humorous speeches were made denouncing the carpet-bag policy of the general government, and this bogus legislation, and protesting against the issue of bonds and granting of subsidies, in confiscation of the private property of the state and city. Reports of committees were read, showing the corrupt character of the numerous projects to which these grants of the state credit referred, and resolutions were passed giving notice to the world not to purchase the bonds thus fraudulently obtained, as they would be repudiated by the people of the state; all which turned out to be futile, however, as the same interests which maintained the carpetbaggers in office shaped the national policy and political sentiment everywhere, and reconstructed the courts so as to sustain all such proceedings.

I have often been struck in the course of my life by the readiness and ease with which the rankest injustice can be clothed with the invulnerable robe of legislative and judicial authority; the hideous features of wrong are thus made to wear the sober face of justice. In our day this is most frequently consummated in the creation of public debts both state and municipal, legalized under the pretext of public wants, but in reality for private gain. Corrupt rings, by manipulating elections and the members of legislative bodies after election, obtain the legalization of their schemes, always on some plausible pretext or other but with the certainty of plundering the industrial classes in the end. No matter how iniquitous or unjust such bonds and subsidies may be in their origin, the taxpayers are always held liable by the courts for their payment. There is no chance of escape for them: the judges of the courts owe their office to the same source of power at the bottom of it; brokers and financiers are interested in it, as public credit in national, state, and municipal bonds is the foundation of their business; the public press is interested in it, because its profits depend on the prosperity and favor of bankers, brokers and politicians all put together. Such is one of the chief methods by which the tax eaters of all classes prey upon the tax payers; and by which the class who live by their wits, and believe the world is bound to afford them a living without labor, are enabled to subsist on the earnings and savings of others. The industrial classes are the real sufferers—they are the taxpayers, whether owners are assessed for taxable property or not. One of the insuperable principles of economic law, or science of political economy, as it is called, is that the user of property or consumer of commodities must necessarily pay the full cost of construction or production, besides a profit to the owner or producer. Hence every one except the thief and pauper pays indirectly his full share of all tax burdens. Bonds of the kind may be without valuable consideration, and the municipal corporation may receive no benefit from their issue, and they may be contrary to law and constitutional rights, and may be issued in amounts exceeding the value of the taxable property of the citizen; but still the ingenuity of the judges can find some plausible pretext for holding

them valid and enforcing their payment. Such has always been the outcome of resistance to this line of public robbery for the past thirty
years or more. There was a time when the law and judicial policy and
public sentiment was otherwise—even as late as the early part of my
professional life it was otherwise. Strict construction and limitation of
delegated authority to state and municipal bodies in contracting debts
was then the rule. Bonds or other securities of such bodies were held to
be utterly null and void, no matter in whose hands they were found,
unless there was clear right and plain statute law and constitutional authority to authorize them. It was held that the purchaser of such securities was bound to look to their consideration and the law and circumstances of their creation, and was not protected by the arbitrary
rules of commercial paper. It was then the judicial doctrine that the
fact of a municipal or public corporation being maker of the obligation
was in itself sufficient notice to the purchaser, and subjected him to all
the equities of the corporation against its payment. But this has ceased
to be the doctrine since the piling up of debts against states and counties, cities and boroughs, became a business of immense profit and
controlling importance to certain classes of politicians and capitalists.
The law as then held was a protection to taxpayers and municipalities;
but that protection has been withdrawn by a judicial construction, and
innovations on the common law. So it is, whilst time and again states
and counties and cities are driven to repudiate such debts on account
of their iniquitous character, we see a general howl raised against them
by the public press. This is inspired by the powerful interests at stake.
The fact of repudiation is held up as a term of reproach, and the government and people of the repudiating community are stigmatized as
dishonest, when in truth and in fact there is in many such cases no
more injustice or dishonesty in their repudiation than would be in the
repudiation of a forged note or check by the party on whom it was
forged. If the industrial classes shall become wiser, and better organized in their own interests, the repudiation of iniquitous municipal
debts will become respectable, and be oftener resorted to, until this
trade of public plunderers is broken up. Such will have to be the result
in the end. It is a wrong principle to allow irresponsible politicians,
mostly without any property interests of their own, to mortgage at will
the private property of the citizens. It must bring about ultimate disaster. Avowed agrarianism or communism is honest and respectable

compared with this system of depredation. Communism would openly and avowedly take property and the fruits of labor from their owners, and distribute them equally to all. There is some show of equity in this. But this thing of contracting debts for other people to pay, and converting the proceeds so often to the subsistence of those who contract them, is communism in the livery of law.

Credit and the power to borrow money is the bane of cities and other municipal bodies of our day. It is a power which all experience goes to prove can never be delegated and exercised with safety. There should be no power to contract debts on the public credit, except that resting in the general government, to be exercised for war purposes alone. It takes all the prudence and caution of individuals and private corporations whose immediate self interest is at stake, to prevent them from overdoing the business of going in debt. But in cities, counties and towns, or other public corporations of the kind, where the power is placed for the most part in irresponsible parties who are benefited by its exercise, those on whom the burden of payment is to fall eventually are left without any adequate protection. It cannot be said that those who have to pay have the power to protect themselves by electing none but honest, competent and prudent men to office. This is not the fact. Those who have nothing to pay with and are indifferent have the numerical majority of votes and elect their own class to office; and however this may be, experience, which ought to but does not teach fools, proves conclusively that universal suffrage does not as a rule place honest, prudent and competent men in power.

If such power did not exist, public improvements in cities and towns might not be rushed on so rapidly, or constructed on so expensive a scale in advance of their needs. If the money was raised to pay for them in the first place, or as the work progressed, more care and economy would be exercised. The progress of cities and towns under such a system, if perceptibly slower at the beginning, would be steadier and greater in the end. How much more prosperous would not Pittsburgh be to-day, without the excessive taxation required to pay interest on her enormous debt! Rents would be lower to the working classes because it would be profitable to capitalists to erect more dwellings if the tax burdens were less; and manufacturers would construct their factories within the city limits instead of seeking locations outside. I suppose, however, it is one of those evils which must go on increasing till its own enormity causes a revulsion of public and judicial sentiment on the subject.

At the time I refer to in New Orleans, property in the city was rendered as nearly valueless from this cause as it could well become. Even on Canal street and the Levee, and other choice business localities of the city, business houses were offered for sale at prices which elsewhere would have been equal to about one year's rent; but the trouble was the rent did not pay the taxes, and the delinquent taxes were in most instances as much as it was worth, and no certainty of any relief or exemption from their payment. Even the improved property of that city was in as bad condition as was the unimproved property of Pittsburgh, which was brought within the city limits under the consolidation iniquity: where the rent fell so far short of the taxes as to confiscate the property in a few years, unless the owner had an independent income out of other sources to meet them. All such government is spoliation, pure and simple, and an evasion of the constitution, which forbids the taking of private property for public use without compensation. It was discouraging to see so beautiful a city in so wretched a condition: business industries abandoned, streets out of repair, and private property dilapidated, all from a system of misgovernment without a parallel outside of Egypt and the Empire of the Turks. It was discouraging because foreshadowing what might be expected to overtake our own cities and counties in the North.

But to return to my narrative. Whilst in New Orleans we made an excursion some forty miles up the river to the sugar plantation of the Messrs. Watson, well known Pittsburgh coal men of our acquaintance. It was said to be one of the finest sugar plantations on the lower Mississippi, and was formerly the property of Judge Adams, who had been for a short time an associate with me on the bench. I had a wish to see one of those plantations which I had heard and read so much about, in connection with the proud slaveholders of the South. We were well received by the proprietors. Bachelors as they were, we could not expect the refinement and delicacy of family life in their home; but the great old house was there and all its appliances, the same as when in other days it had received the softening touches of feminine hands. The matron of the establishment, as we found it, was a very ancient and venerable negro woman, who had been the head of the cooking department under more than one former proprietor; but she had certainly not been a success in the culinary line. Her hoe cake and coffee and pork were rather unpalatable; and these constituted the chief ingredients of our meals.

The building was an oddity; it stood, as did most of the other plantation houses, at a distance of some two or three hundred yards back from the river, and was about sixty feet square, of frame, standing somewhat over four feet above the ground, on brick pillars. The space underneath was entirely open, and as there was a depression in the centre, containing a small pond of water, it had become the refuge of flocks of geese and ducks, which the old darkey woman seemed to pride in, and their continued squawking right under my bed room during the night banished sleep. I never before had realized the full truth of Roman history which relates how that great city was saved on one occasion by the cackling of the geese. I found all plantation mansions erected pretty much in the same way, without cellars, and the first floor at least four feet above the surface of the ground, and open all around to permit the ingress and egress of the water if the levee should break and let the river out upon them, as frequently happens. The house was but one story high, with two or three bed rooms on the garret, lighted from dormer windows; and a wide porch outside extending around the entire building. The roof of the house proper extended from the centre point on all sides with the same pitch down over this porch, leaving no more than nine or ten feet or so between the eave and the porch floor. This gave the large building a low and squatty appearance on the outside resembling my old barn at home, and a rather gloomy or darkened appearance on the inside.

The negro quarters, consisting of twenty or thirty small frame houses, were some two hundred yards back of the main building, and separated from it by a paling fence. These negro lodges were set in two rows about equal distances apart, with a wide street between them, and resembled the miners' dwellings at our coal mines.

I found the plantation in a very fine condition, comprising several hundred acres stretching from the river bank to the swamp, like most others in the neighborhood. Every few hundred yards it was traversed by a deep ditch for drainage purposes, the course of drainage being from instead of to the river. The space between these ditches was filled by straight rows of cane, six feet apart, resembling our corn fields when the corn is cut off in the fall. At the time we were there the young cane had not begun to sprout; it has to be replanted only every four or five years. The sugar-house was the matter of most curiosity to us. There is one on every large sized plantation, and this is the most expensive affair in the business. It approaches to the magnitude of a rolling mill and salt works combined, requiring a large battery of boilers to run the rolls which crush the sugar cane and operate the presses, and also to afford steam to evaporate the syrup: costing altogether, with its vats for molasses, and machinery and buildings, according to its capacity, from $30,000 to $60,000. After crystallization takes place and the sugar is separated, the molasses is drawn off into vats under the building, resembling those in a country tannery, each vat receiving the molasses of its particular grade and quality. And the sugar is separated into some three or four different grades of excellence, the best quality much resembling rock candy. I had never seen any of the first or second quality for sale in any of our groceries at home. Lower grounds in this section of country, too wet for sugar cane, are used for rice, large stacks of which were standing on some plantations, and men were at work with machinery similar to our threshers, separating the grain from the straw.

Our return trip as far as Louisville was by the same road we went, and we then discovered why our fellow passengers on our way down had cast envious looks at the contents of our lunch basket when spread out before us for a meal in the car. We found the meals at the eating houses to consist of very little more than hard stale bread and black coffee, with dishes of beef or pork, seemingly hardened and darkened by successive heatings for the passengers of successive trains. The old darkey's cookery at the plantation was bad enough, but this was worse. She had her table cloth and table furniture clean; but here, in one case at least, I cut out the solid dirt or other substance between the prongs of the fork with the knife. It required a very keen appetite to overcome these difficulties. They are no doubt all changed for the better since then.

It was a curious experience, returning into the cold winter weather at Cincinnati, with snow covering the fields, and everything bleak and dreary—even colder than when we had left it only a week or so before. To be transported from winter to summer, and return to winter again, all in a few days, presented quite a novel condition. It was an experience also which corrected many of my preconceived ideas of the southern country and its resources. The absence of wealth, the scarcity of white population, the poverty-stricken condition of the towns, and the absence of resources calculated to support prosperous enterprise was very remarkable, and different from what I had expected; and made it very clear why the North was necessarily successful in the recent strife. But it suggested the unflattering reflection that it cost the North too much in time, men and money to overcome so weak an enemy. There was evidently bad management somewhere, because it was difficult to see where either men or means could be sufficiently produced in the South to present any serious resistance.

In the following year, 1871, I purchased the lot on which our present banking house is erected, Nos. 512-514 Smithfield street, and improved it, the lot costing thirty thousand and the building twenty-eight thousand dollars; and my time was pretty closely occupied between the attention given the two banks, and the construction of the building.

In 1872 I took an active part in the Greeley campaign. The duplicity practiced on President Johnston by Grant whilst secretary of war, and the corrupt cabinet he gathered about him when he became president himself, and his remarkable capacity for accepting presents from office seekers, had disgusted me with Grant and his administration. The outrageous systems of swindling and theft under the pretext of government, which I had witnessed throughout the South, was well calculated to increase this disgust, and was producing a split in the republican party. Those opposed to Grantism were called liberal republicans, and a large portion of the thoughtful and fair minded took that side. The stalwart or black republicans, as they were called, wanted to hold the Southern states in abject submission under carpet-bag rule. The liberal republicans proposed to restore the Southern states, under proper restrictions, to their former standing in the Union, and allow them the right of local self-government. Grant was at the head of the stalwarts for re-election for a second term, and Horace Greeley the nominee of the liberals, in opposition. Thus three parties were in the field—the stalwarts, the liberals and the democrats.

Apart from his liberal views on the reconstruction policy, I had always admired Greeley as a philosopher and elegant writer.

We did not succeed in electing him however; but we did succeed in turning the tide of public opinion against Grant and Grantism to such an extent that, when proposed for a third term, he and his supporters were swept out of political existence, and Hayes, the exponent of the liberals, if not regularly elected, nevertheless obtained the office. Thus the policy of the liberal republicans succeeded to power in the end, and held it until the success of the democrats in 1884. But my participation in the Greeley campaign did not go beyond a dozen or so of speeches at public gatherings. I felt a satisfaction in thus unburdening my mind on existing evils, and always had an attentive audience, although fun and anecdote and clap-trap declamation calculated to create a laugh, are more acceptable to the majority in the crowds who attend such meetings, than sound reasoning. In this city and county we had quite encouraging prospects; but after all the office-holding federal power was too much for us.

The indomitable Swope, an appointee of Grant, was then in the zenith of his power.[1] He had been appointed the deputy attorney general for the federal courts of this district, and was a remarkably bold, daring and unscrupulous character, with considerable ability. He had set out in the world as a preacher of some kind, and abandoning that profession had studied law. On coming here he surrounded himself with detectives, whom he employed in ferreting out omissions in placing government stamps where required; and as it was difficult always to determine the kind of stamp and the article or document requiring it, and the penalties for omissions were heavy, he succeeded in this way in extorting large sums from ignorant and often innocent people. Poor old Cimiotti, the pawnbroker, was nearly ruined by him. He had not adverted to the fact that his pawn receipt constituted a contract, and required a five cent stamp; and one of Swope's detectives on some pretense or other got a glance at his books. When he was arrested, and his books brought before Swope, hundreds of receipts were found without the stamp, the penalty for which was a five hundred dollar fine in each case. But Swope, professing great liberality, consented to compromise at forty-five hundred dollars cash, as was his habit in other similar cases. Whether the sums extorted in this way from the different parties found their way into the federal treasury or remained with Swope, no one ever took the trouble to inquire; and in either case it was but a species of oppression.

Swope had also a finger in the manipulation of the celebrated city water bonds, large amounts of which had been issued for the construction of the new water works. One John Ross was secretary of the water works commission and custodian of the bonds; and before long it transpired that some thousands in amount of them had disappeared from the city safe, and also that Ross had been quite liberal in supplying his political friends about Municipal Hall with water bonds as collateral security to enable them to borrow money, whenever they were in financial difficulties or in need of aid to promote their schemes. Ross was also a protege of Mr. Swope, who had strong political ambition and was desirous to establish and control a newspaper in his own interest; consequently Ross and Swope both became greatly interested in such an enterprise. A company was formed and a lease obtained of the basement and upper floor of my bank building, and the apartments well supplied with presses, furniture, type and other appliances of a newspaper establishment. The paper had just got fairly under way when the deficit was discovered in Ross' bond account, which made it necessary for Ross to disappear although the paper survived; but a great hue and cry was raised in Councils about his defalcation, and a committee of investigation appointed, whereupon Swope at once insinuated himself upon the committee of Councils as attorney to assist them in their labors. The committee beat about the bush for a time under his guidance with of course no definite or practical results; and so far as Swope's newspaper was concerned the committee did not look under the surface, or discover whether through Ross, or otherwise, any proceeds of the bonds had found their way to its establishment. But, when it was all over, Mr. Swope did not neglect his opportunity to charge the city the neat little fee of twenty-five hundred dollars for his professional aid in the matter.

But his boldest exploits were in the political line. Towards the close of the Grant-Greeley campaign he sent to Washington for an army band and a car load of battle flags and other trophies of the war; and drummed up a business men's meeting here, prevailing on upwards of fifty quiet, modest, conservative business men of the city, unknown to partisan politics, to attend the meeting, placing them conspicuously on the stage as figure heads. It is wonderful how readily smart but politically innocent business men can be used as advertisements by such demagogues to promote their purposes. Extensive performances of this kind of course collected crowds, which were addressed by himself and such of his favorites as he selected for the purpose; and the proceedings were heralded forth to the world as a grand uprising of the business men of Pittsburgh to rebuke the attempt of the liberal republicans to re-establish dissension, rebellion and slavery. It shows what brazen effrontery can accomplish in politics towards deceiving the common public. He was a remarkable character while he lasted; but his career, meteor like, was of short duration.

This, as I said, was my first campaign in party politics; and the manifest advantage of false and impudent assertions, trickery and deception, over truth and merit in the support of men and measures, satisfied me that it was not in my line, and so thoroughly disgusted me that I have taken no active part in politics since.

In 1872 my sons Andrew and Dick were through school, and eager for active employment.[2] Andrew was suited for the business of the bank, but Dick's preference was out-door employment; and I feared lest the confinement and close attention to the banking business at so early an age might be injurious to Andrew's health. Besides, the business in which Thomas and James were engaged was much more profitable than banking; so I concluded to manage the bank for the present myself, and place Andrew and Dick in the same business as their brothers, at some point where they would not interfere with each other. In pursuance of this plan Mansfield, on the Pan Handle railroad, eight miles west of the city, was selected.[3] It was a prosperous point, and afforded a good opening at the time. There I purchased a piece of ground for a lumber yard, and several other pieces in the neighborhood suitable for dividing into building lots.

On these properties Andrew and Dick went to work with a will. In a short time they had their lumber yard neatly and conveniently fitted up, with an office building and the necessary sheds and warehouses, and well stocked with lumber, doors, sash, moldings, hardware and every kind of material necessary for building purposes. They surveyed and divided their other grounds into building lots themselves, as they were competent civil engineers for all ordinary practical purposes. Thus provided they commenced business with bright prospects and obtained a good trade at once. They did the work of retailing, measuring and delivering lumber, and selling lots also, themselves; kept their own books and did their own conveyancing, without any miscarriage or mistakes for the eighteen months they were in the business, and without any other assistance than the necessary teamsters and common laborers. It was their first start and I was curious to see how they would manage, and the result greatly exceeded my expectations. According to the progress they made they would in time have done an equally prosperous business with their brothers, and with equally good judgment; but the collapse came, which speedily ended their operations. Under its disastrous effect however, they wound up their business creditably, with a fair profit for the time they were in it and without losses to any appreciable extent. Seeing what was coming they sold out the stock on hand at cost to other parties immediately, together with a lease of the lumber yard for a term of years as an inducement.[4] This itself was a masterly stroke of business policy as it turned out, for the collapse continued longer and values went lower than at first anticipated. And after ten years or so, when times had changed and property values recuperated, they sold the remaining lots at sufficient prices to cover first cost and interest.

Such was their first business adventure, and although nipped in the bud, gave good promise of the future. When the collapse came we were all on the flood tide of prosperity. Thomas and James were doing a remarkably extensive and profitable business, both wholesale and retail, at East Liberty; and Andrew and Dick had fully entered on an equally successful career at Mansfield; and the business of our two banks was in a flourishing condition. Deposits had flown in rapidly, amounting to nearly eight hundred thousand dollars between the two places, although but recently established.

As already stated, ever since the end of the war I had been doubtful as to the continuance of such remarkably good times, and especially the extraordinary inflation of real estate and other values. History had taught me that undue inflation is followed by a corresponding depression, and I had still a clear recollection of the collapse of 1819, but was hoping against hope, and guessing in favor of our new banking and greenback system to avert the evil: vain hope to expect to change the natural laws of trade. The only good effect of my distrust was to make me rather conservative in the purchase of real estate or other property, not at any time purchasing more than I could readily under any circumstances pay for without inconvenience. Had it been otherwise, and had I purchased extensively during the war or soon afterwards and sold out again before the collapse came, I might have realized an immense fortune. But on the other hand, had I been tempted to purchase beyond immediate ability to pay, I would have been ruined. My conservatism restrained me, and we only purchased in small pieces capable of being divided into building lots and sold speedily, so that when the collapse did come it cost us no embarrassment in regard to private debts or liabilities. The amount of real estate on hand was comparatively small, and the only losses which we incurred in this direction arose from the shrinkage of values in unsold lots, and the inability of those who had purchased to meet deferred payments. The serious trouble which the panic caused me arose from our two banks. Prolonged prosperity of the times had thrown me off my guard. The apparent abundance of money everywhere misled me to believe, as it did everybody, that little difficulty would be experienced in obtaining money on first-class securities at any time, should an emergency arise. First-class securities were scarce and in great demand; but we had plenty of them, and had no reason to fear any difficulty in getting whatever money we wanted when needed. Accommodation paper of the best iron and coal firms was plentiful also, but whilst there was no question about the present solvency I felt suspicious regarding it. This had made it difficult to keep our deposits invested, on much of which we were paying interest at the rate of three and four per cent. Many other private banks were allowing more, as discount rates on mortgages and accommodation paper averaged ten to twelve per cent. The consequence was, as before stated, I invested too much in mortgages in proportion to our deposits, as subsequent events proved. Neither mortgages or other permanent securities, however safe, are of any avail to a bank in case of a panic resulting from a sudden and general collapse.

On the 16th of September, 1873, while seated at my desk, Mr. Whitney, our notary public, on his customary call at three o'clock, looked in and inquired if I had heard the news of Jay Cooke's failure.[5] I replied, no. He said it had occurred that morning, and there was a good deal of excitement over it in New York and Philadelphia. This news did not disturb me, indeed it scarce attracted my attention, as we had no business relations with Cooke or his railroad projects; and I supposed the flurry caused by it would blow over without any serious effect, as it had done after similar failures of others. The same evening however I had occasion to attend a party where many of the bankers and leading business men of the city were present, and found they regarded it seriously on account of the sudden panic it had produced in the Eastern cities. The next morning the cry of the newsboys everywhere on the streets was "All about the panic;" and from day to day it seemed to be playing havoc among the banks and business houses of the East. Instead of calming down and affairs assuming their usual course, the apprehension and excitement spread everywhere, and became more and more intensified every day by successive failures all over the country, until by the lst of October we were in the midst of the most disastrous and extensive panic and collapse since that of 1819.

Chapter XIX

After the Panic

AFTER THE PANIC commenced money matters grew worse daily until a condition of affairs was reached which no one who has not gone through the like could conceive of. Money immediately disappeared from circulation and values of all kinds subsided rapidly. Credit was gone, payment in money imperative but no money for the purpose. Dealings and business transactions had been carried on so generally on credit that everybody was largely both debtor and creditor, and now that clearings could no longer be made by an exchange of mutual obligations, a dead lock and general collapse was the result. Men and firms owning large estates in real and personal property, and extensively engaged in business, were found to owe as much as their property and assets amounted to even under existing inflated values, and of course could not withstand the shrinkage. The demon of credit had destroyed confidence, and suddenly called a halt in the mad career of speculation. There was nothing for it now but for every one to produce the cash; and no cash was forthcoming. The best banks and private parties needed the most of what they had to meet their own depositors and obligations, and were too much alarmed and distrustful to part with any surplus. Nobody wanted property at any price, because it could not be applied in payment of debts, or held without shrinkage of value and loss. Property of all kinds remained, but it was set afloat in search of its true owners, who could only be discovered through the tedious process of judicial sales in the bankrupt and other courts. A, for instance, would appear to be the ostensible or legal owner of a valuable estate, but an examination of the records would show it to be mortgaged to its full value. The holders of these mortgages therefore might

be taken to be the owners until it appeared they had assigned or hy-
pothecated them for money or securities to speculate with, or owed
more to other parties than their mortgage securities amounted to; and
so on along the line, as one was struck by another, they toppled over
like a row of bricks. Nothing but a process of general liquidation could
determine what any man owned or was worth. The stock had to be
boiled down to evaporate the water from it. Real and fictitious wealth
had become so mixed up that the refining process or bankruptcy and
sheriff's sales became necessary to separate the dross from the true
metal. And when in this way the real owners of property and wealth
were ascertained, they were found to be only the few who had paid as
they went, or confined their business and speculative operations to
what was clearly within their power to hold. In the meantime such
banks and individuals as happened to have any money to spare held on
to it to await results; and this aggravated the trouble. No matter how
good or secure the paper, to procure its discount was out of the question. Anywhere from twelve to twenty per cent. was offered for money
without avail. Discounts in the banks were confined to renewals of the
notes of such customers as were deemed sound, but utterly unable to
pay under any degree of pressure. At the same time deposits in all the
banks were rapidly decreasing, not only on account of the distrust produced by the daily recurring suspension of banks and firms and individuals everywhere, but also on account of the stagnation of trade and
demands on depositors to pay their own debts. It seemed as if every
one was overtaken by a necessity for money, and an irresistible disposition to insist on the payment of what was due him. Almost every one
of the numerous savings banks and trust companies established during
the inflation went under and closed their doors. These daily recurring
failures intensified the alarm. Many of them, like ourselves, had been
investing in mortgages and similar unconvertible securities to a degree
rendering it impossible to realize funds in time to meet such an emergency; but indeed most of them were found to be in a rotten condition,
rendering their suspension only a question of time under any circumstances.

As to myself, the storm struck us at an exceedingly inopportune
moment. We had been unusually flush of cash until a few days before
Cooke's failure, when an offering was made of Pennsylvania railroad
paper so well endorsed as to be considered gilt edged. The temptation

induced me to take so much of it that our cash on hand was reduced greatly below our custom or the point of prudence. Only sixty thousand dollars or so was left to meet the deposits in both our banks, amounting to about six hundred thousand dollars at the time. We had good balances in New York and Philadelphia, but unfortunately our depositories in both those cities failed before we secured the funds; and to convert unmatured mortgages or other securities into money, or even to obtain payment of such as were due, or to sell and procure cash for real estate at any sacrifice, was simply impossible. Such was the unpleasant predicament in which we were placed. Our customers were not aware of it, and no one entertained the slightest apprehension regarding our solvency as I was always looked on as impregnable. They were still making their usual deposits from day to day, but in rapidly diminishing amounts owing to their own diminished receipts. And the checks and drafts on us grew rapidly in excess of deposits, and our cash balance at the close of each day showed a steady decline.

Our East End bank was a joint stock company comprising over a dozen of the solid men of that locality, besides myself and sons. Their wealth at the time aggregated many millions. All were individually liable for the entire deposits; but none of the other stockholders were in active business, or in condition to procure or advance any money to assist us, and consequently the whole burden devolved on ourselves. I did my best to collect in over dues from all sources; and my sons Thomas and James had enough due on their notes and accounts for building materials and lot sales to relieve us of difficulty if they could get it, and they sent out runners to collect, at home and abroad, from customers to whom they had been wholesaling lumber. Their success was only partial, but the funds which they secured in this way contributed largely to keep us afloat for several weeks; yet withal it became painfully clear that we could not sustain the heavy drain if affairs did not take a sudden turn for the better. But instead of any change for the better it grew constantly worse. The end was approaching, and no alternative. The securities we held, though perfectly sound, could not be converted into money at any sacrifice; and being absolutely certain that we could pay the depositors every dollar in a very short time, I did not feel called on to make any exceedingly great or extraordinary sacrifice to meet the unreasonable demands of such as I knew did not need their money and were only acting under the impulse of fear and alarm.

It was a bitter pill for me however to acknowledge present inability to pay every demand upon me. Neither myself nor any of my ancestors so far as I knew had ever been in that condition before. In fact it was rather our habit to pay cash and not contract debts at all; but banking is a business founded on credit, and renders the banker debtor for every deposit made. The end was approaching and already in sight. The extremely disagreeable announcement must be made, which I knew would cause a very great sensation, as we were supposed safe if there was safety in a bank anywhere. After all our exertions, the cash balance for both banks fell to nearly twelve thousand dollars, and as our suspension was not to be a failure involving loss to any one, I considered it better to keep this much on hand, to meet any necessitous cases of depositors likely to suffer for want of their funds; and at the close of banking hours on the 15th day of October, 1873, I directed the officers to stop payment the next day to all except special cases, but not to close the doors of either bank: I thought it more satisfactory to customers to keep them open, and continue the officers in their places to explain the situation to those interested. And this did have a good effect in preventing alarm; we had no run nor excitement at either place; and I have ever since felt gratified at the generous consideration with which we were treated. Whilst we met many anxious faces, there was not an unkind word or disagreeable reflection made by any one. On the contrary we were met mostly with manifestations of surprise and sympathy, and offers of assistance in every way except in the only effective way—the use of funds, which none could spare. No signs were shown of fear of wrong doing by any one: indeed at the time of this partial suspension we had managed to pay out and decrease the deposits in both banks to an extent which reduced them to less than one-third their amount when the panic set in. And after all I found the situation not nearly so unpleasant as I had feared, although the contemplation of a suspension, and having actually to succumb at last to a condition which I had never anticipated as possible, gave me more vexation and mortification than all the other adverse circumstances of my business life put together. Many incidents of that trying and disagreeable time are now, since it is long past, only amusing. Two of these may be worth mentioning.

John and Mary Hutchins were an old Irish couple whom I had known many years. They had always been quiet, well disposed, hard working and poor. He was a common laborer and she took in washing. Now he was too old for labor, but she still managed to do work; and soon after I opened the bank in the city they brought me their little hoard amounting to sixteen hundred dollars, which they deposited in her name as he supposed she would survive him, and I gave her the usual certificate for time deposits, at four per cent. interest. She had collected her interest for a couple of years before we suspended, and about a week after the suspension she called one morning in evident excitement and alarm, and tremblingly asked me if it was true that we were broke. I told her it was not so bad as that but we had stopped payment for the present on any who, like herself, were not in immediate need of their money; that she need not be alarmed, as her money was safe and she could get it in a short time if she wanted it, and even some of it then if she needed it. To this she paid little attention: her mind was not relieved by it in the least, and she deplored deeply the calamity which had thus overtaken them in their old age. Without any complaint against me she bemoaned her fate, and described, truthfully I believe, the hardships and deprivations which she and her husband had undergone for over twenty years past in accumulating this little sum by small savings to support them when they got too old to work, and to bury them when they died. But now it was gone, as she declared. It was truly a hard case and her sorrow was well founded in the light she viewed it; and the event would have been as sorrowful to me as to her had it been so, but I felt sure she would not lose a cent, and on that account had less sympathy for her, and tried to console her by the assurance that my sons and I were each and all individually liable and bound for it, and would pay her no matter what would become of the bank, and that we were worth in property and otherwise many thousand dollars for every one we owed.

But this assurance seemed to afford her no consolation: the idea of other people being individually liable for or paying what the bank owed was beyond her comprehension. Her money was gone, as she looked upon it. Nothing I could say seemed to persuade her to the contrary: and in view of the depth of her distress, I had about concluded to direct the cashier to open the vault and pay her the whole sum, when she went on to say, that she and her old man had heard the bank was broke only the evening before, and that their distress had kept them awake all night. They knew me to be a rich man, and had always considered me to be just and honest, and they believed that if the Lord would only put it into my heart to give them my own note they would be safe; and in their sleeplessness they had prayed to the Lord during the night to put it into my heart to take back this bank certificate which they held and give them my own note in its stead, and then they would be sure of their money. This was a queer turn for the affair to take, and it was not for me, under the circumstances, to disappoint their faith in the efficacy of prayer. I tried again to explain to her that the bank certificate was a better security than my note would be, as it held both me and my sons. Her reply was an incredulous shake of the head, exclaiming, "Oh, who ever heard of a broken bank paying anything?"—that if I would only give my own note for it, then they would be sure and satisfied. Although I was not in a cheerful mood her ludicrous notion was sufficient to produce a smile, and remarking I would give her my note if I should never sign another, I directed Mr. Senft, the cashier, to fill one up; and when it was signed and handed to her, she seemed as if a mountain of distress was lifted off her mind and with extravagant demonstrations of gratitude she showered blessings on me, declaring they had always trusted in the Lord, and now the Lord had answered their prayers and saved them from this great calamity. Then leaving in high spirits she only appeared again to receive her interest from time to time for several years.

Another instance had reference to one of our regular depositors, Thomas Coyle, a shoe merchant. He had worked up from poverty to comparative wealth and was consequently careful and cautious, and regarded me as his confidential adviser in business transactions, and gave me the credit in great measure for his previous success. He had some time before purchased my property at the corner of Fifth and Wylie, where his relatives still carry on the shoe business.

When the panic commenced the balance on deposit in his favor amounted to somewhat over eight thousand dollars, and as it was much harder just then to forecast who would not suspend than who would, he felt rather nervous over the situation, but showed no signs of distrust; and our suspension, when it came, caused him surprise, and although he expressed no alarm his frequent visits to the bank showed an uneasy state of mind. I assured him that it would be but a few weeks before we could pay him in part or in full, should he happen to need the money. This gave him a shadow of relief. His money had remained for a year and more, and he evidently had no immediate occasion for it as there was nothing he would venture just then to invest it in. But he soon began to discover, or profess to discover, profitable uses for it, and as we kept on collecting from all sources as rapidly as we could our cash balance increased pretty fast, and in less than three weeks we were in condition to meet all pressing demands: and when I announced to him that his money was ready, it seemed to surprise him almost as much as the suspension had done. However, as he had pointed out so many uses for it, consistency required him to take it when in his offer. He expressed great satisfaction to know that I could pay him without any particular inconvenience, and appointed to call for it the next day; and when returning from dinner a day or two afterwards, I met him with a package under his arm which he informed me was his money: he had just been to the bank and gotten it, and wanted my advice as to where he could deposit it with absolute safety. I named three of the leading banks of the city, any one of which I considered undoubtedly safe, so he left to select one of them; but just before closing the bank he returned with the same package, saying he had been debating in his mind all afternoon where to deposit it and concluded it could be no safer than where it was before, if I would take it back. I consented he might leave it in our vault as a package, but I did not care to reopen an account for it, as I was disgusted with banking and had it under consideration whether or not to wind up the business altogether instead of resuming. He left it with me and afterwards, when I concluded to resume, had it placed to his credit and a good deal more with it—where it remained till his death some years afterwards—forgetful altogether of the many purposes he had conceived for its use. Several instances occurred of a similar kind. We were never closed at either bank, and never entirely stopped payment to those in actual need, and in less than a month from the time we suspended we were prepared to pay all checks as presented; but it was some considerable time before I fully made up my mind to continue the business. Finally, in view of the fact that an office with a couple of clerks was necessary for the transaction of my private affairs, and but little more expense would be required for a banking business in connection with it, and having a very excellent vault and banking room in the city, I decided to continue the business in it and wind up the bank at the East End. Accordingly we paid off the depositors of the East End Bank, and the stockholders the par value of their stock with a surplus over, although we had paid twelve per cent. annually in dividends during its existence.

Whilst the crash of credit and financial affairs was sudden and immediate, the ultimate result of the collapse in many respects was not reached until several years afterwards. The value of real estate subsided slowly and steadily till it touched bottom about the year 1877. Our sales books showed this with great exactness. In the first year after the collapse we sold more real estate, and at higher prices, than we did in the second; and sold more in the second and at better prices than in the third; and so on until in the fourth year it reached zero and real estate was unsalable at any price, and business of all kinds was equally depressed, and employment by workingmen could hardly be obtained. It was a period of liquidation. When the collapse took place we held numerous mortgages both for purchased money and for money loaned, and also many contracts for lot sales on time payments on which less or more had been paid; but in the majority of cases the property was abandoned. Although in most instances no more than a third of the value of the premises had been advanced on any mortgage, yet the value had fallen below that; and so with property sold on contract. Lots contracted for at twelve hundred would not sell for four hundred. In this condition of affairs most parties found it to their interest to abandon the property altogether, and allow it to be taken for the mortgage or contract debt, and lose what they had paid on account. We tried to encourage all we could to hold on, by throwing off the interest and making abatements of the principal and giving them time; and taking advantage of this, the more energetic and well doing among them succeeded eventually in holding their property and saving their original investments.

I remembered when my parents were in the same condition under the collapse of 1819, and their hard struggles and deprivations to save themselves; and the sympathy produced by this early experience inclined me to be lenient and indulgent to all who made any earnest effort of a like nature. We foreclosed no mortgages and forfeited no contracts where the parties were doing the best they could to pay for and hold their property. But notwithstanding all such leniency and encouragement, a large majority gave up. Some were hopelessly incapable through bad habits and extravagant living; others through general thriftlessness, and the depression of wages and employment rendering it apparently hopeless for them to make the necessary effort. Large numbers left the city altogether; and for some three or four years the Sherrif's list at each succeeding sales day was immense. Nothing equal to it had ever been seen in this county and city before. Delay was useless in cases where the parties neither expected nor proposed to pay or redeem their property on any terms, and it was as late as 1880–81 before this process of liquidation was gone through with. From 1879 on, property values gradually recuperated, and sales slowly recommenced and increased until in 1882–3 and '84, when my sons in the lot and lumber business, and Andrew and I in the bank were again doing nearly as well in all branches of our business as before the panic.

In 1883 and 1884 I was enabled to get rid of a good deal of improved and unimproved property which had come to me under the liquidation process already mentioned, not however at much over half the prices ruling before the collapse. Our losses by this panic, whilst in no wise remarkable under the circumstances, were nevertheless serious. Several considerable claims on notes and drafts were lost outright, all the parties to them going into bankruptcy; and when once in bankruptcy, no matter what the previous estate and condition, there is seldom anything realized by the creditor. Such has been my uniform experience in regard to bankrupt laws; and I have been intimately acquainted with their operation, mostly as attorney for others, but sometimes as a creditor myself, ever since 1838. Our heaviest losses resulted from the shrinkage in values of real estate, and the length of time which intervened before we could dispose of it. Part of this loss was afterwards covered however by the increased value which some properties acquired over the amount originally invested in them.

After Andrew and Dick closed out their Mansfield business, Andrew assisted me in the bank, and in time was able to take the entire management of it upon himself and relieve me from the labor of its details altogether. Dick for some three or four years attended to my outside affairs and property, and his next prominent employment in which he had any interest of his own was the construction and operation of the Ligonier Valley railroad.[1]

In 1877 several prominent citizens of Ligonier, interested in procuring a railroad from that borough to Latrobe, offered me strong inducements to assist them in its construction. It required strong inducements as I was averse to outside enterprises of any kind, and it was doubtful whether the business of the locality would support the road when built; but my sons thought well of it. A company had been formed and a charter obtained several years before the panic, and the chief part of the work of grading had already been accomplished. But as so often happens where such an enterprise is attempted on the subscriptions of stock alone, the company failed and the road with its franchises was sold out by the sheriff and purchased by a syndicate of the ablest of the stockholders who, unable to complete the work themselves, applied to me as mentioned. In extent and location the road was not such as could be bonded and the bonds sold in the East; and there was no capital for such an investment just then about home. It had remained on the owners' hands for some five years without their being able to obtain any outside parties to take hold of it. The town and rich valley of Ligonier had no other practical outlet through the mountain ridge to the outside world than by the rough turnpike through the Loyalhanna Gap. The railroad was intended to occupy the same gap, and connect with the Pennsylvania railroad at Latrobe.

The syndicate offered me four-fifths of the capital stock of one hundred thousand dollars, and ten thousand to be raised by subscription among the people in the valley as a bonus; and a mortgage on the road besides, for whatever it might cost me to complete and equip it, to be paid with interest by the net earnings as they accrued. This offer was so tempting that the only question left was whether or not there would be any net earnings; or whether the road, when completed, would pay for the outlay; if not, the stock part of the inducement and the mortgage for the outlay would be worthless, and the question of its paying appeared very doubtful. I found that the passenger travel by the turnpike between the same points was accommodated by a daily trip of a two-horse hack, not averaging over four passengers each way; and three or four wagon loads of lumber and bark or farm produce daily, was the extent of the freight traffic. This presented a very unpromising prospect for a paying railroad. But my sons were more sanguine of the effect of a railroad in developing trade than I was; and the result has more than fulfilled their expectations. Thomas and Dick especially favored the enterprise, and made careful estimates of the cost, showing the risk was not disproportioned to the probable gain.

Accordingly I was induced to consent; but in order to economize and proportion the outlay to the probable trade of the road, we adopted the narrow gauge, which however in five years afterwards we had to change to the standard gauge to accommodate the increased traffic and travel. So I contracted with the syndicate to construct the road, that being their chief object in order to benefit the town and surrounding country in which they were largely interested. They showed much more desire to have the road built, and to have it built within a specified time without any outlay or liability on their part, than for the retention of any stock in it after it was built. When we met in Greensburg to have the contract drawn and executed, and they were asked how much time they would allow, they replied after consultation that they thought six months should suffice. I thought so too, because my sons and I had concluded to make shorter work of it if we undertook it.

It was in the beginning of September, 1877, when the contract was signed, and by the middle of the month Thomas and Dick were on the ground with all necessary tools and appliances, and commenced work. Large numbers of laborers were then out of employment everywhere. The Pennsylvania railroad was paying but ninety cents per day; and no sooner was it known that my sons were about to commence work on the Ligonier Valley road than they were beset by applicants for work in much greater number than they could employ. It was a new role for either of my boys but they soon had their men organized into gangs with proper foremen. They paid a dollar, being ten cents more wages than the market price, in order to obtain good men. A day or two after they commenced work I went out to see how they were getting on, and was pleased to see everything working so smoothly, and amused at the officiousness of some old contractors of Latrobe in giving the boys advice as to the management of the men. One of them said they would never get the work out of them—they were entirely too modest and polite; they must swear at and drive them or they would get nothing done. But this was not our method, and my sons did not adopt his advice. Men in any condition of life will act better if treated as gentlemen; and this was the theory we acted on. Accordingly, after two or three days Thomas paid and quietly discharged some ten or twelve of the shirkers, who were doing little themselves and demoralizing the others; and the next morning told those remaining that he did not propose to drive or urge them to extra exertion, or expect more than a fair day's work, but such as could not comply with this requirement need not expect to be retained. After this and a little more weeding out occasionally in a peaceful way, better gangs of men were never witnessed, and the work progressed quietly and satisfactorily. It was admitted by all who saw the progress made that my sons had the faculty of obtaining good men and good work without noise or bluster. Coincidences sustain the adage that "history repeats itself." The visit to my sons on this occasion produced a serious though interesting train of reflection as I looked across the valley at the old turnpike road. There was the spot where, sixty years ago, I met with my two uncles, then about my sons' age and engaged in precisely the same kind of work as they are now; and my grandfather visiting his sons then for the same purpose as I am visiting mine now. In those sixty years what a web of varied experiences!

Whilst Thomas and Dick thus accomplished the grading, bridging and track laying, James made contracts for the delivery of ties and materials of all kinds along the line; and the progress was such that at the end of sixty days from the commencement the first train entered Ligonier. Most of the track was laid at the rate of nearly a mile per day, so that the shrill whistle of the locomotive sometimes took the Ridgers by surprise. I went out often to see the work progress, and was amused at an incident which occurred on one occasion. They had laid over a mile of track that day, and the locomotive with trucks loaded with materials approached as far as the rails were spiked, and quite a crowd of tow-headed girls and boys had come down out of the mountain to gratify their curiosity. Many girls among them almost full grown had never seen a railroad or locomotive before. It was standing in a deep cut, and the girls, big and little, had climbed upon the fence on the bank above it. They had arrived whilst it was standing still, and were awaiting in anxious expectation to see the thing move; but when the engineer suddenly let off steam with terrific noise several of them dropped from the fence as limp as if shot dead. It was too much for their nerves; they thought the thing had busted, as they said afterwards.

After the road was finished Dick remained and managed it with credit and ability, although but a boy, for over three years; and whilst necessarily antagonizing the self interest of the neighborhood in regard to rates, etc., he did so with the least possible friction, avoiding unpleasant contentions, and gaining the general respect and good will of the community and all having business with the road. He also secured a class of men for employees of a character that could be relied on, and so faithful that most of them were retained for many years afterwards. Such is the history of this little enterprise.[2]

In 1880 my youngest son, George, finished his education, but had as yet indicated no preference for any particular employment. With the quiet, modest manner of his brother Thomas, I found he united the good judgment and executive ability of his brother Andrew. He was now in his twentieth year, and the readiest employment I had for him was house building on vacant property which I wanted to dispose of. Dwellings had become scarce and rents advanced: so much so as to afford six per cent. interest on the cost of house and lot beyond taxes and other expenses. Besides this, the readiest way to dispose of vacant property at the time was to erect a building on it. In this way unproductive property was rendered salable or changed into a paying investment.

I could not give personal attention to details and specifications or to making contracts and superintending the execution of the work. I had always found the details and superintendence of building contracts more troublesome than anything else, and had had so much of it in my time I wished to avoid it, and George showed himself ready and eager for the enterprise. He soon had some fifteen to twenty buildings under way; and I was surprised at the ability and ease with which he conducted the business without contention with any of his numerous contractors or employees. They are of a class more difficult to get along with than most others. But he had all his contracts specifically written out and succeeded, so far as he went, in procuring their fulfillment and making settlements without disputes, managing a large business in that line with remarkable tact and judgment for over a year; and when his loss of health cast on me the task of closing his unfinished business I found his contracts, papers and accounts all remarkably sagacious and correct, his buildings skillfully constructed, and what was still better, that he had the esteem and good will of those he dealt with.

It was early in 1881 that his health began to fail. He was not aware of the serious nature of the ailment, and disregarded it at first; and none of us supposed it to be more than the effect of a bad cold which would pass off in time. But in March, 1881, we had business in Kentucky, when I advised him to take a trip there, as the change of climate and relief from the details of his employment might benefit him. We had a controlling interest in the Pittsburgh, Oakland and East Liberty Passenger Railway,[3] and had occasion to buy horses in Kentucky to replenish the stock. He accordingly, in company with the manager of the road, spent some time in Kentucky and went from there into Missouri to examine some wild lands that we held there; and after three weeks absence he returned with health much improved. If we had known the serious nature of his trouble then and had applied the proper treatment, and he had left off work for a time, his health might have been thoroughly restored in two or three months without any dangerous consequences. But neither he nor any one else was aware that bronchitis had set in and progressed to such an extent that the upperpart of his right lung had become slightly affected; and feeling so well on his return from Missouri, he went to work with new vigor on the buildings he had in progress. But as the weather got warmer and his work more incessant, his appetite and strength began to fail again. It happened that about the first of June I had occasion to examine a large property in West Virginia, the Loope Creek estate, of some twenty-seven thousand acres. It was situated on the south side of the Chesapeake and Ohio railroad, a short distance below the falls of the Kanawha. In order to afford him some relief from his business I had him to accompany me, and we had a quite pleasant and interesting trip. Although his health was rather delicate, we had as yet no idea of the serious nature of the disease. When arrived at the Loope Creek station on the railroad we procured two thin, wiry horses from a blacksmith in the neighborhood, the only available means of transportation. Their owner allowed them to subsist as best they could in a rather wild state in the mountains near by, and whenever a call for them such as ours occurred he sent his little boys in search, and they generally captured them in half a day or so. The roads we were to travel were not fit for vehicles, and even if they had been no vehicle could be obtained. The saddles and bridles were of ancient pattern and in dilapidated condition, the reins entirely too short. But not to be disappointed in hiring their horses, the blacksmith's boys pieced them out for us with their suspenders. The animals could neither be styled horses nor ponies, but some sort of hybrid between the two, rather goat-shaped; but we had not gone far till we found they were the right thing in the right place. It was a clear case of natural selection, and afforded a good illustration of the adaptation of everything to its environments. The horses exactly fitted the mountain paths, and perhaps the paths fitted the horses. In climbing over large boulders and making descents down hills as if by stairways, it was wonderful how these animals would pick their steps and get on at a reasonably speedy gait without ever stumbling. They were used to it. At first we tried to help them by guiding their motions with the bridle and warning them of difficulties, but soon found they got along much better when left to themselves. With heads down, they would pick their steps with undisturbed attention.

Thus we proceeded in single file for three days: it takes a good many miles to traverse such a property thoroughly. We lodged at night with one or the other of the squatters as most convenient, wherever we could get room, which was often very scant, and the fare poor. These squatters were many of them of the second generation, their ancestors having in times past settled in nooks and corners between the hills, wherever a few acres were found level enough for cultivation. They had all long ago acquired good titles for their holdings by statute of limitations; and they and the owners of the general estate had made compromises and surveys, appropriating to each the quantity of land he was entitled to by virtue of his continued adverse possession. Few of these holdings exceeded fifty acres, and were dotted all along the creek bottoms.

Our travels in this vast property were interesting, both in regard to the scenery of the country and the character of the people. The scenery might be regarded as mountainous, yet the elevations were scarcely high enough to be so considered, but entirely too high for hills, and their sides too steep for cultivation; and the valleys between them too insignificant for anything but the smallest patches of farm land. Part way up the sides and in the gulches it was well timbered with immense poplar, sugar tree and some cherry, and occasionally a good patch of white oak. Near the top rock oak, pin oak and other scrubby timber prevailed. The backbone is seldom more than a few feet in width, with rapid declivity on either side. So far as the poplar and sugar extended the soil was reasonably rich and did not present the appearance of mountainous land; but wherever an opening at the junction of streams afforded a few acres of cultivable land it had been squatted on, cleared and cultivated at an early day. Our object was the purchase of the estate, which contained twenty-seven thousand acres exclusive of the lands held by the squatters. Its value consisted in its coal and timber. We found in every hill some five or six veins of good bituminous coal, above the water line of the streams and pretty regularly spaced throughout a perpendicular height of from five to seven hundred feet from the foot of the hill to the upper vein, almost fully equal to Pittsburgh coal for gas and other purposes, and one or two of the veins nearly equal to Connellsville coal for coke. The whole was offered at six dollars per acre, a low price considering the mineral and timber. But we did not purchase, as it required too much personal attention and too great an outlay for railroads, coal works, coke ovens and saw mills necessary to render the investment profitable. We concluded we had enough to do at home.

It was curious to find among these remote mountaineers many of the second and third generation from the first settler, who seldom visited any town or public place and were seldom disturbed with news of what was going on in the outside world. [Samuel] Johnson must have had some such far remote locality in mind when he described the "Happy Valley of Rasselas." Even in these wilds the good effects of civilization are seen: kind and obliging people, earnest in Christian feeling and duties. Pope must have had a similar impression regarding rural life when he wrote:

> Happy the man whose wish and care
> A few paternal acres bound,
> Content to breathe his native air
> In his own ground;
>
> Whose herds with milk, whose fields with bread,
> Whose flocks supply him with attire;
> Whose trees in summer yield him shade,
> In winter fire.
>
> Blest, who can unconcern'dly find
> Hours, days and years slide soft away
> In health of body, peace of mind,
> Quiet by day,
>
> Sound sleep by night. Study and ease
> Together mixed, sweet recreation
> And innocence which most does please
> With meditation.

Thus let me live, unseen, unknown;
Thus unlamented let me die;
Steal from the world and not a stone
Tell where I lie.

Doubtless, however, if we could look under the surface and read the inward feeling and sentiments of those people, we would find every one to have his share of losses, crosses and disappointments. Perfect contentment and peace of mind are to be found nowhere. One man or class of men who admire or envy the happy condition of others do so only through ignorance of what others have to bear. The principle of compensation equalizes all conditions, high or low. To understand this we must study Emerson's Philosophy of Equalization of Conditions, or Burns' story of "The Twa Dogs," which is still better.

Some of the characters to be met with in these regions are quite unique. In one family where we staid over night we found two who made a vivid impression—the grandmother and her bachelor brother. The old lady was exceedingly tall and rather graceful in her motions, with piercing dark eyes, evidently having been a fine looking woman in her prime, and was now verging on ninety. She was silent and observant; regarded by the family as rather in her dotage, but showing no other sign than the habit of bringing her chair up close in front of a stranger and sitting down looking intently in his face, as if about to commence a confidential conversation, but without uttering a word or paying any attention when addressed by the party so confronted. Seating herself in this manner before me or George, she would remain for a painful length of time as unmoved as a statue. It created an uneasy sensation, reminding one of some weird characters of the kind in Scott's novels. Two hundred years ago she would assuredly have been burned as a witch. Her brother was some three years younger, eighty-seven, perhaps, about six feet four inches in height, straight and exceedingly well proportioned for his years, and when in his prime had been a man of fine presence, but without much intellectual force. He was known in the country round about as the root doctor. Unlike his sister, he was communicative, and his conversation in some respects quite interesting, although delivered in fragmentary installments.

He had come with his parents from East Virginia some seventy-five years before; had lived in that neighborhood ever since, and practiced medicine for upwards of sixty years. His stories of the Indians, who

had not all left the country in his early days, and their habits and customs, were quite entertaining. He gave me descriptions of several prehistoric curiosities of the neighborhood which, if time had permitted, I
should have examined. He described an extensive wall, enclosing a
mountain top not far away, which was there when he first came to the
country and is there still: a regularly built wall of undressed stones
without mortar, as he described it, averaging six feet high, solid and
permanent; and concerning which the Indians, or any one else, had no
tradition, and in a location where no one could imagine its purpose.
He also described several Indian mounds, one of which I saw afterwards in a ravine on part of the Loope Creek estate. A settler had built
his chicken house upon it. It was considerable size, and would evidently cost a couple of months time of twenty or thirty laborers of our
day to construct, with the best tools and appliances in use, and so far
as I could learn it had never been opened or explored.

All through this country are wild mountains and glens more imposing in size and romantic in scenery than anything I have seen in Ireland, or the Highlands of Scotland. But these unfortunate hills and valleys are without legendary lore—too numerous and similar to each
other to be interesting. They may have had their bards and historians
to write them up, and if so it is well for the modern world their works
are lost, for it would take a common lifetime to read them if they did
justice to all. This, like other regions, doubtless had its great men and
history in the past which we know nothing about, and presumably as
famous too as that presented in the pages of Homer or Ossian. Nature
produces all heroes and great men of similar physical and mental faculties, with but slight variations; and the differences between them are
chiefly exaggerations existing rather in the poets and historians who
describe them, than in the individuals themselves. Who knows? Some
great Hector, Caesar or Washington may lie under this big mound of
earth. None of them has a more substantial monument than the
mound over this ancient hero, unknown to modern fame. Solomon
was wise regarding human greatness, and the vanity of fame and notoriety as well as riches. Now, and perhaps for thousands of years past, of
what value has been his fame or monumental mound to him or his descendants! Who are they, and where are they? But to return to the root
doctor.

His hobby was vegetable medicine. It had been his bread winner, and his constant recurrence to it made it difficult to extract information from him. You could never keep him off the subject for five minutes together, and he disclosed considerable ingenuity in getting back on to it in every story he related. He had a regular formula which intruded itself into each successive topic of conversation in this fashion: "Roots, plants, barks and gums are provided by nature with medicinal qualities when rightly mingled and applied, to cure all the ills that flesh is heir to." His conversation resembled somewhat the performance of a wheel revolving in machinery, with a broken cog causing a jar at regular intervals. The poor old gentleman's memory was too weak to keep him informed of having made the same observation a few minutes before.

On part of our way the next day we were accompanied by the county surveyor, an intelligent man well acquainted with the country. He piloted us to the top of Ford's Peak, which appeared to be considerably higher than any of the mountains surrounding it, and which we found far more formidable in the ascent than we had expected, when viewing it from a distance. We rode up the zigzag bridle path in Indian file for about two miles, and then dismounted, thinking it safer to walk and lead our horses. When arrived at the top, we found it more extensive than any mountain top we had been on, perhaps fifty or more acres of level land of fair quality, and strangely enough it had been appropriated and the timber cleared off, and for some time subjected to cultivation and human habitation. There was the dilapidated log cabin and stable, and some parts of the land yet fairly enclosed by fence, and well covered with pasturage, with an old, feeble horse as its sole occupant. Other parts, once cleared, had grown up again with brushwood; and around the cabin were still several apple and peach trees, carrying a better fruit crop than any we had seen on the lowlands. Our companion, the surveyor, was well acquainted with the former occupant, who maintained his position upon it for several years but finally gave it up as too stormy and uncomfortable, and entirely too inconvenient of access to the lower world. Although it could hardly be regarded as a mountain peak, yet the difference in the temperature at its base and on its top was remarkable. It was a sultry warm morning in June at the foot, but on the top the temperature was such that we had to keep our hands in our overcoat pockets, to avoid pain from the cold; and we found it was good advice we had taken to bring our heavy overcoats along. It was the first time I had ever seen rain sources. The day was showery, and from our position we could often see a rain cloud approaching and passing by below our level and the rain pouring from it on the land below. It resembled an island in the sea, or more exactly what it really was, a cloud viewed from a point above it, and it was very interesting to see the sun shining out of a clear sky whilst it passed along casting its shadow and rains on the green fields below, like a watering pot in the hands of a gardener. I did not learn the height of this peak, but I should take it to be higher than the backbone of the Allegheny at Gallitzin, as I never experienced so much difference in temperature at either Ebensburg or Cresson.

This excursion in the wilds of West Virginia was an exceedingly pleasant one to both of us, and George seemed much improved by it; but when he returned to his work of house building, and the heated term set in, loss of appetite and weakness returned. He was still reluctant to believe there was anything serious the matter, and unwilling to undergo a course of regular medical treatment. Such advice as he received from our local physicians was unsatisfactory and unavailing. He was advised to visit Bedford Springs, but in a few days found the water and climate there to be injurious; and was then advised to visit Berkeley Springs, but soon found that to be worse. Mineral water, with the damp mountain atmosphere, only aggravated his complaint. He at length became so much reduced in flesh and strength as to greatly distress me. And at this juncture Dr. Dunmeyer of Philadelphia, the brotherinlaw of my son Thomas, happened to make us a visit. On examination he informed us the disease was progressing toward the right lung and of quite a serious nature. This suddenly developed the fearful condition and impending danger, and alarmed me almost to consternation. Was the pain and sorrow of Selwyn's loss to be repeated? I could not bear to see so bright and valuable a life, so dear to me, and just merging into manhood, going down gradually but surely to the grave. It is hard enough for those who have borne the burdens of life past middle age, and have found out how little of unalloyed pleasure or happiness there is in it, to leave the world; but it is doubly hard for the young in the bloom of hope and ambition, and anticipating long years of pleasure here, to see themselves rapidly approaching a sure and certain end. I resolved at once on energetic action, and to leave nothing undone that money or skill might do to save him. Too much time had been lost already on vacillating theories and systems of medical treatment.

It was now early in September, and no further time was to be lost. My own opinion was that climate would be more efficacious than medicine; but our home doctors rather discouraged this, and I went with him immediately to Philadelphia in order to obtain the best medical advice of the profession there, and on our arrival called in our friend Dr. Dunmeyer and also Dr. De Costa, of the Medical College, who had a high reputation as a specialist in lung diseases. They confirmed our worst apprehensions: the upper part of the right lung was found to be already affected; but they hesitated regarding where he should go, or whether it was worth while for him to go anywhere else than home to linger and die. I staid by him and had him remain under their treatment for about three weeks, but found it was of no avail, and then took him South as a last resource, which happened to be the right thing after all, as to it we attribute his rescue. While there was life there was hope, and I desired to leave no stone unturned which might avert the dread result. When I determined on a change the doctors hesitated between the North and the South; but as the winter was coming on, and the northern climate known to be severe, George and I between ourselves concluded to try the South. We have discovered since that both climates are about the same in effect, equally good, both clear and dry, and favorable to the lungs. But as between the two, considering the time of the year and condition of the patient, we happened rightly to prefer the South.

About the middle of October, 1881, he and his mother and I, after a tedious journey in a sleeping car, as he was unable to sit up much of the time, found ourselves at Aiken, South Carolina, where he was placed under the medical care of Dr. Geddings, who is a man of deserved celebrity, a Southerner and a secessionist, of fine education professionally and otherwise. After deriving what benefit could be obtained from the medical schools of our own country he had studied for five years in the medical schools of Germany; then had been on the medical staff of Gen. Lee during the Rebellion, and afterwards selected Aiken, South Carolina, and established it as a sanitary point. He fully understood the climatic differences in all localities for sanitary purposes; and it happened well that we selected that point and him as the physician. He had little faith in the efficacy of medicine, and told me

that all it could do was to soothe and regulate the stomach and diges-
tive organs; that if they could be brought into healthy action it would
improve the quality of the blood, and pure blood would at least retard,
and perhaps prevent further progress of the disease in the lungs, and if
so the climate would cure the damage done. He privately gave me but
little encouragement, however. George's youth, he held, was not so favorable as I had thought it. The change from boyhood into manhood,
he said, was a dangerous period, and the fact that no hemorrhages had
hitherto occurred was not to be relied on as a favorable symptom; that
the form of the disease which produced no hemorrhage was often
more dangerous than that which did.

We all three remained at Aiken for six weeks, under very discouraging prospects. Those six weeks included about the most gloomy and
depressing period of my life, most of the time on the ragged edge of
despair. George had become so weak he could take little or no exercise;
even a ride in the carriage over the smooth roads about Aiken excited
the hectic fever. The doctor gave little hope; and strange enough, with
all the doctor's skill and experience and our desire to understand and
observe his directions, we were following a mistaken course. Doctors
and their patients should be careful to guard against such mistakes.
George and I had studied the nature of the disease, after we found out
what it was, pretty thoroughly ourselves. We had read the best authors
on the subject with close attention, and all we needed was practical experience to entitle either of us to a professional license in that particular department. Fresh air and vigorous exercise was strongly recommended in everything we read, as well as in the medical opinions we
had obtained from all the physicians we had consulted; and Dr. Geddings was particularly emphatic on this point. For pedestrianism or
horseback exercise George was evidently too weak, but carriage riding
was insisted on and we tried it persistently, but it invariably produced a
bad effect—a higher stage of the hectic fever and greater weakness followed it every time. I sought repeatedly for the doctor's explanation of
this, but he would not credit it, and insisted that the apparent bad
effects must result from some other cause. We tried the experiment so
often however, and the bad effect followed so invariably, that it led me
to call on the doctor privately for a fuller explanation. I thought we
might misunderstand each other in the language and terms used, and
asked him to explain his meaning of the term exercise; whether there

might not be certain conditions of the patient in which exercise, in the common acceptation of the term, would be injurious. And after a full consultation I discovered that the exercise must be proportioned to the strength and condition of the patient; that what might be exercise in one condition would be damaging fatigue in another. I concluded from this that the best test was its effects. To be beneficial, the doctor agreed it should produce exhilaration and a comfortable feeling afterwards, instead of fatigue and depression or increased feverishness.

This gave me the clew to the difficulty. Even the exertion of getting up and dressing in the morning seemed to produce lassitude and weariness. His fever had uniformly come on at ten o'clock each day, and after three or four hours left him in a weak and uncomfortable condition; and on the next day after this explanation we concluded to try what effect it would have for him to remain quietly in bed till after the hour of the fever's return. He did this, and to our agreeable surprise the fever did not return at all on that day, although he got up at one o'clock and dressed for dinner as usual. We followed the same course for three successive days with the same encouraging result; and in the early morning of the fourth day I left him to take the train for home, as I had some pressing business to attend to. It was with a sad heart and gloomy forebodings that I left him, supposing his relief to be but temporary, and expecting in a week or so to be recalled to witness his downward course to the end. But it turned out otherwise. After my return home reports continued favorable; and what was still more encouraging, he was gaining in weight and strength.

At the end of March he accompanied his mother on her way home as far as Ashville, N. C., where he remained for a few weeks, still improving and able to take full exercise daily by carriage or on horseback. He continued there until summer set in, when his physicians advised him to pass the hot weather at the White Mountains in New Hampshire, where he remained until unfavorable symptoms were manifested and a sea voyage was advised by his physicians, the incidents of which have particular reference to myself, and will be related in another chapter. I have gone into details regarding his case rather fully perhaps, but the great anxiety it produced furnishes the excuse. Business reverses or pecuniary losses sit lightly, compared with the feelings produced at seeing the life of one near and dear to the heart and affections in such jeopardy.

Chapter xx

Trip to Europe

THE MIND-PICTURE OF my childhood's home always appeared so fresh when recalled, that it often produced a desire to compare it with the original. Regarding scenery and localities I have found errors of memory when absent but a few years, and I was curious to know whether such was the case regarding Camp Hill and Kinkitt and their surroundings, from which I had been absent so long. Another circumstance increased my curiosity. In 1874 my son James with his wife on their tour in Europe, had visited these places at my request, of which I had furnished them a sketch and description. These they found surprisingly accurate; and the photographs of the Camp Hill and our house at its foot, and the river and church and surrounding scenery, which they procured to be taken and brought home with them, corresponded also in every particular with their images previously existing in my mind.

These circumstances, added to an emotional tenderness which I have ever felt for old places and old friends, led me to hope that at some future time I might have leisure and opportunity to see the originals of my early home scenery and mind pictures once again.

In the summer of 1882 this opportunity came, and so suddenly that on the third day after it occurred I was on board the good ship "Celtic" of the White Star line, bound for Queenstown.

My son George, who was in ill health at the time, as already related, was advised by his physicians to take a sea voyage, and it fell to me to accompany him. At four P.M. sharp, on Saturday, the 12th of August, 1882, at tap of the bell, our ship quietly and carefully drew herself back from the pier into the open river, and cautiously turned her head to the

East. There were wavings of handkerchiefs and many farewells, but none for us. Our departure was rather a surprise to ourselves and friends, and we could enjoy its incidents all the more in private. The quiet steady movement of the great ship picking her way out of the harbor, as if endowed with life and a dignified feeling of her own importance, and the apparently receding city of New York and shores of the bay, was an interesting sight.

The voyage out was quite pleasant, the sea all the time was smooth as a pond. Our only disappointment was the absence of sea sickness, which we had expected as a healthful renovation: for its supposed good effect my son's voyage had been prescribed. It was monotonous to sit all day on the deck and see nothing within the entire circle of view but dark, indigo blue water, with but one shade of variety,—the path of the ship, of light green, stretching away far behind.

Although we were in the established track between the continents, where I had expected to see other ships as frequently as vehicles on a public road, we did not see a vessel of any kind for several days; nothing but the solitary waste of water, excepting on the few but interesting occasions when some native of the deep put in an appearance. Twice we had the pleasure of admiring the great whale in his native element, spouting a puff of white spray into the air at regular intervals, like the discharge of steam from a locomotive, and as often some fifteen feet or so of his back would appear on the surface like a canoe turned bottom up. These, with occasional flocks of Mother Carey's Chickens flitting about the ship, comprised the sum of outside life attracting our attention.

On the ninth day out, August 21st, in the afternoon, we sighted the high and rugged shores of the Emerald Isle, not very emerald as viewed from the sea at a distance, but rather gray and bare; and here for the first time we met with a mild type of rough sea, very mild for the locality we were told, as it is mostly boisterous and dangerous, justifying the opinions of the Milesians of Spain in their first invasion, regarding the nature of the coast. But as if conscious of the power of science to propel and protect her, our ship moved proudly along the coast all the afternoon, with evident indifference to the power of the magicians who might be concealed in the threatening rocks. At eleven o'clock at night the pulse of the great engine stopped. We were in the quiet waters of the Cove of Cork. The lighter was soon alongside, ready to receive passengers for Queenstown on its elevated platform, and we were shortly afterwards landed on the pier. Here the excise officers went through our baggage with commendable alacrity and politeness. Only a slight inconvenience occurred from the unlucky desire on our part to give accurate information. The officer shoved aside a paper box in the bottom of the trunk, which we informed him contained nothing but my son's revolver. He looked surprised at our indiscretion, and took up the box, saying he was sorry but in the present condition of the country his orders were positive to seize all firearms. The only remedy for us was to go before a magistrate the next morning and declare our peaceable intentions, when a license would be granted and our pistol returned. This was no unreasonable condition.

Our next want was a hotel. The steward of the ship had assured us the Queen's Inn was the best, and it was but a few yards from the pier, to which our ordinary sized trunk and two satchels could easily be carried by a porter, but it was late and no porter about. Some Irishmen however, were around, with the smallest and most miserable looking donkeys I had ever seen between cart shafts. One of these was retained, and loaded our baggage, about sixty pounds in weight, on his cart. The lights at the pier and on the street were dim and far between, but I was once again in Old Ireland and moved off hopefully in solitary and rather ludicrous procession, for all others had disappeared from the scene. The Irishman walked in front, tugging and swearing at the donkey, and the donkey tugging at the cart; whilst we followed in the rear, all in the middle of the street, as the light was too dim to trust ourselves to the uncertainties of the sidewalk. The further we went the louder he shouted at the donkey. We soon found he had reason for anxiety, for the first depression in the pavement which the cart settled in put a stop to the procession. There was a regular stall. The scene was too ludicrous to be annoying; it made us laugh, although we were sleepy and wished to get to bed, as it was now after midnight. The hotel was but a few yards off, and we advised the man to take the trunk on his shoulder and we would take the satchels. The dignity of his profession would not allow him to stoop to that. He would continue to pull at the halter and shout and curse and kick the poor donkey; it is uncertain how long this performance might have continued if I had not interposed a peremptory protest, and directed him to leave the head of the donkey and go to the tail of the cart: when, with our assistance, both cart and donkey were pushed and guided to the front door of the hotel. Such was our fitting entry into the land of St. Patrick.

As soon as we got the baggage into the possession of the hotel porter on the pavement, we directed him to pay the man the regulation fare and put it in our bill; and then hurriedly withdrew inside and retired to bed as soon as possible, not however without hearing the rising notes of a contention between the porter and the donkey man regarding his charge. How long this contention continued we did not wait to learn, but went to sleep about one o'clock. It might have continued all night for it was the first noise I heard in the morning. The donkey man was still there, clamoring for more. The porter had paid him the legal fare, but he had returned in the morning to see the gentlemen themselves, as he declared that gentlemen always paid him more than the legal fare. I assured him that we were not gentlemen but only common American citizens; but this plea was scornfully rejected, he boldly insisting on our being gentlemen. This was a dilemma—to be, or not to be a gentleman was the question, and we handed over the additional shilling to have a rest. For what followed I may as well use my notes made at the time:

Tuesday, August 22d, 1882

Arose at seven, refreshed after a sound sleep. Came down stairs but found no one astir except the servants scrubbing the passages, and the porter and donkey man engaged in controversy about our baggage fare. After this was settled walked out to view the surroundings. The town is stuck on a steep hillside, resembling our Pittsburgh Southside, but not so extensive, and more stone used for building purposes. Grand bay in front with some war ships and other sea craft. Found a barber shop up stairs, not far from the inn: all barber shops here are up stairs. Whilst being shaved, I asked the barber what was the chief product of this part of Ireland. After suspending his razor a moment he replied, "Troth and its children for the most part, I believe." And from all I saw afterwards, here and at Cork and elsewhere in the south of Ireland, I am satisfied that the barber was right. Telegraphed home our arrival. Returned to the hotel, found more people astir, but very few guests. Asked when breakfast would be served: whenever ordered, was the reply, and the servant proposed to take my order at once. Tired of pastry and rich cookery on the ship, I ordered potatoes boiled with their skins on, mutton chops and coffee, all which was served in due time, as soon as cooked, together with excellent bread and butter.

And in this breakfast I recovered some lost knowledge, which was that Irish potatoes and American potatoes are very different. The Irish potato has a flavor and richness of taste not found in the best American article. When boiled, the skin bursts open—the flowery white substance of the potato bursting through the crevices, resembling a ball of pop-corn. The nearest approach we have to such potatoes in America is when raised in entirely new land, when the forest is first cleared away. The mutton also is greatly superior to ours in the fact of having no flavor of mutton about it whatever.

We were able to see all we cared to see in Queenstown in a short time, and ready to leave for Cork by the evening train. When paying our bill we included baggage transportation to the train, so as to have no more trouble on that score. This subjected us to the annoyance of seeing a poor cripple on his knees, born footless, pushing it to the station in a hand cart. Besides the distressing sight of course we had to satisfy his appeal for charity with as much as would have paid a baggage wagon or a hack for its conveyance; an able-bodied porter could not have appealed to our charity. Such was the ruse! The cripple was doubtless kept for the purpose. George was indignant at the meanness of the town in permitting such a distressing spectacle, and hoped a humane society might some day be established in Queenstown.

But we were soon aboard the train, experiencing the novelty of European railroad cars. Very comfortable and very well upholstered, but with interior arrangements just the same as might be made up by placing some twenty or thirty of our street railway cars on trucks, to be drawn sideways instead of endways. Four to six passengers on each side sitting face to face, the one side riding face forward, the other backward, with no water to drink, or water closet to retire to. The conductor is perched in some kind of caboose in front or behind the train, and embraces the opportunity when the train stops to run along, sticking his head in at the door of each compartment and calling for tickets. If occasion requires, he stops the train a mile or two before it reaches the station, to secure all the tickets. Altogether the train arrangements in this respect are inconvenient and cumbersome; but like the common law of England it is settled by custom, and therefore permanent.

At five o'clock in the evening we found ourselves at the Victoria

Hotel, in the city of Cork. All the first class hotels in this country are named for royalty in some shape or other. Here we find it different from Queenstown. The house is crowded with guests on account of the races, but we fare very well. It would be all pleasant enough but for the obtrusive impudence of the hackmen and Irish hoodlums about the street, especially in front of the hotels. If we look out of the door we are immediately beset with a boisterous and clamorous half dozen or so of carmen and hackmen, and as many others without hacks or cars, insisting on being employed to drive us around or as guides to show us the town. On this account we find it impossible to go about the streets in that unmolested freedom which is always most agreeable.

Wednesday morning we planned an escape from these obstructionists. From our chamber window we selected a cab in the crowd of those lining the street, and having paid our bill and given directions as to the disposition of our baggage, we made a rush from the hall to the street and mounted the selected cab to the surprise of the driver before he was aware of it or any of the others had time to intercept us. Once mounted and driven off, we could look about unmolested. We drove over the chief streets of the city, down by the quay, then at the driver's instance to a well celebrated for its holiness and for the curative qualities of its waters, resulting from its having slaked the thirst and received the blessing of a great saint of antiquity, whose name I have forgotten. But when we arrived at the spot we were disappointed and could get none of the holy water to slake our thirst, for a great stone covered the well, with a large cross cut upon it. This was the only indication of holiness visible, but was sufficient to cause our driver to make the sign of the cross with his hand on his breast. He informed us the stone had been placed on the well many years ago by the proprietor to prevent the people of the city and of other cities, who came there in crowds, from using the water, as he required it all for his brewery; and as the water carried its qualities with it into the beer, the beer had become so famous that its producer was made a millionaire. But he was dead now, "God bless him!" so we were informed. Thus it seems the trick of utilizing ignorance and superstition to obtain wealth and fame is not confined to the Irish political agitator and the American labor agitator exclusively.

Then, having occasion to visit a magistrate to obtain our pistol, left at Queenstown, we drove to the police court where it was said the

magistrates were in session. In our criminal courts at home I had seen
what I supposed was the lowest grade of civilized humanity; but here
was a class below anything I had ever seen before: a class of parties and
witnesses presenting as near as possible a perfect embodiment of arrogance, ignorance, filth and viciousness. Sometimes the atmosphere of
our own criminal court rooms in the large cities is rather unsavory;
but to equal the Cork court it would have to be well supplemented by
an unpleasant scent of stale fish.

We had now *done* Cork to the extent of our ambition, and stipulated
with our hackman to drive us to Blarney Castle, which he said was
about three miles distant. I should judge it is five or six. The country
scenery from the city to the castle was fine and enjoyable, worth seeing
at least once in a lifetime.

Here,

> By nature all is lovely,
> And only man is vile,

because the only thing that marred the beauty of the scenery were
some peculiarly constructed shanties by the roadside here and there,
with miserable and dirty looking women and children about them.
The explanation we got of these shanties was that they were kept on
hand readymade at Dublin, by the Land League; and whenever a family or tenant was evicted for the non-payment of rent one or more of
these shanties were sent out and occupied by the evicted tenants at
some spot in sight of the land from which they were evicted, mostly on
the side of the public road, but sometimes on the land of an adjoining
tenant who had not been evicted but was in sympathy with the Land
Leaguers. And the rule was that whilst the evicted tenant remained in
sight of his former home it was *boycotted:* no one dared to lease or occupy it, or even to crop the land from which he was evicted. If he did
so he was pretty sure to suffer for it in the death of his cattle and destruction of his crops; and very often he paid for his temerity by forfeit
of his life. These atrocities were never committed by the evicted tenant
or Land Leaguers of the neighborhood, but by emissaries from a distance, in order to evade detection. The appearance of the lands themselves showed desolation; and the accounts in the papers of that morning of two families having been slaughtered by the Fenians the night
before as suspected informers, gave ample evidence of the presence of

innate malice and depravity. To our surprise, when we expressed horror at such murders and outrages which our driver related, he seemed
not to take it in good part, and very clearly indicated his opinion that
death was the desert of any one who would take the place of an evicted
tenant.

We found this disposition prevalent in all the hack drivers and other
classes of the kind which we met with in that end of the island; and indeed the aversion seemed not to be confined to the amount of rent, but
to the payment of rent at all, or debts of any kind. The question most
frequently and anxiously asked us had reference to the aid which Ireland might expect from the United States in case of a rebellion. They
seem to have an abiding faith that the United States would sooner or
later send over an army to fight Ireland's battles and gain her independence. The information that it was only the more ignorant portion of
the Catholic Irish of the people of the United States who took much
interest in Irish politics, did not seem at all to please them. Here could
be seen massive ignorance of political possibilities and of the relations
and policy of nations, both at home and abroad; a large class trained in
vicious disregard of law and order, and educated to build all their
hopes and expectations on the coming of an impossible event—the independence of Ireland and its restoration to the Celts. Their ancient
hatred to the Orangemen or Protestants was manifest enough; and
these ignorant creatures who would kneel and make the sign of the
cross in presence of every holy object and never omit the observance of
the mass, would unhesitatingly cut the throats of Protestants or opponents of their pet theories of land tenure, and consider it no sin.

How this comes about can only be understood by a study of the
Irish history for ages past, showing that their religious and political
training by priest and demagogue has left them a legacy of hereditary
bigotry and prejudice which will take them many generations yet to get
rid of.

Arrived at the castle grounds, we were ushered through a gate in a
hedge and through a flock of geese and ducks into a small gate-house
or dwelling, where an old woman proposed the privilege of writing our
names in a book for a shilling apiece: a formality which she declared
she would not for all the world dispense with or give tickets for the
castle to anybody without. Whereupon, after walking a quarter of a
mile or so through a fine meadow and across the castle moat and

through the great gateway of the castle wall in a belt of trees, the celebrated Blarney Castle, in its dilapidated grandeur, stood before us. According to the best informed, it was built by the M'Carthies some six hundred years ago; evidently before the invention of firearms, because its construction shows no anticipation of such method of attack or defense. It was clearly intended as a fortress of defense against the arms and plans of attack then in use. In this view therefore, it affords a very interesting study; and I was greatly pleased with the opportunity to examine its different parts in this respect.

The roofs and floors and all wood work are entirely gone, the strong, thick stone walls alone remaining, and no one dwelling in or about the ruins; and in such a climate as this they may remain many hundreds of years longer if no other forces than the elements are applied. You can walk all around on the top of the wall of the main building at a height of some seventy to eighty feet. The wall there is about four feet in thickness, with a projection of two feet outward near the top, which looks like a cornice and rises to a height of perhaps five feet, with regular openings inside of this parapet wall looking down perpendicularly on the outside of the main wall; thus serving as a breastwork for archers, spearmen and slingers to assail an enemy approaching the castle on the outside, and by the downward opening to destroy, by molten lead or boiling water, an enemy attempting to make a breach. The traditional Blarney stone at one corner near the top, can be kissed without much danger or inconvenience, by all having a fancy for the amusement. The danger to those inclined to giddiness is in following the narrow path around the projections on top of the wall behind the parapet. The effort produces an uncomfortable sensation in a strong wind such as prevailed at the time of our visit. But few tourists forego the gratification, if we may judge from the narrow, beaten path in the grass: the climate here is so moist that grass grows even on the top of a dry stone wall, and shrubs spring from the cracks and crevices.

The whole affair rather resembles the standing walls of a public building after its destruction by fire. The stone work never was very fine, but certainly very strong, and the mortar seemingly as hard and tenacious as the stone itself. The traces of the different stories, one above the other, and their apartments, can easily be seen. The large stone fireplace, about ten feet square, with its projecting architraves, remains in a perfect state, where once was the great hall. If hearth enough remained a good fire of logs could be built in it at any time. The stairways are numerous, of rude stone placed within the walls and towers. Besides these, the donjon keep and subterranean passages afforded interesting subjects of contemplation which my limited time cut short.

George, whose health did not suit the raw cold wind on top of the walls, had left long before I did. But before getting off I was accosted by a woman who made her appearance from a concealed niche and demanded a shilling; she said her office was to show people over the castle. We had not seen her before nor had the benefit of her services, but I gave her the shilling, although the woman at the gatehouse had assured us there was nothing to pay at the castle. But on paying her the one shilling she forthwith demanded another for my friend who, she said, had left without paying her. I replied that in my country the people were too sharp to let any one off without paying; and if such a thing happened no one was silly enough to pay for another. I suspected, as I afterward found to be true, her demand was an imposition. She had stolen into the castle to spring her trap on an unwary tourist. The readiness with which she relinquished her claim for the second shilling betrayed her, because wherever the shadow of a claim exists these people stick to it with wonderful pertinacity. But I left Blarney Castle and its grounds highly gratified with my visit. When I rejoined George I found the castle woman had secured her shilling from him as well, notwithstanding her pretense to the contrary; and we then remembered to have seen her scouting over from the gate-house by a by-path toward the castle whilst we were there.

A visitor in this part of Ireland must expect imposition and importunate exactions and constant begging at every step. The importunity, and not the amount, constitutes a nuisance and discouragement to tourists; so much so that many, as we did, avoid visiting interesting spots on this account. After lunch at the restaurant near by, we drove to the nearest station on the road to Dublin, and dismissed our hackman with a fee for having kept his promise not to pester us with demands for more at the end of our journey than he had agreed to take for his whole day's services at the beginning, a promise which we saw was very hard for him to keep; and therefore we gave him the additional half crown for his fidelity and forbearance.

The train soon came along and we were off for Dublin at three o'clock, in a first class car—coaches they are called here. One or two first class coaches are attached to every train, and are patronized by Americans, plutocrats and native aristocrats. There was but one other passenger in the coach besides ourselves. He seemed an aristocrat or bloated bondholder; and if George and I had been highwaymen or Fenians, I can see how very easy it would have been for us in this kind of railroad car at night to have murdered and robbed and tumbled him out of the side door. So far as regarded detection, there was no one to disturb us until arriving in Dublin, where we could secrete ourselves in any of the hiding places there.

Our companion showed no sign of sociability, but he was in our power, and as we spared his life and purse he could have no reasonable objection to lesser intrusions; therefore I attacked him with all sorts of questions, with as much careless indifference as if he were an ordinary personage or an old acquaintance. The scenery, the state of the crops, and names and history of the places we passed through afforded ample material for the purpose. As soon however as he realized the fact that we were Yankees, he showed an interest and readiness to converse which I had not expected. Before our arrival in the city at ten o'clock in the evening we had become quite intimate, and he gave us his card and the name of the best hotel to stop at, inviting us to call on him if we had occasion for any information or assistance whilst in the city. I was curious to know who our new friend was, and showed his card to the clerk at the hotel, when we were informed that he was one of the wealthiest and foremost men of Dublin.

Thursday Morning, August 24th.

Up early at the Shelburn House, our third day in Ireland. It is midsummer here, so they say; their harvest is just beginning to ripen throughout the country, but so far we have found it comfortable to wear our heavy overcoats all day, and add them to our bed covering at night; and at Cork, as here, we found it further necessary to have fire in our room. An occasional misty, drizzly shower, with intervening glimpses of the brightest sunshine and the bluest sky you would see anywhere, except at Aiken, South Carolina, has been the order here so far. The Shelburn is really a fine hotel. It is peculiar in the magnificent dimensions of its rooms and departments. The stairways I should take to be about ten feet wide, with a conservatory of tropical plants and flowers and a fountain at each landing. And their halls and parlors are ornamented with many fine oil paintings; whilst the table and servants and other appurtenances are all that ought to be expected anywhere. Each guest orders his meals when and of what he pleases. There are no bullying roughs or importunate cab drivers about the doors, as at Cork. The police keep them quiet and orderly, and detail a cab or a coach for you as required. The fare is fixed by law, and no importunity for more allowed. After breakfast we were soon in one of those convenient machines called a hansom, rattling along the smooth street to and through Phoenix Park.[1] Our driver pointed out to us the spot where Cavendish and Burke fell, and the course taken by the car which drove rapidly away with the assassins.

Next we visited the famous Dublin Castle,[2] which, unless pointed out to him, a stranger would not take to be any other than an ordinary square of the city: buildings of nearly uniform height, surrounding a quadrangular court, and nothing imposing in the construction to distinguish them from other old-fashioned looking buildings elsewhere. We drove through an archway and past a forlorn looking sentinel into the open square which reminded us of our Arsenal buildings at Lawrenceville, only tamer and more contracted, and without the show of piles of cannon balls or other military display.

Next we visited the Old Parliament House, now occupied by the Bank of Ireland, although the room in which the lords sat, with its tapestry, is still kept undisturbed; and it was something to contemplate this apartment, which used to ring with the boisterous and abortive eloquence of the historic characters of the renowned Irish Parliament, a body which at all times contained more first class demagogues of the noisy but timid type, than any other legislative body of the same size in the civilized world.[3] And in driving away we paid our respects to the ostentatious monument to Daniel O'Connell, the prince of Irish agitators of his day, but neither the first nor the last of that line of characters of which Ireland has always had an abundant but unprofitable supply.[4] We had now seen as much of Dublin as we cared to see, and were ready to go elsewhere in the afternoon. But the climate, and especially the state of the weather was unsuitable to George's condition, and as his health was the object of our journey we consulted and decided to part, he to go south to London, and I northward towards my early home, which I felt a stronger desire than ever to behold again. Accordingly at two o'clock I was on the train for Omagh, County Tyrone.

It was a fine afternoon, and the scenery of richly cultivated fields and green meadows, with patches of black bog and brown heather and occasional glimpses of the sea, was quite enjoyable. The names of most of the places we passed were familiar and historic; at length we entered Tyrone, and when approaching the ancient town of Dongannon, I thought the small stream along which we were running might be the headwaters of the Strule, to me almost as sacred as the Ganges to a disciple of Brahma, and on inquiry I found that such was the fact.

We soon neared Omagh, my county town, but approached it from a side which I was unacquainted with; and in the dusk of the evening I recognized no objects until arrived at the White Hart Hotel, where the courthouse and jail, and main street stretching down the hill from them, at once broke on my view and revived the old but distinct memory of its appearance long ago.[5] I found the White Hart a very satisfactory stopping place, kept by a quiet, respectable, middle aged widow, and in many respects superior in accommodations to the best hotels in any of the neighboring county towns near Pittsburgh.

Friday, August 25th.

I was up and out early. The morning was fine, and this was the day of great expectation—a sight of my early home. I was all over the town before breakfast time, and saw the hinges and fragments of the identical trap platform, high up on the second story of the front of the jail, where, from the narrow door behind it and projecting beam above, hundreds of criminals had been hanged in the olden time when sheep thieves and like offenders suffered the death penalty more certainly than murderers do now. I remembered the horror with which I had regarded it when pointed out to me in childhood. Now it is disused since executions are limited and take place privately in the jail yard.

Breakfast over, a carman was soon secured to take me to the Camp Hill place in Lower Castletown, some three miles distant. It had been so long since I had seen that queer contrivance called a jaunting car that I feared I might be thrown off at the first rut or obstruction. I felt unsafe and applied to the driver to exchange seats with me—I preferred his seat, and to drive myself. But nothing would induce him to agree to what he considered so ridiculous a proposal. What would the people of Omagh think, he said, to see the gentleman driving, and the driver sitting back on the car in the gentleman's place! I assured him that I did not care what the people of Omagh thought; but he earnestly declared it would render him the butt of ridicule and might cause his discharge by his employer. And I soon found there was no great inconvenience, and not the slightest danger in my proper place. Irish roads are kept in a finer condition than to produce any inconvenience in that line. The jaunting car is a machine peculiar to Ireland. Imagine a low wheeled dray without slides behind, but a broad platform extending over the wheels, with sides reaching downward as low as the hubs, like a cart bed turned bottom upwards; and a foot board extending out from the lower edge of the inverted side, to rest the passenger's feet on. A box with a lid extends along the centre from the driver to the tail end; this contains horse feed and luggage. On the end of this box next the horse sits the driver, and the passengers are placed in two rows, back to back, and facing the road sides and leaning their backs against the central box. Its motions are abrupt and obey every movement of the horse, but it is the right thing in the right place. A stout horse on these smooth roads and easy grades can trot with rapidity with as many as can be piled on the car—over a dozen perhaps. Although without covering and unshapely, it is cheap and serviceable.

My directions were to drive through the forest of Lord Montjoy's domain, by Cappaigh Church, through Upper Castletown, down by the Cross Roads Meeting House and over Cappaigh Bridge on the Strule into Lower Castletown.[6] The driver signified compliance, but intimated that Lord Montjoy's forest and domain had disappeared many years ago; that two successive Lord Montjoys had been so profligate and extravagant as to sink the whole estate in gambling and riotous living, and it had been divided up and sold out under the Encumbered Estates Act; and the purchasers, as the first step of ownership, had cut and sold the timber and converted all the forest lands into farms. Here and there as we passed along, he pointed out a solitary tree or two as relics of the old forest.

We soon approached Cappaigh Episcopal Church.[7] I had never seen it, but had heard it so often mentioned by my parents that it seemed like a familiar object. A small neat stone building in a tidy little enclosure, with a well kept little graveyard attached—such is the ancient parish church of Cappaigh. I devoted a half hour to the old and curious inscriptions on some of the crowded tombs. Here lie the bones of many of those who had fallen in the indiscriminate slaughter of the Protestants by the Catholics over all this part of the country in the memorable rebellion of 1641. Then comes the Catholic Church but a short distance off, very much resembling the other only with the added convenience of an ale house near by. What a pity that selfish ambition and bigotry should ever have been able to engraft the spirit of intolerance on pure and simple Christianity as originally taught by its author! A feature of the present day is the fact that this unnatural spirit is dying out; but it is to be feared the decline of the graft is caused by the decline of the stock on which it is grafted. Perhaps like the other great religions which preceded it, and like Judaism which it superseded, present Christianity also will have but its time, and in the course of evolution will itself be superseded by another modified religion growing out of it to suit the progress of our race. I interviewed the priest for statistics. He was a jolly looking, stout man, with every disposition to be polite and obliging; but I soon found that local history or past events of a secular nature were not contained in the stores of his knowledge.

I next visited Upper Castletown, where I had a view of the old stone dwelling supposed to have been erected by my great ancestor, Archibald Mellon, after his arrival from Scotland; because he was the first who improved and occupied Upper Castletown after the massacre of 1641, but soon afterwards removed to Lower Castletown upon division of the townland between him and his partner, Jack Graham. It is a fine farm, and the descendants of the original Graham occupied it until quite lately, and the story of the last of them is a melancholy one. The late owner, like his ancestors, was thrifty and comparatively wealthy. He had but two children, sons, who aspired higher than farming, and he gave them a liberal education, after which they studied law in Omagh and were admitted to the bar there; but they turned out to be so worthless, extravagant and intemperate as to involve their father seriously in debt, and he was compelled to sell his property. Yet as a fair competence was still left for him in old age, he concluded to leave with his sons and remove them from the evil influence of their companions. They accordingly had emigrated to Australia a few years before, where the old man invested what was left from the wreck of his fortune, some five thousand pounds, in real estate. But no improvement was effected in the habits of the sons. The property was soon again encumbered, and taken from him by judicial sales, when he was left penniless and friendless in a strange land. His family a moral and physical wreck, the world now to him a dreary waste of blighted hopes, he ended his fears and sufferings together, by cutting his own throat. This sad tale I obtained from the present occupant of the place.

I looked around over the nice farm, its well planned hedges and ditches, its beautiful little mill pond and grist mill, and numerous out houses indicative of an industrious and careful proprietor, and was told it was all, or chiefly all, the work of the last of the Grahams. How illusory are human hopes, and how soon the places which know us so well, shall know us no more forever! With these reflections, I was soon rattling briskly along between the beautiful thorn hedges towards a place which to me was of far greater interest, as early thoughts of long ago clustered about it, and I still had a very clear image of it in my mind, the Cross Roads Meeting House.[8] This was the Presbyterian representative of religious houses of worship in the neighborhood, and the altar where my ancestors had worshiped for many generations: in the United States we would call it the Presbyterian Church, but here they have, or did have in my early days, too great an antipathy to popery to use any term in common use among the Catholics or Episcopalians, semi-Catholics, as the Presbyterians regard the latter. They avoid the term church, and call all their places of worship meeting houses; and avoid spires and Gothic arches, which they look upon as devices for the ornamentation of the scarlet woman of Revelation: at least such was the feeling of Presbyterians in this neighborhood some sixty years ago, but this feeling is considerably toned down now. The thinkers and far sighted leaders of all sects are beginning to perceive that the Protestant Reformation was but a rationalistic movement at bottom, and if its democratic principles of self-government and individual private judgment were carried to their logical results, it would lead to the destruction of all power of the clergy over the minds of men. They perceive that, apart from the truth or falsity of doctrine, the Catholic system of church government is the most effective that has ever been devised for the maintenance of sacerdotal power and the procurement of money for religious purposes. Hence it is we see a tendency, unconsciously perhaps, in all branches of Protestantism to retrace their steps and get back into the original fold. It manifests itself in ritualism, in church architecture and religious literature everywhere. Episcopalians are already ripe to enter if the doors were opened by the mother church; Episcopal Methodists are not so far advanced, but ready to take the place of the Episcopalians; and the Presbyterians, though as yet more conservative, show a leaning towards present Episcopalianism of the Methodist type. All in all, admiration of the dignity and power of the Catholic priesthood is at the bottom of it.

But now the old meeting house shows itself through the trees. Here I had been with my parents on two or three Sundays, impatiently sitting still under the sound of tediously long sermons, of course meaningless to a five year old child as I was. But alighted from our car and our horse secured, I am now before the sacred edifice itself.

Here it is! The same long, low stone building in shape of a "T," and roofed with straw thatch, just as I remember to have seen it sixty-four years ago. And there too is standing the same little study, in the corner of the square yard in the middle of which stands the church proper—the study building much resembling our American spring house. I remembered an occasion when, before the service commenced, my father had led me by the hand around the church among the waiting people, and showed me the preacher through the little window, sitting in his study all alone; and of his telling me that Mr. McClintock was in there studying his sermon. I knew very well from former experience what a sermon was, and remember wondering at the time how it could be that sitting in there for a time would have the effect to make him talk so long and so loud up in the pulpit. But the church looks very old and dilapidated and is evidently in bad repair. The reason of this, as I soon learned from my driver, was that it had not been used for many years. A new and finer church building had been erected, which was pointed out in a pleasant location at a short distance across the road. But the new building had no charms for me; it was to this venerable old structure that my associations and sympathies belonged. I approached one of the doors—there is a door in the end of each wing and one in the end of the main trunk. The door was not securely fastened and was easily pushed open sufficiently for admittance. I walked up the silent and gloomy aisle to the pew where I had sat, as near as my memory would serve me. There it was, a square box with a hinged door, a narrow board seat and very high back. I well remembered that the backs of the pews were so much higher than my head that I could not see over. And there too, about half way up on the opposite wall, still remained the little round pulpit with a sounding board some six or eight feet above it, the pulpit much resembling a pitcher, and the sounding board a suspended lid. Eight extremely narrow winding steps led up to a slit in the pitcher at one side, which afforded entrance to this sacred desk of the place. And I remembered inquiring on our way home whether Mr. McClintock could speak like other people if he wished to, or always spoke so loud and cross when at home with his children.

I found my long preserved memory of the place to be entirely correct. But where now was the preacher and his large congregation there assembled on the days to which my memory related? Perhaps only one or two more than myself who were present then are yet in the land of the living. But the preacher of the Cross Roads Meeting House of today is as vigorous, and the congregation as numerous and as earnestly intent on spiritual and temporal affairs as ever. Such is the stream of humanity!

The floor was flagstone, and the pews and pulpit of hand-worked deal boards, a species of yellow pine, yet without paint and still in a good state of preservation. "Why was the old church not pulled down and its materials used in constructing the new one?" I asked the carman. "Oh," he replied, "they never pull down so old a church building as this. They regard it as sacred." I thought to myself, we have not so much respect for antiquities at home, but it is a pleasant and commendable feature of public sentiment. I afterwards visited the old Church Alloway, of Tam O'Shanter memory; and undoubtedly the old Cross Roads Meeting House near the banks of the beautiful Strule, among its trees and in its present dilapidated and uncared for condition, would be a much more fitting place for a dance of witches than Alloway. After leaving the old meeting house we crossed Cappaigh Bridge, where the Strule in all its gentle beauty opens on the view.[9] I had to dismount here and do homage to both bridge and river; both were household words with my parents and grandparents; so much so that they seemed to me like very dear old friends. The bridge is a very ancient stone structure of some ten arches, in an excellent state of preservation. One of the oldest main roads leading from one end of the island to the other, from Dublin to Derry, crosses the river by this bridge, which for generations was the entrance of my ancestors to the forests and pleasure grounds of the beautiful and extensive domain of Lord Montjoy. All along the banks of this delightful stream my ancestors had indulged in the exciting sport of landing the lively trout and vigorous salmon. Many were the exploits with fly and fishhook here, which I had heard related by my father and my uncles. The stream is renowned for abundance of these kinds of fish, as well as for mussel shells containing pearls. I gazed on the river and its beautiful scenery with tender emotions, and could not leave it until I took a walk of several hundred yards along its grassy banks, and dipped and drank of its water with my hands.

After remounting it was but a short distance till we crossed the railroad and were in sight of the place to me the dearest of all—the Camp Hill with our cottage at its foot. Here it lay before me with the river on one side and the heathery turf bog on the other. Through this bog passes the highway between Dublin and Derry, already mentioned, and the railway also, constructed since we left. A strip of fine farm land lying between this turf bog or moorland and the river is what chiefly constitutes Lower Castletown. There I found it all as I had left it so long ago, and just as I still remembered it, with no apparent change whatever. The face of the country and the buildings in the rural districts here are subject to but little change from generation to generation. We drove into the yard in front of the house unceremoniously, where I alighted and directed my driver to unhitch and feed his horse with as much confidence as if the place was my own, and evidently to the surprise of the woman of the house, who was standing in the door.

I introduced myself as having lived there over sixty years ago, and now desired to look over the old house and place; and further explained that I should be greatly obliged, besides compensating her, if she would get us something to eat, to which she cheerfully assented, proposing to send for her husband to show me around. This I declined, I needed no guide; I was at home again, and preferred to be left alone with my thoughts. My heart was full. There was no spot on the place or its surroundings which I did not remember and know where to find. The croft, the river brae with its bright spring well under the holly bush, the holm with its beautiful whin and broom, where the dog and I had so often hunted water rats, and the river at the foot with the turn hole in it below: all were there in their places as accurately as the Camp Hill cottage itself, with the stable and the small orchard beyond the *flush*. I was soon over and around them all, after which Mrs. Steel, the wife of the present owner, had our luncheon ready: good wheat bread, nice fresh butter and milk, and tea, with fried ham and eggs, all as palatable to a hungry traveler as anything I had met with in the great Shelburn Hotel at Dublin. I sat down to this delectable meal in the same spot where I had sat at our meals long before; the same apartment with the same window and door at which I had such an unpleasant adventure with the dog. And there was the great open fireplace, no jambs to it on either side: just a rude stone pilaster protruding a few inches from the wall like a door casing; and the chimney projected from the wall about six feet above the hearth, and wide enough and extending out into the room far enough, like a funnel, to receive all the smoke which might arise from the fire. There was the hearth where I used to stir the fire of nights to afford light to my father to read to my mother from the *American Gazetteer* the glowing accounts of the richness and abundance of the lands, and the liberty and freedom of the people from taxation and rents, in the United States. It was all again before me like a vision of the past. Mrs. Steel assured me that the roof tree and *wattles* sustaining the thatch were the same as when we left the house; that no change in that respect had been made. No other repairs than renewing the thatch and clipping the eaves had been done.

When through with our luncheon I examined the bed room and the niche in the back wall, called there an outset, where my bed had been, and still containing a child's bed. Indeed, the dwelling houses of small farms in the north of Ireland and in Scotland are all alike: a low, one-story stone building about thirty-six feet long by eighteen feet wide, with chimney in one end, seldom in each end, and two windows and a door in front, with two windows in the back, and the house divided into two apartments by a partition. Among the Scotch the apartment containing the fireplace and outside door is called the but; the other apartment the ben. I found afterwards, when I visited Burns' cottage at Ayr, where he was born, that it and ours at the Camp Hill were almost exact duplicates of each other; and the picture of our Camp Hill cottage, which I have inserted elsewhere, affords a good likeness of the Burns cottage also. After going all over the place a second time with Mr. Steel, who had come in, I found nothing wanting from what it had been in my day, except the bright spring well on the river brae, which he told me he had drained off into the neighboring ditch when he improved the land below it. I then visited my grandfather's old place down the lane, passing the cottage where I used to have the desperate conflicts with the irate ganders. But the former occupants of the cottage, as well as the ganders, were all dead and gone, and new generations in their place. I soon found the ruins of my grandfather's house with his initials cut in the stone which had been the lintel above the door. The present owner had built a new house near by resembling the old, but had left the ruins of the latter undisturbed. I remembered the situation well, and Tatinure Wood, which lay across the river beyond it—it was all familiar. And here too was Mark Mellon's house still standing on his little farm which lay between our place and that of my grandfather. Mark's descendants are in West Philadelphia now. The features of inanimate nature remain long the same; only life is transitory. Not one of our name, and not one of the name of those who were our immediate neighbors, is now found in Castletown. But I found elsewhere in the neighborhood one old man of our name and connexion, poor and obscure; and after a pleasant interview, and gladdening his heart with a gold piece, I left him and met his son the next day in Omagh, an industrious laboring man of good habits, who was anxious to obtain my opinion as to the advisability of emigrating to America. When I learned that he had regular and healthy employment and his wife a fair share of custom as a dressmaker, and besides that he received a small salary from a Presbyterian church of the place as janitor: taking all things into consideration, I could not see that his chances would be improved or condition bettered by coming to this country. So I advised him to wait and see what his children might incline to; and when they grew up it might then become advisable to afford them a wider field and better opportunities to rise in the world.

I had now examined all and every part of the place and its surroundings, and after leaving my friend, the old man, it but remained to take a last parting view of my early home with its familiar objects, and tear myself away. It was growing late in the evening, and the scene beautiful. I took a look of last farewell at it all as we passed again over Cappaigh bridge, and out of sight forever. Before coming I had supposed I should want to stay or return here for several days; but I am satisfied: what more could I see or know if I returned again? So farewell to the home of my childhood. Adieu to the reality of its beautiful presence, but its sweet memory will remain to the last!

There is a soft beauty and freshness of verdure about the scenery in this country throughout all the summer season which is only approximated with us in May and June. Its rivers and streams glide through green meadows and grassy banks everywhere; and the water never gets so low or so high as with us. The ease and frequency with which it rains here all the year round prevents the low water of drouths such as our summers produce, and prevents also the thunder storms and rain gusts, and heavy floods of muddy water which we are subjected to. But the water looks dark, which appearance it acquires from the turf bogs, imparting a dark color to the channel. Although in the channel it looks dark, it is clear and transparent when taken up in a glass. The Camp Hill is nothing more than a good sized knoll, well situate between the river and the bog for a fortification or place of defense, and was so used in time of the Danish invasions and received its name from that circumstance. Some vestiges of the ruins of the camp still remained in my great grandfather's day, and there were many legends of hidden treasures connected with it, but none ever discovered. Our cottage was built at its foot on the southwest side, and nothing whatever had been done to change the appearance of the cottage or its surroundings since 1818, when I left it, except removing a few feet of earth from the foot of the hill in its rear.

Bessybell Mountain, about two miles distant, is the only elevation in sight approaching a large hill, differing from our hills in being spread out more; the distance from the bottom to its broad heather-covered top is nearly two miles of a slope, such as might be formed out of a rounded section of our Chestnut Ridge.[10] I well remembered the great pleasure I enjoyed in a pleasant Sunday walk with my parents from our place to its top, where we saw the curious cairn of stones of a kind not to be found about the place, supposed to have been collected there by the Druids for some religious rites; but more probably placed over the grave of some chief of a clan, or other great man. Greatness is a relative term, and evanescent in all conditions. The rough stones remain, but what of the Druids or the chief?

Saturday Morning, August 26th.

On the return to Omagh I met with a new sight which revived an old memory. The long main street was full of people. This happened to be the fair day and they had come to town to do their marketing.

"Chapman billies," that is, peddlers, were auctioning their goods from barrel heads; selling clothing, tinware, crockery and all manner of notions, each according to his specialty. Then, in other places, were long rows of carts loaded with turfs for fuel. Turfs are cut out of the peat bog and dried in shape and size of bricks, but light in weight, and black. Here were women peddling brooms made of heather; and indeed all manner of goods and farm produce was exposed for sale along the curbstones on either side of the street. I had three hours yet until the train would leave, and spent it with much satisfaction among the people, studying their manners and customs. Here were all classes from town and country intermingled; and I must say, that in behavior and general appearance they compared favorably with a crowd similarly collected in Pennsylvania. There was more communicativeness; conversation seemed to commence spontaneously, whether the parties were acquainted or not, but always quiet and respectful, nothing loud or boisterous or calculated to breed excitement and disturbance; and, whilst their whiskey is cheap and drinking places numerous, I saw no indications of its influence on any of the crowd. There was nothing in the conduct of any one requiring the attention of police. It was easy to see that the common people here are different in spirit and character from the same class in Queenstown or Cork or Dublin. Standing at the courthouse steps at top of the street, I could look down over the long dark stream of humanity, seemingly the same I had viewed from the same spot when lifted in my father's arms to see it, on a market day long ago. But now I must make the train and bid farewell to Omagh, its White Hart Hotel and its fair. The train soon stops at Newtonstewart, a little town a few miles below, but I have no time to stop off and little interest in any association of ideas connected with the place. But a few miles further and Victoria Bridge Station is arrived at, where I leave the train and soon obtain a boy with a jaunting car to take me to Kinkitt, about two miles west of the station.

Does he know the road to Kinkitt? "Sure he does." Does he know Samuel Wauchob of that place? "Oh! sure everybody here knows Mr. Wauchob; he is very rich." So we were soon on the Derg road to Kinkitt; a good road, but longer to Kinkitt than I had expected. At the end of two miles or so we left the Derg road and turned up the county road to the right towards Strabane. After a long stretch of up grade the top of the hill was reached, and just on the other side, as if in a dish, the townland of Kinkitt lay before me.

This had been my last abode where I had spent a few weeks before leaving for America. The scenery around it had faded out of my memory, but not the place itself. The house was not the same, for my uncle Joseph Wauchob's family had built a larger and finer one since; but all the locality and spot where the old house had stood was readily recognized, and as plain as ever.

On making myself known I met with a kind reception. My cousin is about my own age, a tall man, but not in very robust health; as tall but not as robust as my cousin Mathew. Everything about the place and the family is indicative of industry, intelligence, thrift and comfort. After a substantial supper I went to rest in a remarkably pleasant and well furnished bedroom, as fine indeed as the spare room of the average wealthy citizen about Pittsburgh. I woke refreshed the next morning at my usual time, a little before six. The sun was rising with a peculiar sort of brightness, such a brightness as at home would suggest the approach of an uncomfortably warm day; but the soft freshness of the lovely verdure everywhere indicated that a scorching day never accompanies bright sunshine here. Just now at home, grass and foliage are parched, and assume a hardened look of darker green.

No one was astir in the house, but such a morning, and such beauty in nature, was too precious to neglect. I quietly made my way out, and enjoyed one of the pleasantest rambles on the neighboring hillsides which has fallen to my lot in a lifetime. All the places round about were connected with stories of domestic history often related by my mother, and highly interesting to me when I was of an age to enjoy romance; and I could easily recognize the different places by the recollection of her oft repeated descriptions. A map of the whole neighborhood had thus been permanently traced on my memory. I could distinguish them all: hill and dale, mountain and moorland, and remember their names and the legends connected with them. All were familiar as the scenery of fairy tales in memory and story; and the beauty and interest of the scene delayed my return to the house till nearly ten o'clock, where the family were anxiously waiting and wondering at my absence. The protracted morning walk over ditches and turf holes and through hedges had left me in a dilapidated condition, both as to strength and clothing. But a good breakfast and my cousin Rebecca's handy needle soon put all to rights again.

But the day was too fine to stay within doors, and with my cousin's son James as an escort I set out again, and soon made the top of Whiskey Hill, an extensive elevation in the neighborhood, nearly as high as Bessybell, with its broad top covered with turf-bog and heather, like its neighbors; and here I investigated the nature and growth of bog. It exists extensively throughout this country and Scotland, and is found to cover the tops of most of the high hills and to spread over much of the low wet lands, wherever they are cold and sour. I should think it comprises nearly a fourth part of the entire country. It is deepest and best for fuel in the low lands or hollows, and is also mostly deep enough to be cut and utilized for fuel wherever it exists on higher grounds. Its thickness varies from three and four to twenty feet and upwards, though not over about five feet in depth is cut out at once; and after the surface is gone over in this manner, another stratum can be taken off, and so on till the bottom is reached, if the drainage is practicable. It seems to be a product of the climate and grows again after its removal, if left undisturbed. It is estimated that it grows at the rate of about one foot in one hundred years. The locality where it has been cut and removed for fuel resembles the neighborhood of our brick yards where brick clay has been excavated. Spades with a flange on one side are used for cutting it. The laborers seem as if engaged in trenching, sinking their spades into the soft, black, soap-like substance, and laying each spadeful on the bank beside them, from which it is taken by off-bearers to a place exposed to the sun, where it dries like sun-dried bricks. These trenches are cut from four to six feet wide, a convenient width to lay the turf by the spade upon the margin on either side. On their fresh cut sides the nature of the growth or formation of the bog is plain to be seen. Whether on hill or valley, it is always wet and spongy. Uppermost on the surface is found the heather, a small shrub resembling our whortleberry, only more slender and finer in stem and branches, and attaining an average growth of about eighteen inches.

The heather is renowned for its beauty in song and story, both in Ireland and Scotland. Its beauty can be seen only when viewed at a short distance, because further off it renders the tops of the hills, and other localities where it exists, of a dark bronze color; but when approached closely at the right season it is found to cover the surface of the ground as a mat, and its slender sprays, provided throughout their lengths with closely inserted tiny purple flowers, produce a scene of loveliness which must be seen to be appreciated. In the sunshine the scene is enlivened and its beauty heightened by swarms of wild and tame bees and other insects reveling in its sweets. Such was its condition on this fine Sunday morning.

Among the stalks, between the surface of the ground and the branches of the heather, is a closely packed growth of a plant resembling moss. This moss is in threads or stems, and forms a compact matting six to eight inches in thickness, under the branches of the heather, and as the threads or stems stand up straight and close together, the water rises among them by capillary attraction and is held as in a sponge. This moss is of annual growth, and its decayed crop makes a layer every year out of which the new crop springs. On the face of the ditch newly cut for turf I could see the gradual conversion of this moss into bog or peat, becoming darker and solider for a distance of from fifteen to eighteen inches from the surface, until it presents a sticky, black, soap-like substance, which is the pure peat used for fuel. Wherever the water is insufficient to afford the necessary moisture the peat is not perfected or utilized. So much for the native fuel, which appears inexhaustible. If this island should sink below the sea level, and deposits of mud accumulate on these peat bogs, petrifying into rock one after another, and the island be elevated again, these peat bogs might afford the inhabitants of a few million years hence some fine coal fields.

But having explored the peat bogs on Whiskey Hill and the patches of ground reclaimed where the peat had been cut off to the bottom or surface of the earth and restored in many places by lime and manure and drainage to a state of cultivation, my guide and I made our way to Concess, the residence of Miss Isabella McFarland and my cousin, John Wauchob. John and Elinor, her mother, were two of my playmates for the few weeks I was here before we left for America; and I remembered them well, even to the spots on her calico dress. But John is an old man now, two years my senior. I have already mentioned the marriage of Elinor with Robert McFarland and their death. Isabella, the only child and heir, owns a good farm here and is otherwise well off, and her old uncle manages her property. We spent a few hours with them in their pleasant home, surrounded with flowers and shrubbery. Here I first saw and heard the European robin red breast, different altogether in song and size from the bird we know by that name in America. The growth of flowers and shrubs in this country is finer than with us; pansies in the borders of flower beds looked like butterflies. But the growth of the forest trees, such as the fir or pine, and ash and other woods, do not seem as luxuriant as with us. We are home again for dinner at three o'clock, served in as good style as at any hotel, after which the fatigue of the morning prevented any more extended excursions, and the remainder of the day was spent in conversation with the family.

This was to me a memorable Sunday—one of the few gala days of a lifetime, which can never be forgotten; a feast of soul and sense upon the realities which had before been so cherished in imagination. We sat late in pleasant converse of the past. The only drawback to my pleasure was the sad reflection that now there was no one living to enjoy what I could tell of the old persons and places when I returned home. My father and mother, and all who would take delight or care to know what I had seen and heard at Castletown and Kinkitt, which afforded me such pleasure, and which would have afforded them still keener pleasure to hear of, were now dead and gone. I had remained away from the scene too long!

Monday morning early, August 28th, after many earnest adieus to my kind friends, the family conveyance, the traditional jaunting car, one of the neatest construction I had seen, was brought into requisition, and Victoria [Bridge] Station was reached in good time for the train, although on our way down we experienced the heaviest rainfall I had yet met with. What Irish raindrops lack in size they make up in numbers. It comes on so readily and so often, without any effort or warning, that rain here appears to be regulated differently than with us. There is such bluster and exertion and thunder and lightning and wind in our system, the liquid is jumbled together in larger drops. With us the rain seems to come through trouble and difficulty; but here it comes with all ease. A gray cloud may be over your head, drenching you effectually as with the tiniest spray, when the clearest blue sky and beautiful sunshine is in view everywhere else. This is the secret of the soft freshness and beauty of the verdure which very appropriately gives to this country the name of the Emerald Isle.

I am soon safe from the rain however in the comfortable railway coach, and rolling past the great Sion Mills or linen factories, a few miles below Victoria Bridge on the Strule. Next we pass the ancient town of Strabane, and our little river soon widens at its reception of the tide water into Loch Foyle. As the train passed down from Victoria Bridge to Derry on the west side of the Strule, I could see the road on the east side by which we went to Derry on our way to America; and when in sight of Derry I could see the bridge over which we crossed from the east side of the river into the city, on that occasion. On leaving the train and securing a luncheon at the Jura Hotel, I set out for the old walled town of historical celebrity.[11] I knew the direction to find Bishops gate in the city wall near which we had lodged long ago, and had not far to go till it appeared in view. I remembered it well and that an old woman sat beside it at a stall selling penny's worth of the nutritious sea weed called *dulce,* and candies. And there now was the gate all the same as I had left it; and sure enough an old woman, the counterpart of the one I had left there sixty-four years ago, and with the very same kind of stand and merchandise. After buying and tasting some of her wares, in memory of former transactions of the same kind at her stand when with me half pennies were scarce, I sought and mounted the stone steps to the top of the wall, which I again traversed as when a little boy led by the hand of my father, feeling very much the same as then, only my thoughts now were tempered more with sadness. I could still remember the cannon and other important objects. I made my way around the entire wall, stopping and inspecting each old gun and the date of its manufacture. Here they remain and are kept in reasonably good condition; but still time has produced heavy pock-marks upon them, notwithstanding the repeated coats of paint. They are in their positions to rake an enemy and protect the ramparts, just as in the time of the memorable siege; and to all appearance Roaring Meg and her sisters could open fire and do good service on an enemy yet. She would have to be elevated considerably however, or would play havoc on the surrounding buildings; because more of Derry is now outside than inside the walls. Captain John Walker, a stubborn Presbyterian preacher and indomitable fighter who commanded the besieged, still keeps one hand on the open Bible whilst he grasps a sword with the other, on the summit of his tower: a shining example of the former force of religious opinion.

The wall is about twenty feet high and a little over forty feet wide on top, with parapets or breastworks on each side. Its circuit can be made at an easy walk in an hour and a half. After making the circuit and descending from the wall, I obtained admission into the ancient Cathedral of Derry and made my way up into the steeple, where hang the celebrated old Joy Bells of Derry, whose chimes, morning and evening, had so delighted me when a child during our stay in the town. Ten of these are the same which were presented to the cathedral by King Charles; two are of the same metal, but were smashed by a cannon ball during the siege and recast afterwards.

From the balcony of the steeple I had a splendid view of the city inside and outside the walls, and of the Loch and surrounding country. On leaving the church, old memories were again aroused by strains of music produced by a blind man on the streets. The air came to me like an old friend long absent; easily recognized but the name forgotten. From the child in whose plate I put a few pennies I learned the air was "Derry Walls Away." Produced as this blind man produced it on his pipe, no music that I have ever heard could excel it in exciting the passions or putting "life and metal in the heels" of those inclined to dance. Those old Irish and Scotch airs have their origin in the wild depths of human feeling, and are eloquent of the history and sentiments of their time.

But I had now seen all I cared to see of Derry; indeed, all I cared to see of Ireland. I had seen again the places and people near and dear to me as old friends, around whom my early memories clustered. All else were unrelated to me, and strangers: so at three o'clock I was again on the train for Belfast. Many objects along the road were quite interesting; at one point I could see from the car one of those remarkable round stone towers whose origin and purpose is entirely unknown, their construction dating beyond the period of either history or reliable tradition. What can be said regarding them is imaginary and inferential. Several of them, similar in size and structure, are scattered over the country. But we now approach Bunker Hill for which our Boston Bunker Hill was named; then arrive in Belfast, the first city I had met with so far of such regular squares and wide streets.

Tuesday morning, August 29th, got up early to explore Belfast, and had a drive of several miles in an open cab before breakfast. The result of the flax growth of the country centres here in the linen trade, and is apparently productive of great wealth, judging by the fine blocks of buildings and the reputed capital engaged in it. Irish cities do not equal our American cities in height of the buildings or elegance of display of open fronts. I rode through the chief parts of this city during the day, and was now ready to leave it. To me there is very little variety in the general aspect of cities, and one build of city is pretty much the same as another; and as to the population of Omagh, Derry and Belfast, I find very little difference between the English speaking people here and those of Pittsburgh.

The boat moves out for Glasgow at eight o'clock. By nine we are clear of the bay and getting out to sea, and we go to bed. The stateroom is rather diminutive for four occupants, but conveniently arranged, two on each side, one above the other and about two feet between the berths. I had gotten into the lower berth and gone to sleep, but was soon awakened and would then have preferred an upper one. The boat was pitching and rocking in all directions, and the man above me and the one opposite seemed to have a contest between them in the upheaval business; and more space and better ventilation would have been pleasanter. But after they became quiet I slept again till daybreak, then got out to view the shores of Scotland and the Clyde. The entrance was at first broad and magnificent, but soon began to contract till it became so narrow as to leave very little spare room between boats when passing; and for a very considerable distance below Glasgow it is walled up on either side, and kept dredged out at great expense, to allow the ingress and egress of ships. Nearly all the way both banks are covered with ship yards; the din of the sledge hammers on the rivets is deafening and indicates an immense business, and the wealth manifest at Glasgow shows it. We breakfast on board the boat and at eight land on the pier.

Wednesday morning, August 30th, St. Enoch's Station is in sight a few blocks off. I hand my satchel to a boy, and when deposited at the station found in him another pest equal to any of those across the channel. One shilling was entirely unsatisfactory and unacceptable, although sixpence was the regular fare; but I finally got rid of him for eighteen pence just in time to get a ticket for the town of Ayr. I did not notice the right window to get my ticket at, and when showing it at the entrance the conductor referred me to a second class car; this explained the exceedingly low fare for a forty mile ride. I found it an improvement however, on my previous car traveling experience: no dif-

ference or inferiority in the car itself and more lively, being pretty well
filled with as respectable looking people as are met with on an American train. Sitting face to face is more conducive to conversation, and
less reserve is maintained among the passengers than with us. Among
them was a merchant, a minister, and their families and some ladies, *en
route* for the different watering places on the coast, chiefly Trune, and
general conversation soon sprung up. One lady passenger beside me
was quite obliging in giving me the name and history of the different
objects and places which we passed. She was evidently educated, and
refined in manner, and her dress indicated good society. She was "gaun
doon ta Trune," she said, to rejoin her family, which had been there
bathing for a couple of weeks. It is novel to converse with the intelligent, well educated Scotch, and find that they, equally with the lower
class, retain the Scotch or Doric dialect and accent. It rather surprised
me that people should feel any disposition to bathe in this country
where I found my heavy overcoat indispensable to comfort even in the
car; but she said it was nice, for it was warmer in the water than "oot."
I told her I was on a pilgrimage to the birthplace of Burns, and wished
to pay my respects to his town of "honest men and bonny lasses;" and
that I was pleased to meet with such as herself in that part of the country, justifying the poet's eulogy on the fair sex. I found she took the
compliment in quite good humor.

But now we were at Ayr itself, down by the sea, no very picturesque
place; rather flat, and with no such ancient appearance as a stranger
would expect.[12] Here is the celebrated Ale House indicated by a figure
of Tam O'Shanter over its door, but it is not a place to accommodate
tourists; and after dinner at the Queen's Arms the next thing in order
was a cab with an intelligent driver for Burns' monument. And this
was of easy procurement, being in daily demand by the numerous visitors who come to the place from all parts of the world for the same
purpose of worshiping at the shrine of the poet.

Going out, I followed the way of Tam on that memorable night. Being in broad daylight and a rather open and level country, I was unable
to call up Tam's emotions as he passed along; but considering his views
of the supernatural in witches and warlocks, which at that day men of
much higher enlightenment believed in,—such as our great Blackstone
for instance, who declares that no one can disbelieve the existence of
witches without disbelieving the truth of the Holy Scriptures—it was

perfectly natural, indeed rather unavoidable, for Tam to connect the darkness of the night and the force of the storm with some special business the de'il had on his hands; and in view of the muddled condition of his brain, he might readily become involved in such a performance as he conceived going on at the old deserted kirk. After crossing the Doon some little distance below the place, we passed up on the other side through a beautiful avenue of ancient trees, their branches nearly uniting over the road; and after crossing back again over a substantial stone bridge, a short distance below the old one where "Maggie lost her ain grey tail," we confronted the celebrated Burns monument, a very fine affair, and the grounds about it very carefully kept. It stands right on the brae or bank between the two bridges.

The young poet looks the clever, jolly fellow that his pictures and his poetry exhibit him; but whilst the expression of his features indicates the wit, humor and satire of his poems, it does not indicate the wonderful pathos and keen discriminative philosophy of his heart and mind. From the monument a good view is had of the "Bonnie Doon" and its banks and braes; and the old brig, the terminus of that memorable race, is still in good passable condition, though disused.

The Doon is a rapid brook from forty to fifty feet in width, but not nearly so beautiful or attractive as the Strule at the Camp Hill; it runs between steeper banks and more resembles an American stream. Yet doubtless there are many spots along its course of great romantic beauty. Near by and a short distance below the monument, Tam and Souter Johnnie have their alcove; and whilst Burns occupies the position of honor, these two are the real heroes of the place. Tam and his companion rather disappointed me however. Such a noble, well preserved, trimly dressed, Quaker looking gentleman was not the dilapidated, "blethering, blustering, drunken blellum" which I expected to see. Souter Johnnie may do, but he would do better to represent a fat deacon of the church rather than a cringing social parasite.

But now for old Church Alloway; and here we are just in front of it, with fine cut stone steps leading up to its gate, and a tasteful modern iron fence in front, separating it and its churchyard from the road.

You see the roofless and windowless walls of a square stone building of moderate size, and masonry of very rude quality, with its little graveyard in the same enclosure, much resembling Cappaigh Church, and indeed all other old-fashioned churches and graveyards in this country. But here I was disappointed again. I expected an ancient mysterious looking ruin, in a remote place, something like the Cross Roads Meeting House which I had lately seen. But there was a freshness and smartness here which took off the spell of mystery. Its importance to the world has destroyed its repose. Instead of an old tumble-down building in a graveyard of broken, leaning and misplaced tombstones covered with moss and weeds, and the whole place concealed by ancient trees, as I expected, there is an almost total absence of trees or shrubbery; every gravestone is set as primly, and the grounds kept as neatly as if the whole place was constructed recently. The old walls are standing, but where is the ivy, or some other natural garment of time, which ought to cover them? The changed surroundings and undue care conferred upon it have nearly destroyed Burns' picture of the place altogether. Any child would understand that if "the de'il had business on his hand" he would not choose a place so liable to interruption as this to hold his conclave. "Tam did not come down this road past the front of this church, surely," said I to the sexton who shows visitors over the place for a shilling. "Oh, no," he said, "he came by the old road which went around the other way behind the church; it is closed up now:" and he pointed out its course to me. Then I could see the proper picture of the whole concern as in the mind of Burns. From the road as located now, Tam could have had no such view of what was going on in the interior of the church. In the light streaming from the back and side windows across the old road, it was easy for Tam to see the loups and flings of the dancers and the horrible display of relics on the holy table; even "Auld Nick in shape o' beast," could be distinctly seen in his niche. But the old road is gone, and the surrounding hedge obstructs the view: and worse still, as if intended to mar the tourist's fancy of the "unco sight" which Tam might have seen, some lady has built for her husband a white marble tomb in shape of an immense upturned dry goods box, about eight feet high and ten feet long. Why such shoddy display so out of place is allowed, is unaccountable. In material and architecture it displays no beauty, and is wholly inconsistent with the surroundings.

So goodbye to old Kirk Alloway. I must pay my respects however to the cottage where the poet was born. It is not over a mile or so distant, and now we are at it, with its two rooms, the but and ben, and its thatched roof like my own birthplace at the Camp Hill, the picture of which I prize more highly after seeing this, as it serves for both. It is really something worth crossing the seas for to enter those sacred precincts, and revive the associations connected with them. Here was the lowly dwelling place of the humble plow boy, his bed and the household goods and furniture all suited to his worldly condition and the customs of his time: the birthplace of the poor Scotch gardener's son who brought so much sunshine and wisdom into the world. This place and the surrounding scenery awoke the first flashes of his wonderful spirit of poetry and philosophy! Here pilgrims come from the remotest regions of the earth to worship at the shrine of his wonderful genius. Luckily for this one object, it still remains truly original, and its sacred associations are not marred by extraneous ornamentation. The bed is kept made up in the original style in which the poet's mother kept it. I felt inclined to draw the curtains for a closer look, but the lady stayed my hand—visitors are not allowed that freedom; but she showed me many curiosities, among other things the lease by which the poet's father held the little farm, together with the original manuscript of Tam O'Shanter, in the poet's own handwriting. All about this place is sacred, and I parted from it with more regret than from the monument or the kirk.

I was nurtured in the moral, social and religious sentiments of the Scotch—for the Scotch and Scotch-Irish are the same in their characteristic elements; and it may be on this account I am so warm an admirer of Burns: because none but those imbued with the Scotch nature can fully appreciate the truth and beauty of his poetry. He above all others has revealed the inward springs of the Scotch disposition. Some of his expressions, it is true, regarding the sexual relations may seem indelicate to refined taste, but we must consider the time and state of society in which he wrote; and his satires on sectarian dogmas and religious characters may seem occasionally to reflect on religion itself, but no one can say they were undeserved under the circumstances. A solid substratum of truth underlies and justifies it all. He dared to be true to nature, even at the risk of seeming undevout and unrefined, but is none the less beloved by every virtuous and religious Scotchman on that account; and whatever be their nationality, all lovers of truth must admire him. In fact, any seeming departure from propriety arises only from lack of the varnish applied in modern society; and any specks of apparent coarseness found in some of his fugitive pieces are overshadowed by the truth, beauty and delicacy of his chief productions. In graphic description what words could be put together or language found better to depict the type of a prevalent class, than "A blethering, blustering, drunken blellum?"[13] And what could better represent patient endurance, wise reflection and excusable indignation of the wife of such a character, than the relations of Tam and his "ain wife Kate?" Or what could be more beautifully descriptive of the evanescent nature of sensual pleasures, than the lines beginning, "You seize the flower, its bloom is shed?" Or what literary production presents such keen irony and subtle humor as is embodied in that unique tale of "Tam O'Shanter?"

Then, as a picture of the rural cottager's life of his day, what could exceed his "Cotter's Saturday Night?" Where can we find such portrayal of the true Scotch character for earnest loyalty to home and family, religion and duty—or such a picture of parental and filial affection, mingled with a due proportion of commendable family pride among the poor and lowly? Or can anything exceed the presentation of the finer feelings of a generous heart, or the black-heartedness of the betrayal of an innocent girl and its consequences, than is found in the following verse?

> Is there, in human form, that bears a heart—
> A wretch! a villain! lost to love and truth!
> That can, with studied, sly, ensnaring art,
> Betray sweet Jenny's unsuspecting youth?
> Curse on his perjured arts! dissembling smooth!
> Are honor, virtue, conscience, all exiled?
> Is there no pity, no relenting ruth,
> Points to the parents' fondling o'er their child?
> Then paints the ruin'd maid, and their distraction wild?

And what other author has ever given, in such small compass, wiser and more practical worldly advice, or a sounder moral code, equal to every day wear yet good enough for holiday dress, than is found in the "Epistle to a Young Friend?"[14]

> "Ye'll try the world soon, my lad,
> And, Andrew dear, believe me,
> Ye'll find mankind an unco[15] squad,
> And muckle[16] they may grieve ye:

For care and trouble set your thought,
Ev'n when your end's attained;
And a' your views may come to nought,
Where ev'ry nerve is strained.

I'll no say men are villains a';
The real harden'd wicked,
Wha hae nae[17] check but human law,
Are to a few restricted;
But, och! mankind are unco weak,
An' little to be trusted;
If self the wavering balance shake,
It's rarely right adjusted!

Yet they wha fa' in fortune's strife,
Their fate we should na censure,
For still th' *important end* of life,
They equally may answer;
A man may hae an honest heart,
Tho' poortith[18] hourly stare him;
A man may tak a neebor's part,
Yet hae nae cash to spare him.

Ay free, aff han' your story tell,
When wi' a bosom crony;
But still keep something to yoursel'
Ye scarcely tell to ony.
Conceal yoursel' as weel's ye can
Frae critical dissection;
But keek[19] thro' ev'ry other man,
Wi' sharpen'd, slee inspection.

The sacred lowe[20] o' well-placed love,
Luxuriantly indulge it;
But never tempt th' *illicit rove*,
Tho' naething should divulge it:
I waive the quantum o' the sin,
The hazard o' concealing;
But, och! it hardens a' within,
And petrifies the feeling!
To catch dame Fortune's golden smile,
Assiduous wait upon her;
And gather gear[21] by every wile
That's justified by honour;

Not for to hide it in a hedge,
Not for a train attendant;
But for the glorious privilege
Of being independent.

The fear o' hell's a hangman's whip
To haud the wretch in order;
But where ye feel your *honour* grip,
Let that ay be you border;
Its slightest touches, instant pause—
Debar a' side pretences;
And resolutely keep its laws,
Uncaring consequences.

The great *Creator* to revere,
Must sure become the *creature;*
But still the preaching cant forbear,
And e'en the rigid feature;
Yet ne'er with wits profane to range,
Be complaisance extended;
An Atheist's laugh's a poor exchange
For Deity offended!

When ranting round in pleasure's ring,
Religion may be blinded;
Or if she give a *random sting,*
It may be little minded;
But when on life we're tempest-driven,
A conscience but a canker—
A correspondence fix'd wi' Heav'n,
Is sure a noble *anchor!*

Adieu, dear amiable youth!
Your heart can ne'er be wanting:
May prudence, fortitude, and truth,
Erect your brow undaunting!
In ploughman's phrase, 'God send you speed,'
Still daily to grow wiser;
And may you better reck the *rede,*[22]
Than ever did th' adviser!

   The beauty of Burns' pictures of character lies in their exact correct-
ness; no strain, no exaggeration. Every Scotchman is well acquainted
with the Tam O'Shanter type; and the Cotter's humble but upright
family is to be found on almost every farm; whilst Andrew, the young

man, ardent but afraid to start, and anxious to learn the right way to success in the battle of life before him, is found in many Scotch households. All know the originals, but have never before seen them so clearly depicted.

Thursday, the 31st, I am on the morning train again for Glasgow, where I arrive at ten o'clock, and have just five hours to do that great city before the train leaves for Edinboro, which the inhabitants here mostly pronounce "Edbro." Procuring a hack in Glasgow, I tell the driver to drive me where most can be seen, or where there is most worth seeing; and I am driven accordingly through many fine streets of business houses and others of elegant private residences, and among other things was made to inspect the celebrated old *busted* cannon, kept in a conspicuous position for all strangers to see, and the New College, and many other places of attractive architecture. But I wished rather to see the Old College, the scene of so much student life in the far past, and so renowned in fact and fiction; pretty much appropriated to other purposes now, yet its outlines, in nowise attractive to the lover of the magnificent, still remain. Was there no place yet to see? Yes, I was told there was a great old church near by of ten or eleven hundred years standing—I forget its name now.[23] On entering I found it not quite so imposing as I had expected because at first sight the interior magnitude of great buildings is not taken in; but after passing up and down its numerous aisles among its tall fluted columns, and after being shown the ancient part and the modern additions to it, I began to comprehend the wonders of a structure of an age when labor was cheap and religion had power. And whilst admiring the architecture, I was made to apprehend the difference between the emotional and the rational in religion. I had been brought up a Presbyterian or Rationalist—because the Reformation itself was nothing but a Rationalistic movement against ritualistic formality—and I had the idea that there was nothing in the ascetic or emotional in religion; but here I was, for the first time, convinced of my mistake. The antiquity and magnificence of the building itself was calculated to produce a feeling of awe; but whilst admiring it, a sound commenced as of distant rolling thunder, and came on swelling and increasing in volume until the whole building was filled with peals of music, the grandest and most inspiring in its effect of anything of the kind I had ever experienced, and I stood spell-bound until it ceased.

In one end of the building, between four pillars, I noticed a small congregation of twenty or thirty, seated on rude looking benches, alternately kneeling and praying, and engaged in religious exercises. A similar congregation were worshiping in another part of the building, at such distance from the first as not at all to interfere with the sound of the priest's voice at either end of the building. The great organ (invisible by an enclosure in the centre of the building) furnished the music for both congregations. I can readily understand how splendid music and magnificent architectural dimensions may affect the untutored mind, and produce a sense of awe and fear calculated to promote veneration for the invisible and regard for the priesthood, and lead rude men to a better life. The great medieval cathedrals were not without a purpose when Baconian methods of investigation did not exist.

But the time for the train to Edinboro approached, and I was again in St. Enoch's Station, one of the finest structures of the kind I have ever seen. Its plan and appointments are surely as near perfection as can be reached; and the whole space roofed with colored glass, gives an abundant light of an agreeable mellow type which casts a shade of elegance over the extensive scene. I had supposed our Pennsylvania new station at the head of Market street in Philadelphia could scarcely be excelled, but it falls much short of this.

Again on the train, whirling across to the ancient capital where can be seen Holyrood Palace and Arthur's Seat, and so many other objects interesting in story.[24] Time is saved the traveler by the convenient proximity, in this country, of all places he wishes to visit. I found myself in Edinboro at five o'clock, and that I could *do* a great deal of the town yet before nightfall. So, after a luncheon, I commenced by a trip on top of a street car drawn by a dummy engine, going seven miles out to Dunfermline. Returning, I made a circuit of the north part of the city, known as the New Town, on top of a horse car. All street cars here are double decked and provided with safe and convenient seats on top from which a better view can be had than from a carriage.

Next morning, Friday, September 1st, on board a train for Melrose Abbey, Abbotsford, and Dryburgh Abbey, forty miles distant.[25] At Melrose Station, about twenty other tourists alighted from the car on the same errand. Pilgrims to the shrine of Walter Scott are even more numerous than to that of Burns. Unfortunately it commenced raining just as we reached the ruins of the abbey, and we were compelled to tramp around and among the old dilapidated walls with considerable discomfort. It was curious to see the depressing and irritating effect which the drenching rain produced upon the many enthusiastic lady admirers of the ruins, and to witness their futile attempts to use their sketch books and pencils, under the stinted shelter of umbrellas. I confess my taste for the aesthetic was not sufficiently developed to produce an overwhelming degree of enthusiasm: Scott's poetic description of Melrose overdoes the business, or had led me to expect too much. High old walls of rough masonry, here and there indicating the outlines of a very large and solid building, and the masonry and construction not otherwise remarkable than in profusion of carvings of the cut stone in some of the facings, and the tall slender stone shafts yet remaining in the great window. The most favorable light to view it is in Sir Walter's descriptive poetry, which relieves it of much of its rudeness. Those who have viewed it from that standpoint will only have their mental picture marred by coming here. In many places the walls are covered with inscriptions, mostly very difficult to decipher; and there are many ancient gravestones in and about the ruins, with inscriptions in like condition. In one corner is a square stone block with the inscription, "Here the heart of Bruce lies buried:" the great historic hero still revered by the Scots. My talented preceptor of that name, formerly president of the Western University, was undoubtedly one of his descendants—so I learned on this tour; the ancestor was able with the sword, the descendant was able with the pen. Nor can the sons of the Pittsburgh descendant be regarded as degenerate, or unworthy of so illustrious a sire. It is quite interesting to see relics of objects we have read about and characters we have admired, but not at all essential to comfort; and regarding the whole scene of ruined walls, situate in one corner of a mean looking little town, I would much better have held to the picture which the "Wizard of the North" had drawn for me instead of going so far for the original on so wet a day.

I was soon afterwards to witness a ruin at home, which in dimensions and dilapidated walls and Grecian portico with fluted columns, compared favorably while it lasted with any of these old concerns which people go so far to see. Any Pittsburgher who saw our ruined Courthouse after the fire need not go to Europe to hunt up old abbeys and castles. The chief difference between an American and European ruin is that the one remains but a few weeks until removed and replaced by a new structure; whilst the other remains undisturbed for centuries, and becomes venerable and venerated through the enchantment of age and its consequent traditions. Those of Europe are paying institutions. Streams of tourists visit them continually, and are all taxed for admission or otherwise in some shape. Our people are behind the Europeans in this line of thrift. We have no difficulty at home by means of our mobs and conflagrations in producing elegant ruins of great splendor on short notice; but we are too impatient to wait a few centuries for the profits to be realized from their preservation. The tradition and story to render them interesting could easily be supplied. Incidents and characters commonplace at first would magnify into importance by lapse of time. Our ruined Courthouse, for instance, would produce enough stories of schemes and mysteries, pains and troubles of parties and criminals to supply all attractions in that direction, if properly written up by a Walter Scott.

It had rained every day since landing at Queenstown, but the alternations between rain and sunshine had been so fine and frequent as to render it all the more enjoyable; but this day there was no let up of the constant and increasing drizzle, so I made my way to the small inn near by for shelter and a dinner, intending to return to Edinboro by the next train. After a good dinner, although the rain was heavier than ever, I felt in better spirits, and admired the perseverance with which a young Londoner was canvassing the tourists congregated in the inn for companions to share with him the expense of a drive to Abbotsford and Dryburgh Abbey, some five miles distant. Although well dressed and genteel, his means seemed to be limited and economy an object with him. He feared if the present opportunity was lost he would never have another; and though these objects were in the programme of the day's performance of most of them, the rain discouraged everybody so that none were found willing to venture out. I felt an inclination myself to see those other celebrated places, and rather than see him fail I mustered courage to join him; and procuring a cab as nearly waterproof as could be found, we were soon on our way to Abbotsford. Arriving there in a drenching rain, we dismounted and made our way to the house under cover of umbrellas.

It is a rather commonplace looking structure from the direction in which we approached it, certainly nothing imposing about it; such as we would pass by the dozen in the vicinity of any of our large cities without attracting attention. It is situate below the road at the foot of a hill, which detracts from any beauty it would otherwise present. A flat meadow lies between it and the Tweed; but we were told that when viewed from the road on the other side of the river, it appears to much better advantage.

Admitted to a plain basement room of ordinary size and finish, we are directed to wait there until the inspection by the company preceding us was ended. More tourists visit here than elsewhere, sometimes amounting to fifty or more in a day. They are received into this basement waiting room and admitted to the inspection of the apartments above in the order of their arrival, not exceeding ten or twelve together at a time. After being shown over the establishment they are dismissed at another door, each having paid the established shilling. Then another company is admitted and disposed of in the same manner, and so on as they come. Soon the company that preceded us was dismissed, and four or five others having dropped in in the meantime, our company of half a dozen or more were admitted up a narrow stairway into the rooms above. An expert lady attendant, with a stick like the cue of a billiard table, received us at the head of the stairs and led us from one room to another: that is, the rooms open to the public, four or five in all—the residue of the house being occupied by Sir Walter's niece and family as apartments. Our lady attendant pointed out with her cue each object in every room and on every shelf and table, giving the name and a few words of explanation, not stopping or dwelling on anything in particular. I discovered her duties were performed automatically and by rote, as she could give no further account nor explanation of anything than the few words which she uttered; and it was difficult to restrain her from going on too fast, because the place presented an extensive and perfect museum of most interesting objects. Sir Walter had all his life been an industrious collector of rare curiosities, and had received numerous valuable presents from most of the kings and queens of Europe of his day; and here you find the entire collection carefully preserved and properly displayed.

I very soon found ample compensation for the discomfort of our journey. Here were actual and well preserved specimens of every kind of firearm used or in fashion from the time of the invention of gunpowder up to the time of Sir Walter's death. Here also were full suits of every kind of armor used by warriors at different periods of the past, before the time that firearms rendered such protection useless. And here were swords and battle-axes, and the weapons of war of all countries. To wield some of those double-handed swords, and bear up under the weight of suits of armor which we saw, certainly would require men of greater strength than is common in our day. Then there were relics of kings and knights and warriors of renown—purses and pocket books and pen knives, and rare curiosities of an early stage of society. Some articles, such as the fire grate from the library of a great church functionary of three hundred years ago, I think could not be improved upon, either as regards taste or convenience. It is made of wrought iron, oval and movable, and rather a handsome ornament to stand in a fireplace.

Then one of the camp kettles of Caesar's army when in England, of cast iron, with a high narrow neck and long feet, suitable to admit of a fire under it when set down anywhere, attracted attention. Here stands the remarkably fine writing desk, of great value, presented to Sir Walter by the prodigal King George IV, and other articles of *virtu* too numerous to mention. And here in the library is the well known writing desk and arm chair where this Wizard of the North produced all his wonderful tales; and on the shelves of this same room stand all his collection of choice books; and in an alcove close by, out of view from the library, lies the plaster cast, giving the exact figure and appearance of Sir Walter in death, as laid out in state—a rather startling sight.

But after viewing the steep, narrow, crooked stairway in the corner by which Sir Walter crept to his dormitory overhead of nights when exhausted with his labors, we are through, and our good lady bows us out. We have received, however, far more than the worth of our money and time or discomfort. We had seen much which was well worth coming here to see, even through the rain.

But in nowise daunted, my companion and I resolved to see Dryburgh Abbey also, still further on. On coming to the Tweed it was found too high to cross with the team, there being only a swinging foot bridge similar to ours at Idlewild over the Loyalhanna; and we dismounted, leaving the carriage in care of our driver, to make the remainder of the journey, about a mile, on foot. The Tweed is about the size of the Conemaugh at Lockport, or the Youghiogheny above Connellsville. The rain had somewhat slacked, but the paths and roads were drenched and spongy. It was no time to turn back however, and the mile was made with reasonable alacrity, and in the end we were more than repaid for our exertions.

Here were the ruins of an abbey of a much greater extent and in a better degree of preservation than those of Melrose, and the grounds connected with them were extensive and beautiful; avenues of trees which were planted six hundred years ago, and all the surroundings indicative of the wealth, power and antiquity of the order which once dominated here. Here was the great council hall of the monks, there the chamber of justice; and elsewhere their great dining hall and cloisters, storerooms, kitchens, chapels, etc.; below were their underground prisons where heretics were tortured. In one place a hole is drilled through a projecting stone, just sufficient to admit the hand and arm so that the hand can project on one side and two or three inches of the arm below the elbow on the other side; the hole is formed in an oval shape to admit a wooden wedge on top of the arm to be driven tighter and produce intenser pain from time to time. And this is placed at that height from the floor which would prevent the wretch from either sitting, kneeling or standing, compelling him to remain in a stooping posture—most admirable invention for cruelty! Surely no one but a crank would entertain heretical opinions for a moment under such pressure, unless under a very strong belief in a future state of rewards and punishments. Numerous other appliances for the expulsion of error from the mind by the injection of pain into the body were visible, but none so pronounced as this stone socket for the arm.

Query: Will the experience of the past be sufficient to prevent the union in the future of spiritual and temporal power in the priesthood? Of course it will as long as the present state of civilization lasts; but will it last? It must either advance or go back. No doubt the priesthood who inflicted these punishments were as fair-minded and conscientious in the performance of their duty as the average priesthood of our own day. They believed, no doubt, they were doing God service in the punishment of disbelievers, just as the priesthood of a later day, in the Irish rebellion of 1641, believed they were doing God service when assuring the rebels that it was not murder to kill a heretic. Then we must remember that all institutions grow out of the condition, temper, habits, and beliefs of the people of the time to which they belong.

These are the most interesting ruins and contain more suggestive objects than any others I have met with. I must not omit to mention an ancient coffin exhibited here. From its form and the locality in which it was discovered it is supposed to have been the tomb of a Roman governor, and to antedate the Christian era. It was hewn out of a solid block of stone about eighteen inches in depth, sides about four inches thick and bottom about six inches, with stone pillow as a rest for the head, a hole in the centre of the bottom as an outlet for water, and the lid a flag of equal thickness with the sides—an admirable contrivance for the preservation of human remains.

And here lies buried the remains of Sir Walter. His tomb, surrounded by a light iron fence, stands in a corner of the great council hall, the only part covered by roof as originally constructed of stone and cement. Those wild ruins in this solitary domain, with nothing of the modern world in sight or hearing to disturb the repose, afford a most appropriate resting place for what is perishable of so renowned a man.

But we must hasten away, as we have little enough time to make the train at Melrose station. The labor and discomfort of the afternoon was richly repaid by the gratification afforded; my companion and I had Dryburgh all to ourselves, the rain having deterred other tourists, and I found him to be a man of reading and reflection; so agreeable that on our return I insisted on bearing the expense of the journey myself. After reaching Edinboro it was too late to do any more sightseeing that day; and I received a telegram from George at London saying our ship sailed on the Tuesday following, and passage in another might not be soon attainable. I must have a day in London, and to do so must leave Edinboro to-morrow. So for Holyrood Castle I will have but an hour or two before the train starts.

Saturday Morning, September 2d.

Out early; at Holyrood by nine. Had but an hour to look around, but it was sufficient. After casting a hasty glance from Arthur's Seat, the projecting nose of a hill behind Holyrood, over the celebrated Old Town of Edinboro, I made my way to the train and was soon *en route* for London, a long stretch of railroad line for this country, but which at home would be regarded as short. Long and short, either in space or time, and great and small, swift and slow, are only relatively so, as every one knows who has read Gulliver's Travels or Herbert Spencer's "First Principles."

When I had "crossed the border" and left Scotland behind, the rest of Britain had little interest for me. Scotland has an interest to me and to all human beings, as the country of men of thought and ideas energetically carried out. The Scotch and Scotch-Irish—the latter but a Scotch colony—monopolize business and wealth, and almost dominate politics and religion wherever emigration carries them. They owe this to their qualities of thrift, economy, intelligence and industry. But apart from Scotland's "canny" business qualities, she is queen of the emotional and philosophical. When or where has Scotch philosophy been excelled in the analysis of the intellectual and emotional faculties? The readers of Reid, Stewart, Brown and Hamilton can answer. The keenly discriminative quality of the Scotch mind is established in her religious catechisms, as well as her poetry and fiction. When or where have Burns and Scott been excelled in beauty, depth or variety? Burns, the man of the people, or democrat; Scott, the aristocrat, the champion of the artificial in society—each a born master. The mission of Burns to exalt the lowly by bringing the hopes and fears and joys of their hearts into respect and admiration, teaching them contentment and reliance on their own efforts and resources of enjoyment; the mission of Scott to preserve what good might be extracted from that wild admiration for rank and caste, and that disinterested spirit of chivalry which Don Quixote, the French Revolution, and modern democracy have dispelled. But railroads play havoc with the odor of reverence and poetry pervading highland glens and moorlands. We whisk along through them so fast they look like commonplace ravines and hills in America.

The journey occupied the entire day and until nine o'clock at night, nothing very interesting by the way except great stretches of well-lying, beautiful and highly cultivated farm lands. The buildings on them make very little show. We pass through several historic towns presenting a rather dingy, dirty appearance from the railroad; necessarily so, because railroads seldom pass through the finest part of any town. London presented a novel appearance at night from the cab in which I was driven about two miles from the station to Morley's Hotel in Trafalgar Square, through some streets nearly in darkness, and others again ablaze with lights of all kinds, as if lighted up for market purposes. George was awaiting me at the hotel, and rather improved in health. He had been consulting the celebrated Dr. Bennett, who had taken much interest in his case and had encouraged him greatly.

Sunday Morning, September 3d.

Before people were much astir or on the street I walked down to the Thames to pay my respects to that ancient river, so important in historic events and so much written about in fiction. It is about the size of our Monongahela slackwater, but the stream rushes along with far more rapidity, is deeper—perhaps by dredging—and the water seemingly thickened with dirt. Our muddy Mississippi is crystal in clearness compared with this! There is no wharf sloping into the stream, so far as my observation extended. It is walled up with solid masonry on both sides like the Clyde, and at intervals piers are projected out forty feet or so into the stream, with stone steps leading down into the water at each side of the pier, affording safe and convenient boat landings. London bridge did not seem nearly so great in length in crossing as our Smithfield street bridge over the Monongahela. George and I kept a hack in use all day visiting the parks, the Albert Memorial Monument, the Tower and numerous other places and objects worth viewing from the exterior.

Monday Morning, September 4th.

I took a ramble through Westminster Hall and Westminster Abbey, and the splendid new building in course of erection for the law courts. I was able to afford two hours or more to the interior of Westminster Abbey—time well spent. This is another, the greatest of those magnificent old church edifices the like of which will hardly ever be replaced when they are gone. The human race is becoming too practical and rational to waste its time and energies on pyramids and edifices for idle wonderment.

The chief attraction of Westminster Abbey lies in its wealth of statuary—statuary of all ages and schools, stuck in and piled up in every square foot of space. Here and there, between the great tall rows of pillars which support the roof, is an altar with a few plain wooden benches for a congregation to hear a sermon and perform their religious exercises. These so-called chapels or places of worship are not separated from other parts of the building, but far enough apart not to interfere with each other. At one place some thirty or forty were at worship as I passed by. The throng of tourists flows on in every direction without interruption, except the occasional suggestion from an usher to some thoughtless gentleman to remove his hat whilst in the vicinity of the worshipers. Much of the statuary is so particularly nude that modern taste would forbid its exhibition in any other than so sacred a place.

I then visited old St. Paul's Cathedral for the purpose of getting a good view of the city, such as I had obtained of Londonderry in a similar manner. The steeple of this church is very high, and the balcony surrounding it accessible from a narrow crooked stairway, and much resorted to by tourists. But after climbing this stairway, which seemed in its windings to be interminable, I arrived on the balcony thoroughly exhausted with fatigue; and lost my labor, because although the atmosphere was not particularly smoky—not quite so much so as the usual condition of our Pittsburgh atmosphere—yet the line of vision was quite limited, and what I did see was so far below me as to present nothing distinctly. Merely a broad extent of roofing of houses, intercepted with numerous lines crossing each other, in which could be seen crowds of men and vehicles, looking like noiseless pygmies.

The very ancient books and manuscripts in the libraries of this church would have been far more interesting if time had allowed their examination. But a short tour of shopping closed my survey of London, as we had to be on the train for Liverpool at two o'clock.

I could observe little difference between the people of the north of Ireland and those of Scotland or England in intelligence or respectability of appearance; or between them and the same classes whom we are accustomed to meet with at home. I would note this general difference however: the people met with in the streets of the cities and at the stores and depots in these parts of Europe—the common public, we might say—seemed to have a greater desire to appear decent and respectable, and to manifest a less percentage of bluster, rowdyism or rudeness than is to be found in the same class in the United States; and they seemed to wear their clothes for a greater length of time, judging from their general threadbare appearance and frayed look of collars and linen, indicative of limited earnings. But something very nearly similar may be seen in the crowds of shopmen and shopwomen which pass down and up Chestnut street, Philadelphia, and Broadway, New

York, of mornings and evenings. The Scotch and Protestant Irish are evidently of the same stock and with but slightly different accent of speech. Between both and the English, the distinguishing feature is the trouble which the English have with their "h's." And I noticed no perceptible difference in the general appearance of streets and buildings in the chief cities of Ireland, England and Scotland. The general aspect is not so lively or attended with so much display as in the American cities. A feature in that part of London where we were located was the frequency of the ringing of bells, some of them very fine in tone; and the chimes of some of the churches were quite musical.

The general appearance of the country between London and Liverpool struck me less favorably than that between Edinboro and London. We arrived in Liverpool at nine o'clock, and experienced the great convenience of having a first class hotel in the station, as at Glasgow.

And here ended my two weeks' travel in Europe. We had escaped rain whilst in London, but now, on Tuesday morning, it poured down again. So we had little opportunity to see much of Liverpool before going on board ship at eleven o'clock. Bad as it was however, I made out to obtain a drive through some of the main streets, and to spend a few minutes in a celebrated second-hand book store where I found some rare curiosities in the book line of the olden time, particularly the History of St. Bartholomew Fair, which greatly relieved the tedium of our sea voyage home. We were now on the "City of Montreal" of the Inman Line, not so modern or commodious in its appointments as the "Celtic" of the White Star Line on which we went out; but better than to be delayed nearly a month in London for another chance, especially so as London was unsuitable for George's condition of health. We had a nice afternoon out from Liverpool, and the next morning found ourselves again in the extensive and beautiful bay in front of Queenstown. Here we had to lay at anchor for five hours awaiting the Irish passengers and mails, entertained however by the beauty of the scenery. It was amusing to see the great flocks of white sea gulls, as large as geese, gather in the air and dart down with screaming noise, scrambling for scraps of all kinds whenever the cooks would throw out a bucket of slops and fragments. From our ship the bay seemed enclosed on all sides by hills; around what hills or how we were to leave could not be seen; but when at last she moved in a direction different from what I had expected, the broad outlet opened up before us, the hills receding on either side. It is as tedious to lie at anchor motionless on shipboard as to remain on board a train of railroad cars at rest; and we were glad to get away. With the prow of our great ship turned westward as the shades of evening came on, the barren lofty coasts of Ireland disappeared, and I bade it farewell forever, with a pleased feeling of satisfaction with my visit, but a consciousness that a repetition or more protracted stay would be undesirable.

The voyage home was without incident until within about one thousand miles of New York. In securing our berths, both going and returning, we had regard to the best supply of air on George's account. This, in its highest condition, could only be secured by personal negotiation with the officers of the ship. The chief officers have separate staterooms on the upper, or what steamboatmen would call the hurricane deck. These bunks or staterooms are of large and commodious dimensions, and quite attractive to novices. They have the advantage of being free from the closeness and heat and smell to which those below occupied by the passengers are subject. Before leaving New York, having first paid our regular passage money and obtained our berths as other passengers, we paid the chief steward fifty dollars to exchange his room for our berths. His room was very eligibly located on the upper deck and about ten feet square, with two separate berths, well furnished and plenty of light and air at all times; and it afforded us an enviable and very pleasant place on our voyage out, as we had no rough weather whatever. Returning, we made similar exchanges with the chief engineer, and first mate or second officer of the vessel. No officer's room on this vessel had two berths; consequently we had to purchase two of these rooms, costing double what the same convenience cost us on our outward trip. But the difference in comfort and convenience was adequate compensation under the circumstances; and all went well and satisfactory until about two-thirds of our way home, when a circumstance occurred which caused us some alarm and would make me hesitate before adopting a similar course again.

So far we had no rough weather—all had been fine and smooth; but we were now to experience a storm at sea, and when it came on in its force and fury it was soon rendered very evident that our safety would have been much better provided for by being below inside the ship among the other passengers. Whilst before, the passengers who were shut up below stifling for want of air had reason to envy our open and airy position, now we had reason to envy their security. The rope-like streams of lightning were incessant, but the fury of the wind and sea and rain drowned all sound of thunder; and as one heavy sea after another bounded against the outside of our bunks and over their roof, falling in front with a thud on the deck, making the place tremble and shake as if a rock had fallen, it became uncomfortably suggestive. As the water was ordinarily three or four feet deep on the outside in front after each successive sea had broken, we could not venture out; and to have done so would have been useless, as access to the interior of the ship was cut off, the hatchways being closed to prevent ingress of the water. We were also separated from each other, each in his own bunk, while the storm lasted. On my part, though I cannot say that I felt any terror during the interval, I was well aware of the unpleasant possibility that something serious might happen. The exposed condition which might render our apartments unpleasant in a storm had been mentioned to one of the officers when we hired them and was hooted at. But after the storm was over we learned from the steward that on their way over in the previous November they had encountered a similar storm in which these very bunks had been broken into by the waves and the furniture washed overboard; as would the occupants also perhaps, had they been in them and as unused to sea life as we were.

The storm passed over however without accident, and its dangers were measurably compensated for by the sublimity of the scene afterwards. Any one who has ever ridden a fine horse at his best speed has felt an exultant and exhilarating effect in the performance; and the same sensation is experienced, only in much higher degree, on the deck of a great ship when she is riding the waves after a storm. About two hours after this storm had subsided the great swells of the sea were at their highest, but not of that angry nature which breaks over the ship's decks; and I never had so grand an experience as when standing on the extreme verge of the stern, holding on to a rope and looking forward to the stem or forepart of the vessel, whilst the ship, as if with straining effort, was climbing over each successive hill of water. Alternately she would sink in front, whilst the stern where I stood was lifted in the air, her point going down and down more and more in the water as the trough between the swells was reached, till I would feel as if there was no other way out of it but that she must go under. But just as if in time to shun the catastrophe she would groan and shake herself, and by herculean effort begin to recover and rise above the water in front, and continue so with a corresponding sinking of the stern till I would feel so much danger of being submerged that I could hardly resist the impulse of trying to escape from pending ruin. Thus for hours, slowly rising high above the sea and then sinking again to its level, with all manner of conceivable lateral motions, she would bound on, whilst the sensation was that of riding a great monster over the mighty waves of the deep sea. Nothing could excel it for magnificence and exciting interest.

But we are in the bay of New York again at last, where we had to lie at anchor over night according to a rule of the Custom House, because we did not reach the dock before sunset. The evening was pleasant and spent in music and dancing by those who enjoyed it; and the next morning, Sunday, the 17th of September, 1882 at ten, we set foot again on terra firma. It was our twelfth day out from Liverpool; the ship was slow and we were retarded somewhat by the storm.

Such was my trip to Ireland: a flying visit of thirty-six days, twenty of them on the sea and sixteen on land in the Old World, rather too short to afford interesting material for so long a chapter. Nevertheless it was the most interesting and pleasurable trip I have ever experienced; one of those which we like to go over again in memory, affording some of that enjoyment which makes life worth living.

Chapter XXI

Changes of a Lifetime

ALTHOUGH THIS BOOK has already grown to a much greater size than at first intended, its purpose would not be fulfilled without mention of some of the important changes which have come about in my time, and the way I regarded them. It has been a memorable period of material progress, the most so perhaps in the world's history; and the changes of public sentiment and condition of society have not been less remarkable. I shall confine myself to such of those changes as have come under my own observation. Whether such conclusions as I may draw from them are correct will be for time to tell.

We live in a world of change, and are in a constant state of change ourselves. There is nothing *steadfast* and *sure*: even the *everlasting hills* are no more everlasting than the grass on their slopes, but have been formed and are being transformed by the elements around them. And men not only change their faith and practice individually, but collectively as societies and states, changing their laws and institutions to suit the changes in their environments.

In the short voyage of a lifetime, we can see the eddies and ripples upon the surface, but not the under-currents changing the main channel of the stream. History alone can determine the deep seated causes which had been at work to bring them about; but history is made up of observation of the present. Each notes what he sees; and those who come after him apply his facts to the results which followed, in order to ascertain and establish the relationship of cause and effect. In this way the world profits by experience. As in the physical world, so in the world of living, thinking being. The causes of the moral, social and political changes which are constantly at work, and which at length produce marked results, are generally so slight and slow of progress as to be imperceptible by the living observer at the time of their operation. The effects are only discoverable by others at long intervals.

In the Augustan age, when Rome was being transformed from brick to marble, and ornamented with statuary and painting of highest art, and literature and eloquence had attained to a degree of perfection which has supplied the world with models ever since: no one at the time among the wisest of the Roman people discovered the canker at the root which resulted eventually in the decline and fall of the Roman empire, and the destruction of its wealth and civilization.

Life is too short for an individual to forecast the ultimate effects of what is going on around him. Conscious of this I hope I may be mistaken regarding the general drift of my own time, for its tendency seems to be in the wrong direction. I am unable to take so rosy a view of the future as I should wish, and I fear those who come after me will not have their lines cast in as pleasant places as mine have been; will not have as good opportunities for well-doing and bettering their worldly condition; and will not be blessed with such peace and prosperity. Such are my fears; but I am aware of the effect of years to cast a sombre shade on men's views and opinions, and therefore would hope that these fears may be unfounded. In youth we look forward with eager expectation. Nature, to encourage us on, tinges the object and prospect before us in shining colors. But after we have gotten over the summit and experienced the stern realities of life, she casts a more sombre shade over the scene, to let us down easier on the other side, and with less regret. On the latter part of the journey, therefore, we are rather inclined to look backward, and, forgetting disappointment in attained objects, continue to cherish the brighter memories of them as they appeared in early hope. Hence it is that people are apt to deceive themselves and to think the opinions, institutions, and condition of affairs in their youth were so much better than in their declining years.

But prosperous and happy, and in the enjoyment of excellent health, I have no reason whatever for despondency or dissatisfaction with the world. I shall only relate what is within the scope of clear memory, and may hope that the ultimate results will be better than present appearances would foreshadow. And one of the first which occurs to me, although perhaps of least importance, is

THE COST OF LIVING,

Which, although of little moment to some, is of vast importance to the multitude. Now, in 1885, it is at least double what it was in 1825. And this applies to all localities and conditions, to the rich and poor alike. Its recent rapid increase is caused chiefly by the rapid material progress of our day; but it has steadily advanced or declined in all past time with the advance or decline of civilization. The difference between our civilization and that of the ancients in this respect is remarkable. We are astonished when we examine the details of expenditure in domestic life among the Athenians, the most civilized people of antiquity, and find that ordinarily the wealthy among them did not spend as much for food and clothing, or house and furniture, as the common laborer does at present. Their tastes and habits in these respects were extremely simple and frugal; it was only among the higher orders of the governing class that luxurious living was indulged in, either among the Greeks or the Romans. And as regards houses and furniture, food and clothing, the kings of England, but a few hundred years ago, lived less sumptuously than our well-to-do farmers of today.

There are special causes contributing to this change in our own country which do not exist in others. The wide extent and richness of our lands and inexhaustible mineral resources, afford easy access to a good living for all who will take the right way to get at it. Such abundance naturally develops more costly tastes and habits.

But there is another, a different and more discouraging cause, chiefly confined to our cities and towns; that is, increased taxation resulting from extravagance in the management of public affairs. Ignorance of economic principles blinds our governing class to the evils of extravagance and undue public burdens, increasing the cost of living to rich and poor alike. They succeed in evading the odium justly due to their folly by pretending that the burdens of taxation fall upon the rich alone, and thus mislead the non-property holders to believe that they are not prejudiced by tax burdens. Even our school system, as shaped by the politicians, excludes economic science from the curriculum; and thus the masses are kept in ignorance of the fact that with or without taxable property they are compelled, by the increased cost of all that they use or consume, to bear their full share of all public burdens.

Whilst all taxes are collected directly from the property owners, the tenants pay them indirectly by increased rents. Capitalists do not build houses until their scarcity insures a reasonable interest for the investment over and above all taxes, insurance and repairs. And so with all the necessaries of life. The grocer's rent of his store, his water tax and business tax, and vehicle license and other exactions, must all be paid by his customers, and a reasonable profit to himself besides. Indirect taxation equalizes the property holder with the non-property holder in this respect, and if taxes were less, prices would be lower all around. Competition would soon produce that effect.

Another cause of increased cost of living in this country is our unduly expensive system of government. It is the most expensive system which the world presents at the present day. All its machinery is duplicated and triplicated, as relates to cities and towns. Other nations have but one supreme power to support—one executive, legislative, and judicial system. But we have one sovereign power over the whole, and another sovereign power over each state; two executive, two legislative, and two judicial systems, with all their costly appliances for the industrial classes to support: a system of wheels within wheels, and all operated at present under the most extravagant methods. It may do till the country becomes more populous and the masses more severely pinched for a living, when a violent remedy may become necessary.

Another cause may be found in the greater facility of production by new inventions and improved machinery. The first impression would be that greater facility of production of commodities would lessen their cost, and thereby lower rather than raise the price to the consumer; but so far this has not been the result. The seeming inconsistency arises from the fact that the greater facility for production and consequent over production tends to more expensively constructed articles of every kind, and educates up to a higher standard of living in all classes, producing and intensifying a variety of artificial wants. People are not satisfied with the simple and plain style of their forefathers, and do not economize now as they did formerly.

The effect of this increased cost of living has, according to my observation, been injurious. So far as brought about by the cultivation of artificial wants and a desire for luxuries, it results in disappointment and discontent, and produces misery to rich and poor alike.

For a young man of the middle or wealthier class to marry now, he must have a secure income to support so expensive an establishment as custom demands. The expense has increased to such an extent as to deter prudent young men in large numbers from the marriage relation altogether,—too many are beginning to regard a wife as more ornamental than useful, and too costly a luxury to be indulged in. The consequences are in most instances neither conducive to their own happiness or the good of society. And in regard to the poorer class, and working men generally, who are less governed by prudential considerations, marrying improvidently without regard to the future, they soon find themselves in a condition that to accumulate is hopeless even where the desire to accumulate exists. They are compelled to live from hand to mouth as best they can, better or worse, according to circumstances. Discouraged, they often become intemperate and reckless: hence an increase of separations, divorces, pauperism, crime, insanity and suicides. The difficulty appears to be in this: whilst the wealth of the country increases generally and is distributed between capital and labor fairly under the natural economic laws, each getting his due proportion, yet the increase to either rich or poor has not fully kept up with the growing luxury and cost of living. If people were satisfied with the simple but comfortable style of living in fashion sixty years ago, all classes who chose to save part of their profits or earnings could grow rich.

AVERSION TO LABOR

Another change in my time is a growing indisposition towards common labor. There is an increasing desire to make a living without hard work or drudgery of any kind. Apprenticeship to a trade for an occupation through life has gone nearly out of fashion. This arises in great measure from the fact that most of what was done by hand sixty years ago is now done by machinery, and the practice of attending a machine can be acquired in a few weeks; and it is so easy to change from one machine to another that a specialty in any craft, or skilled labor of any kind is not so much in demand as formerly, and the motive to seek reputation as a fine workman is lost. Another cause of this aversion is a mistaken notion of education. Young people are led to believe that its chief end is to enable them to live without work. Hence the commer-

cial and other colleges and normal schools, and professions, are over-
crowded. I cannot explain this difference between the olden time and
the present better than by the following lines which went the rounds of
the press at the time of our Centennial:

Centennial contrasts—first as copied from Poor Richard's Al-
manack—1776:

> Farmer at the plough,
> Wife milking the cow,
> Daughter spinning yarn,
> Son threshing in the barn,
> All happy to a charm.

And this is the modern improvement—1876:

> Farmer gone to see a show,
> Daughter at the piano,
> Madam gaily dressed in satin,
> All the boys learning Latin,
> With a mortgage on the farm.

Another cause of it is the increased wealth of the country, and the
greater abundance and variety of commodities produced by our wonderful inventions. This has created costlier tastes and artificial wants to
an extent which the wages of the common laborer or mechanic can
hardly hope to gratify, and therefore a dislike arises to remain in the
ranks of common labor.

But what is most unfortunate for society is the fact that this dislike
to labor works in the wrong direction. It would be all right if those
affected by it would work up and out of the necessity of labor by honest methods, by sober industry and thrift in their occupations, until
their earnings rendered them independent. In that case their own happiness and the good of society would be subserved. But unfortunately
the tendency is to crowd into pursuits for which nature did not intend
them, or to become idlers, waiting, Micawberlike, for something to
turn up.

NEW INVENTIONS

In this direction most remarkable changes have been brought about in my time, and the end is not yet, and the ultimate effect uncertain. It has been a time of industrious cultivation of science, and the subjection of natural forces to human wants. I have lived to see the solid turnpike take the place of the clay roads of the time when we traveled from Baltimore to Westmoreland county in a Conestoga wagon; and to see the canal in great measure supersede the turnpike; and ultimately to see the railroad supersede both. The changes which these improved methods of transportation have produced, and the ways in which they affect the interests of the people, are too numerous to attempt any description.

When I came on the scene steam had not yet been harnessed to do the world's work. It was being experimented with as a propelling force for boats in rivers and harbors, but no one had dreamed of its application to ocean navigation; and railroads as common public highways had not yet been projected. Appliances for the use of steam were in so rude a state as to be dangerous and unduly expensive, but these have been improved and extended, and the efficiency of steam promoted by labor saving machinery until it is safe to say that two-thirds the old time labor has been displaced. And of late a still more subtle agency is at work, and bidding fair to become a serious rival to steam. Electricity is already producing wonders, and no one can forecast the future of its performance. It is replacing darkness with the light of day, and carrying messages around the world at a greater rate of speed than the sun travels, and, by the telephone, is enabling the inhabitants of cities and towns at long distances apart to converse with each other as if personally present. All this has come to pass under my own observation. Science, ever since Bacon pointed out the proper method of its application, has been going on utilizing the forces of nature for man's benefit at a surprising rate. I have seen the harvest gathered by the slow and painful labor of the sickle and the scythe, and the grain threshed by the equally tedious process of the flail, or horses' hoofs; but now the reaper, the mower, the thresher, and the portable steam engine do the work. Now we have the sewing machine in every house; and no longer is the flax or the wool spun by the ready hands of the farmers' wives and daughters, or woven on their hand looms as in my youth. The fulling mills and carding machines which were once scattered everywhere through the country, and the little tanneries, and the tailor and shoemaker shops have disappeared from the rural districts. Machinery, driven by steam, is doing their work in the cities and towns. The tendency is to supplant hand and mind labor in combination, and substitute for it the cunning accuracy and patient endurance of the machine. The effect of the change so far has been an increase of products, and an increased demand for them, to such an extent that the labor required to make and keep the machines in repair, and to manage them in the process of production and the application of the power to them, has increased the demand for labor in this direction in proportion to the old time hand labor dispensed with. This arises however not so much from the labor needed to make and operate the machinery as from the cheapening of products and improved style of living, and artificial wants produced by the material progress and wealth of the country. It is to be hoped that this condition of affairs may last, and thus tend to keep up the equilibrium between the wants of the workingman and his opportunity for employment. We can have some conception of this tendency from the number of carpenters it would require to do the work by hand as in my boyhood, which is now done by the planing mill; or the number of sewing girls it would require to do the work of all the sewing machines now in use; or the number of nailers required to make all the nails by hand, as formerly, which are now made by machinery. Yet the labor of all these carpenters, sewing girls and nailers is still needed in one direction or another, and their wages are better than before. The increased product of all the different machines is now needed: the style of living demands them. Strike them out of existence, and the style of living would have to be lowered and a corresponding amount of labor dispensed with and wages reduced. The consumer could not afford the enhanced cost of the product which a return to hand labor would occasion. Thus the demand would be diminished, and wages lowered to what they were before machinery was introduced. I do not regard the invention of labor saving machinery as otherwise than beneficial; the advantages of performing such an immense amount of labor by the forces of nature must necessarily work for good. But whatever may be the ultimate effect of such a radical change on the condition of the world, it appears as yet to be exercising an influence for the worse in some respects. Doubtless future readjustment will be required in order to regain an equilibrium.

Formerly workingmen were individualized in character and condition. They were distributed throughout the country and associated with other classes, and better influences surrounded them than now. The example and progress of their neighbors in other vocations was calculated to prevent class prejudices, and to incite emulation in well-doing and a desire for respectability. The weaver, the tailor, the shoemaker, the miller, the tinner, the wheelwright, and the blacksmith, were in a better moral atmosphere to promote self-esteem and moral sentiment, when distributed among the farmers and villagers throughout the country, than they are now as collected in masses in the cities and manufacturing centres.

In another respect their collection into separate distinctive communities has a bad influence: it tends to separate and antagonize labor and capital. The more generally capital is diffused and united with labor in the same persons, who perform the work and transact the business of the community, the better it is for all concerned. Small proprietors who own their own tools and work on their own materials are better contented and make better citizens. And this in a great degree was the condition of workingmen in my youth. The shoemaker had his own little stock of leather, the blacksmith his own iron, the wheelwright and carpenter their own lumber, and so with the other trades; each was put on his good behavior for public patronage, and was his own employer. A healthy competition was thus promoted between workingmen themselves, and no room was left for discontent or antagonism to capital or employers. It is very different now, under the system of aggregated capital invested in extensive mines and mills and factories. As it was formerly, the mechanic or tradesman had fuller opportunity to better his condition, and fuller opportunity to benefit by his own merits and ability; in other words a better opportunity for the free exercise of all his faculties. Industry, thrift, and good habits gained him custom and enabled him to increase his business with a prospect of ultimate independence. His mere muscular labor was not all he had to depend on, but now it is all. He has now no direct interest in the success of the establishment where he works, and perhaps but slight acquaintance with its proprietors. His only interest in the establishment is to exact the highest rate of wages from it, but his individual honesty and good character are no longer a means to that end, and the intimate and friendly relations which ought to exist between employer and employee are displaced by a state of antagonism.

Another effect of labor saving machinery is that its tendency to the division and subdivision of labor is so great as to afford the individual workingman the exercise of only a few muscular motions which he soon performs automatically, and is thus reduced to the condition of a mere machine himself. And the crowding of men and families of the same occupation together has a demoralizing effect; it dwarfs individuality, reduces all to a common level in a monotonous condition, and creates a caste feeling and discontent with their lot. The stimulus to improvement by the moral effect of associating with others of different occupations and of other conditions is removed. The employees and their families in the larger manufacturing and mining establishments are often designated each by his number, and live in numbered tenements, and are all subjected to the same routine, and treated alike: too much like the soldiers of an army or the inmates of a prison. The opportunity to work up and out and better their condition is rendered so remote as to appear to them hopeless. A man is never in so healthy a condition, morally and physically, as when his natural disposition to improve is stimulated by his surroundings.

The general effect of new inventions so far has been beneficial. But there is no unmixed good in this world, and the foregoing are some of their evil tendencies which may create serious trouble before entirely eradicated,—as doubtless they will be if civilization and the progress of true social science continue.

INCREASE OF CRIME

Another change in my time is painfully obvious in the increase of crime. I wish I could believe myself mistaken in this, but statistics concur with both memory and observation to prove that there is a far greater ratio of criminality to the number of inhabitants now than formerly. Besides, this is confirmed by the observation of much younger people than myself, and the details of crime in the daily press. Murder, robbery, and violence of every degree of atrocity, and fraud, embezzlement and dishonesty have become so common as to attract little attention. Such was not the case fifty years ago. A crime was not then uncommon, but not so common as to take from it the sensational character which naturally belongs to it. Besides common crimes occurring in the ordinary way, there is a most remarkable increase of suicide, and murder in connection with it; and insanity, whilst not in itself criminal, may yet be mentioned as a prolific cause of violence, and its increase is alarming. I see by the report of a charitable institution that the number of the insane in the cities of New York and Brooklyn has increased two and one-half times in the past eleven years. Insane asylums are crowded, and new ones and additions to old ones have to be provided; and so with prisons and penitentiaries of every class.

I cut the following from the published report of a recent sermon preached by an eminent divine which, although seemingly exaggerated, cannot be far from the truth:

> The most fearful atrocities are perpetrated in a time of plenty in a country that provides the means of gaining an honest livelihood for all who are willing to work. It is said that in England, out of every ten thousand deaths seven are through crime; in France, eight; in Ireland the same, while in the United States there are twenty-one. That is, in this land there are three times the amount of the highest kind of crime that there is in England. In the latest report of the prison association of New York it is stated there has been an increase in the criminal population of the state of 33 per cent. over the highest estimate of 1870, while the population has only increased 20 per cent. In the various prisons of the state there are 15,600 convicts. This report says: "It is estimated that the proportion of the criminal population at present in custody of the state is only one-fifth of the entire class of criminals, which gives us the appalling showing in a population of 5,000,000 of 75,000 persons directly and indirectly interested in the success of criminal practices, preying upon property, endangering human life, contaminating society."

In the same sermon the causes of the increase are attributed to the spread of atheistic sentiments, the spread and popularity of secret societies, impunity of crime, and increased use of intoxicating liquors. To these I would add idleness, neglect and insubordination of youth—the want of compulsion to require children between certain ages to attend school, and keep off the streets; the crowding together of the working classes as already mentioned; the perfunctory character of religious exercises; and the inadequacy of moral training and instruction.

And criminality is not confined to individuals alone, but is beginning to show itself occasionally in organized force. At the present writing the papers furnish us daily accounts of new atrocities in the mining regions, coal property and mining machinery and bridges burned, and railroad tunnels blown up by dynamite; and striking miners drilling under anarchist leaders, armed with repeating rifles, in preparation for conflict with the state authorities. The industrial population of this county and city is paying annual tribute to meet the interest on the three millions borrowed to compensate for the property destroyed by the mob of 1877; and a similar mob, actuated by similar motives, is now menacing the towns and country of the Hocking Valley in Ohio. And it is but a short time since the courthouse and other public buildings of Cincinnati were destroyed in the same spirit of lawlessness. We have daily reports of the proceedings of organized bodies of men in the different cities boldly and openly advocating the entire overthrow and destruction of the present social system.

This country has lately served as an asylum for the spendthrifts, the desperadoes, and other criminal classes of the Old World: which may fairly account for the disproportion of crime here over what exists there. Every thief, or crank, or cut-throat, for whom it is made too hot at home, makes his escape, if he can, to America. He knows that ours is not a strong government, and that his chances for impunity are better here than elsewhere; and that when everything else fails him his vote is as good as the best; and if unsuccessful in depredating on society in the criminal line, he can turn politician and get into office, and rob the public under form of law if he is smart enough. His previous bad character will not be prejudicial to his success in that direction, according to present tendencies. Our rural population, however, still compares favorably for virtue, thrift and intelligence with that of any other nation.

But the disproportion of the depraved and dangerous classes bodes no good to our future peace and safety. Such elements in any community are as explosive and dangerous as the dynamite they boast of as their weapon of aggression.

EDUCATION

Education is more general and varied now, but not more thorough than when I was at school. It is now spread out over a much broader surface, owing to the increased number of studies; but my memory and observation incline me to the opinion that what is gained by expansion in this respect is counterbalanced by superficiality. Since my college life a notable change has come about in the importance assigned to the classics. Formerly they held the chief place in the college course. No education was deemed adequate without Greek and Latin. Now the foremost colleges are giving diplomas for proficiency in whatever studies the pupil may select. This is on the theory that life is too short for proficiency in all departments of knowledge, and that the time of youth should be applied to acquiring such knowledge and training as may be best calculated to prepare each for the special vocation he intends to follow. I have no doubt this is the right principle, and yet I feel regret that a time is coming when the elegant literature of the Greek and Latin will be cultivated only by a few specialists, as the Sanskrit and the Hebrew are at present. I have observed that, whilst the classics do not contribute directly to fitting the student for any particular profession or calling, except perhaps the ministry, yet they confer an air of refinement or culture sufficient to distinguish, in the active pursuits of life, those who have had the advantage of such an education from those who have not.

It is held by some eminent writers that education should be left to the private enterprise of the parents and guardians. They claim that parental affection and self interest will produce greater efficiency in the pupils, at less cost of time and money, and with better results in the end, than can be obtained under government supervision. My own recollection of the keen interest taken by parents in the education of their children when the duty devolved entirely on them, before the public school system was introduced, rather favors this theory. The separation between parent and child now is too great, and the power of the parent in directing the child's studies and in the choice of its teachers is too much weakened. It discourages and disposes parents to abandon the education of their children to the public altogether. The better policy would be to leave it entirely to the parents themselves, wherever they are competent in means and morals to perform the duty, and only educate at public expense where private means and qualifications are wanting; but in all cases to enforce the duty in the one way or the other. It is not likely however that the present policy will be changed, not at least till people become much more enlightened than they are.

The spirit of the age tends rather towards socialism, or the performance by the state of duties which ought to be left to individual enterprise.

Another class of writers holds the somewhat singular doctrine that the fabric of society will eventually be destroyed, if all classes are educated: that superficial education is but an *ignis fatuus* to lead men astray, and anything like a sound and good education is calculated only to make them discontented with their station in life, and raise hopes which in the great majority of cases must necessarily be disappointed. There must be "hewers of wood and drawers of water," they say, "scavengers and coal heavers, day laborers and domestic servants, or the work of society will come to a standstill;" that "great numbers are only fit for such vocations, but if you educate and try to refine them all, none will be content to assume these functions, and all the world will want to be gentlemen and ladies." Herbert Spencer, whilst he favors general education, as every intelligent man must, seems not so hopeful of its efficacy on politics, judging from the following passage from his essays, "The Man *vs.* the State."[1]

> We must educate our masters [the people]; yes, if the education were worthy to be so called, and were relevant to the political enlightenment needed, much might be hoped from it. But knowing rules of syntax, being able to add up correctly, having geographical information, and a memory stocked with kings' accessions and generals' victories, no more implies fitness to form political conclusions than ability to play cricket implies proficiency on the violin. Facility in reading opens the way to political knowledge. Doubtless; but will the way be followed? Nine out of ten people read what amuses them, or interests them, rather than what instructs them.

According to my observation, the general public is only educatable to a certain extent, no matter what are the facilities afforded. The generation which preceded me, my ancestors in Ireland one hundred years ago and later, had about as poor educational facilities as can be imagined: no free schools, no trained teachers, or comfortable school rooms. The pupils carried the fuel to heat the room, as well as their books and dinners, with them every morning. And yet there were few children who were not as thoroughly educated in reading, writing and arithmetic as those of our day. And after all, these elementary studies are the foundation on which all education is built, and greater facilities do not further proficiency in them to any appreciable extent. In my own boyhood, without free schools, and with what would now be considered wretched accommodations as to buildings and teachers and methods, the children of the neighborhood were as generally and thoroughly educated in the elementary branches as they are to-day. I have made it a point to inquire into this recently when in my old neighborhood, and find it to be a fact. The intellect of the general public will only absorb a specific quantity of knowledge, and it is useless to try to cram it. Select any common school, and you will not find over one in a hundred perhaps whom you can force much beyond the elementary studies. You may cram them with history and geography and a smattering of science to some extent, but they will not have left school a year till it is all forgotten. Whilst the real student, the one in a hundred, will have progressed and would have progressed, however poor his or her educational facilities, to a fuller and more complete knowledge than any common or high school can afford. Every one can solve this problem for himself who will take the trouble, as I have done, to look around him among his acquaintances and ascertain the proportion of solid readers and thinkers. He will find them indeed very few. The general public becomes intelligent over the newspaper and transient literature of the day, but needs no more capital than reading, writing and arithmetic to begin with for this purpose.

In whatever way it is to be brought about, however, the world will be benefited by enlightenment. All classes, whether high or low, rich or poor, have arrived at a stage where general enlightenment is demanded; and if popular government is at all practicable, this is essential. I see the evils of ignorance around me everywhere. It affords too great facility for demagogues and ignorant agitators to gain power and depredate on the industrial classes. In fact ignorance is the breeder and supporter of all kinds of imposture. It exposes to error and deception in every direction. Wherever you see a new or absurd religion, or any sensational or false theory of society proposed, those propagating it invariably seek the lowest and most ignorant for their proselytes. The Mormon converts and Mormon missionary labors afford an illustration of this; and it is among the extremely ignorant and degraded classes that the propagandists of anarchy, nihilism and socialism live and thrive. So too among our own working classes, we find that the more recent their arrival from other countries, and the lower they are in the scale of intelligence, and the more degraded their condition, the

readier they are to be duped and made contribute to demagogues, and
to submit themselves to the direction of leaders in abortive strikes and
labor troubles. They are not intelligent enough to see that whilst they
may injure themselves and their employers, they can never force wages
against the natural laws of trade. Wherever you see a wild or foolish or
absurd public movement, contrary to social science and natural law,
you may be sure that narrow minded ignorance directed by selfishness
is at the bottom of it.

But our school system is subject to three glaring defects: first, the
absence of all compulsion on those whom it was intended to improve
to accept its benefits. Political economists and standard sociologists,
such as Spencer, regard the common school system supported at public
expense as a socialistic measure, and indefensible on any other ground
than the public policy: it is for the good of the state that all its citizens
should be enlightened and intelligent. There is no more reason for
compelling one man to pay, not only for the education of his own children, but for the education also of other men's children, than to compel him to feed and clothe other men's children: unless he receives
value for it in the greater security to his person and property. The public school system is justified on the theory that the education and enlightenment of the people is essential to the existence of popular government. Notwithstanding this theory, and the expense incurred to
carry it into effect, vast numbers of children do not attend school at all,
but are utterly neglected, and the public receives no benefit for outlay on their account. They are allowed to grow up in ignorance and
vice. Instead of seeking some useful employment, or being put to ap-
prenticeships, they afford recruits for reform schools and workhouses,
whence they are graduated to the penitentiary or gallows. This is
wrong, if the common welfare of the state depends on the intelligence
and good behavior of its citizens; and where the owners of property
and the industrial classes, for their own protection, contribute the necessary means, it would seem but reasonable that all should be made to
accept its provisions.

The second defect in our system is found in the fact that whilst the
intellectual faculties are educated, the emotional or moral faculties are
entirely neglected. This part of our nature receives no education whatever under our present school system, although so far as the making of
good citizens is concerned in the matter, the right training of the moral

nature is more important than the training of the intellectual faculties. If the heart or feelings and passions are evil, education of the intellect only extends the capacity and sharpens the wits for rascality. In my experience as a judge, I found the adroitest thieves and crooks were always among the best educated inmates of the jail. I am aware of the difficulty, perhaps I should say the impossibility, of educating the moral or emotional faculties in school, but I believe the elementary or first principles of ethics ought to be taught there. This kind of knowledge is the most natural and easily understood by the child, and a catechism of fundamental principles of ethics, and their relation to the affairs of life and the happiness of the child itself, as well as to the good of the community, might well be made one of the studies. I base this opinion on my own experience of the effect of such training, although it was not strictly moral training. When a boy at school the Westminster Catechism of the Protestant faith was part of our course. It took up little time of the regular school hours. Every pupil was expected to be able to repeat a question and answer each morning, and on Saturdays to repeat what he had gone over from the beginning without the book. In this way a pupil of any degree of brightness was soon able to repeat the catechism from beginning to end; and whilst I can not claim to have received much benefit from the religious dogmas thus acquired, I must say that, by the mental and ethical training and logical method of reasoning inculcated by that early exercise, I have been benefited more or less all my life. It is because the homes and circumstances of many are incapable to afford it, that mental training is provided by the state: and if to make good citizens is the object, moral training is still more essential. Not only the welfare of society, but of the individual also, depends so much on moral training that it should not be thus neglected. Parents under our system are induced to leave the education of their children to the public, and on that account are too apt to excuse themselves of the duty altogether, unmindful of the fact that the state provides for mental education only, and still leaves the physical and moral education to the parents. Nor would the elementary ethical training I have in view involve the difficulty of religious sectarianism in the schools. Moral training has no necessary connection with religious teachings. Apart from whatever the child's good luck may be in the way of moral instruction through home influence, the only institution we have for its benefit in this respect is the Sunday school; and we find that, from its connection with religious teachings or other causes, its influence on the morals of youth is exceedingly slight.

The third defect is the absence of all instruction in sociology or social science. Sociology includes the science of political economy, government, and all political rights and duties—the whole philosophy of society; and yet our educational system affords no knowledge whatever of this science paramount to all others in its importance. It is a singular fact that whilst our political system assumes that every one should understand the duties of officials and the rights of citizens, and the true principles and policy of government, yet even our high schools and colleges afford no instruction on the subject. There has undoubtedly been a decline in the popular knowledge on this subject in the last fifty years. I remember when there was a much clearer conception of civil liberty and social rights and duties in the popular mind than at present, and a corresponding regard for them. In confirmation of this, let any one refer to the writings of Franklin, Jefferson, Adams, Madison, and political writers of this country generally at and about the time of the declaration of our independence, and it will be seen that a much better perception of the principles of social science prevailed then than is to be found among our statesmen of to-day.

If education was made compulsory, and sociology was thoroughly taught, we would secure an improvement in our legislation and the tone and character of our office holders, with less ignorant agitation over impracticable measures, and less encouragement to schemes of socialism and anarchism.

POLITICS

In my time there has been little change in political party machinery, or the methods of operating it, but quite a change in the spirit and character of politics. The solicitude to maintain a high standard of character which was formerly paramount has nearly disappeared, and even the desire for fame, which came next to it, is now in a measure subordinated to groveling desire for office and its emoluments; and that high toned sentiment of honor which once prevailed among public men is losing its force. Indeed common honesty in the management of public affairs is decreasing rapidly.

In early years I had great faith in our form of free government to preserve the blessings of individual liberty: but of late, seeing the way political power is obtained, and the character of those who obtain it, I begin to lose confidence, and feel that the form is no protection. As a popular writer aptly says: "It is the form from which the substance of freedom may most easily go." When popular government becomes corrupt, "despotism advances in the name and with the might of the people. * * * In a corrupt democracy the tendency is always to give power to the worst. The best gravitate to the bottom, the worst float to the top. While as national character must gradually assimilate to the qualities that win power and consequently respect, that demoralization of opinion goes on which, in the long panorama of history, we may see over and over again transmitting races of freemen into races of slaves."

I greatly fear our country is drifting in this direction. Person and property is not nearly so secure as half a century ago. Justice is not administered with the same degree of certainty and expedition now as formerly. The same writer already quoted, illustrates it thus:

> It is a matter of fact, that in spite of our laws, any one who has money enough and wants to kill another, may go into any one of our great centres of population and gratify his desire, and then surrender himself to justice, with the chances as a hundred to one that he will go free or suffer no greater penalty than a temporary imprisonment and the loss of a sum proportioned partly to his own wealth, and partly to the wealth and standing of the man he kills.
>
> And so, if a man steal enough, he may be sure that his punishment will practically amount but to the loss of a part of the proceeds of his theft; and if he steal enough to get off with a fortune, he will be greeted by his acquaintance as a viking might have been greeted after a successful cruise. Even though he robbed those who trusted him; even though he robbed the widow and the fatherless; he has only to get enough, and he may safely flaunt his wealth in the eyes of day.

Such is too much the case. It is only the small fry of criminals that are caught in the net of justice; and it costs the public more to catch them than the catch is worth. And whilst this condition of affairs arises in some degree from the inefficiency of the law and its officers, unfortunately it arises still more from a demoralized public sentiment, which does not condemn but regards criminal conduct with indifference, and even with approval if the criminality is successful in a pecuniary or political point of view. I remember when a boy that if any well founded suspicion got abroad, concerning a member of the state legislature or any county or town official, that he was influenced in his official conduct by personal or private ends, he was far more sensitive on the subject than at present, and always made strenuous efforts to defend his character. And failing to clear his skirts of it, not only his political prospects were blighted, but his social standing was seriously affected amongst his neighbors at home. Now almost the only quality required in a candidate is ability to help his party and political friends.

This lowering of the standard of moral sentiment arises from various causes. The unprecedented prosperity of the country during the past century is one of them. All the past history of the world goes to show that continued peace and prosperity produce luxury and idleness, which in turn corrupt the morals and deteriorate the character of the people. The counterpart of our republic in this respect can best be seen in the history of the Roman republic. We are about in the same stage in which Rome was at the time when Marius and Sulla, and Cicero and Julius Caesar appeared on the scene of action. Wealth is gradually accumulating and concentrating in few hands with us as it was then in Rome. At Rome the working of small farms by their owners was abandoned and the lands worked by slaves under wealthy proprietors, and the common people were crowded into the cities and towns. This is becoming too much the case with us, but from different causes than at Rome. With us it is not slavery but manufacturing and machinery which is drawing the working classes from the country and crowding and demoralizing them in cities, and mining and manufacturing centres; and our working people, like those of Rome, are becoming more and more clamorous of what they suppose to be their rights, and more regardless of their moral and social duties to themselves and to the public. They claim a more general or equitable distribution of wealth, but disregard the prudential virtues and habits of thrift, sobriety, and self-restraint necessary to acquire or retain it when acquired.

Sixty years ago our national congress contained proportionally a greater number of great men than now. The representative men of the country in character and ability found their way there. Senators were selected for their talent and statesmanship. Now they buy their seats as was done at Rome. There must be value received for it either in money or party service to be rendered—or both; and like the Roman senators our congressmen use their position for personal emolument. The Ro-

man senators enriched themselves from the spoils of conquered provinces; the American senators mostly through the interests they obtain
in land grants, railroad subsidies, and the other numerous private enterprises of the time. Few of them leave public life now without having
acquired a fortune, mostly displaying it by the erection of a palatial
Washington residence.

It is true our constitution is an improvement on the Roman constitution: it makes all equal before the law, and admits all classes and localities to equal rights and privileges; the Roman constitution did not,
and hence the state was subjected more frequently to political conspiracies and factional strife. But if venality and corruption continue to
grow with us as rapidly in the future as in the past sixty years, it must
result in revolution and civil strife at last; in a disruption of the union,
and anarchy or monarchy. These are the natural consequences of such
causes. And unfortunately the consequences of the venality and corruption of our legislative bodies are not confined to spoils for the
members and their political friends, but manifest themselves in a still
more damaging way—in the quality of the legislation they produce. In
the olden time legislative bodies acted more as constitutional conven-
tions do now. They considered and enacted wise general laws having
for their object the good of the whole people in promoting general
prosperity. But now, whatever time is not consumed in devising party
schemes, is taken up with special and class legislation for the benefit of
some favored few in order to secure their services at primary elections,
or to promote some private enterprise. The chief object of legislators
now would seem to be self-interest. And this deterioration in public
sentiment and in the character of representative bodies is not confined
exclusively to our national congress, but equally permeates our state
and municipal legislative bodies. The interest of their constituents or
the general public is not now so much regarded by them as formerly.
Hollow pretexts now take the place of earnest regard for the public
good. Unfortunately also, this decline of honest regard for the people's
interests is not confined to the legislative and executive departments of
our complicated system, but makes its appearance in our higher courts
of justice. We see no such sensitive regard now in judicial opinions for
constitutional limitations and restrictions as are found in the older
Pennsylvania reports. The laws were then construed more favorably to
individual rights and the encouragement of the industries of the peo-

ple, and less favorably to the privileges and emoluments of the governing class. It matters little now if the people do procure constitutional amendments limiting the power of state and municipal encroachment and interference with private rights; and it matters little now if the people do succeed in worrying a measure through the legislature to protect themselves against such encroachments: the courts, by the power of construction which they exercise, are almost certain to nullify everything of the kind. A sentiment prevails that state authority is the people, or embodies the power and majesty of the people, and that majorities can do no wrong. The individual citizen who complains of oppression or encroachment on his rights, or opposes public measures on constitutional grounds, is regarded as contumacious, and wherever judicial construction can do it he is sure to be hustled aside: and it is difficult to imagine what judicial construction cannot do.

It is too clear to leave room for doubt that the political tone and sentiment of the country has rapidly degenerated in the past half century. Professions of reform in party platforms are abundant, but no reform ever comes of it; and I fear that if degeneracy progresses at the same rate a catastrophe will be reached before the end of another half century.

I am not alone in these views of the situation, and can scarcely hope to be mistaken. Though often doubting the certainty of similar unfavorable views of public affairs, I have generally found that when time tested the question, they turned out as apprehended. And I find too many now entertaining the same opinions, to regard them as exceptional or unwarranted. People are beginning not only to think, but to act in conformity with them. An apt illustration of this is afforded in the change of practice in the celebration of the Fourth of July, the national birthday. Formerly it was celebrated cordially by public meetings for jubilation and congratulation over the success of popular government and free institutions; the liberty of the citizen, the encouragement to industry, and safety to person and property which our government afforded. This has fallen into disuse of late. People rather feel ashamed of any demonstration on the Fourth, in view of the deterioration of our boasted liberty and independence. The celebration of the day is now left to the small boy with the firecrackers. Sober, earnest people feel the inconsistency of congratulation and praise over a condition of affairs which no longer exists. I extract the following article, headed "The Fourth," from the Pittsburgh *Sunday Globe* of July 5th, 1885, which shows this tendency:

> Yesterday was the "Glorious Fourth," with the "glorious" part left out. Even the usual rehash of the "blessings" handed down to us by our forefathers was omitted, and instead there was a liberal flow of "booze" and 3c. beer patriotism. Among the "blessings" flowing from the glorious "declaration" we should not fail to recount ring domination in all the large cities; the supremacy of ignorance in councils and the legislative halls; a list of presidents of whom but few have been statesmen or even gentlemen, two of whom were murdered, and one of whom stole the office. Nearly every department of government, national, state and municipal, a den of thieves and vulgarians. A territory larger than the original thirteen states dishonestly given to swindling corporations. An army and navy degenerating into an army of gamblers, drunkards and embezzlers. Our streets full of acquitted murderers; bank smashing and embezzling at a premium; and mobs everywhere. Nearly every man with property perjuring himself to escape exorbitant taxation. A school system whose "high pressure" is crowding penitentiaries and insane asylums. A press that follows public opinion because it is afraid to lead it, and is subject to unworthy influences. A tax system heavier and tenfold more iniquitous than the stamp tax against which our forefathers rebelled. Lynch law approved where jury justice fails. Blockheads who should be sawing wood, in high places: and scalawags aspiring to political leadership. Nowhere respect for law; little of it meriting respect. A nation without a conscience, a body politic without a soul. These are some of the "blessings" it has been our happiness to inherit, and our study to debauch. Let us celebrate it with the customary orgies.

This is a sad but too true a picture of a country which in my young days was really and truly an asylum for the oppressed of all nations— "the land of the free, and the home of the brave." But notwithstanding all this, I am not discouraged. An energetic, industrious people can bear a great deal of exaction and misrule, and at the worst there is always room for the survival of the fittest. It may result badly if things do not take a turn for the better; but the turn may come; a change for the better may arise when we least expect it. I have faith in the principle of regeneration. It works for preservation through evolution and change, and belongs to social organism of every kind, as well as to individual religious hope. Were it not for this recuperative or regenerative principle in humanity, society and the race itself would have gone to destruction long ago.

SOCIALISM

Nothing has appeared in my time which threatens more serious consequences than socialism. It is only of late that it has shown itself in this country in an aggressive or rabid form, but it is on the increase, and demands more attention than usual.

It appears now in three stages of development: the voluntary or harmless, the aggressive or compulsory, and the rabid or nihilistic. In all its forms it springs from the same root, the desire of him who has nothing, to share with him who has; the desire of the idler, the worthless and good for nothing, to place himself on a footing of equality with the careful, industrious and thrifty. This is the hidden force which unconsciously to many, and unobserved by most, propels the movement, and provides the numerous plausible theories put forth for its justification. When traced to a logical conclusion, its tendency in every form presented is found to be downward.

It antagonizes the present system of social order, and is confined to those of the industrial class engaged in physical labor—that is, to workingmen in the common acceptation of the term. It ignores all brain work except as subservient to the interests of labor. It may pass through the three different stages of development in the same individual, or each stage may apply to a separate group of individuals, some of the groups differing so widely from the others in purposes and methods as to be scarcely recognizable as belonging to the same system. They all agree, however, in some essential elements, as for instance, in asserting the right of workingmen to supremacy; that labor alone is the producer of wealth, and that the present rule of the distribution of wealth is inequitable and unjust.

Formerly socialism was known, and is yet frequently spoken of, as communism. Both terms have nearly the same meaning, but its adherents of late prefer *socialism* as indicating relationship to social science. There is a relationship, it is true, but it is rather that of the spurious to the genuine. Socialism, and what is regarded as true social science, both relate to the improvement of man's social condition, and both favor greater equality in the distribution of wealth, but differ widely in the method of bringing it about. "It is here," says Mr. Orpen, the translator of M. De Laveleye, "that social reformers definitely part company with socialists. The latter say that nothing short of revolution, peaceful or bloody, will be effectual. The laborers must, by force if necessary, take possession of the land and capital of the country, and appropriate it without compensating the present owners. Production for profit must be abolished, competition done away with, and the work of production and exchange must be carried on in some undefined way by industrial and agricultural armies, marshaled by the state. Social reformers, on the other hand, say that a revolution of this kind, apart from its gross injustice and accompanying reign of terror, if successful at all, would be ineffectual, and could only lead to anarchy, faction, and despotism; that the real revolution, if such it is to be called, must take place in the minds and hearts of men; that this revolution can only be brought about gradually—must, in short, be an evolution, and is in fact going on at present; and finally, that they do not consider production for profit necessarily a crime, nor competition necessarily an evil, while they look upon the vast extension of state action contemplated by socialists as giving the death blow to progress and substituting comparative slavery for comparative freedom."

Such is a pretty fair description of the difference between socialism and true social science. It is true that socialism is countenanced by a class of writers such as M. De Laveleye, Henry George and Prof. Ely, who would base their theories on economic science, but it is economic science of their own invention, unsanctioned by the established principles of political economy. Their doctrines favor state interference and control in all industrial pursuits and social relations. They aim at restricting individual liberty, and appropriating individual effort directly to public benefit; whilst orthodox social science aims at the greatest degree of liberty of the individual for the exercise of all his faculties which may be compatible with an equal degree of liberty to every other individual of the community, and would restrict the function of civil government to the protection of life and property, and the exercise of public duties incapable of private enterprise: thus indirectly benefiting the public by increased individual effort and greater general prosperity. The latter theory is maintained by the best English and American economists, especially at present by Herbert Spencer. Socialism would introduce state interference in everything as it existed three centuries ago. True social science, or sociology, would maintain that spirit of liberty which was inaugurated by the declaration of American indepen-

dence. The one means parental restraint by the state over the actions of
the citizen; the other allows him freedom of action in so far as he does
not interfere with like freedom of action of his neighbors. So long as he
is willing to live and let live, the orthodox school would allow him a
fair field and equal rights in the pursuit of life, liberty and happiness.
In short, sociology aims at a state of society where the individual is
governed the least; socialism at a state where he is governed the most—
where his individuality is merged in the community.

In the reported speech of an anarchist delivered Sunday, May 31st,
1885, before the Liberal League here in Pittsburgh, the orator declares
that "anarchists believe in no authority on earth or beyond the skies.
They repudiate all laws, rules, officers, civil or religious, all government, and all rights of private property." And in a morning paper I
find the following: "Chicago, June 8th, 1885.—The Central Labor
Union had a picnic at Ogden's Grove yesterday [Sunday]. In the procession to the grounds there were numerous banners inscribed with
such mottoes as 'Down with the Throne, the Altar and the Money-
bags.' Twenty-two red flags and one solitary American flag were carried. At the grove socialistic speeches were made, one speaker saying
that if the people would organize against the capitalists they might enjoy a picnic every day. In their fights, he said, 'they must employ the
little insidious missiles that would destroy the palaces of their
masters.'"

The vicious classes, as well as the "good for nothings generally,"
seem to be greatly on the increase at present, or at least show more
boldness than ever before. It indicates a demoralized condition of public sentiment, which may require blood to purify. Intellectual aberra-
tions are various in degree and character, and if they are epidemical, it
would account for the wide extent of such monstrous doctrines, and
the boldness with which they are flaunted in the face of modern civilization.

It may seem strange that rational men would entertain such purposes, or if proposed by cranks and criminals, that rational men would
listen to them patiently. But it is true, nevertheless, that very large
numbers who claim to be rational not only propose but are working
might and main to propagate and carry the principles of aggressive
and rabid socialism into effect; and although surprising, it is nevethe-
less true also that they are rapidly making converts. It is also true that

honest workingmen, who would regard it as an insult to be charged as anarchists or socialists, are nevertheless imbibing socialistic sentiments from every labor newspaper which they read, and every labor agitator whom they hear. The doctrines and sentiments of our labor journals and agitators are traceable to Rousseau, Proudhon, Marx and Lassalle, and their disciples. Those who retail them to the workingmen of to-day may not be aware of it, but this is the source from which the leaven is derived that is leavening the whole lump and cropping out all over the surface of labor agitation. Whoever receives the virus, unless protected by good common sense, advances from one stage of socialism to another, until he arrives at the logical conclusion of the theory—nihilism and anarchism, dynamite and assassination. At first he becomes possessed of the idea that the present system is not as it should be and does not suit him, that he does not get his full share of the good things of the world. He never looks for the cause of this in himself; men are never inclined to do this. He never thinks of reforming his own conduct to suit society, but forthwith concludes that society must be reformed to suit him.

But when, in this dissatisfied mood, the disinherited, as in Germany they prefer to call themselves, set about to devise a new system as a substitute for the present one, their trouble begins. They at first yearn for the equal-division millennium, and see nothing in the way of its immediate introduction. But soon an unexpected obstacle arises. They fail utterly to get an adequate number among themselves to agree on any new system. They soon discover that it is not as easy to invent an artificial substitute for a system which has taken ages to grow up in the natural way, as they had supposed; that whilst every crank or visionary theorist has his pet hobby, yet no adequate number of them can be induced to give up their own and agree on that of any one else. This was the rock on which the great International Workingmen's Association split; and Kropotkin, seeing that destruction of the present social system was the only purpose which all could agree on, concluded to take a new departure and to rigidly exclude all substitutes or plans for reform, and strictly adhere to the purpose of destruction, nihilism, or nothingism, as the term implies. There is little danger to be apprehended from this rabid element, however. Society is not likely to lose its common sense entirely, and devote itself to destruction. The real danger to our liberties is from the aggressive element, the socialism of the state—the insidious encroachments of legislation on the domain of personal liberty and private enterprise. Our legislation seems to be drifting of late towards a condition where no principles of civil government of any kind are regarded; where the sole motive of action is expediency and the immediate interests of the legislators themselves. Our present danger is not from blatant social theorists, but from the ignorant hoodlum and political demagogue, void of theory or principle of any kind.

RELIGION

Born and reared as I was in the spirit of puritanism, religion was the first subject to which my attention was directed. The Old and New Testaments were my school books, and the Westminster Catechism and Confession of Faith my guides to opinion; and as an earnest nature led me to regard their teachings seriously, the questions which they presented pressed continually on my attention for solution. If the doctrines were literally true as expressed, the consequences of disobedience were momentous. Yet I saw that the great majority of people lived in disregard of their requirements, and the minority yielded but a superficial conformity. My religious instructors led me to believe that all men were already condemned, their guilt predetermined, and an endless and horrible punishment awaiting them, with but slight chance of escape for the smallest possible number; and that this small number, according to the doctrines of election and predestination, were personally designated and foreordained from all eternity.

If religion in this form was calculated to excite fear rather than devotion, it nevertheless presented problems which afforded admirable exercise for the intellect; and I was placed between two forces; religious teachings drawing one way, and the rational mind another. The knowledge obtainable from the popular religious books of the day, such as Boston's "Fourfold State," Allan's "Alarm to the Unconverted," Baxter's "Saints' Rest," and Bunyan's "Pilgrim's Progress," drew a dark shadow after them, and impressed me with the idea of God as an infinitely powerful, stern, and vigilant monarch, of a jealous and vindictive disposition, ready to punish everlastingly any one who transgressed His rules—rules relating more to what we should believe concerning Him, than to the duties which we owed Him; and that want of knowledge or inability to entertain the correct belief, afforded no excuse for disobedience.

Without cherishing any spirit of skepticism, I could not help a slight feeling of uncertainty. It seemed to me strange that God, who was infinite in power and wisdom, and had made and could unmake or reform everything, should leave His Works in a condition requiring His constant personal attention to keep them in order, or that He should visit with such condign punishment any slight mistakes of opinion as to His will or personal attributes, or as to the origin, nature, or future destiny of man himself.

I could not understand it then, but I think I do now. After passing through all the different phases of religious thought, and taking into consideration the wider sphere of knowledge now afforded by science and comparative history, I am satisfied that these old beliefs in a humanized or anthropomorphic deity, though they may appear grotesque, were well founded relatively to the mental conditions in which they prevailed. The Bible contains great truths embodied in figurative language—the language best understood in Biblical times. Personification of natural laws and vices and virtues has been the method with every people in a primitive state.

But it is of the changes which have taken place in religious thought and sentiment during my lifetime, and under my own observation, that I wish to leave some account. Religious ideas or convictions concerning God and creation, and man's position here and hereafter, were more real or intense sixty years ago than now. They had a hold on life then which has since become relaxed. I remember when they afforded an agreeable topic of conversation in every social gathering, and were discussed not only in the pulpit, but everywhere else, thus showing a living interest in them. Men regarded the subject more earnestly then; not that religion itself is more real or true at one time than another, but that the intensity of belief and profession differs at different periods. Hypocrisy would be too strong a term—indifferentism would more nearly express the present condition. In consequence of this, religion of to-day has less effect on conduct than formerly. A living belief in anything produces corresponding action: the loose band slips on the pulley and transmits no motion; or, as Roland Hill puts it, religion of to-day resembles a child on its hobbyhorse, it has all the motions, but makes no advance. I greatly fear it is falling into that state of atrophy in which heathenism was found at the beginning of the Christian era. History tells us that the temples of all the deities at Rome were well supported and highly adorned, and the sacrifices abundant. The magistrates and politicians believed religion useful to the state. Society believed it respectable. But philosophers, and the intelligent classes for the most part, regarded worship of the gods with derision. Froude says of the pagan religion at this period: "It had ceased to touch the conduct, and flowed on in an unceasing volume of insincere and unreal speech." Such, it seems to me, is the approaching condition of affairs with us at present. Religion is apparently in a transition state, and what is commonly called the philosophy of evolution is promoting the transition. Religious exercises are now performed in an artificial or perfunctory manner. Plenary inspiration of Scripture is rather kept in the background, as also the existence of a personal devil and material hell. Religious teachers cannot insist on doctrines which the people mostly regard as shaken by science. Religion used to have its stronghold in the lower classes; but now it is supposed that hardly one in ten of this class attend church or pay any attention to it whatever. Their common excuse is, the churches are too fine, and they cannot afford to attend; but in fact it is rather the leaven of skepticism which keeps them away.

Hypocrisy, skepticism and atheism existed always, but there is less hypocrisy now and more skepticism than formerly. There is less motive for hypocrisy and more inducement to skepticism. Religious work and institutions are still as well sustained materially as ever they were, but spiritually they don't seem to possess the same vitality. Contentions between different sects about their doctrines have disappeared. Religious people would seem to have adopted Pope's view of it:

> For modes of faith let senseless bigots fight,
> His can't be wrong whose life is in the right.

And this may be accepted as an improvement, if not the result of indifferentism.

There is also a wide difference between the kind of skepticism which existed sixty years ago and now. Then it was the skepticism of scoffing and wit, now it is the skepticism of philosophy and science. There has unquestionably a change taken place in the religious spirit, but the causes which have led to it are difficult to describe. Generally they may be ascribed to—

1st. Decline of public virtue.
2d. Superficial knowledge.
3d. Science.

Every reader of history knows that piety declines as the people of a nation become corrupt, and that every nation which prospers greatly in wealth and power becomes corrupt in time. The advance of our nation in power and material prosperity in the last half century has been unprecedented, and we find what might be expected, a corresponding decline in public and even in private morals and virtue.

There is no such keen sense of honor and integrity among our public men now. Disinterested motives do not govern them in obtaining office and discharging public duties to the same extent as formerly.

Superficial knowledge is also a cause of decline in religious sentiment. The masses hear of a conflict between science and religion, but have no other knowledge of the conflict in question than what they gather from the newspapers. Consequently, they can have but a confused notion of what it relates to, and readily conclude that, as in the past, scientific discoveries triumphed when they conflicted with religious doctrines, so it will be in the future. As science advances, they suppose religion must recede, and with that readiness of decision which always accompanies superficial knowledge, they conclude there is no truth in religion whatever. In this condition a rationalistic spirit has grown up which regards everything religious as bordering on superstition. Under its influence lack of knowledge is no impediment to decision. Whatever is too serious for easy solution is treated with contempt. The average citizen feels hurt at the seeming insult to his intelligence by a suggestion that some spiritual problems deserve his further consideration. He retires all such problems to the realm of witchcraft and superstition; and at the Liberal League or a socialistic meeting of a Sunday afternoon, he will mount the rostrum and talk more glibly of the absurdities of religious doctrines and their contradictions, than if he had taken a regular course of both theology and science. I have seen many such blatant skeptics who, when they went further and learned more, became modest and conservative.

> A little learning is a dangerous thing;
> Drink deep, or taste not the Pierian Spring.

But after all, science and philosophy are the most serious obstacles in the way of the old orthodox faith. On this account the alleged conflict between religion and science demands more than a passing notice.

That department of science which is supposed more especially to conflict with orthodox religion is what is commonly known as Darwinism and the development theory or philosophy of evolution. Science investigates and discovers; philosophy arranges scientific discoveries into systems, according to their co-relations. The scientist is the quarryman, the philosopher the architect and builder. Darwin, Wallace and others are the modern scientific quarrymen, whilst Spencer, Huxley, Fisk and others are the architects or builders of what is commonly known as the evolution theory.

The difficulties which have agitated the minds of men in all ages regarding religious doctrines, and the conflict which exists, or is supposed to exist, in modern times between them and the discoveries of science, disposes many good people to give up all discussion on the subject in despair, and relegate religion to the emotional instead of the rational side of our nature, and rest it on faith alone. But neither theologians nor philosophers are willing to take this course. Both sides claim that religion addresses itself to our judgment as well as to our emotions. Prof. Hodge, of the Princeton Theological Seminary, in his excellent little book, "What is Darwinism?" says that "religion is a system of knowledge, as well as a state of feeling. The truths on which all religion is founded are drawn within the domain of science, the nature of the first cause, its relation to the world, the nature of second causes, the origin of life, anthropology, including the origin, nature and destiny of man. * * * The great fact of experience is that the universe exists. The great problem which has ever pressed upon the human mind is to account for its existence. What was its origin? To what causes are the changes we witness around us to be referred? As we are a part of the universe, these questions concern ourselves: what are the origin, nature and destiny of man?"

And Prof. Huxley, one of the foremost among scientists, declares: "The question of questions for mankind—the problem which underlies all others, and is more interesting than any other—is the ascertainment of the place which man occupies in nature, and of his relation in the universe of things. Whence our race has come, what are the limits of our power over nature, and of nature's power over us, to what goal are we tending, are the problems which present themselves anew and with undiminished interest to every man born into the world." This is common ground on which both sides stand. Hence, according to theologians as well as philosophers, religion and science must stand on the same basis of scientific truth. Each professes to give an account of the material and spiritual universe, and their accounts must agree or one or the other be erroneous. Nor can we ignore the fact that a conflict between their accounts in some respects has long prevailed. The discovery that the earth is not an extended plane, with the starry heavens as a canopy overhead, and the sun and moon making their appointed rounds for man's benefit as the chief object of God's attention; and the fact that all creation is not a thing of yesterday or of five thousand years ago, but that the earth had an existence of millions of years before man appeared among the living things upon its surface, and that some hundreds of thousands of years have elapsed since his appearance; and similar discoveries, have long had a tendency to disturb serious minds. But plausible explanations were given for these discrepancies and a truce was had which lasted until a quarter of a century ago, when Darwin, Wallace and others disturbed the peace of theologians by a new theory of the arrival of man at his present state. It was nothing more than an application to man of the same principle of being which had long been established as applicable to all other animals, and to vegetable life as well—the evolution theory, or principle of development and variation, enlarged so as to include not only individual life, but the continuous life of race and species, and existence of all phenomena whatever, animate or inanimate, mental or material, and every institution, system or doctrine of any kind. As a law of being all things fall within its sphere of operation. Darwinism is only that branch of science which connects man with this general system. As to man and animals, the following are the principles on which it is based:

First. "Heredity, or that by which like begets like. The offspring are like the parent."

Second. "The law of variation, that is, while the offspring are in all essential characteristics like their immediate pro-genitor, they nevertheless vary more or less within narrow limits from their parent and from each other. Some of these variations are indifferent, some deteriorations, some improvements, that is, they are such as enable the plant or animal to exercise its functions to greater advantage."

Third. "The law of over production" in both plants and animals, allowing lavish expenditure of life in order to promote improvement by a struggle for existence.

Fourth. "The law of natural selection, or the survival of the fittest. That is, if an individual of a given species of plant or animal happens to have a slight deviation from the normal type, favorable to its success in the struggle for life, it will survive. This variation, by the law of heredity, will be transmitted to its offspring and by them again to theirs. Soon these favored ones gain the ascendancy, and the less favored perish; and the modification becomes established in the species. After a time another and another of such favorable variations occur, with like results. Thus very gradually great changes of structure are introduced, and not only species but genera, families and orders in the vegetable and animal world are produced."

It is claimed that there is no limit to the effect of these laws or causes in varying the form and structure of living organisms, provided time enough is allowed for the purpose. And the science of geology would seem to afford all the time wanted. Scientists claim that the development theory applies not only to the physical constitution of animal and vegetable life, but to the mental or psychical faculties also. Prof. Fisk shows how, in accordance with the principle of natural selection and survival of the fittest, a slight departure or variation for the better in the intellect or brain power of the early man commencing forty thousand years ago, or even later, would fully account for the difference of intellect between man and the highest of the other animals at the present time. That a very moderate degree of progress after such departure had taken place in the brain power would account for all the difference at present existing between the man and the monkey. The variations which are constantly going on in form and structure of body and in mental qualities of the lower animals, and their transmission by heredity, are calculated to countenance this theory. And on its own merits, and as corroborated by other scientific facts, the Darwinian theory, as it is called, seems now to be rapidly gaining ground. It is not susceptible of the same degree of scientific evidence as the heliocentric system of the planets or the earth's antiquity. It cannot be shown in what condition man existed at the beginning, or when or how a variation of nerve force or brain power began, which went on improving until in time it elevated him to his present high estate. It is here that evolution in its widest scope comes to the aid of Darwinism, and this renders it necessary to explain that theory.

Evolution is not a recent discovery, as some suppose. It has been recognized in the principle of dualism, or continual state of conflict and change going on in nature and life, in all past time: production, destruction, reproduction and variation, now and always, has given rise to various conjectural hypotheses concerning the beginning and maintenance of the universe. To this duality, or universal conflict in nature and life, is ascribed the idea of good and evil spirits; of angels and demons; a preserver and destroyer; a God and a devil; and it had afforded a prolific source of speculation long before science pointed out the way to its utilization. Before correct methods were applied to scientific research, speculations of this kind were left to the imagination. According to the logic of Aristotle and the methods of the ancient schools, speculations about occult causes, quiddities and entities, passed for knowledge. Of course they could account for everything so long as there was no attempt to test the truth by actual experiment or practical analysis of mental conception. But after Bacon pointed out the correct method of investigation, the scientific world began to scrutinize the operations of nature with more profitable results, and soon introduced a more orderly method of inquiry into the nature and causes of things. The theory of cause and effect was established as universally applicable to all phenomena alike. That remarkable genius, Bishop Berkeley, was the first who gave an impetus to this inquiry; and after him David Hume, and then Prof. Thomas Brown, of the University of Edinburgh, contributed a valuable treatise on the subject. Men had already begun to comprehend that the changes constantly going on might belong to a universal plan independent of immediate personal agencies. The doctrine of occult and efficient causes, maintained in the old philosophy, was discarded. It was found that the innate or moving causes of phenomena are incident to their nature and as yet undiscovered; and that all we know is that one thing, under certain conditions, follows another in uniform sequence.

The antecedent in the process we name as the cause, and the subsequent the effect: what invariably precedes the happening of anything in like conditions is the cause, and what invariably follows under like circumstances is the effect. This is all we know about it, and this is also all we know about the laws of nature, which are not, as some suppose, enactments ordained like human laws, but are simply the uniform methods of nature in her different spheres of action. Hence the laws of cause and effect and the laws of nature are convertible terms, and apply equally to mental and material operations. And indeed all we know about nature herself is her manifestations, or the different appearances in which she presents herself to us; and the uniformity with which these appearances succeed each other under the same circumstances is the foundation of science, and this invariability of presentation under like circumstances is what is termed the chain of causation or universal ongoing. We can neither discover nor understand the ultimate essence or innate principle of either matter or mind, nor can we know the relation which exists between the cause and its effect. But as some invisible relation between them is supposable, we give it a name and call it the power to cause, but what that power is in itself we know not. Scientists divide and subdivide by the aid of the microscope and chemical analysis to the utmost extent, and can only discover that some invisible power or force connects all things, material and immaterial, from the highest to the lowest; and sift the connection as they may, when they have resolved all into what is practically imperceptible, nothing is left but an inscrutable power or force, magnetic or electric, which some scientists suppose to be the nearest manifestation of God to our senses. The invisible relation between things in like conditions, which produces the change, is unknown and supposed to be unknowable. All we can discover is a chain of sequence, which in like circumstances is ever uniform and invariable, and which we never can trace to the last link.

Scientists have therefore given up the search for the occult relation between cause and effect as well as for the last link of the chain or final cause, and confine themselves now to the investigation of actual phenomena or the appearances of things. And on this plan of investigation, knowledge—useful and practical knowledge—in modern times has rapidly increased. The changes constantly going on in the realms of matter and mind have been closely watched and important inferences drawn from them. It is found that everything in being is evolved with more or less variation out of something of the same nature going before. So radical may have been the change brought about by these variations in the course of production and reproduction in ages past, that nothing can be claimed to exist now as it was created at first, nor in the same shape or condition it was at first presented. This applies to animate as well as inanimate nature; to the domain of mind as well as matter, and is the process of development to which the term evolution is applied. Thus the doctrine of evolution resulted from investigations into the nature of cause and effect.

The conclusion arrived at is that the universe, and all that is therein, is but a succession of effects following their antecedent causes, each in its line; each successive effect becoming in its turn the cause of a subsequent effect. And every one of these lines of causation regarding any object or subject, when followed back towards its source, link by link, leads us eventually to a final or first effect for which we can postulate no antecedent cause whatever. This first cause of all causes, whose operations and relations we cannot discover or comprehend, we designate as God, the creator and maintainer or father of all. And according to our mental constitution under universal experience, we can understand nothing to exist without a cause, or some antecedent of which it is the consequent. We are therefore compelled to postulate Deity or God as this first cause. Hence we may take the chain of any line of causation of mental or physical phenomena and follow it up, and in doing so we must necessarily come to the last link of which we cannot fathom the cause or power which produced it. As already mentioned, this inscrutable or final cause is assumed to be God. It is the most rational and logical assumption we can make, as to assume a final cause of some kind is a mental necessity. Thus the belief in a God is forced upon us independently of special revelation.

By this philosophy every mental process or material product is found woven into the warp and woof of causation. Every system and form of religion as well as of civil government, and every institution and doctrine of belief, are all found to have been caused and developed each from something similar going before. It appears that this incessant growth and decay, or change and reproduction, and never-ceasing state of development, is conducted in strict conformity to a universal and unvarying plan; and that so far as human penetration can go, nothing happens by chance.

It was this investigation into the operations of nature on the principle of causation which resulted in the establishment of the development theory. It was observed that everything was but the product of something else which had preceded it. It was seen that it could not be affirmed of anything that it was established and unchangeable, or that it still existed in the same condition in which it had been created at first; and this universal principle of change, of ongoing or development of everything in the universe, is what is commonly understood now as evolution. It is not new, for it was held as a philosophic theory in India among the Aryans before the time of Moses, and had become a leading doctrine of the Buddhistic religion long before the time of Christ. But it was not until after the time of Bacon that it received such critical attention of modern thought as to produce useful results. In the mind of the general public the doctrine of evolution is regarded as a new philosophy developed by Spencer, Huxley, Fisk and others of the present day. Its newness relates only to its greater extension, so as to include all systems of society and institutions of men, and mental as well as physical operations. And the gentlemen just named have contributed so largely to this extension that the system itself is attributed to them by the public. The importance attached to it arises from its supposed antagonism to orthodox religion. It is shown that it applies to every thought of the mind as well as to the germ of a decaying seed, and to all institutions, moral, civil and religious, and all customs, habits and systems of government; that whatever exists is the offspring of something which preceded it, and must, according to the universal plan, in the fullness of time give place to something of a similar kind. And although everything appears after its kind, nothing which succeeds is the same as that which went before, but appears in endless though limited variety; and the principle of variation itself is subject to the same law, and may proceed in time to such an extent as to almost transcend the limit of recognition. This expansion of knowledge regarding the principle of natural development, and the inclusion of man within its operation, is all that present scientists and philosophers can claim credit for. And it is by this including man within its scope that it is supposed to conflict with orthodox religion.

Scientists claim that in its far-reaching influence and effect, it is sufficient to account for everything, without supernatural or miraculous interference. They claim, indeed, that nothing can be supernatural, as nature is God's method of being, or presentation of himself. And whilst something new may appear, of which we have not discovered the character or antecedent cause, yet in view of our experience regarding all that we do know, and in view that all which we do know of God's providence is that it proceeds on a uniform plan, "without variableness or shadow of turning:" we must infer that what appears to us wonderful or supernatural is only so from our lack of knowledge. Under this new philosophy scientists account for the existence of man and animals as we find them, without holding that they were always in the condition in which they now appear; thus tracing the origin and variety of the different species from primordial germs; and the same law applying to man as to other animals, it cannot be claimed that he is an exception or has remained the same ever since his creation.

But the development theory of the origin of things does not, after all, differ so very materially from the Bible account of creation. The terms *Genesis* and *nature,* when traced to their roots, simply signify *becoming* or *being born,* which is the central idea of evolution. It is claimed for evolution also, that it establishes the existence of a God on scientific evidence, that a future state of existence is consistent with it, and that atheism is unthinkable. And it is claimed to be consistent with the Christian doctrine of divine inspiration; and this may be so, if by inspiration is meant production under natural laws of thought. As God is the author or first cause of thought as well as of everything else, it may well be said that all thought and product of thought is of God; and in this sense the Bible is undoubtedly an inspiration of God. "It is the inspiration of the Almighty," says Carlyle, "that gives us understanding." Scientists regard the Bible with veneration and respect, but hold there is no rule of evidence by which the degree of plenary inspiration claimed for it can be tested or established; the question of its inspiration must rest on faith alone. But they claim that the book of nature is a Bible about whose authorship there can be no question, as every line of it is in God's own handwriting. This new philosophy regards the law of nature as supreme, emanating as it does directly from God Himself in an unbroken chain of causation.

And it is claimed also to be consistent with the doctrine of the efficacy of prayer. Prayer, to be answered, must be offered in a manner and for things agreeable to God's will; that is to say, in accordance with natural laws, as natural laws being ordained of God must be taken to be His will. Prayers in accordance therewith must therefore be successful. If a man takes the natural, which is always the most efficient method to accomplish a purpose, he will succeed just in proportion to the force of his effort, that is to say, the fervency of his prayer. This corresponds also with the definition in the catechism, that "prayer is an offering up of our desires to God for things agreeable to His will." The difficulty in the way of this theory of prayer to the orthodox believer, however, lies in the implication that it would be equally applicable and successful whether the object prayed for is good or evil. But, it is replied, that the choice of good or evil is left to man's free will, and the one as readily accorded to him as the other, subject to the inherent consequences of reward or punishment. Scientists regard the Old Testament as the fullest knowledge and highest truth possible relatively to the time and condition of the people to whom it was given. The relativity of knowledge and God's established plan of progressive development, are relied on to sustain this view. And as further proof, they refer to the fact, that as in course of time the New Testament and Christian religion were evolved from the Old Testament and Jewish religion, so must new developments or dispensations in religion, as well as everything else, succeed and be evolved out of each other in time to come.

The foundation of the scientist's religion is law, and obedience to law—the law of God as established in man's nature and throughout the universe—the only way of salvation. Their religion knows no special providences. Whilst it does not preclude the efficacy of prayer, its efficacy relates to the party praying in leading him to greater effort and a knowledge of the better way of obtaining what he prays for, that is, to a knowledge of God's will manifested in His laws. Scientists do not hold that the wonderful contrivances in the organs of plants and animals, and the design manifested throughout animate and inanimate nature, is due to blind chance, but to the divine power working by and through the uniform laws or methods of progression. They hold that God's infinite intelligence conferred qualities and capacities on His works which act as causes, producing the intended effects and purposes throughout all time and that in this way all things come about in their appointed time and place, appearing as effects of secondary causes, and becoming in turn the causes of other effects following them in the chain of being.

This doctrine differs from the common orthodox theory in the supposed method of operation. The orthodox belief holds that the universal plan was at first perfect, but was broken in upon by the spirit of evil, the devil, and has ever since been obstructed by the same agency; and that after this occurred God provided a way of salvation or escape from destruction for all who would avail themselves of it—the propitiatory sacrifice of his only Son.

According to the scientist, God is truly regarded as "a spirit, infinite, eternal and unchangeable, in whom we live and move and have our being;" according to the orthodox Christian he is the God-man, who has taken upon himself humanity, assuming human sorrows and cares, making himself acquainted with our griefs and hardships, and pardoning our sins and shortcomings. The Christian regards God and appeals to him, as a child would to a parent possessed of human attributes and feelings. It is on this account the scientist charges the orthodox believer with anthropomorphism, or making to himself a God in his own image, with human form and attributes. Whilst on the other hand, the orthodox believer retorts the charge of agnosticism—that is, the scientist, if he worships at all, worships a deity whom he declares to be unknowable, and whom, according to his own doctrine, he never can understand or know anything about. The scientist replies, that it is impossible for the finite to comprehend the infinite, but that whilst he cannot expect to know the essential nature of God or the beginning, he can by constant, fervent prayer, that is to say, earnest study and investigation, learn so much of God's will and ways as may guide him with comparative safety through life. And so far as he can find out and obey those moral and physical laws, that is, conform his conduct to the laws of nature, he is sure to be preserved from evil; whilst every transgression of them is sure to be visited by its prescribed punishment without possibility of escape.

The scientist regards all thought, and moral and religious beliefs and institutions, as subject to the law of evolution. It would appear, however, that his religion leaves no room for a personified conscious spirit of evil, or power independent of the deity. He holds that God is not thus antagonized, but has for his own inscrutable purposes implanted in nature and life a principle of conflict, of aggregation and segregation, in other words, of growth, decay and reproduction, to which all are subject, and under which all objects appear and disappear, giving place to others continually; and that in living, sentient animals, acts which promote growth or preservation are accompanied with pleasure, and acts tending to the contrary are attended with pain, in order to give warning of the consequences. This rule applies to our physical, mental, and moral nature, and as we conform to natural law in these respects we derive pleasure and escape pain, survive or perish; and thus, according to the scientist, to every one is meted out the measure of his deserts.

On the whole the new faith is greatly more severe and exacting in its requirements than the old; but the misfortune is, the uneducated and unreasoning masses do not see it in that light. Inferring from the scraps of information which they pick up concerning Darwinism and evolution that they discredit orthodox religion and the existence of a hell or devil, or state of future punishment, they jump at the conclusion that the idea of future rewards and punishments is a myth. They do not perceive that if hell and the devil, and punishment in a future state of existence, are eliminated from religion, it does not follow that the consequences of good or evil conduct are abolished. They do not perceive that all experience, whether scientific or unscientific, goes to prove that every act and thought is attended with its good or bad consequences to the party concerned in this life and to his posterity after him. He who violates the laws of morality or health, trade or industry, in other words who disregards those principles by which the affairs of life are regulated, must and invariably will suffer the just penalty duly proportioned to the nature or degree of the violation. The clergy are somewhat to blame for the popular misapprehension on the subject. They combat fiercely every discovery of science which seemingly encroaches on Bible doctrines, and combat the development theory as they did the Copernican system of planetary motion, and the science of geology regarding the age of the world. All such opposition to science is futile. Whatever is true must be accepted. The only question is, whether or not it is true; because if true, it must be the work of God, and any Scripture or interpretation of Scripture contrary to it must be erroneous. There really can be no conflict between true science and true religion, whatever there may be between erroneous theories concerning either; and the sooner a reconciliation is had between them the better it will be for society. If the fundamental principles of religion can be established on a scientific basis, as Herbert Spencer and others of high scientific authority claim they can, so desirable an object should be accomplished as speedily as possible, even if it involves some modification of orthodox creeds. And it is gratifying to see that many of the ablest theologians are beginning to take this view of it. Knowledge is relative, and all theories and systems to continue true, have to be modified to suit changed conditions.

I have treated of the decline of religious sentiment and feeling in my time at more length than may seem necessary, but not beyond its importance. No nation has ever existed without the restraining power of religion in the masses; and whether organized society itself can exist without it, and be sustained by the light of science alone, is yet an experiment. So at least thought De Tocqueville, one of the ablest thinkers who has ever written on civil polity. And whilst science ignores religious creeds or special dogmas as beyond its sphere, it regards two great principles or central truths on which all religious creeds and dogmas rest. First, that there is an eternal power—a God; and second, that this eternal power makes for right. My own opinion of the conflict between religion and science corresponds with that of the author of "The Conflict in Nature and Life." "The law-deity of science," he says, "is a poor abstraction compared with the anthropomorphic deity of theology. The former can be looked to for none of the sweet comfort which comes of the consciousness that providence has a personal interest in us as individuals, and cares for us as a parent cares for his children." Whatever the world may come to be in the future, it is not prepared to dispense with its religion at present. And the misfortune is, as the same author declares, "the working people are becoming quite extensively afflicted with the leaven of skepticism. It is in the air, and like a contagion seizes on the minds of men. If faith in immortality should be lost, it will be a loss which in the present state of humanity nothing can fully repair. If all mankind could become philosophers we might imagine them forming a society so exalted that they could get along without the consolations which religion affords. But no such society is possible, and even if scientific in form, it must be composed mainly of mediocre people; and if these may lose their religion as they are losing it, the loss is a real one for which it is difficult to conceive an adequate compensation."

Chapter XXII

Conclusion

AT THE OUTSET I purposed continuing my narrative until near the end of life, but whether that event is near or remote, I must hasten to a close, as my book has now grown to a size far exceeding my original intention.

Although now in my seventy-third year I feel little the effect of age. Possibly this may be owing to regular and abstemious habits. I have all my life avoided late hours and excesses, and exercised full control over my appetites; and have been a light eater of plain food, seldom using any stimulating beverage, and no tobacco. The injury resulting from stimulants is manifest to every one, but that resulting from tobacco, though less manifest, is not less certain. I have just been to see an esteemed friend, Hon. Edgar Cowan, at his home in Greensburg, who has been suddenly compelled to abandon his worldly pursuits, and prepare for death by the lingering torture of a cancer in the tongue, produced by smoking, as he is advised by the best medical authorities at home and abroad, and as he fully believes from his own experience. Similarly has ex-president Grant's life been shortened of late by the same habit. Whilst we know that every unnatural appetite is necessarily injurious, yet strange it is, that our godlike reason and boasted intelligence do not protect us against such pernicious habits as are shunned even by the lower animals. Though fully enjoying most kinds of pleasure and amusements, I had no inclination to others. I have never seen a horse race or boat race, or played a game of cards in my life, or incurred any extra hazardous risks—never speculating in property of any kind without I saw a sure thing in it.

By way of personal description, I may mention my height as five feet nine inches, and average weight as one hundred and sixty pounds, with dark eyes, dark complexion, and thick hair once jet black though now white, but not bald as my photograph would indicate.

Whilst I do not attend to the details, I have not yet remitted my daily attendance at the bank during business hours. The bank parlor is a convenient place for those who have occasion to consult me regarding public or private affairs; and for over a year past I have spent the intervals between such calls in writing this book. For five years past I have allowed myself to be elected to the select council of the city, and have recently been elected for two years more, a term which, if I am spared to fill, shall be my last in that line. No more unsatisfactory position could be held by one of my disposition. I have for over forty years been combating municipal abuses without any appreciable effect. The drift has been steadily towards folly and extravagance, and those who oppose it are usually in the minority. Whilst not successful in reforming public affairs, however, I cannot complain of want of success in my own, where I have been able to overcome obstacles and to master the situation by care and persevering industry. I have for many years been rated as a millionaire, and perhaps justly so. But gratification or happiness does not increase proportionately with wealth. Beyond a competence sufficient to produce a feeling of independence and afford the ability to help one's family or a friend if in need, or the opportunity to indulge in some such harmless extravagance as this performance which I am now about finishing, wealth adds nothing to enjoyment.

But if happiness does not increase proportionately with wealth, it is to be remembered that hardships and discomforts never fail to increase proportionately with poverty, and that the lower you sink, or the lower you find yourself, the harder it will be to work up and out financially. You may take this consolation, however, if poverty is a cruel master you will find it also a great coward, and utterly unable to withstand courage, industry and economy. Courage and hope in poverty are golden, and the time and place to begin the battle is just at once, and wherever you find yourself. Never wait for something better to turn up. Engage in whatever you are best fitted for, and make yourself useful to others: remembering it is not favor but self-interest you must appeal to. This course will secure patronage or employment when no other will; and once you are fairly started, all that is needed is perseverance and constant saving of some portion of your earnings or income. Saving is of vital importance, and has never been properly appreciated by any economist except Franklin. It does not involve niggardly parsimony, but to overcome poverty you must accumulate, and to accumulate you must save, and to save only requires a proper adjustment of your expenses to your condition, to secure a sure surplus over. The reward is great. The savings will soon begin to accumulate of themselves, and independence be secured. And when independence is secured, your accumulations will grow more and more until your labor and care is transferred from accumulating to holding what you have.

According to my experience, it is more difficult to keep wealth when you have it than to accumulate it. Fluctuations in value, panics, unjust laws, maladministration of justice, frauds, accidents, and the constant importunity of schemers, as well as grinding taxation and other influences, tend constantly to the disintegration of wealth. More especially so at a period of life when the masterly spirit is weakened, and the stimulus of success no longer allures to renewed exertion, and we are more inclined to repose than activity. In that condition we are more likely to lose than gain. I now no longer wonder at so many of my business contemporaries having acquired wealth in the prime of life, and letting it slip through their fingers in old age. Without prudent children, or others competent to guard it, it is a natural consequence that a man's wealth will begin to waste away with his mental and physical energies.

This reflection has a saddening effect, and sometimes the heart sinks. But when we look abroad on nature, we see the autumn has its place in the animal as well as the vegetable kingdom, and is not without its tranquil beauty. Leaf and fruit must fade and drop to make way for a new and fresh crop in its turn. Man is as the grass. There need be no regret: it is the way; and the way of nature is a revelation of God.

Family affairs stand thus at present:

My son Thomas has his elegant and comfortable home adjoining mine, and is happy in the possession of a most excellent wife and three interesting children. Alexander, the oldest, with much of his father's nature, and Edward, with the good traits of both father and mother, are now at school, and in the attachment and companionship between them and their father they remind me much of a similar intimacy once so gratifying to myself. Their bright little daughter Mary is not yet sufficiently developed to disclose much of what she is to be.

My son James occupies a home equal to that of his brother, immediately across the avenue from me. His son William, now a young man of seventeen, already taller than his father, bids fair to become a credit to himself and his parents. Just out of school, he has taken the situation of shipping clerk in his father and uncle's firm, and works industriously every day from seven o'clock in the morning till quitting time in the evening, giving promise of steady habits and attention to business highly commendable. Little Tom, his brother, now of the age at which I left my early home in Ireland, a bright boy of an inquiring and thoughtful disposition, and amusingly careful to be correct in what he says, bids fair to satisfy parental hopes. They both owe much to the assiduous care of a wise and affectionate mother.

Andrew, the only son now at home with us, manages my banking business with eminent ability and success. Although of a proper age for marriage he shows no desire to change his condition. This may possibly be accounted for by an unhappy experience which he passed through. Being of a social disposition, he at first went into society a good deal, and a mutual attachment sprang up between him and a young lady acquaintance. She was of good family, and in every way worthy of him; and the attachment between them ripened into a marriage engagement which was entirely satisfactory to both families, and would have been consummated in the spring of 1882, but her health began to fail, and as the disease developed, it proved to be of so serious a nature that by the advice of her physician marriage was deferred till the result would be known. She continued to decline slowly, however, until all hope was abandoned, and died in about a year afterwards. Since then he has gone but little into ladies' society, and become more and more absorbed in business pursuits.

Dick, the successor in form and disposition of our lost Selwyn, is equally a model with his brothers in the management of business affairs. In 1833 he and his brother George located themselves in the banking and real estate business at Bismarck, Dakota, chiefly on account of George's health, for which the climate was deemed favorable. They have been reasonably successful so far, but whether the location shall be permanent is as yet unsettled. Wheat growing seemed profitable, and having plenty of lands suited for the purpose, George, who superintends their agricultural department, broke up over one thousand acres of prairie during the first summer, and seeded it with wheat in the spring of 1884: which though it yielded over twenty-five bushels to the acre afforded but little profit, as wheat fell in price during that season from ninety to sixty cents. It was arranged between them that Dick should superintend the bank and real estate sales in the city, whilst George should enjoy the open air and exercise of the country. But the latter's health is still deemed too tender to bear the rigor of a Dakota winter, and as yet he has had to spend his winters in the South.

With him, whilst worse was once greatly feared, the break down in his health has been a serious drawback. In 1880 he gave high promise of energy, industry, and first class business capacity. Although but a boy he showed the ability of a man of experience; and his ambition for active employment was so strong that when his health failed and we took him to the South, in the winter of 1881, on meeting with other invalids like himself, some of whom had spent three successive winters there, he declared that if such was to be his fate he would rather die at once than spend so much time in tedious idleness. He has become inured to it, however. The past is the fourth winter he has spent in the South. His business at Bismarck is thus so much interrupted as to destroy the continuity of regular pursuit, and what the ultimate effect will be yet remains to be seen. I still retain the hope that robust health and vigor will restore his desire and capacity for regular employment. But however that may be, or should his health not be so fully restored, I rely upon his good common sense to restrain him at all times within the bounds of his income.

Such is our present history.

A long life is like an ear of corn with the grains shriveled at both ends. The few years at the end of an old man's life are of as little account to him or others as the few years of childhood at its beginning. But I am neither dissatisfied with life nor greatly concerned for its long continuance. And when the time comes, my hope is to depart in peace, with as little pain and suffering as possible, and to be laid quietly, without display of public funeral, between my parents and only brother, with room for my loving wife beside me, if she has not preceded me; and there to rest as I have lived, quietly and unostentatiously, with merely a modest stone to mark the spot. My life on the whole has been a pleasant one, but my capacity for usefulness as well as for physical enjoyment is declining, and already I begin to feel desolate. On looking back, it is with a shade of sadness I find that all, or nearly all, of my contemporaries who knew me intimately in active life, and would be interested in me or in what I might write or say, are gone; and nearly all of my friends and associates whom I would feel an interest in communicating with are gone also. To the general public which surrounds me now, I am as a stranger in a strange land. I have still the gratification, however, of the society of a devoted family. And the only excuse for what I have written is, the hope that after I am gone I may continue in some degree as a mentor to them and their descendants. But happily as to my sons, I have outlived the necessity even for this. They no longer need my guardian care. It was when they were young, and their hearts and minds open to all manner of influences, that death had terrors for me. I feared the possibility of exclusion from guiding and helping them on their way. But all has gone well. And now, whilst the dark shadows of the evening of life are extending towards me, I may as well end this task; and to-day, the 22d of August, 1885, the forty-second anniversary of my marriage—the luckiest event of my life, is the fitting time.

FINIS

Afterword

Mary Louise Briscoe

"Wealth, fame and position arise so often
from mere fortuitous circumstances, that little for
good or evil can be predicted of them."
—Thomas Mellon

THOMAS MELLON FINISHED his autobiography on the evening of his forty-second wedding anniversary, giving the finale of his narrative a special significance, as he had many other important events in his life. He and Sarah Jane cared a great deal for the rituals of Thanksgiving and Christmas when they gathered their family for festive, if quiet dinner celebrations, though they apparently had little interest in the social life of Pittsburgh. Especially in their later years, Sarah Jane seemed happiest when their extended family was together in the big house on Negley Avenue. Thomas wrote affectionate letters to his sons on more than one Christmas day, noting that their love and success was the greatest gift he could receive. In 1890, they chose February 3, their double birthday celebration, to transfer all their real property to their son Andrew. Coincidently, it was on February 3, 1908, that Thomas Mellon died; Sarah Jane would outlive him by less than one year, for she died on January 19, 1909.

When he finished his autobiography in 1885, Thomas Mellon was seventy-two years old, he had completed three different careers—lawyer, judge, banker—and he had helped each of his five sons establish himself in a promising business career. All of the Mellons had become successful in real estate, construction, and banking, learning the business from the ground up. Except George.

George was the youngest Mellon, said by family members to be warm and charming, and probably somewhat spoiled by his parents, especially by his father who was forty-seven when George was born. When George was diagnosed as having tuberculosis, Thomas and Sarah Jane got the best available medical opinions on this mysterious disease and ultimately stayed with him for several months near a sanitarium in Aiken, South Carolina, which they found to be a pleasant place; Sarah Jane returned to Aiken on at least one occasion hoping to find relief from an asthmatic condition she suffered from occasionally. George's health improved somewhat after traveling to Britain with his father, who then sent George and Richard to Bismarck, in the Dakota territory—the northern climate was thought to be good for consumptives—where they opened the Mellon Brothers Bank and invested in real estate, farming, and cattle. Richard was not only the elder but clearly the more stable and shrewd in business ventures.

In 1882, with the coming of the railroad, Bismarck seemed on the way to becoming a boomtown. Letters Thomas wrote to Richard from 1882 to 1886 are filled with fatherly cautions on business investments, comparing his own earlier experience in Leavenworth, Kansas, where the boom from railroad expansion was short-lived.[1] While Richard's enthusiasm was keen for several years—he thought of living there permanently—the Bismarck ventures never went as well as expected. Thomas continued to worry over George, not merely for his health but also his inability to stick with projects successfully. In January 1883, Thomas wrote Richard that George was indignant because his salary in the Ligonier Valley Railroad, then managed mostly by his son Thomas, would be reduced to $1,000 and that his son was anxious to have George out of the project. George spent more money on himself than his father thought wise or prudent, and comments in several letters suggest that he simply did not know how to manage his money. Thomas finally cut off George's accounts at the Bismarck bank and forced him to charge only to his father's account, with any arrears to be subtracted from his share of the family estate. He worried constantly about George, his health, and otherwise, as he wrote Richard: "It is doubtful however even if he does get well whether his long idleness won't take all the sand out of him for business. I hope not. A man has a poor excuse to this world who could spend all his life as a *dude.*"[2] Finally, in December 1886 Thomas advised Richard to get his Bismarck ventures in a "safe condition" and return to Pittsburgh to join Andrew

in the bank. Although he wrote that he understood George was determined to go to Denver, in the spring he would set George up in the
Pittsburgh business he had started before he became ill, building and
selling houses.

George's trip to Denver was an adventure of several months. Leaving
Bismarck with a team and a buck wagon with a compass attached to
the dashboard, he traveled through the Badlands, the wilderness of
Wyoming, and the Colorado Rockies down to Denver. Outdoor life
and adventure seemed to agree with him. William Larimer Mellon,
who remembers sharing a tent with George on the Dakota prairie,
acknowledges that he came to believe that George never had tuberculosis, given his delight in the rugged life of the frontier.[3] Once George
made it to Denver, however, he was stricken with spinal meningitis and
died within a few days on April 15, 1887. The family was devastated.

Shortly after George's death, Richard joined Andrew at T. Mellon
and Sons' where they became equal partners, though Richard had the
title of vice-president. With adjacent offices separated only by a swing-
ing door, the two brothers formed an unusually close working relationship that enabled them to make business decisions on each other's
behalf, buying, selling, or investing with an equal share of responsibility and profit. The phrase, "my brother and I," became commonplace in
their dealings with clients.

Throughout the eighties, Thomas Mellon continued to be involved
in business affairs, though Andrew was officially in charge of the bank.
His letters to Richard and Andrew make reference to a variety of real
estate transactions in Pittsburgh, Greensburg, and Leavenworth, but
his hunger for land over the years had led him to explore new markets
in many other states, especially in the West, where he bought whole
townships along the new Northern Pacific Railroad. He and his sons
bought properties in Maryland (many in Baltimore), Missouri, the
Dakota territory, and Wisconsin. As Andrew once said, the Mellon
name "was sprinkled all over the title records of certain states, particularly Dakota, Colorado, and Idaho."[4]

It was land that Thomas Mellon understood as an economic base,
and it was land from which he made his fortune. A product of the
preindustrial world, he did not have the capitalist vision that would
make his sons famous. During his prime in mid-century, those discov-

eries by Drake, Westinghouse, Carnegie, and others—oil, natural gas, electricity, steel, and aluminum—were beginning the base of an industrialized Pittsburgh that Thomas Mellon observed but did not invest in, as his sons would later. He did what he knew best, and it is perhaps for this reason that, after giving his estate over to Andrew in 1890, Thomas Mellon abruptly left Pittsburgh and went to Kansas City, leaving Sarah Jane in charge of the household on Negley Avenue.

Apparently he intended to stay in Kansas City for only a few weeks, but although he made frequent visits back to Pittsburgh, Kansas City became the center of his life for the next five years. By this time, the Mellons owned considerable property in Missouri and Kansas; Thomas's two older sons had married women from Leavenworth, which was only about twenty miles upriver from Kansas City; and the son of his brother Samuel, William A. Mellon, was one of several relatives then living in the area. Although initially Thomas may have intended merely to check up on his property and relatives, his stay in Kansas City resulted in much more. Letters written to "Dear Ma" from Kansas City are buoyant with his pleasure in this frontier outpost, where he slept well, ate well, and enjoyed life and good health.[5]

In 1890, Kansas City was experiencing a lively period of growth. Its railways controlled one-third of the railroad mileage in the United States, and it had more miles of cable road in operation than any other city in the world. It ranked second after Chicago among American cities in packinghouse and stockyard business, in railroads entering its Union station, and in volume of depot business. And it proudly claimed that it had not had a single case of smallpox or any other disease in epidemic form during that year.

Like Pittsburgh in the early 1800s, Kansas City by mid-century had become an important "gateway to the West" for settlers heading across the plains, and when Thomas Mellon arrived in 1890 he saw opportunities for development that he knew and understood. One of these was the opportunity to build incline railways, as he had done so successfully in Pittsburgh. In his excitement about this new venture, he bought land, brought in his engineers from Pittsburgh, and sought a franchise from the Kansas City Council to begin construction. Opposition from several councilmen led to a bitter court battle in which Mellon accused them of seeking payoffs before granting him the franchise, and as a result the speaker of the council and three leading councilmen were indicted. Mellon became something of a local hero by fighting graft in city politics, gaining popular attention by writing editorials in the *Penny Press,* a struggling newspaper run by his nephew, William A. Mellon, and distributing thousands of broadsides denouncing the corrupt councilmen and proclaiming the virtues of his incline plane. "I rather enjoy the opposition," he wrote to Andrew, and to Sarah Jane he wrote, "it affords me amusement."[6] It also gave him the opportunity to help his nephew's newspaper; in addition to writing editorials, he backed it financially, and in 1890, Richard B. Mellon was listed as the publisher of the press, which died out by 1891. By 1894, however, William A. Mellon was the agent for the Kansas City Incline Plane Company, and business was progressing.

Thomas Mellon continued reading, or being read to, in his later years, when his eyes failed him. One book he asked Andrew to send him in Kansas City was his copy of Edwin Arnold's *The Light of Asia,* a study of Buddhism. He also continued to explore spiritualism, which had attracted his interest during the early days of its broad popularity in the 1850s. Although he deemed it "unscientific," he still believed there was "something in it." He attended several seances in Kansas City, hoping to make contact with his dead sons, but it was in Cincinnati where he believed he saw the spirit of Selwyn: "If there is a future life for man it is natural there should be spirits and if there are spirits of the deceased there, I have no more doubt that he was my son in the life he now enjoys than I have of my own present existence or his former existence on earth."[7] Andrew accompanied his father to seances on several occasions, and though he himself was not a believer, he thought them a harmless comfort to his father in old age.

Thomas Mellon was never interested in public philanthropy, but he took care of needy family members and friends of the family for many years. In a letter to his sons dated September 24, 1895—the only document he left that resembles a will—he asked them to continue providing for a woman named Henrietta who had been brought up in the family and for the children of William A. and Lillian Mellon, his brother Samuel's grandchildren. In his words, "my heart and hand was always open to relieve the actual distress of worthy objects of private charity. I have given in this way what might have been given to public charity with more praise and display, but private charity was always what attracted my feelings most." Sarah Jane was involved in charitable work, however, in the East Liberty Presbyterian Church, the Home for Aged Protestant Couples, and the Home for Aged Women in Wilkinsburg, where she was vice-president of the board of managers until she died. Public philanthropic interests of the Mellon family, particularly in education and the arts, would come much later, long after the death of the family patriarch.

During his last years, Thomas Mellon enjoyed visiting with journalists—after returning from Kansas City he even thought of starting up a paper himself—and literary figures in or passing through Pittsburgh. Occasionally he wrote features for the local press on his early days in Pennsylvania, some expanded from sections in his autobiography, or on issues of current interest. Six months before he died, the University of Pittsburgh gave him a doctor of law degree in honor of his lifelong interest in education and his extraordinary contributions to the development of the regional economy.

One distant but vivid memory of Thomas and Sarah Jane Mellon still lingers in the mind of their living great-granddaughter, Rachel Mellon Walton, who was nine years old when Thomas died. With her grandfather, James Ross, living just across the street, every Sunday she and other young Mellons would be taken to visit their elderly great-grandparents, who greeted them from a pair of rockers on the porch or in the parlor. And every Sunday the old man in his rocker would look at them, with a glint of humor probably too droll for their comprehension, and ask, "Who are these children?"

The house at 401 Negley remained in the family until 1956, when it was torn down and the property sold to a developer who, following the pattern of Thomas Mellon, divided it into lots and built a dozen little ranch houses in its place. By that time the house had twenty-two rooms, with a walled-in tennis court and golfing greens, as well as the original stable, carriage house, and springhouse. The backyard included a vine-covered stone bell tower, remembered by some family members as a kind of Irish tower, that was rimmed with statues and busts of prominent figures in the family. All that now remains of the original family estate is one massive stone gatepost.

FAMILY HISTORY
GENEALOGICAL CHART
NOTES
BIBLIOGRAPHY
INDEX

FAMILY HISTORY

———◆●◆———

*"If you would know yourself, begin with the study
of your forefathers."*

Chapter I

Name and Nationality

POSSIBLY INVESTIGATION as to the origin of one's own name, and names in general, may seem more curious than useful, but curiosity is a natural feeling, and deserves some little indulgence on such an interesting subject. A good name, according to Shakespeare, is everything; but Shakespeare has reference to the quality of the article, and not to the tab attached to it. If asked what's in a name, I should reply, very little. If its possessor has nothing else to recommend him, he is poor indeed. Still, every one entertains a natural love and affection for his name. It is so closely related as to seem part of himself. Then again, it is a family keepsake which has come down from his remotest ancestor; the oldest, and perhaps the only, bit of ancestral property which he holds.

Proper names are of two classes—those of ancient and those of modern origin. The name Mellon belongs to the first of these, and is so ancient as to be prehistoric. It is first to be found among the Thebans, and must have come from the Scythians or Greeks. We find General Mellon highly eulogized by the Greek historians for his co-operation with Pelopidas, and the services he rendered in accomplishing Theban independence.

Thus, among other accounts, Plutarch says of Pelopidas and Mellon, they were "men of noble families, who in other things loving and faithful to one another, were constant rivals only in glory and courageous exploits." [*Plutarch's Lives*—Pelopidas and Mellon][1]

Illiteracy and difference of language and dialect have, in both ancient and modern times, occasioned some differences of spelling. In Greek authors mostly, it is "Mellon"; in the modern version of Plutarch it is "Melon," and in modern use it has assumed various shapes, as Melon, Malon, Mellen, and Milan. But genealogists regard these as corruptions, and Mellon as the proper orthography.[2]

The name Mellon originated among the Greeks, where, in the Theban dialect, it meant "future hope." Even in modern times there was a newspaper published in one of the Greek provinces headed "The Mellon." Perhaps it is in existence yet. Its object was to advocate the future hope of Greece. Thus the meaning of Mellon, in the language where it originated, did not signify the melon fruit of our modern English; but is one of those ancient names of that period of society when each individual possessed but a single descriptive appellative; and according to the meaning of our name, therefore, in the language where it originated, every young Mellon may be truthfully regarded as a "young hopeful."[3]

I can scarcely claim Irish nationality, but as Ireland was the land of my birth, and home of my immediate ancestors for over two hundred years, a chapter concerning it may be interesting; and apart from all ancestral connection, I know of no other country whose history is more curious and suggestive. Certainly no history presents a richer field for the sociologist to trace the effect of laws and institutions, civil and religious, on national and private character. There it may be learned how the passions and emotions, as well as the intellectual faculties and tastes, may be intensified and transmitted by heredity. No other spot of its size on the earth has produced such marked variety of human character, or suffered greater vicissitudes of condition, or succeeded so long in attracting the attention of the rest of the world by its incessant strifes, atrocities, and abortive political agitations.

The ancient Irish began the cultivation of letters at a very early period, and their bards and druids, and afterwards their Christian priests, took great pains in collecting and preserving the history and traditions of the people. Like the history of other countries professing to go far into the prehistoric age, it can be but legendary; but even legendary history always contains some basis of truth; and it is wonderful how facts wrapped up in fiction have been preserved in this way, and how far, in some instances, they have floated down in the traditions and folk-lore of the people, before the period was reached when they were crystallized into permanent shape by writing.

We find the Irish annals more full and particular, and claiming greater antiquity than those of most other countries. It appears their pagan priesthood possessed about the same facilities for writing, and an equal knowledge of the arts, at nearly as early a date as the Egyptians. Their annals and ancient psalters—especially those of Tara and Cashel—the books of the Four Masters, and similar records, translated from the Gaelic, and collected and published by modern Irish historians, are the sources from which I draw the following information concerning them. Much of their early history, like the early history of other nations in the same stage of development, must be unreliable as regards dates and precision; but it is not uninteresting nor useless on that account. A comparison of the similarity of thoughts, actions and popular beliefs existing among all men in the same conditions of development, cannot be otherwise than instructive. In the infancy of society, or savage state, imagination begets belief, and in great measure takes the place of knowledge in accounting for the causes of natural events. In that stage the emotional greatly exceeds the mental in man's nature.

The early Christian Irish historians profess to be able to begin at the beginning: thus the Four Masters tell us that "God the Father, Son and Holy Ghost, was from all eternity; and in the beginning of time created red earth, and of red earth framed Adam, and of a rib out of Adam's side, fashioned Eve." This would indicate that the ancient Irish had no conception of black men, or they would have mentioned that God had created some of peat bog or black earth. After thus relating how Adam and Eve were created, the annals then go on to say: "After which creation, plasmation and formation, succeeded generations as follows." Then is given what they claim to be the regular line of descent from Adam to Noah, who, we are further informed, allotted to his youngest son Japhet, Asia beyond the Euphrates, and Europe to Gades, modern Cadiz, in Spain; and that Asia was the birthplace, and Spain the subsequent place of sojourn, of the Milesian Irish before reaching Ireland, their present home.

This may be true or not. How Noah divided his extensive estate is uncertain, as his last will and testament is not on record; but it serves the purpose of the early Irish annalists, as that part of Asia corresponds with the country of the Scythians, one of the greatest nations of antiquity, from whom they claim their descent.

From the same narratives we derive other rare bits of information, such as that the mother's name of Shem, Ham and Japhet was Titea, and that Noah had a son named Bith by another woman, whose name and position as wife or mother is not related. But, considering the loose habits ascribed to Noah in Bible history, the story is sufficiently probable.

The ancient Irish were of course savages, and their customs in war and the education of youth were no better, if no worse, than those of other savage nations. War and strife was the rule; self-preservation and depredation, the sole business of life; and, of course, all habits and pursuits were directed to that end. They drank the blood of slain enemies, and smeared their faces with it. The first solid food of which a male infant was allowed to partake, was presented to it upon the point of a sword, with much ceremony. This was its baptism into those ways of life which they considered the chief end of man; and as soon as it was able to draw the tiny bow, its breakfast was suspended to the top of a pole, or the branch of a tree, where it had to cut the string by its arrows to let it drop, before it could partake of the morning meal; and the food thus suspended was elevated still higher, from time to time, as the strength of the child increased. Thus it was trained for the chase and for war.

Cannibalism is not attributed to them; but it is related of the nurse of one young princess, that she fed her charge with the flesh of other children, to render her more beautiful and charming when she should arrive at womanhood.

The Scythians, whom they claim as ancestors, are well known to history, and were a very powerful and numerous people; but how much of their blood runs in the veins of the modern Irish, is problematical and inconsequential.

Fenius Farsa was the inventor of letters, [father of Niul], grandfather of Gael, and king of the Scythians, the ancestors of the Phoenicians, through whom the language was at one time called Phoenician; and the letters of which Cadmus, the Phoenician, according to Greek and Roman history, had the credit of introducing into Greece. By some, it is held that Cadmus was a brother of Fenius Farsa, and that they existed about the time of Joshua. It is true the Gaelic and Phoenician languages contain the same number of letters—sixteen, which is the number the Greek historians report to have been brought into Greece by Cadmus. It is also contended by some of the Irish authors, that this Scota was the Pharaoh's daughter who found Moses in the bull rushes; on which account Moses afterwards entertained a fraternal feeling for the Gaels, and other members of the Niul family: so much so, that when young Gael, the son of Niul, was bitten on the neck by a serpent, he was forthwith taken to Moses, on account of the latter's great fame for miraculous cures; and Moses at once cured him, by simply laying his rod upon the wound, and nothing but a green scar was left on the young man's neck, from which he obtained the nickname Gael Glas, or Gael the Green. This incident, it is said, originated the Irish preference for green, still perpetuated in their flags and uniforms. Moses, however, did not stop at this favor, but blessed him, and declared that forever afterwards no venomous serpent should be able to live in any country inhabited by Gael or his posterity. The same writers claim that indubitable proof of this miracle is found in the fact that in Ireland, and elsewhere inhabited by the descendants of Gael, no serpents are found to exist—a notable instance of the illogical; but however that may be, it takes the wind out of the sails of the common tradition, ascribing the miracle of snake banishment to St. Patrick, and would relegate that saint's fame to his other virtues. Climatic influence on snakes was unsuspected.

According to good authority, much of the Irish history, even within historic times, is purely mythical. Many writers hold that St. Patrick himself is but a mythical character; and indeed, the oldest legends do not claim his authority as apostle of Ireland from the Pope, but by the direct miraculous appointment of Christ; and more and greater miracles are related of him than are ascribed to Christ himself in the New Testament.

There may, or may not have been, a priest of the name of Patrick. Patricus is a Latin general term, signifying position or distinction, as in Patrician; but if there ever was a priest of that name, with pretensions to piety and sorcery, it is easy to see how his fame might increase. In a savage or barbarous state of ignorance, whenever any one gains some notoriety for a particular quality or virtue, as for physical strength, wit, bravery or piety, there is a tendency to add freely to his claims, especially so after his death. In this way, most of the heroes and saints of old were either created, or greatly magnified.

Indeed, this tendency has not yet entirely disappeared in civilized and enlightened nations. In our own day we have seen President Lincoln, because of his eccentric manner and humorous sayings, get credit for all the wit and humor and notable anecdotes of the time; and so, too, regarding President Garfield, who gets credit for a degree of piety, honesty and wisdom, surprising to his personal friends. It may be on this account that heroes are said to look small when you are close to them, and prophets are not honored in their own country.

All such legends are seriously related as facts, by those who wrote at a period when few could read, and knowledge of the natural causes of things was limited; and whatever was written or said by men regarded as learned and wise, was received as absolute truth in perfect trust and confidence. Scepticism of any kind had not infected popular credulity, or begun to disturb profound belief in the marvelous.

[In 1155 A.D.] the church of Rome, which at that time exercised plenary power over kings and nations, as well in temporal as spiritual affairs, transferred the temporal sovereignty of the kingdom of Ireland to Henry II of England. Whilst Ireland existed as a separate nation, it appears jealousy, feuds and wars between the chiefs of its clans, by courtesy called kings, and savage atrocities among the people, constituted the normal condition of the country. War and strife was ever prevalent in one part or another. This, with the plague and famine always consequent on such a state of affairs, reduced the population to a minimum, and kept the country a wilderness.

We find in all people trained for ages in this mode of life, where the passional or emotional part of their nature receives more scope and training than the judgment or intellectual faculties, the passions and emotions acquire the ruling power and direct the actions. It is the savage condition of humanity in which blind passion of the malignant type prevails. The lower the scale of humanity, the more unreasoning and more violent the passions for good or evil. Of course where hate, fear, jealousy and revenge are in constant exercise, these malevolent passions are the most developed, and predominate. We find precisely the same conditions resulting from the same causes among our North American Indian tribes, and among the tribes of interior Africa, and wherever else the savage state exists: producing a sparsity of population and a state of degradation approaching the nature of the predatory animal. These bad qualities were so long and thoroughly cultivated among the Irish, and so perfectly ingrained into their nature, that modern civilization has as yet been unable to extract the virus. Their improvement by connection with England has been exceedingly slow. Blindly ignorant and superstitious, although subject to the dictation of the priests so far as their prejudices are not interfered with, and scrupulously observant of their religious rites under all circumstances, no religious influence of the kind brought to bear on them has been able to subdue their evil propensities. The gall and bitterness of malice, nursed in the heart from generation to generation, has become a second nature, which the genial rays of Christianity and civilization has not been able to change; and it still crops out in plots and conspiracies to murder and destroy.

The Fenian, Hibernian and Invincible societies of Ireland, and the Clans na-Gael and Molly McGuire[4] associations in the United States, are some of the poisonous weeds springing from this root. Political considerations afford neither excuse nor palliation for the atrocities committed under these combinations.

England's policy towards them, it is true, has been unwise and unfortunate. But its unwisdom has been on the side of too great leniency and toleration. Government of the Irish, to be beneficial to themselves and safe to others, must be with a firm and steady hand: as one able historian expresses it, "A government strong, just and impartial, is Ireland's sovereign necessity." They have always admired and respected power; but despised weakness and vacillation. Cromwell was the only ruler who understood their nature, and governed them accordingly. Had his policy been continued, Irish agitation and Irish grievances would long since have disappeared, and the Catholic population would at present be enjoying the same peace, prosperity and contentment as the Protestant part of the population.

Their connection with England all along has been one of discontent, complaint and strife; and their condition, in the main, one of poverty and wretchedness. They have never assimilated with the rest of the population of Great Britain in spirit and feeling, and to this day manifest much of the malevolence, deceitfulness, indolence and reckless unthrift of the original savage character—good workers and industrious when compelled by necessity and led by a boss, but careless, wasteful and shiftless when not under restraint. The slightest leniency and relaxation by England of her power over them has always been followed by increased clamor against the government, and atrocities committed among themselves. They have never been able to attain the same degree of thrift and industry as the Protestant part of the population of Ireland and Scotland. The constant agitation of demagogues on their turbulent nature has frequently brought upon them punishments, and subjected them to restraints they would otherwise have escaped. Their incessant atrocities and defiance of law and order in the times of Elizabeth, Charles I and Cromwell, and William and Mary, almost drove the English government to measures for their expatriation or extermination. The policy of banishment was actually put in force in the northern counties of Ireland: in consequence of which the Celts were mostly expelled from that section, and the lands repeopled by emigrants from Scotland, Holland, France, and elsewhere. And if we compare the condition of these northern counties and their Protestant population to-day, with the southern or Celtic part of Ireland, it is very manifest that it would have been well for Ireland, and well for Great Britain, had this policy of expatriation been carried into effect throughout the entire island.

The cruel atrocities they committed in the rebellion of 1641–2 equal, if they do not exceed, in savage brutality the worst massacres which have ever been committed by our North American Indians upon frontier settlers.[5] Nor, indeed, was their wild ferocity much less in the rebellion of 1798, and subsequent outbreaks. And, in our own day, their widespread secret organizations against life and property, and law and order, supported openly by contributions of money from all classes among them, and the assassination of innocent victims, show that the old savage disposition is not yet extinct.

A singular peculiarity exists in the Celtic nature, consisting in a periodic overflow of temper, moving in cycles, and terminating in outbreaks. It is found in the individual as well as the community. In the family relations, however kind and affectionate ordinarily, the husband and wife among the lower classes have their periodic quarrels. The turbulent feelings rise and swell till they burst the bounds of restraint, and relief is afforded as if by electric discharge. So, too, among the Irish working people, men or women; they cannot be together in any employment for a length of time without this periodic ebullition of temper showing itself in outbreaks towards each other or their employers. It can hardly be inferred the Celtic Irish derive this innate rebelliousness of temper from Scythian, or other ancient barbaric blood running in their modern veins, or from a Spanish malignity acquired when they inhabited that country; that they are distinctive from other nationalities in this respect, is certain. I incline rather to believe, however, that their remote ancestors are not accountable for it because we find Celtic descendants in the Scotch Highlands, and parts of Wales, and even in parts of France, without this Irish peculiarity of disposition. I incline to the opinion that this feature of their character has grown out of the continued irritation and consequent exercise of the evil passions from generation to generation, in a people naturally emotional and excitable, and involved in gross ignorance and superstition. For religion not founded on reason is but superstition; and the exercise of reason must be founded in knowledge. They have been thoroughly trained into the acceptance, on faith and trust, of all religious and political ideas; and, as far back as history discloses, their feelings of malevolence, rather than benevolence, have been cultivated and promoted by both spiritual and temporal advisers. It seems this aggregation of animosity has become intermittent, and at intervals produces an eruption.

Such a tendency to violence and rebellion has been traced back by historians for seven hundred years; and even in my own time I can recollect several outbreaks of the kind.

So soon as the line is crossed from the Catholic into the Protestant end of the island, a marked difference is seen: no talk of oppression, or political complaint is heard. You find the people thrifty, industrious and attentive to their private pursuits; resembling the better industrial classes of Scotland and the United States. Rent in arrear is a rare exception. You find the farmers who hold their land under lease laying up more money, after keeping their families and paying rent and expenses, than the farmers on rented farms of a much larger size in our own country. So too, when you cross the channel into Scotland, you find a thrifty, prosperous and contented population, as much so as the Protestant Irish, and all under the same government, laws and conditions. What is the reason of all this difference?

It certainly would be a blessing to the Irish themselves, if by some social force they could be scattered over all the earth, and not a vestige of them left on their own soil. They would soon become absorbed by other races; and by intermarriage, and life under other influences, in a few generations the mixture would be an improvement of both, as is already shown in the population of the United States and elsewhere.

What I have said in the foregoing must not be taken, however, as applying to all the Celtic Irish. I have known many good, honest, industrious and humane people among them, of both sexes; but these are the exceptions to the general rule, and as usual in all such cases, they are overborne by numbers, and helpless to oppose the folly and wickedness of their countrymen. Indeed, their lives would not be safe if they showed opposition. And among the educated, there is no want of talent and ability; but in the mass, they are an eyesore upon the civilization of Europe.

I shall close this chapter here. It will suffice to give a sketch of the nationality to which birth attaches me. And whilst tradition would assign me to that ancient Celtic family of Ulster at a period long before the Reformation or Protestantism existed, yet if I should be allowed to judge from the un-Celtic character of myself and my forefathers, as far back as I can trace them, I would take it we are of the Teutonic, rather than the Celtic race. We are of the same stock, whatever it may have been, from which the modern Irish Protestants and Scotch are descended.

It can make little difference, however, what we were in the past. Different surroundings make wide differences of character in a few generations; and it is not so much what we have been, as what we are now, that counts. No country in the world possesses greater natural beauty, or can afford a pleasanter home, or is calculated to produce warmer attachment to itself in the breasts of its people. And whether of Teutonic or Celtic origin, birth and ancestral residence for upwards of two hundred and fifty years, gives me some title to claim it as my nationality.

Chapter II

Ancestry

THE ANCIENT Mellon family of the province of Ulster is reported in the Irish annals and heraldic registers to have been numerous and powerful. But, in the unsettled state of orthography of those times, proper names were spelled according to sound, rather than by any fixed rule in the use of letters; therefore we find the name of this family sometimes Malon, and sometimes Melan, and again Mellon. It appears to have been wiped out entirely in the fifteenth century, however, as no trace of it is found afterwards; although individuals of the name, who are probably descendants, have always been scattered over the country. As was usual with all families of any importance in those days, and as yet, with the wealthy classes of Europe, each family had its coat-of-arms, or heraldic insignia, and it seems the Mellon family was no exception to the custom, as its coat-of-arms is found in several old narratives of Irish pedigrees.

As a tradition existed that we belonged to this family, my uncle Thomas, to gratify his curiosity when traveling in Ireland, had an examination made at the Herald's office, Dublin, where he found a drawing of the coat-of-arms of the Mellon family, together with a genealogy of its successive heads: and procured a copy, which I insert here as an interesting memento, whether we have any ancestral connection with it or not. Its motto at least is worth preserving,—"Virtue is the safest defense;" which is nearly an equivalent to the modernized sentiment, that honesty is the best policy. It fits our family character better than those mottoes, most numerous on coats-of-arms, which commemorate heroic exploits of ancestors in war. Our ancestors, as far as known, and all the modern branches of the family, avoided soldiering, except as a necessary duty, confining their energies to the industrial pursuits of private life; and were notable only for good habits, and paying their debts. Coats-of-arms originated from the use of seals by men who could not write their names: which was the case with all gentlemen a few hundred years ago; only clerks or clergy could write. Every one who had any estate to manage, or affairs to transact, adopted some device or other, which he had engraved on a seal; this he carried in his pocket, or attached to some part of his person, to be used whenever it was necessary to authenticate a contract or voucher, or anything else now accomplished by signature. In time, the device or seal became the distinguishing mark of the individual, or his family, and was stamped or painted on their armor and panels of their coaches, or wherever it was desirable to indicate the proprietor. Serfs and peasants who held no property, and had no business to transact, needed nothing of the kind, and it was therefore confined chiefly to the landed proprietors, or aristocracy. The practice grew out of illiteracy, but pride retained it after the art of writing became general, and its necessity ceased. We see a tendency even among our own shoddy aristocracy to ape the folly of Europeans in the same direction.

But I wish it distinctly understood that I disclaim all title to this or any other family escutcheon; nor do I claim to have descended from the family to whom it belonged. My descent from it is but traditional, and the tradition itself too shadowy to be relied on, amounting to little more than a possibility; and if a reality, my branch of the family must have journeyed long in the wilderness of Scotland, before returning to the promised land of Ulster. Though not improbable, it is entirely unimportant in every point of view; and judging from their nature and character, religion and habits, as far back as they are known, I should take it, my ancestry have more of the Teutonic than of the Celtic blood in their veins—more Danish or English than Gaelic.

My first authentic ancestor I find in an emigrant from Scotland. His previous history, or how or when he came to Scotland, or his genealogy cannot be traced. He was certainly a farmer. His ancestor may have been an emigrant from Ulster to Scotland, as he was afterwards an emigrant from Scotland to Ulster; for in the wars, emigrations and exterminations which prevailed in Ireland from the earliest period, one family or tribe was constantly disappearing, and another taking its place. But, however that may have been, is immaterial.

Our particular family tree is therefore of Scotch-Irish growth. The greatest depth to which its roots extend in antiquity is a little over two hundred years, or shortly after the time of the massacre of the Protestants by the Catholics in 1641. By that event the Protestant population in the north of Ireland was nearly destroyed, and the country laid waste; but the Catholic population was soon afterwards driven out under the vigorous policy of Queen Elizabeth.[1] This left large tracts of country vacant, and land then being obtainable on easy terms under the English owners, a wave of emigration set in, chiefly from Scotland. It was during this period, according to our authentic traditions, for we have no written records, that our first ancestor, Archibald Mellon, above mentioned, with his wife, Elizabeth, put in an appearance from Scotland, and settled in the county Tyrone, province of Ulster.

Harriet Mellon, the celebrated Duchess of St. Albans, was of our Fairy Water branch.[2] There is a bit of romance connected with her history which I may relate here. She was the daughter of George, the son of Andrew Mellon, who resided near Ardstraw in our neighborhood. George, like so many sons of farmers of the period, found it necessary to emigrate in order to better his fortunes, and he enlisted in the East India Company's service. The East India Company at that time maintained an army and exercised the power of sovereignty in India, and young Mellon soon attained the position of lieutenant. But a few years' residence in India undermined his health, and he came home on a furlough to recuperate. The physicians directed his stay at a health resort in England, the name of which I have forgotten. Here, in a small room on the upper floor of a lodging house, he was confined in comparative solitude for some months—among strangers and without companions. From his window he could see into another small room across the narrow street directly opposite, whose sole occupant was a pale, delicate looking sewing girl whose ever constant application to her needle, night and day, attracted his attention. Without being aware of it on her part, her presence there, and persevering industry became interesting to him, and a source of comfort to his solitude; she seemed as a companion in adversity, and he would often forget the tedious hours in fancying what might be her history, and thoughts, and hopes, whilst so constantly employed. He resolved, as was natural, that if he recovered he would make her acquaintance, and learn how the reality might correspond with the pictures of his fancy; and he kept his resolution. It would seem he found the reality satisfactory, for they were married; and his convalescence appeared so complete, that in a short time afterwards he was ordered to rejoin his regiment in India. He had no money to bear the expense of a companion on the voyage, and in consequence he and his young wife were forced to part, until he could save enough from his pay as a soldier to send for her and restore their happiness. The long and tedious voyage on a sailing vessel, however, was too much for him, and as soon as he re-entered the hot climate of the Indian ocean his disease returned with more virulence than ever, and he died before reaching land.

Harriet, the pledge of their love, who in time became the Duchess of St. Albans, was born after his departure for India; and although in extremely straightened circumstances, the mother seems to have maintained herself and child becomingly, and after a few years of widowhood married again. The second husband was a musician of some note, and possessed of a reasonably fair salary as the leader of the orchestra in the theatre. He turned out to be a kind and considerate husband and stepfather, and it was through him Harriet's attention was turned to the stage. He had her educated for that profession, and introduced her in small parts whilst yet almost a child. She was bright, good looking and intelligent, and attracted many friends and admirers as she grew up. Some ladies introduced her to Sheridan, the celebrated author, who was struck with her abilities, and procured her an introduction on the London stage, where she soon became a star of the first magnitude. In this position she met with Thomas Coutts, the great London banker, who fell in love with and married her. He was reputed the wealthiest banker in London at the time: "being able, on one occasion, to furnish half a million pounds sterling at three hours' notice." Queen Caroline, of George IV, and other magnates, kept their bank accounts with him; and the royal family of England are said to still keep their bank account with the same house. Her marriage with this great banker retired her from the stage, and at his death left her one of the wealthiest widows in England, and not yet forty years of age. Of course, she would have many suitors; and among them was the celebrated Duke of St. Albans. Although noted for great beauty and attractions, it is probable that it was her wealth which most attracted the duke, who in due time wooed and won her. She thereby became the Duchess of St. Albans and a peeress of England; and according to all accounts, she and the duke lived happily together till her death. Her first husband, Coutts, was so exceedingly devoted that he left his whole immense fortune to her absolutely. This was the more remarkable as he had no children by her, but had numerous relatives; and to me it only manifests weakness in the great banker. In the first place, to marry an actress at all was too much risk; and in the second place, to leave all his fortune to a young and handsome widow, was a still greater piece of folly. But the result would seem to have justified his trust, for she did not allow her second husband, the duke, to spend much of it, although he was a spendthrift. She declared that she regarded the wealth as belonging to the Coutts family, and at last willed it all to the niece of her first husband, Miss Burdett Coutts, since then so celebrated as a philanthropist.

But if the uncle was indiscreet in marrying an actress, the niece has been, in her old age, equally indiscreet in marrying a young American adventurer, named Brown.

There must have been something good in Harriet Mellon, for notwithstanding her profession, and varied life, and progress from poverty to wealth and fame, and the possession of such personal attractions as brought the greatest banker of the day, and subsequently a peer of England, in his turn, to her feet as suitors, she retained a good moral character throughout. London society journals and periodicals of the time give her character as "a lady of great beauty and fascinating address, and, what is less usual in her profession, an excellent and virtuous woman also; and that, as Duchess of St. Albans, she was amiable, humane and charitable."

Returning to my own direct line, whose history is authentic and relationship well known, I find they have all been of the common industrial class; and it is of these I wish to give a more particular account.

It is related that Archibald Mellon, already adverted to, soon after his marriage emigrated from Scotland to Ireland, about the year 1660, A.D., and settled on a farm near Newtonstewart, county Tyrone. Tyrone is in that part of the province of Ulster which was then known as the Scotch settlement. Some time afterward he sold his Newtonstewart place to a party named Wylie, and in connection with a friend named Graham purchased the townland of Castletown, in the parish of Cappaigh. A townland has no relation to a town: it is merely a sub-division of a parish. Castletown comprises about four hundred acres, a third of it bog and heather. The wild Catholic natives had been driven out of six counties or so of Ulster for their atrocities, at an early date, by the English government, as history relates, and replaced by a civilized Protestant population who were massacred by the Catholics in 1641, and the country again laid waste. But after Cromwell restored order a tide of Protestant population again set in from Scotland, England, France and Holland, but chiefly from Scotland. It was in this period that our first ancestor, Archibald Mellon, arrived from Scotland. All before this as to my ancestry is virtually prehistoric, as already stated; and of this first ancestor I have only his name and his cane, and the tradition that he was a tall, athletic man of great energy and agility, and of fine personal appearance. The cane has been carefully handed down as a relic from father to son; and was delivered to me, as the present head and representative of the family, by my uncle Archibald Mellon, shortly before his death. It is a rather plain looking article, but not less valuable as a relic or memento on that account. This Scotch ancestor was the first to build and reside in Castletown after its depopulation in 1641.

It is related of this, our first ancestor, that he died at a good old age, leaving several sons, one of whom was named Archibald, who at his death left three sons, Archibald, Mark and Samuel. The sons Archibald and Mark, retained the homestead, and Samuel, my great grandfather, was provided for with a farm on the Fairy Water, near Omagh, at the Poe Bridge.[3]

[The Crawford County Mellons] are all farmers, and whilst none of them have manifested extraordinary talent in accumulating wealth, yet as far as I have ascertained they are the owners of good farms, and in comfortable circumstances.

A brief sketch of the history of Alexander, as I gathered it from himself and others, will illustrate their general character and condition. He is a man now in his sixty-fifth year, and was brought up by his father, Andrew, to hard work on the farm. When about twenty years of age a kindly feeling sprung up between him and an orphan girl who lived with her guardian uncle in the neighborhood: nothing more apparently at first than the ordinary civilities between young people of the opposite sex. She was about four years his junior; and, as young Alexander's attentions became more pointed than the uncle approved of, to remove her out of harm's way, as he regarded it, he sent her off to live with a distant relative. This nettled Alexander, as it implied as much as that he was not good enough for her; and so, love's young dream ended for the time being. Lizzie was poor, both were poor—too poor to marry. But she had beauty, an excellent but dangerous substitute for either money or other good qualities in a lady; and at her new home she had many suitors, whom she treated coolly for a time, her thoughts still going back to Alexander. But when more than a year had expired, and he neither followed nor wrote her a line to say he cared for her, she felt miffed, as I had it; and accordingly, as resentment took the place of affection, she showed more favor to new suitors. One of them, a Mr. Clark, was so strongly recommended by her friends that she favored him most; and in due time they became engaged, and the day was appointed for the wedding. But just three weeks before the appointed day, and considerably over a year after she had left her uncle's, or had had a word from her early admirer, who should appear on the scene but the long lost, but not forgotten Alexander. It was hard: she had liked Alexander, but now liked Clark almost as well, and the trouble was to decide. But she was an honest girl and dutiful withal. She had not been to a female college or fashionable boarding school, but had mental and moral philosophy enough in her nature to know that honesty is an abiding duty, whilst the tender passion is temporary and evanescent. She was possessed of good practical common sense also, and knew that bread and butter is as necessary to a happy life as sentiment; and she would not, therefore, involve herself in any new complications. Level-headed young people avoid escapades and elopements, or thoughts of suicide—such courses are for the weaklings. So she gave Alexander a decisive no. It was no use for him to urge his suit, or plead his secret love—he was too late. He had not been to see or even written to her; and when she supposed he no longer cared for her, she had plighted her faith to another, and would keep her word. "It is too late," she said, and bade him good bye.

So Alexander returned, dissatisfied with himself in particular and womankind in general; while she was married and lived happily with her husband till, in a year and a half, he sickened and died. And, in the further lapse of time, after his death a year or more, it so happened that she and Alexander accidentally met again, and his former interest in her was revived. He had no opportunity of speaking to her at the house where they met, and had another girl with him in his buggy; but he contrived to forget his umbrella on starting, and leaving his girl to hold the reins whilst he should return to the house for it, he succeeded in whispering to her, who was then the widow Clark, that he would like ever so much to talk to her for an hour or so; and wished to know how long she would be at the place where she was then, and whether he might come to see her there. She did not object, and he came again soon; and in four weeks they were married.

They were both young—she but twenty, and he but twenty-four—young enough to marry. They were both poor, but liked and suited each other, and went to work with good heart and strong will. Farming was the only pursuit which either of them understood; and I know of no situation where it is more difficult for a married pair to start without means, and yet become the owner of a farm and independent. Such was the condition of Alexander and his wife. But not discouraged, he purchased on credit a good farm of over two hundred acres, heavily timbered; indeed, with but ten acres cleared, and poor buildings. It was a herculean undertaking to improve and pay for such a farm out of its own products. When they moved to it he had little more than his axe and team, and she, little more than some furniture and household utensils. They worked on, however, happy in each other and in overcoming successive difficulties until the farm was paid for chiefly out of the timber upon it; and some forty years afterwards, when I spent a day with them, in 1884, they were still hale and hearty, with their farm in first-class condition, and occupying a fine house, and independent. Theirs is the foremost farm in the neighborhood. It is only a farmer who can realize the amount of labor it required to bring such a farm, so heavily timbered, into such condition; and to do this with the proprietor's own labor. He never could have done it had he not gotten a wife who was a gem in her way; a first-class specimen of true woman-hood, fulfilling that normal, but almost forgotten relationship of the wife to the husband: that of helpmate, which implies companionship and equality as well as help, and also the minor qualifications of fellow feeling, tastes and disposition, in order to constitute a happy mating. But they had good health, and work was a pleasure to them; not only would she attend to her household duties, the milking of her cows, and the care of her poul-try, but would spin and sew—not for herself alone, but also for others—in order to earn money to pay for the farm. And yet she is ready on the shortest notice, as I found, to get up a meal for a transient visitor not to be excelled at a first-class hotel.

There is a great deal of humbug and nonsense afloat about people breaking themselves down with hard work. I have never known hard work to hurt any one in good health and strength, if the work and will went together.

Alexander and his wife have had their sorrows, however; they have but one child living—Mrs. Reed—having lost two fine boys, one at the age of twenty-nine, and the other at the age of thirty. The only child by the first husband, Clark, is living near by with her husband, on a small farm given her by her stepfather, who, it is said, always treated her as tenderly as any of his own children.

I learned also, in regard to this Crawford county branch of our family: that whilst the first and second generations were exempt from consump-tion, the third generation and their children have been greatly thinned out by it, in its different phases. That was what carried off Alexander's two sons. All that country around Conneaut Lake was rendered exceedingly unhealthy by the Erie and Pittsburgh canal, whilst it existed. The outlet of the lake was closed, and the water dammed up to a considerable height as a reservoir and continuous feeder of the canal, being near the summit between the lake and the Ohio river; in consequence of which, a large scope of land was covered by water, in addition to the actual lake, which produced an epidemical malaria every season, causing the death of large numbers of the inhabitants and injuring the constitutions of the survivors. Since the canal was dispensed with, and the lake drained again to its natural level, the malaria and fevers which it produced have disappeared.

But this is more of a digression than I had intended. Let me return to the main stem, my grandfather, Archibald Mellon, who eventually settled in Westmoreland county. He was the second son of Samuel Mellon, as already stated, and after residing some time on the Fairy Water, he sold his farm there and purchased the greater part of the Lower Castletown place from his cousins—descendants of Mark Mellon—and returned to the ancestral home, where he and his family resided until their emigration to the United States in 1816. He was born in 1756, married in 1780, and died at his home at the Crabtree, in Unity township, Westmoreland county, Pa., September 5th, 1835, aged seventy-nine years. He was a kind and affectionate husband and father, and popular among his friends and neighbors; and was an object of attraction and admiration to his grandchildren and young people generally, for his agreeable pleasantry and exhaustless fund of anecdote and story. Although old age was weighing him down, yet in my boyhood he still possessed such magnetism as to attract me more to him than to any youthful companion. His visits were always hailed with delight. He was slightly over six feet in height, and straight as an arrow, of sandy hair and complexion, with regular features, and Roman or aquiline nose; and was remarkably agile and active. Until near his death he invariably preferred walking to riding on horseback or otherwise. With cane in hand, a walk of twelve miles seemed but a recreation to him; and in his journeys the public road had no special attractions—he would make crooked paths straight by crossing fields and woodlands. Such was the Mellon family down to and including my grandfather; and now it comes in place to relate what knowledge I have of my grandmother's side of the house.

My revered grandmother, Elizabeth Armour, was a daughter of Samuel Armour, of Lignabrade, near Castletown. Armour, in the German and Old English tongues, signifies farmer, and farmers they were, and well-to-do farmers too: for they were always reputed "well off," or in good circumstances for that occupation.

The original Armour came from Scotland about the same time as our ancestor Mellon, and settled at Auldaughal, near Newtonstewart. I have no authentic record of other members of his family, but this Samuel, the father of my grandmother, was his great grandson, and married a Miss

Smith, of the county Down, and had five children; two sons and three daughters. The sons were Hugh and John, and the daughters Nancy, Isabella and Elizabeth.

The father, besides being well-off for a farmer of that time, seems to have been of a pious turn of mind, because before he died he gave each of his children a sum of money for the purpose of educating a son for the gospel ministry; but the results would indicate that some of this good seed must have fallen on stony ground, or was gathered by the fowls of the air, because the crop of preachers from it was small. His son John, however, did comply with the request and educated one of his sons, Samuel, who preached during his lifetime with much credit and success to a large Presbyterian congregation at Drumqueen. My grandmother also set apart her son Thomas for the purpose, but, as will appear hereafter, he did not take to it cordially and preferred to emigrate to America.

My grandmother, Elizabeth Armour, was one of those devoted wives and mothers who are happy in self-sacrifice when promoting the happiness of husband and children: kind, intelligent and unceasing in attention to her family duties. To her is due some of the best qualities in her children and grandchildren. Of her children, my uncle Thomas and aunt Annie most resembled her in disposition. She was of medium stature; born in 1760, married in her eighteenth year, and died September 13th, 1847, in her eighty-seventh year, at the house of her daughter, Mrs. Annie Graham, of Ligonier. In my boyhood, when allowed the usual summer vacation of a week from work, it was my delight to spend it with these grandparents and my cousins, the children of uncle Armour, their nearest neighbor. My grandmother's kind and constant attention to my wants, and her care by good advice to try to promote my future welfare, left an abiding impression on me of her goodness of heart. Both these grandparents are buried in the cemetery of Unity Church, near Latrobe. Such is the history of the Armour family.

As Margaret Wauchob of Kinkitt married Samuel Mathews, the son of John Mathews and Isabella Armour, and Margaret's sister Rebecca married Andrew Mellon, the son of Archibald Mellon and Elizabeth Armour, the Armour and Wauchob families became thus doubly connected, as already stated. And Rebecca and Andrew being my parents, it comes in place here to give the history of the Wauchobs of Kinkitt.

My grandfather on the mother's side was Samuel Wauchob of Kinkitt, three miles west of Strabane. He was the grandson of Samuel Wauchob of the same place, who came to the country from Holland, as a lieutenant in the army of William, Prince of Orange, and acquired the townland of Kinkitt, in the Parish of Urney, about the year 1690.[4] After the defeat of the Catholic Irish under King James, in the battles of the Boyne and Aghram, and the destruction of the Jacobite power, many districts of the north of Ireland were left comparatively depopulated, as already mentioned, the Catholic natives being mostly driven into the southern part; and many of the soldiers of William, who by the terms of their enlistment were entitled to discharge, and preferred to remain in Ireland, and others whose time of service had nearly expired, were granted permission to remain there, where lands were cheaper and opportunities better than in Holland or England at the time. Such of those who remained as were married, sent for their families to join them, but most were single.

This first ancestor on my mother's side, Samuel Wauchob, was one of those Hollanders who remained; and he soon after married a woman of Scotch descent, and acquired the townland of Kinkitt, which has remained in his family ever since. I am therefore of Dutch descent on my mother's side, and I have much of her in my nature. I may ascribe to this source some of my best qualities, such as they are. It is not generally known to those unfamiliar with the history of Europe, that the Hollanders at an early period were far in advance of the English in civilization and the arts, and are fully their equals yet.

According to this it may be regarded as creditable, rather than otherwise, to be the descendant of a Hollander—the more so if these good qualities of nationality are reflected in my ancestor and his posterity.

This ancestor, Samuel Wauchob, had two sons, Matthew and Samuel, between whom the townland of Kinkitt was divided.

Samuel was my grandfather, of whom I have a distinct memory, although I last saw him when on a visit to our house in Castletown when I was but four years of age. He was then a quiet old man of dark complexion, rather slender, and about five and a half feet in height; in marked contrast, both in appearance and manner, to my grandfather Mellon; and according to my best recollection I much resemble him now in my old age, as he appeared to me then. He died in his seventieth year, shortly before we left Ireland. I well remember the distress it caused my mother. He had been twice married. His first wife was Annie Cunningham, from near Derry, my grandmother on the mother's side; his second was named Mathews, no relation, however, of the Mathews' connected with the Armour family. The children of the first marriage were Joseph, Elinor,

Rebecca (my mother), and Margaret. After Elinor's marriage, she and her husband and her half-brother, Andrew, emigrated to the United States. Her husband's name was Wauchob, a second cousin. They settled in Washington county, Pennsylvania, where he was killed at a barn raising, after which she and her three daughters removed to Richland county, Ohio, near Truxville, where her brother Andrew had settled on a farm. These, and my mother, were the only members of the Wauchob family who have ever emigrated from the old country to America. Joseph, my uncle, remained at the homestead in Kinkitt, and died leaving three sons, John, Joseph and Samuel, and one daughter, Elinor. John and Elinor were my playmates for the three weeks I was at their house before leaving for America, in 1818. I had the great pleasure of meeting with him and my cousin Samuel when I visited Ireland in 1882. Elinor married Robert McFarland, of Concess, adjoining Kinkitt. She and her husband are both dead, leaving one daughter, an only child, Isabella, who is yet single and living on her father's farm, with my cousin John managing it for her. Joseph married and died without issue. Samuel married Miss Taggart of Baronscourt, and has four children, two sons and two daughters, and he and his brother John have reacquired and hold the entire townland of Kinkitt, upwards of three hundred acres.

All these Irish cousins are comparatively wealthy, and intelligent, prudent and industrious people. But I shall not anticipate what I have to say of Kinkitt before I come to describe my visit to it, in 1882. Rebecca, the second daughter, married my father, and Margaret, the third daughter, married Samuel Mathews, as before mentioned.

Chapter III

━━━◆ ◆ ◆━━━

My Grandfather Mellon's Family

AS ALREADY RELATED, my grandfather emigrated to the United States in 1816, and settled at the Crabtree, in Unity township, Westmoreland county. His family consisted of nine children, seven boys and two girls, in the following order: *Margaret,* born in 1781, died November 23d, 1848, aged sixty-seven. My aunt Margaret, who was, in a measure, my nurse in childhood, spent her life with her parents, unmarried, and died soon after her mother, at her sister Mrs. Graham's, in Ligonier. She was kind and tender-hearted to a degree amounting to weakness, and would give away anything she possessed, no matter how useful, if she found any one else who she thought needed it more than herself.

Armour, born in 1783, married Miss Sarah White in 1808, and emigrated to the United States the month after marriage, settled on a farm in Unity township, Westmoreland county, which is yet in possession of his grandchildren. He died March 23d, 1855, in his seventy-second year.

Andrew, my father, born February 7th, 1785, married Rebecca Wauchob, second daughter of Samuel Wauchob, of Kinkitt, as already stated, April 12th, 1812, emigrated to the United States in 1818, and settled on a farm in Franklin township, Westmoreland county, three miles east of Murraysville, in 1819; and again removed in April, 1833, to a farm in Allegheny county, one mile north of Monroeville, where he died October 11th, 1856, aged seventy-one years.

Samuel, born June 26th, 1788, engaged in merchandising, and died unmarried at Holmesville, Mississippi, in 1826, of yellow fever, aged thirty-eight.

Thomas, born 1790, emigrated with his brother Armour to the United States in 1808, married Miss Eliza Toby, of Philadelphia, October 14th, 1819, and died January 15th, 1866, aged seventy-five years.

John, born 1792, emigrated to the United States in 1816, with his father, married Miss Sarah Larimer, 1820. Resided for a time in Westmoreland, then for some years in Allegheny county, and finally removed to Beaver county, where he resided on his farm until the time of his death, February 19th, 1868.

Archibald, born in 1795, emigrated to the United States in 1816, engaged in contracts and public works for a short time, then settled on a farm in Unity township, Westmoreland county; married Miss Elizabeth Stewart, February 22d, 1827, then removed to a farm near New Salem, and finally into the town of New Salem, where he resided till he died, November 10th, 1883, aged eighty-eight years, and childless.

Annie, born in 1798, married in 1821 Richard Graham, a farmer near Youngstown, Westmoreland county, who afterwards engaged in merchandising in Youngstown, and again in Ligonier, where they both died, she on February 1st, 1872, and he on February 21st, 1883.

William, born in 1800, emigrated with his brother Archibald to the United States as already stated in 1816. He married a Miss Caroline Stovall, of Mississippi, and died of cholera in 1832, aged thirty-two.

It was for my Uncle Thomas that I was named, and, next to my parents, he was the best friend I ever had. His example and encouragement first inspired in me the ambition to better my condition and rise to something higher than common farm life; and his encouragement extended not only to words and presents of books and other material assistance, but to that manifestation of sympathy and concern for my future welfare which is so necessary to strengthen and uphold good resolutions when the young heart is liable to despond, and would give up the struggle if there was no kind friend to encourage. From the time he discovered my inclination for letters, and long before I ventured to declare for a course of education, he neglected no opportunity to supply me with such books as fell in his way and might interest me and excite my taste for reading. Scarcely a year passed that I did not receive a box packed by his own hands with books and other things useful and interesting, showing his kindness and disposition to promote my happiness and welfare. His care and concern for me in particular was marked and special, but not confined to me alone. His nephews and nieces in Western Pennsylvania were numerous, and seen by him but seldom; yet he remembered them all, and all were the recipients of his favors in ways so various, but so well suited to their different tastes and wants, as showed he kept them all in mind.

This too at a time when he was bringing up and educating a numerous family of his own. It seemed he knew exactly what would particularly please or benefit each and every one of us. He was always on the alert to make such purchases, at auctions or otherwise, as would best suit for such presents. The return for his trouble was the pleasure he derived from making others happy. His generosity and kindness of heart to any one whom he deemed worthy of it was unbounded; but he never involved himself in business complications or the risks of suretyship or endorsements.

When a boy, his brightness showed him so well fitted for an education, that his mother for a short time entertained the hope that he might some day "wag his pow in the pulpit," the hope nearest the heart of every Scotch Presbyterian mother of the farming class of that day. His own ambition never rose higher, however, than the profession of medical doctor. His cousin, Robert Mathews, was at the time a successful practitioner at Drumqueen; a circumstance which inclined him to that profession. With this view he had, for a year before his departure to America, been attending the Wood End Grammar School, kept by *Domine* Donnelly at Newtonstewart. This *Domine*, according to my uncle's description of him, was a type of the schoolmaster of the period, whose learning all lay in Latin and English words, of "learned length and thundering sound." He had an abiding faith that outside of the Gaelic the Latin Grammar and language included everything worth knowing; but as a Celt, he regarded the English as vulgar trash in comparison with the pure, euphonious, comprehensive Irish-Gaelic. But whilst his young pupil's progress in Latin was excellent, he was unable to inspire him with his own peculiar educational theories. The circumstances, however, under which my uncle commenced his classical course, like my own, were discouraging; and his own experience elicited his sympathies for me in like condition. Times were bad then in Ireland, and the hardest on the middle class which had been known for a generation or more. The protracted wars in which England had been engaged had rendered taxation oppressive. Every method was resorted to to raise revenue. Every hearth and window and head of livestock, and every business transaction was separately and oppressively taxed; and after paying the rent and taxes, little was left to the farmer.

The hardships experienced by my grandfather's family and my own parents, from oppressive taxation, became so thoroughly ingrained in my nature, when a child, that I have always felt a strong opposition to it, and to all measures rendering an increase of taxes necessary. It was the universal complaint which drove our people from their homes, and swelled the flood of emigration to America at that time. In this country we have not yet learned the sad effects of heavy taxation on public prosperity. We have not yet experienced the hardships and suffering which it inflicts on the industrious poor. But in view of the growing profligacy of government of every kind among us, from the state and federal to the lowest municipality, its evils will be felt soon enough. A most mischievous degree of ignorance prevails in regard to taxation. It is supposed to be only wealth or property which bears the burden: that property holders alone are the taxpayers. They are the immediate objects of assessment, it is true, and pay directly; but a very slight examination into economic principles shows that there is no escape of the poorest from the payment, indirectly, of his full proportion of every public burden on everything he uses or consumes. He pays it in increased rents and increased prices. Whatever adds to the cost of building or production must be made up by the user and consumer, and increases the cost of living. But returning to the narrative of my uncle:

His father and brothers had their separate posts of employment assigned in the labors of the farm and loom; for at that time every farmer manufactured the flax grown on the farm into linen. Spinning and weaving was united with farm labor in every household. In the Mellon household, although the family was large, there was more than enough work for all; and notwithstanding his studies, Thomas had his share of the work to perform, morning and evening. As soon as he returned from school at Newtonstewart, a distance of nearly two miles, he had to change his school suit for his working clothes, and with canvas apron, attend to housing and feeding the farm stock. This service was unavoidable; and the prospect of support at college was slight—and a college education, in his opinion, was essential to respectability in any profession.

At the same time he was thus engaged he had a romantic admiration for the New World, and a desire to seek his fortunes there. And just then a favorable opportunity occurred for the gratification of this desire: the marriage and emigration of his brother Armour. As the family was large and its means limited, and no opening existed for Armour to support a wife and children at home, emigration to America was the alternative, and Thomas accompanied them. The circumstance of his having a sisterinlaw on the voyage was fortunate. It was when the English were rigorously exercising the detested "right of search," which in a short time afterwards led to the war of 1812 with the United States. Britain was pressed for soldiers to fill the ranks of her army, depleted by her wars with Napoleon and the United States, and was drafting all able-bodied single men, and considered the emigration of this class as a grievance; and claimed the right to intercept them on the sea by searching all vessels which sailed from her ports, whether under her own or any other flag.

The British cruisers were overhauling every vessel they sighted; and before many days the ship in which my uncles were passengers was overhauled, and every single [unmarried] man, excepting Thomas, carried off, to be subjected to a tedious term of military service: a fearful calamity to an enterprising young man like him. When the cruiser bore down on their ship, and their fate seemed inevitable, with the aid of his sisterinlaw he dressed in a suit of her clothes, and in a jaunty cap presented to the press gang of the cruiser the tableau of a fresh young Irish girl busily engaged at her knitting. His slight form, smooth face and florid complexion favored the deception.

On arriving in Philadelphia he found a hearty welcome and a situation in the grocery house of Hugh Cooper, who was originally from the same neighborhood in Ireland, and acquainted with his father. Here he remained two years, when he accepted a more lucrative situation, offered by John Hagan, another countryman of his, in his counting house in New Orleans. Mr. Hagan soon discovered his business capacity, and in a short time admitted him as a partner in the house known afterwards as Hagan & Mellon, of New Orleans. He remained in this firm for several years, attaining a high reputation for business capacity and integrity. His industry and attention were unremitting, and the business highly profitable. He was of pure moral habits, high minded, and honorable in all his transactions.

The firm dealt chiefly in sugar and cotton, often chartering a vessel and one or other of the partners going out as supercargo, when the voyage was important. At one time he contemplated a voyage of the kind to France or England, intending to call at Londonderry and bring his father's entire family to the United States on the return trip; but the troubles brewing with England interfered, and finally the war of 1812 broke out.

When New Orleans was attacked by the British, he volunteered for the defense of the city, and gained marked distinction for bravery in the final battle on the 8th of January, 1815; where he stood in the front rank firing on the enemy from the rampart of cotton bales which the Americans had constructed from the river to the swamp; the front rank firing from the rampart whilst the second and third ranks stood below and immediately behind, re-loading the guns for those who fired. In this way the guns of all three ranks were brought into active service on the approaching enemy, and did execution equal to repeating rifles.

Before the battle, the British had prepared bundles of tall cane cut from the swamps, sufficient to fill the ditch in front of the ramparts and afford a passage over. In this way they approached, each soldier of the front rank of the storming column carrying one of these bundles upright in his arms, to shield him as much as possible from the American bullets, and afford him a footing to cross the ditch when he reached it; and each in the second rank carrying a scaling ladder to climb the rampart. But, although they marched at double quick from the time they came in range of the American muskets, the few minutes that intervened before reaching the ditch sufficed for fearful havoc among them. True to orders and strict discipline, however, the ditch was partially filled with the cane bundles, and a desperate attempt made to scale the rampart, but to no purpose; each one was shot or bayoneted and tossed back by the Americans, as he reached the top of his ladder. My uncle wrested the gun from one of the enemy who had reached the top of the ladder in front of him and was trying to gain a footing on the rampart; and he retained the gun all his life afterwards as a trophy, and after his death the soldiers of the war of 1812 placed it in the old State House at Philadelphia, where it remained with other mementoes of the war for many years.

Such, substantially, is the account of the battle given me by himself, and which agrees with the account given of it in history. In regard to the gun, it was said he bayoneted the soldier from whom he took it; but on this point he would not converse. He described his feelings on the occasion to be such that excitement dispelled fear, and as being too busy to think of danger till after it was over; and then his feelings were rather those of remorse and pity at sight of the dead and wounded.

A circumstance which particularly shocked him was the death of Sir Edward Pakenham, the British general.[1] He had known him well before leaving Ireland. Pakenham, then a young officer, was stationed for a time with his regiment at Omagh, a few miles from Castletown, and whilst there made numerous fishing excursions with his friends to the river at my grandfather's place. They were in the habit of leaving their extra luggage and lunch basket at the house, so that the fish might be cooked and the luncheon set out for them by my grandmother on their return. My uncle, then a boy, and some of his younger brothers, had often accompanied the general in these excursions, making themselves useful in gathering bait, and otherwise.

The business of his firm was very profitable during the war, and for some time after: so much so that he felt justified in retiring from business altogether, withdrawing from the firm, as his share, nearly a quarter of a million. This step was hastened by reason of his having married Miss Eliza Toby, of Philadelphia, whose health was found unequal to the New Orleans climate. She was the daughter of Capt. Simon Toby, for a long time president of the Insurance Company of Pennsylvania, and well and favorably known in business circles there. Capt. Toby had been interested in coast shipping between Philadelphia and New Orleans where my uncle formed his acquaintance, which resulted in marriage with the daughter.

After retiring from business he concluded to settle permanently in Philadelphia, and built a spacious dwelling, No. 716 Spruce street, then the most fashionable neighborhood of the city, and here spent the remainder of his life in comparative retirement and the enjoyment of domestic comfort, with an affectionate wife and family.

He had three sons, Thomas, Charles H. and George W., and four daughters, Eliza, Julia, Clara and Amanda, besides others who died in childhood. Twice he established his son Thomas in business in Philadelphia with a capital of ten thousand each time, but without success; and then placed him on a farm in southern Illinois, where he became a prominent Methodist preacher, a calling for which it seems he was better fitted by nature than for trade.

Every substance has its own specific gravity—that is, its weight compared with its bulk or space it occupies; and consequently it rises or falls till it finds its level or equilibrium. In like manner, every man who comes into the world has his own peculiar qualities, and must find his level before he can accomplish his mission satisfactorily. He must rise or fall, or flounder about till he finds his proper place. Faculties, aptitudes and abilities are infinitely various, but all are equally worthy and deserving when rightly applied.

> Act well your part, there all the honor lies.

The great misfortune to thousands is, they never find out what they are good for, or not till after great sacrifice of time and energy.

Thus, my cousin Tom—I knew him well—without any bad habits, and with a good business education, trained by his father from infancy with a view to merchandising, and with a strong desire himself to succeed in that line, failed every time he tried it; and when success in merchandising became hopeless he was placed on a farm, with very little better success. But by chance he slid into a pulpit which happened to be his proper place; and in it he found himself at ease in his profession, and reasonably successful. Had it been known at the beginning that this was what suited him, and he had been trained and educated specially for it, he might have been still more successful in his profession, and would have saved time and money, as well as regret and disappointment.

Charles married Miss Fotterall, of an old and wealthy Philadelphia family, and died December 8th, 1862, leaving a widow, a son, Charles H., and three daughters, Mary F., Matilda F. and Clara. George W. died single, February 3d, 1859. Eliza, the oldest daughter, with her husband, Mr. Rodgers, still occupies the old mansion in Philadelphia. They have but two children, Thomas M. and Charles. She inherits a share of the sarcastic philosophy for which her father was noted, as will be seen from the following extract from a letter she wrote me in reply to one I had written her making inquiries concerning some items of her family history: "To my mind," she writes, "it matters very little, after you and I have passed away, to leave any trace of our ancestry. The people of our day care nothing about ancestry, or fathers and grandfathers, unless they were distinguished for wealth or position. As for mere honesty, sobriety and thrift, these count for nothing. My revered father claimed nothing in the line of aristocracy, but used to say that his best recommendation as to ancestry, was as the son of a poor but honest and industrious farmer."

She was mistaken if she thought I preferred wealth and aristocracy to honesty, sobriety and thrift in ancestry. Poor but honest farmers, or any class possessing honesty, sobriety and thrift, are the right kind of ancestry to produce a healthy and vigorous young growth.

Julia and Clara married two brothers named Harriman, engaged in business in New York; where also Amanda resides, having married Mr. Waller, a merchant of London, now deceased.

Although retired from active business pursuits for over twenty-five years, my uncle did not waste his time in indolence and ease, or impair his fortune by speculation. He was cautious and avoided hazardous enterprises, but kept his means profitably invested. His favorite subjects of investment were real estate securities and municipal or railroad bonds, or

other reliable stocks; and he was noted for sagacity in making and changing investments. He built a block or two of business houses in St. Louis
and Mobile, which afterward became very valuable; and he was one of the
chief promoters of the Pennsylvania railroad, and an active director of that
company for some twelve years. He eschewed party politics, although
nominally a democrat, but took a lively interest in political science and
public affairs. His devoted wife died May 20th, 1851, in her fiftieth year.

A kinder or more generous friend, or more affectionate and indulgent
husband and father, I never knew. He was widely known and highly
respected during life, and at his death left an estate of about half a million.
Some time ago I visited his tomb in Laurel Hill cemetery, and copied from
it the following inscription: "Thomas Mellon, died January 15th, 1866,
aged 75 years. A native of County Tyrone, Ireland. Served in the battles of
December 23d and 28th, 1814, and January 8th, 1815, at New Orleans,
under General Jackson."

My uncle *William* emigrated with his brother Archibald to the United
States, as already stated, in 1816, and taught school during the first winter
after his arrival in Derry township, near the present town of Derry. He was
only sixteen years of age at the time, but got along with his school quite
satisfactorily, and was popular with his scholars. This was much to his
credit, considering his age and the rude character of the boys attending
winter schools in those days. He had only received the advantages of a private pay school in Ireland: there were no public free schools then either in
Europe or the United States; and it is a singular confirmation of Mr. Herbert Spencer's doctrine on the subject of education, that the youth are
more thoroughly and practically educated when their education is left to
the parents and pupils themselves, on their own resources, without state interference. My uncles, who had received but a meagre allowance of schooling in Ireland in the humble pay schools of the period, were certainly
more thorough in the elementary branches as far as they had gone, and
more capable of teaching reading, writing and arithmetic, trigonometry
and mensuration and like practical branches of study, than the average of
those who at the present day go through a whole course at the public
school. Somehow or other in our public schools the time is frittered away,
and there is a want of earnestness of application; whilst in the old time pay
schools, where every pupil was made to feel that it was his precious opportunity, there was an earnestness of effort, and emulation among the pupils
to excel each other, which does not exist now. The parents also paid more

attention and took a deeper interest in the progress of their children when they had the selection of the teacher and the management of the school in their own hands, and were made directly to bear the expense. It gave them as well as their children a better appreciation of the importance of the process, and a keener interest in the value received from it. I received my common schooling before the era of free schools myself, and my recollection of the tone and sentiment which prevailed with both parents and pupils then, and the eagerness of study and thoroughness which it produced, confirms me in the accuracy of Mr. Spencer's observations. According to him government's only legitimate function is protection, all else should be left to the people themselves; in other words, that the people who are governed the least, beyond actual protection of person and property, are governed the best.

After a term or two of school teaching, and a short time in a counting house in Philadelphia, William joined his brother Thomas in New Orleans, and remained in the counting house of Hagan & Mellon until he went to Raymond, Mississippi, and entered into the mercantile business there, with marked success. In 1825 he married Miss Caroline Stovall, a highly educated lady of refined manners and prominent family connections, and soon afterwards went into cotton planting, and became the possessor of a large plantation, well stocked with slaves.

I well remember him and his young wife when on a visit to the North in 1830. They were several days at my father's place, with their little boys and their nurse, a negro wench, prototype of Topsy in Uncle Tom's Cabin. The presence of the nurse was impressed on us by two circumstances, the one that she was a slave, and the other that she would persist in washing the children, whilst they remained at Ligonier, by pumping water on them, when soiled with mud or dust. My aunt Caroline, as I remember her, was a lady of great personal beauty; but what particularly attracted me was her brilliant literary attainments. She seemed conversant with the British classics as well as the current literature of the day, and was then reading "Eugene Aram," one of Bulwer's novels that had just appeared, which she presented to me, and in return I presented her with a copy of "Watts On the Mind," which I prized highly. In fact I always inclined to metaphysical studies rather than mathematics; and "Watts On the Improvement of the Mind" is the most practical form in which I have ever seen the old-fashioned mental philosophy presented.

My uncle William was also very attractive in manner and conversation:

young, energetic and full of hope and endowed with much of the lively pleasantry of his father, his conversation afforded pleasure to all around him. His pictures of the negroes and their peculiarities, and the attractions and rosy prospects of cotton planting, inspired me with so much admiration of Southern life that, had other considerations not interfered, nothing would have delighted me more than to have gone home with him to become a manager of his plantation. But I was rather young and inexperienced to assume so much responsibility; and we parted on the understanding that when I could leave home he would write to say what could be done for me if I concluded to go South. Three years afterwards, however, when the cholera epidemic swept the country, he fell a victim to it, and is buried in the little cemetery at Raymond. My aunt Caroline, after remaining a widow for some years, married Colonel Thomas Robertson, a distinguished lawyer, and removed with him to California. They had one child; but parents and child are now deceased.

My uncle William left two sons, Thomas Armour and William Francis.

William was sent North for his education, and spent some two or three years at Jefferson College, Canonsburg, and visited frequently at my house during that time. He finished his classical education at Princeton, where he graduated with high honors. He then entered with ardor upon the study of medicine, and in 1853 graduated as a medical doctor with much credit at the University of Louisiana. But on the very threshold of his professional career, with a bright future before him, he was stricken down, and died at the residence of his brother Thomas, after an illness of a few days, on the 30th of June, 1853, in the twenty-third year of his age; and was laid beside his father, who had died twenty years before.

Thomas A., his brother, was more energetic, and had a more chequered and extended career. He was an enterprising and very successful businessman, but had the elements of generosity and faith in his fellow-men so strongly developed in his nature as more than once to destroy the results of his efforts. He was inclined to assume too many risks, and too much disposed to help his friends. He was possessed also of a strong military spirit. When but nineteen years of age he volunteered for the Mexican War, and served throughout as a lieutenant. After his return, in 1853, he married Miss Fannie C. Liddell, of the South Carolina family of that name, and receiving considerable property with her, entered extensively into cotton planting, and afterwards engaged in railroad construction.

But when the Rebellion broke out, as he was born and raised in the South and all his affiliations and property were there, it was natural for him to go with the South; and as whatever he did it was his nature to do with all his might, he immediately raised a company known as the Downing Rifles, of which he was made the captain, and entered the Confederate service in 1861. He was soon made colonel of the regiment, and was in active service in many important battles, being severely wounded in the battle of Atlanta, Georgia. The battle of Champion Hill, in which he was also engaged, was so near his own residence that his wife and children could hear the sound of the artillery, and their anxiety may well be imagined. The messenger whom they dispatched after the battle to discover if possible the fate of the husband and father, never was heard from afterwards, and is supposed to have been killed.

After the fall of Vicksburg, in 1863, the wife and children journeyed in a carriage one hundred miles into the pine woods to a place they owned there, and which they supposed safer from the enemy. He was towards the last appointed a brigadier general, but always preferred the title of colonel, as he said he had fully earned it.

At the end of the war his property as well as his slaves was gone, and he was left with but twenty dollars of good money to begin the world anew. But possessed of indomitable energy, he recommenced with a will, and was prospering till overtaken by the greatest calamity he had yet met with, the loss of his excellent wife, a lady of rare qualities, who died May 25th, 1870, in her thirty-seventh year.

This dispirited him, but he worked on under considerable financial difficulty until 1873, when, after some time of enfeebled health, he succumbed on the 15th of May of that year, and was laid to rest in the cemetery at Raymond, with his wife and kindred.

He had, in some measure, restored his shattered fortunes after the war, and was the founder, and indeed at one time owned the greater part of the flourishing town of Bolton, where his family still resides; but his kindness to his friends, and his misfortune of engaging in business enterprises beyond his means, crippled his prospects, and he died comparatively poor. The public verdict on his decease, as expressed at the time, was that "The name of Thomas A. Mellon will live in the hearts of many for years to come, for his nobility of feeling and indomitable energy and perseverance."

Whilst of an amiable and peaceable disposition and gentlemanly manners, it would seem he was possessed of bravery to a degree bordering on rashness. I should judge so from a slip taken from a newspaper relating an encounter he had at one time. It is as follows:

"Colonel Mellon, an old resident of this place, while returning home from Vicksburg, was at twelve o'clock last night attacked by a gang of desperadoes who were in ambush at Champion Hill. One of the men halted the colonel and demanded his money. The colonel told him 'not much;' and at the same time shot at the fellow with his revolver. He then made for the nearest tree and defended himself. After discharging his revolver several times at the outlaws, killing one or two of them, as is believed, and wounding others, he made his escape with but one severe wound on the back of his neck, and several bullet holes in his clothes. He is now at Dr. McKay's office having his wound dressed."

He was proud of his children and loved them dearly. When at my house a year or so before his death, he showed me the pictures of his two daughters whom he seemed devoted to; and as the pictures indicated, they really were beautiful and interesting girls. At his death, his five children—the oldest, Kate, but seventeen, and the youngest Liddell, but four years old—were left orphans in straightened circumstances. But it happened Kate was equivalent to father and mother all in one. She devoted herself to raising and protecting her sister and little brothers, and sacrificed her youth and its prospects to their interests. She has not married, and still continues the head of the family in the old mansion at Bolton.

Mollie Caroline married a man named Wasson, who proved to be indolent, thriftless and heartless, and she is now a widow and home again with her two children. Thomas A. and Frank are clerking in stores in Bolton, and showing fair promise of good business men. Liddell is yet a schoolboy.

In the summer of 1884 I had occasion to write to a mutual acquaintance at Jackson, Mr. E. E. Baldwin, to make some inquiries regarding the family. He replied: "The children of Colonel T. A. Mellon are all living together at the old homestead. Miss Kate has never married, but is the ruling spirit of the family; and has devoted herself to the bringing up of the boys and the keeping of the family together. Tom and Frank are both active business young men, and are clerks in the town. Liddell is a bright boy of about thirteen or fourteen. They have seen some pretty hard times to make both ends meet, but Kate is a courageous little woman and fought it out."

This was the first I was made aware of their straightened circumstances, and I wrote to Kate regarding it. Her reply, which I have before me, shows the true womanly delicacy and sensitiveness of her nature. She modestly says: "You ask me to tell you of the struggles we went through. It is a time I never like to recall. Some persons can become eloquent about their misfortunes, I never could. We had been shielded from every care by a fond and indulgent father. At one time he owned nearly all of Bolton, besides other valuable property, and lost it all by trusting and putting too much faith in men whom he thought his friends. * * * We had a home consisting of thirty acres of land, and converted what we could into a cotton and corn field, and have always managed to make something on it. * * * I have done anything that opportunity offered; have taken boarders and sewed, and have managed to keep out of debt, which was our great horror."

It is remarkable how accurately the words of this girl, unacquainted with her father's relatives or ancestry, describes the leading features of their family character—a readiness to conform themselves to their circumstances and condition, indomitable energy and industry in making their own living, and a horror of running in debt lest they should not be able to discharge their obligations.

Here was a family brought up in the lap of wealth and luxury, left orphans when scarce more than children, and reduced almost to penury; yet, with self reliance and courage clinging together, meeting and overcoming all the hardships and deprivations to which they had been before unused, they continue self sustained in the family home, cultivating good and industrious habits, and availing themselves of the best education the place afforded to fit them for the duties of active life. Truly there must preside over them a beneficent ruling spirit, not in Kate alone, perhaps, but pervading them all.

A family of children losing their parents and property at such an age, holding together under such circumstances, and coming out educated and intelligent and of good habits, seems to me to be more to their praise than anything which the utmost amount of inherited wealth could bestow; and I feel gratified to find them so creditable to their relatives and friends, and so worthy of the share to which they are entitled in their uncle Archy's estate.

It may be observed of my uncles on the father's side generally, that for a family of boys approaching manhood when they arrived in this country, they behaved remarkably well and were very successful. Young Irishmen, strangers in the land, without money or influential friends, they arose from a lower to a higher plane of life rapidly. It speaks well for their habits, energy, industry and good sense. Thomas, arriving with no more money than brought him over, appeared in a few years afterwards as a leading merchant in New Orleans; and in a few years more had amassed sufficient fortune to enable him to retire. William, though but a boy, was able to teach and conduct a school successfully, when almost any other young Irishman would have made himself ridiculous in such a position. And Samuel and Archy, with little more than one hundred dollars to begin on, at once launched into contracting for public work, and made money at it, Samuel emerging into a profitable mercantile business, and Archy accumulating enough to purchase a good farm. And those of the brothers, and the father, who stuck to their hereditary occupation of farming, also succeeded in a short time in becoming the owners of good farms, and prospered in their line much more than the average farmers of the time. Except Samuel and Archy, who died childless, all of them brought up thrifty, industrious and intelligent families, producing a generation of good citizens. I think it would be difficult to find a family coming into the country under similar circumstances which has done so well; and, looking back into their antecedents as far as we can penetrate, it will not be claiming too much should their posterity claim to be descended of good stock.

All, without any exception that I can find, were people of vigorous constitutions and robust health, and mostly long lived. I do not find a trace of hereditary disease of any kind, or a speck of insanity among them. Morally and mentally they were, as a rule, sober, earnest and industrious. Whilst not generally wealthy, I find none among them to have been poor or destitute. All were self sustaining, generally rather well-off in the sphere of life they occupied, strict in performing contracts and paying debts; none who were not well-doing and respected among their fellows. And, what is particularly noteworthy, I have not, in all my researches, found a single instance of any one among them or among their relatives, who was ever charged with a criminal offense of any kind, or who was addicted to dishonesty or bad habits. Whilst I do not find any who were distinguished for great exploits or shining qualities, or who attained to high position in wealth or fame, I do find a remarkable uniformity of such solid and reliable qualities as constitute good citizens.

It is important to know the mental, moral and physical qualities of one's ancestry, because the effect by hereditary transmission of ancestral traits is of momentous consequence. Qualities of person and character, both original and acquired, are always transmitted to some extent to offspring. I believe in the evolution also of families. A family of particular cast and character originates and grows to perfection and decays and dies, just as religions, governments, nationalities and all other institutions. It is a law of nature. A family of good, healthy stock, and good mental and moral qualities, rises from the common level, prospers till prosperity produces the canker of deterioration and decay, then sinks again and eventually disappears. For this reason it is much better to form relationships with rising than declining families. Where a family has enjoyed their career of wealth and prosperity for a generation or so, we may expect "degenerate sons;" not invariably, but more frequently than otherwise.

Chapter IV

My Father's Family

THE HISTORY of my parents is so closely interwoven with my own that it may be postponed until I come to speak of myself. I may say this much of my father, however, that he was an incessant worker. Inured to work from his childhood, it became so natural to him that the lines of Cowper regarding business men would equally apply to him as a farmer:

> Hackneyed in business, wearied at the oar,
> Which thousands once fast-tied to, quit no more.

His case also strongly illustrates the power of habit. When I had attained to a lucrative practice in my profession, and was yet single and wished to again enjoy the comforts of my former home, he having arrived at an age requiring more rest, I persuaded him to give up the farm and come to the city with my mother and unmarried sisters. I expected thereby to accomplish a double purpose: to secure myself a home, and relieve him from hard work. He consented, and after we were comfortably established in town was well pleased and contented for a month or two; but he soon grew discontented and unsettled, and in less than six months his discontent increased to such a pitch that he could bear idleness no longer, as he declared, and thereafter, until the term expired for which he had leased the homestead farm, he spent most of his time in the country repairing his buildings and fences. And when, with the family, he returned again to the farm and was reinstated at his regular farm work, he seemed to rejoice, declaring himself more happy and contented than under any conditions of idleness.

He was a man of sound common sense and temperate habits, and was strictly honest; pleasant and agreeable in his manners, and of an obliging disposition, he was popular with his neighbors and acquaintances.

He read a good deal, and had fixed opinions on most subjects of the day; was an advanced thinker for one in his position, but quiet of manner, and with no disposition to obtrude his views on others. In politics he was what was known as an old line whig, but despised party politicians. In religion he was a Presbyterian, without any tincture of bigotry—rather, indeed, inclined to rationalism. Whilst a kind and provident husband and parent, yet he could not enter into the plans and purposes or sympathize with the views of his children as our mother could. When returned to the farm in 1844, he engaged in the farm labor as energetically as when in the prime of life, and it was this which I conceived at the time broke him down. His health began to fail early in 1856, from disordered action of the liver and catarrh of the stomach, as the physicians regarded it; but if I were to suppose an ulterior cause I would say that this condition was brought about by over-work at a period of life when the system was unable to recuperate the vital energy thus wasted. For nearly six months before the end he was unable to work from sheer debility; his appetite was impaired and sleep rendered difficult. He did not complain of pain or suffering, but only excessive weakness and fatigue. "I am so tired!" he would exclaim; and towards the last, whilst yet able to walk about, he often earnestly expressed a wish for death, and rest in the grave. He was not confined to bed till the last day or two, and his mind was perfectly clear up to the last moment. Some few minutes before he died he noticed a neighbor woman who had called to see him entering the room, and immediately drew my mother's attention to her by name. Then a hemorrhage—the first one—ensued, and all was over without a convulsive movement. To him death's approach had no terrors; in fact, in the many death-bed scenes I have witnessed I have never seen it otherwise. Nature does her work quietly and peacefully, and leaves the mind to amuse itself with its ordinary thoughts and purposes until the torpor of death closes the scene.

As to my mother, I can hardly venture to describe her character or enumerate her good qualities, because I always regarded her goodness as in the superlative degree. But I can remember that as a wife she was a helpmate in all the qualities indicated by that forcible term; and as a mother she was all that tenderness and self-sacrifice could make her. With her, woman's wit served the purpose of much learning; and her strong common sense made her a valuable adviser even in the most important affairs. Her ability in this respect many times surprised me. She had a philosophy of her own by which she gauged everything that transpired, and believed in the wisdom of desiring neither poverty nor riches, but struggling for wealth and competence as affording independence. She shunned extremes and approved the middle course in life. Her favorite books were the Bible

and Burns' poems. Although not entirely reconcilable, yet, with exceptional passages, she could find wisdom and piety in both. She survived my
father for eleven years, living for a time by herself in a part of the homestead on the farm; but when she grew too feeble to live alone she went to
reside with my sister Eliza, where she lived happily and well cared for till
her death. The immediate cause of her death was an asthmatic affection,
which grew upon her in her last years and precipitated what debility of age
was preparing; and when the end came, with seeming unconsciousness
she quietly dropped into her final sleep in my arms, on the 9th day of May,
1868, at the age of seventy-nine years.

Elinor, my oldest sister, was born the year after our arrival in this country. She was a bright, intelligent child, but of a nervous and extremely sensitive disposition. After receiving such education as the country schools
could afford, she spent several sessions at Dr. Lacy's Female Academy,
which in its time was regarded as the best boarding school for young
ladies in the city; and in this way she obtained a rather superior education.
Her marriage with David Stottler, a young farmer of the neighborhood,
was entirely satisfactory to our family. He was a man of intelligence, enterprise and fair promise, and the owner of a valuable farm which afforded a
ready method of securing the livelihood for a family: which is a circumstance never to be disregarded in matrimonial alliances.

They lived very happily together for several years, improving their farm
and accumulating money from its products. But in the prime of life, and
in the midst of his usefulness, he was stricken down by typhoid fever, and
after a short illness died on the 20th of July, 1848, leaving her a widow with
three children, two sons and a daughter: Andrew, Manuel and Rebecca.

Andrew was educated at Jefferson College, Canonsburg, studied law
with me, and practised his profession till 1872 when his health failed, and
he died of pulmonary consumption, at my sister Margaret's, in California,
February 15th, 1873, where he went in a vain attempt to recover his health
by change of climate. His father's family were to some extent subject to
this disease. He was a young man of much promise, and was rising rapidly
in his profession when he was thus suddenly cut off at the outset of a prosperous career. Manuel married the daughter of J. C. Bidwell, Esq., and is
in railroad employment in Kansas. Rebecca married James Evans, a prosperous and respectable lawyer of an old and influential McKeesport family
in this county. Elinor, my sister, died at the residence of her daughter, Mrs.
Evans, on the 10th day of March, 1884, aged sixty-five years.

In temper and disposition she differed considerably from the rest of us.

Although a worthy and affectionate wife and mother, and a kind friend, she was possessed of a nervous temperament subjecting her to fretfulness and discontent, and disposing her often to attach blame where none existed: not however to an extent affecting her mind, or her character as a good neighbor and an estimable woman. I only mention this peculiarity of her disposition as a curious instance of the transmission of hereditary qualities. Our grandaunt McFarland, nee Armour, sister of our grandmother Mellon, had precisely the same disposition. My sister *Eliza* was quite different from Elinor in this respect, quiet, patient, but equally industrious. Her marriage was also happy. George M. Bowman, her husband, was by profession a civil engineer, and the owner of a good farm near McKeesport. He died of pulmonary consumption, November 6th, 1879, leaving her and six children surviving him; four boys, Andrew, Samuel, George and Harry, and two girls, Lizzie and Ella. Their mother has managed the business affairs of the family with admirable ability since their father's death. The oldest son, Andrew, and the two daughters, Lizzie and Ella, are married, and doing well.

My brother *Samuel*, shortly after he attained to manhood, left home and entered a counting house at New Orleans. Although brothers, and alike in most respects, yet in some particulars no two men could be more different. From boyhood a marked difference existed between us in our views of the world and its pursuits. We never could agree on the same business policy, or on the merits and demerits of any enterprise whatever; and now after life's race is run with him and nearly so with me, if results would determine which was in the right, the decision would be in my favor: for I have been successful in every enterprise which I seriously undertook, whilst he failed in most. I have been prosperous, whilst he never got his head much above water. When in need of means I have supplied him several times; but assistance oftener resulted in loss to himself than otherwise. To his credit, however, he invariably managed to pay whatever he owed to any one, and was correct and honorable in all his transactions, but was always subject to business misfortunes whenever he got far enough ahead to have spare means. He never broke up, although often reduced to comparative poverty; the reason was he never went in debt beyond his ability to pay. This family trait he retained in the highest degree; in consequence of it he could always get a stock of goods in the East or at Galveston on credit to any extent he wished. Two causes held him down financially: although never extravagant or wasteful, he was always liberal beyond his means; but the chief cause was credulity and lack of discrimination of character. Any plausible and designing schemer who would obtain his confidence could persuade him into ruinous transactions; and needy parties without the ability, and often without the intention to pay, could insinuate themselves into his good graces, and obtain credit in his store to an extent which too frequently resulted in loss.

He had no bad or immoral habits whatever, was extremely kind and affectionate in his family, and strong and abiding in his friendships. His industry was unceasing, and his desire to accumulate wealth as strong as mine; but the failings already mentioned prevented success. When he was about fifteen years of age I had just emerged into a successful law practice, and naturally desired to lead him into the same profession. Accordingly I took him into my office, the better to superintend his education. But I soon found that he had no ambition to progress beyond the common English branches. He would read and inform himself correctly on all subjects of general interest, but despised the professions, particularly that of the law. Seeing that he could not be induced to prepare himself for admission to the bar, I tried to interest him in dealing in notes and other money securities, but found he had no inclination to make money in that way; and, even if he had, that he did not scrutinize the character and ability of the parties sufficiently to render that line of business safe. After a trial of two years, we both concluded that it was better for him to adopt some other pursuit than that which I was engaged in, and accordingly he returned home, and arranged with my father to manage and operate the farm on condition of a fixed share of the profits. One year sufficed to disgust him with farming, however, and he resolved on going to New Orleans to strike out for himself. There he entered a counting house in a wholesale merchandise establishment, a position for which his education in my office had prepared him, and displayed such ability that he was soon promoted to the management of a department of the concern; and after remaining for two or three years opened a retail store of his own in Jasper, Texas, where he was very successful for a time.

Merchandising was his *forte*. Nature fitted him for that employment. No man can feel at ease or succeed in any profession or calling for which nature has not fitted him. He could purchase goods with better judgment, handle more of them and keep his store in neater order, and obtain more customers than any of his competitors in any place where he ever did business. All he lacked was the ability to hold his own. After he was in business for some time in Jasper he married Miss Angelina Maund, daughter of the Baptist minister of that place, who made him an excellent wife. He remained in business at Jasper until the breaking out of the Rebellion, when he was drafted into the Confederate army, and all his property swept away from him. The close of the Rebellion left him without any means whatever; but he nobly commenced the struggle anew, and with some little assistance from me and his good credit in the East recommenced business at Beaumont, Texas. At Beaumont he retrieved his fortunes to some extent, but was driven out by the effect of the malarial condition of that district on his health, and he recommenced business in Lampasas, Texas, where he remained with measurable success until his death. He died at my house, September 15th, 1879, aged fifty-three years, and lies buried beside his father and mother in the Allegheny cemetery. The circumstances surrounding his death were singular and sad.

He had come North with his daughter Nellie, on a visit to his friends for a summer vacation, with a view to improve his own health and to afford Nellie the opportunity of meeting with her relatives in the North and seeing the country. The visit had been looked forward to by both with pleasurable anticipations; and when he arrived here and for some weeks before he expressed himself in better health than usual, although his sunken eyes and haggard expression rather alarmed me. His cheerfulness and buoyancy, however, indicated no fear or alarm on his own part. He had become so accustomed, he said, to prostration from malaria and inaction of the liver, that it only disturbed him while the trouble lasted; and so far it had only tended to reduce his vigor and general strength. As if in anticipation of the last opportunity we should have, he and I spent several days together visiting the scenes of our boyhood. At the old homestead farm in Allegheny county he found many marks of his handiwork still remaining; and after calling upon as many of the old neighbors as still survived, we visited the older place in Westmoreland county, where I had spent my boyhood and he his infancy.

It was more dear to me on account of my longer association with it. We then spent a day with our good uncle Archy and kind aunt Betsy, of Salem, taking in the old stone church at Monroeville on our way home. Here, on effecting an entrance, we sat down in our father's family pew, where in times past we had endured many a tedious sermon; and in the solitude we could repeople the surrounding pews with the familiar faces of former neighbors who had been their occupants long ago, but most of whom were now in the little cemetery outside. Then, after a stroll through the burying ground to learn from the gravestones how many of our early friends had gone to their rest, and after examining the little enclosure which my brother had himself constructed, on a former visit many years before, around the graves of our parents, and which was still there although I had since removed the remains to the Allegheny cemetery, we arrived home again after one of the most pleasurable excursions I ever experienced. A day or two afterwards he visited our friends in Beaver county, returning in good spirits and hopeful of the good effect on his health which his trip North seemed to produce. But in a few evenings after this, suddenly and without any premonitory symptoms of warning, he was taken with a violent pain in the right side towards the back. Medical aid was ineffectual to afford relief, and his sufferings did not abate until he succumbed to the disease, four weeks afterwards. His wife, who had come on, and his daughter Nellie were the only members of his family present at the time of his dissolution. The doctors attributed his death to a diseased state of the liver, superinduced by long exposure to malarial influences. They regarded the change of climate as calculated to irritate the disorder and produce the acute paroxysm which resulted in death. This event affected me deeply. After our parents, his was the first break in the family. Before his burial, when alone with the corpse in profound sadness, the incidents of our lives whilst together passed rapidly in review. Afterwards I made the following memorandum in my note book of my thoughts as they occurred then:

"O, brother! my only brother! how forcibly all the incidents of our long intimacy, from your childhood up, now crowd upon me. And here it all ends! How wild the emotions which that significant expression on your pale, silent features excites in my heart. Your fixed smile of sarcastic indifference would seem to indicate surprise at the hollow mockery of life, and the undue value we set upon it. What wonderfully calm repose is reached when life's poor play is o'er! The racking pain and disturbing thoughts are gone. No wonder the sages of old regarded this as 'Nirvana,' or everlasting rest. When anxious care could do no more for those you loved, all thought regarding them then ceased to trouble you. One after another their images left your wandering mind. Your little boy, Robby, was the last to disappear: 'My little Robby,' were the last words to pass those silent lips. Yes, dear brother, now all is well with you. If I interpret that silent countenance aright, it is well with you—better than with those you leave behind. Your going leaves bleeding wounds in the hearts of a bereaved wife and children, and brings sadness to a brother and sisters which it would be useless at present to try to assuage or comfort. In such case time alone is the only comforter.

"Twice, dear brother, you have filled my heart with sadness; first when forty years ago, a boy, filled with the ardor and ambition of youth, you disregarded the remonstrances of parents and friends, and departed to seek your fortunes in the dangerous climate of the distant South, among strangers. Then, with a sad heart and fearful forebodings, I watched the boat that bore you away, as far as my eyes could follow it. On that occasion there was still a gleam of hope, but now, in this second separation there is none. This is the end! The end of all our pleasant interviews, as well as our differences of opinion and friendly disagreements. Here is an end of it all, finally and forever. The question of success or failure is nothing to you now; worldly cares have ceased to trouble. You feel no more interest in the passing events of to-day, than if your span of life had been cast a thousand years ago. You care no more for what is going on around you here than you did a thousand years before you were born. Alas, of what weak and contradictory elements we are composed! Whilst my heart is bursting with emotion, and my tears cannot be assuaged, my judgment keeps whispering to me that we need not grieve on your account; that you are at ease, and happier than any of us who feel the sad event so keenly."

He left a widow and five children, four boys and one girl, surviving him—the youngest child, Robby, a boy of only a few years. The daughter, Nellie, married D. M. Phillips, November 3d, 1879, a prosperous merchant of Lampasas. The widow continues the business at Lampasas, with what result is yet to be seen. My brother had great confidence in her; and I think his confidence was not misplaced. He willed his store and property, consisting of some ten or fifteen thousand dollars worth, to her absolutely. And so far she has shown good judgment and great energy in the management of the business. My brother owed me three thousand dollars at the time of his death; she has paid me two thousand, and I have acquitted her of the residue. The only danger I apprehend is on account of the children: boys left fatherless at an age when it is exceedingly difficult for a mother to control them. How they will turn out time can only tell.

My sister *Margaret* married Robert Shields, a Greensburg merchant possessed of considerable means which he had inherited. They lived happily enough for a time, but he neglected his business, and found it necessary to migrate with an impaired capital to Omaha, Nebraska. He arrived there at the right time to have made a fortune, had he been the kind of man to achieve success. As it was, some vacant lots and other property around the city, which he purchased when he went there, increased in value so rapidly as to have made him rich had he behaved properly. But by indulging in drink, gambling, and their kindred vices, and branching out beyond his means to build blocks of warehouses he failed a second time.

The next move was a fatiguing journey of many months by wagon across the plains to California. There was no railroad then. Here, with the residue of the patrimony which I transmitted to my sister from her father's estate, a farm was purchased, a dwelling erected, and farming inaugurated with fair results. He had carried his bad habits with him however, and prosperity was out of the question. Finally he became so habitually dissipated and intemperate, and violent in abuse of his wife and children, that she was compelled to resort to the law for protection, and after repeated disappointments in the hope of his reformation, at last under my urgent advice, applied for a separation and divorce, which was obtained.

His was not the first instance I have seen of the demoralizing effect of drink. It blunts and finally destroys the sensitive and better qualities of human nature, and brings out and strengthens the bad qualities more readily and speedily than any other evil habit that man is subject to. I have known many in my time who, before falling into this habit, were kind and affectionate husbands and fathers, anxious for the happiness and comfort of their families; but as the habit of intemperance grew upon them they became harsh, unfeeling and finally cruel, until in time their whole nature seemed to change to the reverse of what it had been before, and an unnatural selfishness would arise and assert itself to such a degree that the appetite for stimulants would be gratified even should the wife and children be compelled to go without food or shelter. It had this effect on Shields. Naturally he was of a kind and generous disposition; but dissipation changed him into a heartless, unfeeling persecutor of his family.

After my sister was released from his interference and had the farm under her own management, and the crops were exempt from liability to be swept away for his debts, the situation improved, and she was able to not only pay off previous encumbrances on the farm but to secure additions to it, and to make permanent improvements by Artesian wells for irrigation, and otherwise, to an extent which has made the farm valuable and placed her and her family in comfortable circumstances.

But she has had other sorrows to contend with; all of her children but one have died of pulmonary consumption, and that one, James, is liable to the same disease. He, and a grandchild by her deceased daughter, are all that are left to her; and how long they may remain is uncertain, as consumption was hereditary in the Shields family.

Margaret is of the Wauchob side of our house, as I am in some degree myself. Samuel was of my father's side, as were Elinor and Eliza, Elinor being a full representative of her grandaunt, as already mentioned, and Eliza of her grandmother, nee Armour. I have always observed, as I suppose most others have, that in every family the children can be designated and assigned to that side of the house or parentage which they most resemble in nature and character.

Such is a brief sketch of a family of remarkably earnest, energetic and industrious parents and children.

Chapter v

The Negley and Winebiddle Families

A SKETCH of my wife's family history will come in place here more appropriately, perhaps, than elsewhere.

Jacob [Negley], my fatherinlaw, was a skillful land surveyor and mechanical engineer, and a man of great energy and enterprise. He married Anna Barbara Winebiddle, June 2d, 1795, in her seventeenth year. She was the daughter of Conrad Winebiddle, a tanner. In his lifetime my fatherinlaw accumulated a large estate, exclusive of that which he had inherited. His estate, however, was wrecked and almost swept from him in the memorable collapse of 1819, which left scarcely a dozen solvent business men in Pittsburgh; and the worriment and distress of mind consequent on his reverses and efforts to avert the calamity aggravated the disease which terminated his life a few years afterwards. His property was chiefly in real estate, which suffers the most in such a general and disastrous collapse as that which then occurred, and which again occurred in 1873. Exclusive of what his wife had inherited from her father, he had acquired and owned at the time nearly all the land, except that of his brother Casper, which is now included in the Nineteenth ward, and a considerable portion of the Twentieth ward, besides a good deal of adjoining property, comprising an area of about fifteen hundred acres, on which he laid out a town at the junction of the Pittsburgh and Greensburg turnpike and Frankstown road, and long known as Negleystown, afterwards as East Liberty, and now as the East End of the city. He had not only acquired and paid for this extensive body of land, but had improved it and brought it to a high state of cultivation. At the time of its acquisition that portion lying between what is now Stanton avenue and Penn avenue was mostly covered with a dense growth of white oak and hickory timber which he cut off, converting the land into an extensive meadow. He also continued to operate the grist and fulling mills on Negleys run, a short distance above what is now the Brilliant oil refinery; and in 1808 he built what was then regarded as one of the three finest residences in or about the city, and is now known as the old Negley mansion house, at the intersection of Stanton and Negley avenues, locating what is now Negley avenue in a direct southern line from his front door to the Pittsburgh and Greensburg turnpike. He had also planted, and in fine condition, several apple and peach orchards on his extensive property, and had it all so well fenced and cared for that it presented the appearance of one of those great estates to be seen in Europe.

But, out of debt and the possessor of wealth and unbounded credit, he unfortunately aspired to still greater enterprises. He was an intimate friend of Cadwallader Evans, of Pittsburgh, the inventor of the high pressure steam engine. Evans was the only machinist of the place at that time, for the construction of steam engines, and united science and enterprise with practical ability. This friend persuaded him that his newly laid out town and fine property would be vastly benefited by the establishment of a steam flouring mill; and he saw that such an enterprise would be profitable, as milling throughout the country was done by rudely constructed mills on small streams which went dry, and the mill stood idle throughout the summer, often causing great inconvenience and sometimes partial famine for want of milling facilities. He accordingly engaged in the enterprise and constructed the first steam flouring mill west of the mountains. That kind of machinery was then very costly, and his mill, before he was through with it, cost him in the neighborhood of thirty thousand dollars, which was an exceedingly large sum for the period. Besides this, he had contracted some debts for building dwellings and stores, to help the town which he had laid out; and, almost entirely at his own expense, had erected the first Presbyterian brick church of the village. But whilst absorbed in these enterprises, chiefly on credit, the collapse already mentioned came upon him, and money, which had before been so abundant, at once disappeared. The circulating medium to pay debts was gone, and the values of property and commodities collapsed. Debts alone, the money of account, remained in full force and magnitude. In such cases the figures remain undiminished, whilst convertible values of property to balance them shrink and disappear. He made a hard battle, and struggled alone under the load for five or six years, but went down at last, and eventually sickened and died. His death occurred on the 18th of March, 1827. Besides being a man of great energy and enterprise, he must have been very intelligent for his day and condition, and was evidently possessed of fine literary taste. Much of his library and papers came into my hands after I entered the family; and, judging from the large number and choice selection of his books, he must have been a man of extensive reading—re-markably so, indeed, for one who had not received a classical education. Such of his work also as a surveyor and civil engineer as I have come across, would indicate considerable professional skill; and the documents and contracts and the like prepared by him which I have seen, indicate clear business comprehension. He appears to have also been a leading man in the local enterprises of the time, such as the construction of roads and turnpikes. He was a director in the Pittsburgh and Greensburg turnpike, and instrumental in procuring its charter. I have often heard it asserted by old residents that the bend in that road, now Penn avenue, on the hill west of East Liberty, was for the accommodation of his, Negley's, Black Horse Tavern, which stood where the Ingleside house of Richard Dale now stands, near the corner of Penn avenue and Rebecca street, and was a no-table stopping place for stages and travelers for many years, and gave the place the name of Black Horse Hill. The name arose from the large swing-ing sign of a black horse.

After his death the Sheriff administered his property. At this juncture a powerful and very valuable friend of the family appeared on the scene, and interposed his money and influence to save part of the estate for the children. This was the Hon. James Ross, at one time United States senator from this end of the State. He had long been Negley's friend and legal ad-viser, and it was only through him that anything was saved for the family.[1] As the Sheriff's sales of the property took place from time to time, he be-came the purchaser, wherever in his opinion it did not bring its value. He did this without consulting the widow or children. But some time after the entire property was disposed of, and they were anxious to know when they should be dispossessed, Mr. Ross rode out to see them, and had a meeting with the family, as my motherinlaw related it to me; and, after in-forming them of the aggregate amount of money he had advanced in the purchases, said that he had taken this course as well with a view to a safe investment for himself, as also to benefit them if times should improve and the boys showed themselves worthy of their father, and were well-doing and industrious. If so, they might in time be able to redeem the property, or part of it, at least. He felt this course due to the friendship he had borne their father; and they could remain in possession of the mill and the property he had purchased until it would be seen what could be done in this direction.

This was joyful news to the widow and her children, two of whom, Ja-cob and Daniel, were nearly men grown. It inspired such fresh hope and courage as approaching help brings to those in a sinking ship. After this, all who were able went to work with a will; but the success which resulted was due mainly to the persevering industry and excellent management of the mother, and the steady attention and labor of her two sons, Jacob and Daniel. The other boys, George and Alexander, were too young to be of much account in that memorable struggle.

The mother took the farm under her own care, and gave it personal attention. It still comprised about one thousand acres. She has often related to me how, after preparing the evening lunch, she would pack it in large baskets suspended on each side of a steady horse; and, mounted on his back, would transport it to the distant field where her farm hands, from ten to twenty in number, were harvesting or engaged in other work. And not unfrequently, after laboring in this way from before sunrise until dark, she would have to ride at night five or six miles into the country to visit some family distressed with sickness: because her skill was looked upon as equal to that of most doctors, and people unable to pay for or procure professional services were constantly resorting to her for advice and assistance. Like women of her day similarly situate, the roots and herbs of the garden constituted her medical laboratory.

Jacob and Daniel ran the mill, one of them attending market regularly twice a week with the flour and meal. They had a stall in the old Diamond Market House, which they kept constantly supplied with their products. A considerable portion of the land lying between the mansion and the river was yet uncleared. From this the timber was cut and disposed of, and the proceeds of the farm and the mill and the timber, as received, were all turned in to Mr. Ross. After a time, prices were offered for portions of the land which, with Mr. Ross' consent, it was thought advisable to accept; and the money on these sales was turned in likewise, from time to time as received: until finally he was refunded for his outlay, debt and interest, declining to accept anything for his trouble and services as adviser. When this was accomplished, it was left to Mr. Ross to divide among the children the remaining property as he saw fit—the widow disclaiming any share or dower, considering her own patrimony from her father's estate sufficient for her support. Whereupon Mr. Ross, after procuring the services of Robert Hilands, the County Surveyor at the time, had the remaining land plotted and divided into eight shares or parts, but not of equal values. The shares of most value he allotted to the sons, deeming them the more deserving; and on the 15th of December, 1837, delivered a deed to each for his or her share. From this plot and survey, the name of the surveyor was conferred on Highland avenue. After the debts were paid, about five hundred acres remained to be divided in this manner among the children: not much of a fortune to each according to land values just then, but in course of time as values appreciated, those who retained their shares realized handsomely. Even at the time of the division by Mr. Ross, under the favorable prospect in the near future the average value of each share could not have been much less than fifty thousand dollars.

Had it not been for this financial cyclone the Negley family, in the extent and value of its real estate, would have equaled in wealth the Dennys or Croghans or Rosses, or any of the other old families of the city who became so wealthy by retaining their real estate.

James Ross was a remarkable man in his day. Of great talent as a statesman and profound learning as a lawyer, he stood at the head of the bar. Before I was admitted to the profession I heard him make his last address to a court and jury, and it made an indelible impression on my mind. He was then old and feeble; but whilst leaning on the railing of the jury box his arguments, forcibly put, in clear sentences and simple words, I have never heard surpassed. He was a profound politician but no partisan. Sought after in all important cases he was a laborious practitioner, and accumulated a large fortune from his practice upon exceedingly small fees. I have been surprised to find his itemized receipted bills for professional services among the papers of my fatherinlaw, and those of another client of his, John McMasters of Turtle Creek, containing items as low as fifty cents and not exceeding in the aggregate one hundred dollars for services which would now command five times as much. But whilst he charged moderate fees he worked hard and accomplished much, and saved and invested and reinvested his earnings with great care and attention; and hence the large fortune which he left at his death. I need not say more regarding him, as he is an historic character of those times. I admired him so much as to name my son James for him.

By the time the property was redeemed and divided, and the family on their feet again, three of the boys, Jacob, Daniel and George, were married and doing for themselves. Notwithstanding their pecuniary embarrassment, Mr. and Mrs. Negley had not neglected to give their children a proper education, as far as the best local facilities could afford: and now that affairs were more prosperous and a brighter future in view, Mrs. Negley sent her two younger daughters, Sarah and Isabella, to Mrs. Olver's Seminary at Braddocks Field to complete their education. This was the institution in highest repute at that time, where most of the young ladies of the best families of the city were educated. Alexander, the youngest son, received his education at a college in Ohio.

The general type of the Negley family, so far as my researches have extended, is bodily health and energy coupled with good practical common sense; for the most part long lived and exempt from hereditary disease, either physical or mental—anything to the contrary has been casual and accidental. The men were mostly of large stature. Some years ago when it became necessary to remove the remains of Alexander, the aforementioned ancestor, from the churchyard at the corner of Smithfield street and Sixth avenue to another burial place, the great size of the skeleton was a surprise to those present. His sons Felix, Jacob and John were also men of large size; and the same physical type is reproduced to some extent in his great grandsons of the present day, General James S., son of his grandson Jacob, and Major William B., son of his grandson Daniel.

Loyalty to religion and its support is also a strongly marked feature in the Negley character, which may have descended from the ancestral disciple of Zwinglieus.[2] Their ancestor, Alexander, was a strong supporter of the renowned Father Weber, who accomplished so much in Westmoreland and Allegheny counties at an early day in organizing German Reformed churches. A peculiar trait in the character of Father Weber was his forecast in obtaining and attaching to each organization of the kind a farm or large plot of ground, which contributed much in after years to its support. Weber was the originator of the German Reformed Church at the corner of Smithfield street and Sixth avenue in this city, and secured to it an entire square for church purposes, which has been a source of revenue to the congregation ever since. His associates in this enterprise and among the first trustees, were Alexander Negley, John Beitler, F. Lorenz, William Eichbaum and many others whose descendants are among our well known citizens, although not now attached to that denomination. Alexander and his family worshiped there during his lifetime; and he was buried where the present church edifice now stands, but his remains were afterwards removed as already mentioned. His son Jacob, my fatherinlaw, was equally liberal in the support of religion, but with common sense too strong to allow his zeal to become fanatical. Whilst foremost in contributing material aid to the church and zealous to promote Christian morality and due respect to religious worship, he never became officious or meddlesome in church affairs. As already mentioned, he erected the first brick church building on the same piece of ground at the corner of Penn and Highland avenues where the present church edifice now stands. He built it almost exclusively at his own expense, on the grounds which he and his wife donated for the purpose. It was not a very large or expensive building, but as well proportioned to the wants of the congregation at that time as the present edifice is to the wants of the present congregation. Ever since then their descendants have contributed liberally to the cost of the successive church edifices which have been erected on the same spot, as well as to all other religious objects.[3] And the last important act of my motherinlaw's life was to donate, at a cost of fifteen hundred dollars, the bell which now calls the congregation to worship. Under these circumstances it is natural for their descendants to feel an interest in and disposition to attend that church in preference to any other. Few of the members of the congregation which now worships there know or care about what transpired so long ago, and we claim no distinction nor consideration on that account. We prefer to allow the new comers to have their own way in selecting and dismissing pastors, and managing the church affairs. We only care to have the privilege of worshiping at the old altar when we feel so inclined. Such is the history of the Negley family.

Winebiddle is a translation of the German words *wein* and *bydle,* and in sound and meaning are nearly the same in both languages. Wine beadle means wine steward, as Winebrener, another proper name, means wine refiner. Such offices were once common in the Rhine wine districts.

My motherinlaw as already mentioned was the oldest daughter of Conrad Winebiddle. He was a thrifty and well-doing tanner who at a very early date settled and established his tannery on a tract of land on the bank of the Allegheny river, at the mouth of the Two Mile run. His tannery and dwelling were situate between the mouth of the run and the present United States Arsenal grounds. My motherinlaw would often relate how fleets of canoes, filled with Cornplanter Indians, used to pass her father's house periodically, going to and coming from the town below them.

Her father died in the prime of life, and was one of those energetic, industrious men of his day who accumulated rapidly. I judge so from his will dated September 3d, 1795, probated the 17th of the same month, and recorded on page 87 of the first Will Book of the county. He devised his property to his widow Elizabeth, and his four children, Barbara, Philip, Catherine and Conrad. Besides dividing among his children a considerable sum of money and some slaves, he was able to give them two houses apiece in the "Town of Pittsburgh," situate on Water, Market and Wood streets; and also divided between them five hundred and fifty acres of land in what was then Pitt township—now the Nineteenth and Twentieth wards of the city, exclusive of the farm he occupied on the bank of the river. This body of land was held by the devisees until their deaths respectively, and was bounded by what is now the Allegheny cemetery property, the lands of Col. Croghan, Jacob Negley's heirs, Centre avenue, the Pennsylvania railroad and lands formerly of Woolslayer and Ewalt's heirs; and most of it was held till recently by the Negley, Winebiddle, Baum and Gross families, heirs and devisees of the Winebiddles. My homestead is on part of that allotted to Mrs. Negley. As expressed in his will, Conrad Winebiddle appointed his beloved wife Elizabeth, and his beloved sonin-law Jacob Negley, executors.

I introduce one clause of this peculiar will in order to illustrate the manners and customs of the times in which it was made: "*Item,* I also give to my beloved wife Elizabeth, her choice of two of my cows, also a horse, also her bed and furniture and the bed and furniture for the youngest children, and my desk and clock, cubbard and two pewter dishes, six pewter plates and six spoons, two iron potts, a duch oven and a ten plate stove, and her tea equipage and a copper kittle and frying pan, two smoothing irons, a skimming ladle and flesh fork, a small iron pott and skillet, also my negroe boy Jacob and my negroe girl Nell, also a cask of sugar and a bushel of salt, and six hundred pounds of flower, and the money that she has gathered by her own industry, amounting to £40 or £50."

He then goes on to devise his property generally, including his slaves, among his children. Slavery had not yet been abolished in Pennsylvania— only the time of servitude was limited. What is noteworthy in the foregoing extract is the peculiarity and minuteness of the items. He was a man of very considerable wealth for his time and was well known not to be of a close or penurious disposition; and yet his bequest of pots, kettles, spoons and pewter plates is unique in its line. Although rich, he did not despise the day of small things; or it may be that if his will was drawn by a skillful lawyer—and there were very skillful lawyers at the Westmoreland and Allegheny county bars of that early day—the peculiar enumeration of household articles may have been inserted by design, in order that the will might show on its face that the testator was of sound mind and memory. It affords a vivid picture of the household of a well-to-do German of that day. The pewter plates and dishes, the Dutch oven and ten-plate stove, and skimming ladles and flesh forks were essentials in every well appointed dwelling. Their enumeration revives in me a clear impression of such a household. Many a good time and hearty meal I have enjoyed when a boy, in just such a home with one or other of our German neighbors.

The type of the best country dwelling of the day was a hewed log building one and one-half stories high, usually 32 x 24 feet square, with a partition at one end cutting the interior into two unequal parts, leaving about two-thirds of the space on one side and one-third on the other. The smaller part, having the front and back doors, was used for kitchen and mostly for dining room also; the larger apartment, having its sole entrance from the kitchen and two small windows for light, was used for parlor, general sitting room and dining room on particular occasions: and if large enough to spare it, a small bed room was partitioned off on one side for the old folks, the other sleeping apartments being on the second floor. In the centre of the partition dividing the kitchen from the sitting room was the large stone chimney, with wide fireplace intended for wood fuel for the kitchen on one side, and a hole for a stovepipe on the other.

The plasterer's art had not come into use then in the rural districts. Well worked mortar, consisting of tough clay and straw well mixed, firmly closed the spaces between the logs; and all partitions were of rough boards, which were made from the timber of the farm cut into boards at the neighboring sawmill. It was always an object to have the general sitting room quite large, from eighteen to twenty feet square, and in the centre stood the ten-plate stove, named from its being constructed of ten cast iron plates—not of the light pasteboard type of the present day but nearly an inch thick. The stove stood on feet about eighteen inches above the floor, and was in shape a square box usually four or five feet long, three feet deep and three feet wide, with a square opening through the centre from eighteen inches to two feet in length and about a foot high. On each side of this opening was a cast iron door, and the opening itself served well for baking, broiling and other culinary purposes. The stove, with its pipe rising from one end to within a couple of feet of the joists supporting the floor above and extending to the chimney, kept the room at a comfortable temperature in the severest weather. Wood alone was used for fuel, timber being plentiful and coal not yet introduced.

Benches were placed around the walls; and these, with a large table and a few split-bottom chairs, formed the chief furniture. Light in the evening was afforded by a small sheet iron lamp set on the stove to keep its contents in a liquid state. The grease to supply it was collected from the beef and bacon in the process of frying and broiling.

Here the entire family, with any visitors who might drop in, congregated and spent the long winter evenings, and on any festival occasions, which occurred often. The light was dim, but the spirits of those congregated around it were bright. The boisterous mirth and hilarity was such as can never be equaled under the restraints of more refined society; and the close communion into which it brought all the members of the family, old and young, at all leisure hours, so thoroughly inoculated the children with the views and sentiments of the parents that in thoughts, tastes and habits the coming generation exactly reproduced the one going out. There is no other family system wherein the young can be so thoroughly imbued with the nature and disposition of their parents. All, from the smallest to the largest, joined in every topic of conversation, each expressing his or her views; and the views of even the four year old were always received with deference.

The Dutch oven was not our modern outside bake oven, but a large flat-bottomed pot about a foot deep, with a close-fitting lid around which was a perpendicular rim of about two inches high. This was used for baking pone, apple pot-pie or even a loaf of bread in emergencies: the plan being to rake out a layer, about two inches in depth, of burning coals upon the hearth, and set the Dutch oven on them—the feet holding it about an inch above the coals; then placing the lid upon it, and covering the lid also with burning coals to the same depth. These coals would burn till reduced to ashes, and cook the contents of the oven thoroughly in the operation. Of course no other fuel but good sound wood would serve the purpose, and as coal was introduced for fuel the Dutch oven went out of use. Pewter plates and dishes were almost exclusively the table furniture; and as the good housewives of those times were exceedingly particular in regard to cleanliness, the tables and table furniture and cooking utensils were always kept well scoured and brightened up. Table cloths were used only on rare occasions, but the planks of which the table was composed were scoured so smooth and white as to serve equally as well; and the pewter ware was so susceptible of a shining polish that a good set of it, placed on edge in the open cupboard, made a fine display. A strong spirit of emulation was encouraged by the mothers in the growing daughters, to see who could keep their pewter and knives and forks and spoons in the brightest condition. A superstition existed in regard to this, which evidently arose from a desire on the part of the mothers to stimulate the daughters to persevering effort. It was fully believed by many girls that by brightening the

pewter dishes to a high enough degree to reflect their image, whilst ordinarily she would see but her own likeness, yet, if she had been wicked and
unmindful of her duties or disobedient to parents, she might some time or
other be startled by the image of the devil appearing in the plate; and on
the other hand, if a good girl and industrious, she would sooner or later
be favored with a sight of the young man who was to be her future husband.

[I]f luxurious ease and expensive living were at a discount in those
days, Conrad Winebiddle did not neglect his children's education. The facilities may not have been great or the branches extensive, but in the essentials of reading and spelling, writing and arithmetic and general intelligence, they were thoroughly trained; and thorough training in educational
matters is of far more importance than superficial extension.

His children, with one exception, became staid and sober, wise and respected citizens; and the son Philip, although erratic in his manners, possessed equally with the rest the faculty of holding on to his property to a
high degree. All of them whilst they lived retained the real estate acquired
from their father, Conrad, unimpaired; and although the father died in
the prime of life, the children all lived to a very old age and were noted for
uniform good health, physically and also mentally, with but a slight exception. Whilst in the Mellon, Wauchob and Negley families and their different branches, no speck of insanity or mental obliquity of any kind has ever
appeared; and whilst no insanity appears in the Winebiddle family, yet a
slight idiosyncrasy or peculiarity of mind has appeared in some few of its
members—an obstinacy of disposition and misanthropic distrust particularly of friends, and an inclination to adopt unfounded prejudices against
others. The brothers, Philip and John C., were tinctured with this disposition. Philip was boisterous, opinionative and overbearing, with a spice of
Rip Van Winkleism in his nature. John C., on the contrary, was taciturn
and unsociable. On the other hand their two sisters, Anna B. Negley and
Catherine Roup, were as intelligent, liberal and fair-minded women as
may be met with anywhere. And the peculiarity adverted to has not reap-
peared in the descendants of any of the brothers or sisters except in a
slight degree in Catherine, the daughter of Anna B., and William, the son
of Philip, neither of whom have married.

The marriage of Anna B., the oldest daughter, with Jacob Negley took
place before the death of her father, and came about in this way as she related it to me:

The country was pretty wild then and the roads to the town very bad in the winter time, so much so that to attend church in town was difficult; and as the country was settling up and considerable of a population scattered about, Alexander Negley had a preacher, mostly Mr. Weber, to come and hold religious services at his house about once a month. And she, then about twelve years of age, whilst attending one of these meetings with her parents, was observed by Jacob who on sight, as he told her afterwards, formed the resolution in his own mind of making her his wife, if he could, when she grew up. He kept this resolution; for in five years afterwards they were married, whilst she was yet but seventeen.

And I must add a word or two more in this connection regarding her, because she was in many respects a very remarkable woman.

Doubtless every man's experience has made him acquainted with some few women whom he was led to believe as superior to any others he had met with. In selecting the three foremost in my mind I would select my mother, my motherinlaw and my wife. My motherinlaw combined the qualities of a wise, affectionate and self-sacrificing mother with first-class business ability and judgment, without in the least impairing the refined manner of the lady. Her business management of their extensive property was admirable; and she was not only a worker, but a reader and thinker. After I was married I lived in her family for over a year, and in the closest intercourse afterwards until she came to live with me some five years before her death; and what is unusual between the motherinlaw and soninlaw, her society was always agreeable, and from the time that I entered the family, in 1843, till the day of her death at my house, in 1867, not the slightest unpleasantness or misunderstanding ever occurred between us.

Although I supposed myself as shrewd in business as the average, she would not unfrequently make suggestions which I found it wise to observe. I remember on one occasion of her placing in my hands a bill of rents and other matters against her son Daniel, with a request to obtain his store bill for goods, and have a settlement made and bills receipted. After mentioning it to Daniel it was inconvenient at the time to make out his bill and the matter was neglected for some time, when her frequently expressed wish to have it attended to excited my curiosity and I inquired why she was so particular with a son; when she said it was not with a view to be exacting or troublesome, but in all her experience she had observed that, wherever friends or relatives dealt together, frequent settlements were more necessary than in dealings between strangers. That principle had not before struck me, but I have observed its truth ever since.

She suffered severely from neuralgia of the stomach for nearly a year before her death, but bore up under it with wonderful patience and resignation, and to the very end manifested her natural good feeling and practical common sense. For a few hours before her dissolution a lull had taken place in her sufferings, but the physician in attendance observed that she was sinking, and according to an old-fashioned idea of giving timely warning of the entrance into another world, he deemed it his duty, he said, to inform her of the approach of the dread moment. Accordingly, whilst the family stood by her bedside, he told her in a solemn tone that she had but a few minutes more to live and it might be well to turn her attention to that solemn event so near at hand. She did not seem in the least alarmed, but recalling her wandering thoughts and looking up into his face she carelessly said, "Well!" Then pausing a few moments, she continued, "If it was not to be for a couple of weeks yet I would rather—but we must submit." This was her last utterance. Her head soon inclined to one side, and in less than half an hour she quietly ceased to breathe. Such was the end of this excellent woman.

Her mention of two weeks had surprised me, and on adverting to it afterwards to her daughterinlaw Sophia, who had been present at the bedside with us, she said she understood it perfectly well at the time; that, not long before the doctor had made the announcement, she had communicated the fact to her that my son James was to be married in two weeks, at which she expressed much concern and a wish to see his wife before she died. James was her favorite, and his presence and attention to her in the evenings after his return from business had always seemed to have a soothing effect on her sufferings.

Thus nature takes us out of the world in the exercise of our ordinary commonplace thoughts and feelings, as she brought us into it unconsciously before the exercise of thought began; and, except for the interference of fellow mortals or alarmed and excited relatives and friends, we drop out again without alarm into that unconsciousness from which we were awakened on coming in. Not only this but all other death-bed scenes at which I have been present lead me to this belief.

Genealogical Chart

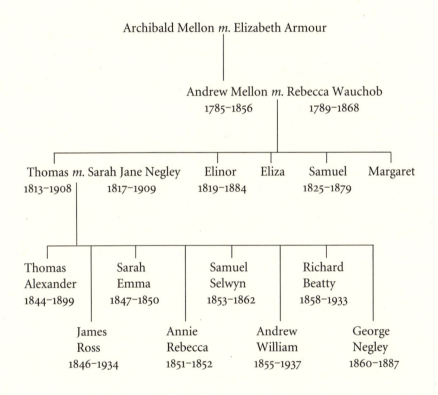

Archibald Mellon *m.* Elizabeth Armour

Andrew Mellon *m.* Rebecca Wauchob
1785–1856   1789–1868

Thomas *m.* Sarah Jane Negley   Elinor   Eliza   Samuel   Margaret
1813–1908   1817–1909   1819–1884   1825–1879

Thomas   Sarah   Samuel   Richard
Alexander   Emma   Selwyn   Beatty
1844–1899   1847–1850   1853–1862   1858–1933

James   Annie   Andrew   George
Ross   Rebecca   William   Negley
1846–1934   1851–1852   1855–1937   1860–1887

Notes

◆ ◆ ◆

Introduction

1. Letter of Jan. 11, 1897, courtesy of Paul Mellon.

2. An unpublished biography of Andrew W. Mellon by Burton J. Hendrick, commissioned by the family in the early 1940s, refers to Thomas Mellon's letter books, interviews with friends and family members, and other materials that appear to have been lost over time. I am grateful to Paul Mellon for making a portion of the Hendrick manuscript and a small collection of Thomas Mellon's surviving correspondence available to me for the preparation of this edition. See Hendrick, "Andrew William Mellon," ch. 4, p. 20.

3. Paul Mellon, with John Baskett, *Reflections in a Silver Spoon* (New York: William Morrow and Company, Inc., 1992), p. 28.

4. Hendrick, "Andrew William Mellon," ch. 4, p. 20. A note on his present to President Coolidge appears in the unpublished diary of Andrew W. Mellon, March 2, 1929.

5. The magnificent structure of the central bank is still in operation on Smithfield Street, but adjacent skyscrapers now house the expanded business offices. Though Franklin's statue was moved inside in 1922, no one is sure when it was removed or where it may now be stored.

6. W. L. Mellon and Boyden Sparkes, *Judge Mellon's Sons*, privately printed, 1948, p. 22.

7. Benjamin Franklin, *The Autobiography of Benjamin Franklin*, ed. Leonard W. Labaree et al. (New Haven: Yale University Press, 1964), pp. 135-36. For an extended discussion of Franklin's work and influence, see G. Thomas Couser, *American Autobiography: The Prophetic Mode* (Amherst: University of Massachusetts Press, 1979).

8. Mellon, *Reflections in a Silver Spoon*, p. 65.

9. Thomas Mellon includes few details of his voyage to America, for as he would later tell his great-grandson, Matthew, "it was such a horror he did not want to describe it in the book." The ship was small, carrying about seventy passengers who had to supply their own food. For meals a cauldron of boiling water was available in a central cabin, where each family would lower a bag of food attached to a string, pulling it out when the food was cooked. The berths below deck were stacked four high, with one berth for each family, and given the roughness of the voyage, seasickness, and primitive sanitary conditions, the stench was unbearable. The young Thomas stayed on deck as often as he could. From taped interview with Matthew T. Mellon by John Gilmore, Ulster-American Folk Park, 1980.

10. Unpublished letter to Uncle Thomas, March 23, 1833.

11. Unpublished letters to John Coon, April 28 and August 16, 1834.

12. James Ross Mellon, *Letters Exchanged Between James Ross Mellon and His Parents Judge and Mrs. Thomas Mellon*, preface. These letters were privately published in Pittsburgh in 1928.

13. Hendrick, "Andrew William Mellon," ch. 4, p. 6.

14. Mellon and Sparkes, *Judge Mellon's Sons*, pp. 184-85, 186. W. L. Mellon believed that the market value of the Mellon property was closer to $4,000,000; he also notes that each son was worth an additional $600,000, though Hendrick, "Andrew William Mellon," ch. 4, pp. 10-11, indicates that that amount was the sum of the share each received from Thomas Mellon.

15. Unpublished letter, courtesy of Paul Mellon.

16. Burton Hersh, *The Mellon Family* (New York: William Morrow and Company, Inc., 1978),

and David E. Koskoff, *The Mellons: The Chronicle of America's Richest Family.* (New York: Thomas Y. Crowell Company, 1978). See also Mellon, *Reflections in a Silver Spoon.*

17. Privately printed in 1885 by Wm. G. Johnston & Co. of Pittsburgh, Mellon's autobiography was reprinted in 1969 by Kraus Reprint Co., but has been otherwise unavailable until this edition. A much abridged version was prepared by Matthew T. Mellon for the opening celebration of the restored Mellon family cottage at Camp Hill, County Tyrone, Northern Ireland, in 1968. As he wrote in his preface, his limited selections were not "an adequate substitute for the book itself," and in fact he hoped it would provide incentive for young Mellons, at least, to read the unabridged book.

Autobiography
Chapter I. Childhood

1. A restoration of the Camp Hill Cottage was undertaken by the government of Northern Ireland and funded by members of the Mellon family and opened to the public in 1968. In 1975, twenty-six acres surrounding the cottage were developed into the Ulster-American Folk Park that also includes a replica of a log cabin that was Thomas Mellon's first American home, a log farmhouse, and a Conestoga wagon similar to the one on which the Mellon family traveled to Westmoreland County in Pennsylvania. The Ulster-American Folk Park was sponsored by Enterprise Ulster and the U.S. Bicentennial to demonstrate links between Ulster and the United States, and the contributions of eighteenth- and nineteenth-century emigrants. The chairman of the Folk Park, Eric Montgomery, is also secretary of the Scotch-Irish Trust of Ulster, the foundation that now supports the park's maintenance and development.

2. Armour, his new wife, and his brother Thomas emigrated to Westmoreland County in 1808. Their uncle John, who left Ireland in 1796, had by then moved from New Alexandria in Westmoreland County to a farm near Conneaut Lake in Crawford County. After a short term of farming and a business venture in New Orleans that led him to be a volunteer in the Battle for New Orleans in 1815, Thomas settled in Philadelphia.

3. In Robert Burns's narrative poem, "Tam o'Shanter," a somewhat inebriated Tam, pursued by witches, rides for his life in the darkness of night. Because of Burns's popularity, the phrase became part of common language. When Thomas Mellon traveled to Britain at age sixty-nine, he visited the home of his favorite poet and followed Tam's route, which he describes in chapter 20.

4. The unsuccessful 105-day siege of Derry by Catholic forces in 1689 is still a rallying cry. A solid Orangeman throughout his life, Thomas Mellon was moved by this childhood memory when he revisited the scene in 1882, described in chapter 20.

5. Sea *dulce* is an edible species of seaweed with bright red, deeply divided fronds, still sold on the northern coast of Ireland.

Chapter II. Boyhood

1. The Conestoga, a covered wagon for overland freight hauling, originated in Lancaster County, southeastern Pennsylvania, during the early eighteenth century to carry furs from the country towns into Philadelphia. It was used extensively between 1750 and 1850 to carry freight across the Appalachian mountains and into the Ohio Valley. The prairie schooner, a lighter and more compact descendant of the Conestoga, became popular in the settlement of the West.

2. The Stoystown-Greensburg Turnpike, one of the first roads cut across the Allegheny mountains, was later replaced by the present U.S. Route 30.

3. The St. Vincent parish was founded in 1790 by Reverend Theodore Brouwers, a Franciscan monk. In 1846, Reverend Wimmer of the Benedictine Abbey of Metten, Bavaria, founded the monastery that became the St. Vincent Archabbey on the same land near Latrobe.

4. The site of the Mellon homestead on Duff's Hill is located near Murrysville on what is now

the corner of Cline Hollow Road, named after the descendants of Jacob Kline, who sold Thomas's father seed oats in the spring of 1819, and Hill's Church Road, named after the church (now the Emmanuel Reformed and Lutheran) that was built on land donated by Peter Hill, Jr., and Philip Drum in 1828. Peter Hill, Sr., and his brother John had purchased the land on Duff's Hill after emigrating from Germany. A bronze plaque was set on a boulder in front of the property in 1975 commemorating the boyhood home of Thomas Mellon.

5. These lots are in what is now the center of downtown Pittsburgh, near those eventually purchased by Thomas Mellon for his first bank on Smithfield Street in 1870.

6. The area described was at the center of the city's central district. In 1994, the streets—Fourth, Fifth, Diamond, Smithfield, and Market—still house major commercial establishments in downtown Pittsburgh.

Chapter III. Material Progress

1. The Whiskey Rebellion by farmers in western Pennsylvania was a reaction to a law of 1791 that imposed a tax on distilled liquors. A major reason that mountain farmers distilled their grain was economy of shipping: A packhorse could carry only four bushels of grain, but when the grain was converted to whiskey it could carry the equivalent of twenty-four bushels. Arguing that the tax violated their rights, angry farmers eventually forced President George Washington to call out the militia to quell their rebellion in 1794.

2. The Pennsylvania Main Line, a system of canals and railroads connecting Philadelphia to Pittsburgh, was completed in 1834. Work on the Western Division, begun in 1826, opened traffic from Pittsburgh to Johnstown in 1831.

Chapter IV. Our Neighbors

1. Census data from 1790, when the population of Pennsylvania was 422,000, indicate that 38 percent (161,365) was German, 15 percent (63,061) was Scotch-Irish, and 7 percent (30,636) was Irish.

2. Major George Ament was a farmer and mill owner as well as a blacksmith. Many of his descendants, like those of Kline, Hill, and Duff, remain in the Turtle Creek Valley.

3. The Battle of Bushy Run (August 5–6, 1763) was a turning point in Pontiac's War. In the spring of 1763, the Indians had captured nine British forts, and Fort Pitt and Fort Detroit were under siege. Fort Pitt was saved when the Swiss-born Colonel Henry Bouquet defeated the Indians at Bushy Run.

Hannastown, the first county seat of Westmoreland County, held its first court in April 1773, in the house of Robert Hanna, who kept a tavern on the Forbes Road. The town of some thirty buildings was sacked and burned by Seneca Indians on July 13, 1782, and never rebuilt.

Chapter V. First Visit to the City

1. Given the fact that his first visit to Pittsburgh was in early spring when the ground could be worked, and that his birthday was on February 3, it is probable either that Thomas was ten years old at the time, or that the year was 1822.

2. By 1820, women represented 8 percent of the industrial workforce in Pennsylvania, primarily in the textile industry. Thomas Mellon's youthful impression of the relative ease of their labor was no doubt affected by his participation in his family's preparation of flax and linen in their home that he describes in chapter 2.

Chapter VI. School Days

1. John Rogers (1500?–1555) was burned at the stake during the reign of Mary Tudor.

Chapter VII. The Decision

1. *The Port Folio,* published by "Oliver Oldschool, Esq.," in Philadelphia (1801–1825), was a popular "monthly miscellany of literature, science and history."

2. Alexander Pope, *Essay on Man,* Epistle IV, line 193.

Chapter VIII. Academic Course

1. During his last weeks at Tranquil Retreat Academy, Mellon wrote enthusiastically to his friend John Kuhn (also Coon) about the quality of his education there. He noted that there were never more than five students in a class, sometimes only one other than himself, and that most, like him, did not attend regularly. He attended only half of the last session. Unpublished letter to John Coon, April 29, 1834.

Chapter IX. College Course

1. The Canonsburg Academy for Men, founded in 1794, became Jefferson College in 1802, and in 1865 joined with Washington Academy, chartered in 1806, to become Washington and Jefferson College in Washington, Pennsylvania, about ten miles from Cannonsburg. Both academies were founded by Dr. John McMillan, who taught Latin and Greek, and also organized many of the churches in the region. Benjamin Franklin donated fifty pounds to Washington Academy in 1790 for the purchase of books. In 1970, Washington and Jefferson College became coeducational; it currently enrolls 1600 students.

2. Western University of Pennsylvania evolved in 1819 from the Pittsburgh Academy, founded in 1787 by Hugh Henry Brackenridge, who used Benjamin Franklin's Philadelphia Academy as a model. In 1904, Western University became the University of Pittsburgh.

Mellon writes that he decided to attend Western because it was more serious in purpose, but letters to his Uncle Thomas and his friend John Kuhn (also Coon) suggest that money and time-to-degree were also important factors. He hoped to enter as a sophomore and graduate in eighteen months, though it eventually took three years, and he was twenty-four when he received his degree.

Dr. Robert Bruce, president of the university from 1819 to 1843, was born in Scotland and educated at the University of Edinburgh. When Thomas Mellon began his studies in 1834, there were four other faculty and only forty-three students. The full course of study was seven years, four of preparatory work, called the classical section, which Mellon had completed with Mr. Gill at Tranquil Retreat Academy, and three of the collegiate section. Tuition was thirty dollars a year, one-half payable in advance.

After the Great Fire of 1845, the university was located at different times on three city sites until 1889, when new buildings were erected in Allegheny on Observatory Hill, where the university had installed a thirteen-inch refracting telescope in 1865. It was not until 1908 that the university moved to its present site in Oakland's Civic Center. In 1921, A. W. and R. B. Mellon donated Frick Acres, then worth $1.5 million, to the university and paid off $600,000 in university debts.

3. The Tilghman Literary Society (1821–1844) was organized by students at Western University in honor of Judge William Tilghman, Chief Justice of the Pennsylvania Supreme Court, 1806–1827.

4. "The Point" refers to the geographic point of land in downtown Pittsburgh where the Monongahela and Allegheny Rivers join to become the Ohio River.

5. Old Economy in Ambridge was the third and last home (1825–1905) of a utopian religious community founded by George Rapp and some five hundred German followers who came to America in 1803. They first settled at Harmony in Butler County, moved to Indiana in 1814 where they founded New Harmony, and returned to Pennsylvania in 1825. Builders of an industrial empire, they adopted celibacy in 1807 and eventually died out.

Chapter X. Study of Law

1. Herbert Spencer, *Education: Intellectual, Moral, and Physical.*

2. Following the tradition of the English legal system, in Pennsylvania the prothonotary is the chief clerk or registrar of the Courts of Common Pleas.

Chapter XIV. Professional Life

1. Samuel W. Black was killed at Turkey Hill during the Seven Days Battle near Richmond in June 1862. Black had been appointed by President James Buchanan as a judge of the U.S. Court of Nebraska, and later as governor of that territory (1859–61). His letters from this period are included in the memoirs of his granddaughter, Elizabeth Moorhead, in *Whirling Spindle: The Story of a Pittsburgh Family* (Pittsburgh: University of Pittsburgh Press, 1942).

2. Brackets included in original text.

3. Samuel Butler's mock-heroic poem, *Hudibras,* published 1663–78.

4. The Great Fire of 1845, said to have started in an Irish washerwoman's laundry shack, destroyed fifty-six acres, nearly one-third of the city of Pittsburgh. Some one thousand buildings were lost in the fire, including the entire Market area, the Monongahela House, the covered Monongahela Bridge, the Customhouse, and Western University. About twelve thousand people were left homeless, and the damage was estimated to be between five and eight million dollars.

5. Allegheny City was located on the north bank of the Allegheny River directly across from Pittsburgh. During the 1860s it became a fashionable residential district for the newly rich who wanted to escape from the industrial pollution of Pittsburgh.

6. "Wall's accommodation" was a coach of the Wall Street Railway Company, one among dozens of similar horse-drawn conveyances in the city at this time. By the 1890s many small companies such as Wall Street were consolidated and converted to electric traction.

Chapter XV. Judicial Life

1. In Pennsylvania, the Courts of Common Pleas are general trial courts at the county level. They still have jurisdiction over civil and criminal cases, but also include Family Division and Orphans' Court. The Allegheny County Court of Common Pleas had fifty judges in 1994.

2. On April 29, 1862, Captain David G. Farragut and the federal navy took possession of New Orleans. Two days later, Major General Benjamin F. Butler arrived with the Union occupation forces. Butler already had a reputation for wartime looting and pillage, but during the occupation of New Orleans, he became notorious for his cruel treatment of its citizens, his strict adherence to military law, and his deftness in taking over the wealth of the city, for which he received the nickname "Spoons." His brother also became wealthy by confiscating cotton, as well as other goods, such as Thomas Mellon's coal.

3. While it is clear that Thomas Mellon had little confidence in the city's ability to defend itself, considerable effort was invested in the plan. Fearing a raid by the cavalry forces of J.E.B. Stuart, Pittsburgh's leaders decided to suspend business on June 14, 1863, and hired two thousand of their own workers at $1.25 per day to begin digging rifle pits around the perimeter of the city. On June 25, the city was warned by telegram that Stuart's troops had occupied McConnellsburg and were moving toward Pittsburgh. The next day there were 11,828 men at work on 32 separate defense installations. The Union victory at Gettysburg in early July removed the immediate threat to Pittsburgh.

Chapter XVI. Vexatious Litigation

1. The details of Mellon's "vexatious" cases well may affect readers differently as well. Those with the patience to follow him through this sometimes laborious account of litigation will see his idealistic, principled notions of the law and the value of a man's word pitted against the realities

of human behavior and legal practice. In earlier chapters, Mellon has referred to occasions when friendship, softness of heart, or bad judgment of character led him to make unwise business decisions, all of which are reflected in the litigation described here. This chapter, more than any other, offers direct advice to his sons and heirs about how to avoid errors in legal and business decisions. It was cut from the second "private" printing that Mellon ordered.

2. "A" is probably J. B. Corey, with whom Mellon did business in coal until 1863. It was the Corey coal shipment that was confiscated in New Orleans during the Civil War. Mellon's troubles with Corey suggest a possible source for his fervent belief that it was far better to have his sons as partners in business enterprises than to depend on others on whose competence and honor he might not rely.

Chapter XVII. Private Life

1. Thomas and Sarah Jane Mellon's home at 401 Negley was passed down through the family of their eldest son, Thomas Alexander, and was finally torn down in 1956, when the property was converted into lots for a dozen small brick homes. Only one of the original gateposts remains.

2. Sarah Emma, born December 26, 1847.

3. Annie Rebecca, born January 26, 1851.

4. Samuel Selwyn, born February 11, 1853.

5. Richard Beatty, born March 19, 1858.

6. James was only seventeen when his father sent him north.

7. The year was 1865, and James was only nineteen years old.

8. Both Thomas and Sarah Jane were decidedly against James's desire to join a regiment of one-hundred-day volunteers to guard Washington. On May 17, 1864, Thomas wrote to James: "Don't do it. I have written." Sarah Jane wrote to her son in even briefer terms: "Come home!" James Ross Mellon, *Letters,* pp. 97, 100.

9. Rachel Larimer's father, General William Larimer, had been a coal baron in Westmoreland County before he moved to Leavenworth. Later he became one of the founders of Denver, Colorado.

10. When their eighth child, George, was born, Sarah Jane was forty-three and Thomas forty-seven years old.

Chapter XVIII. Before the Panic

1. Henry Boucher Swope (1831–74), U.S. District Attorney for Western Pennsylvania, was hated by many of his fellow attorneys and feared by criminals who appeared before him in court. His legal colleagues often referred to him as a "persecutor" instead of a "prosecutor," and even his obituary comments on his relentless pursuit of criminals.

2. In 1872 Andrew was seventeen and Dick fourteen, both extraordinarily young to be involved in this business venture. Andrew left Western University before graduation, and Dick did not attend college at all.

3. Mansfield, now known as the city of Carnegie.

4. According to Hendrick, "Andrew William Mellon," ch. 2, p. 39, Andrew foresaw that the boom would come to an end, and when he woke one morning in the fall of 1873 to discover that the lumberyard of his chief rival was on fire, he offered to sell him his own flourishing business only weeks before the panic began.

5. Jay Cooke (1821–1905) made his fortune selling government bonds to small investors during the Civil War. His company continued to be the largest dealer in government bonds after the war until the firm was overextended in railroad loans and securities, especially Northern Pacific, and was forced into bankruptcy by the financial strains that led to the Panic of 1873.

Chapter XIX. After the Panic

1. Although Mellon remembers the railroad as Dick's first major project, it involved a joint effort by Thomas, James, and Dick, who were then aged thirty-three, thirty-one, and nineteen; once completed, Dick managed the railroad for three years.

2. In 1878, Thomas Mellon obtained from William M. Darlington four hundred acres near Ligonier to develop Idlewild Park, a picnic resort that he hoped would attract business for the railroad. Railroad schedules and rates were widely posted in the Pittsburgh area, with adult round-trip fare from Pittsburgh at seventy-five cents, children under twelve, fifty cents. The *Ligonier Echo* noted in the summer of 1881: "The Ligonier Valley Rail Road did a monstrous business today. Their long trains and an observation car were constantly running from Latrobe at one end and Ligonier on the other to the campgrounds at Idlewild." Today Idlewild Park remains a popular attraction for western Pennsylvanians.

3. Formed in 1872, this line connected the city to Oakland, which later would become the Civic Center, and East Liberty, formerly Negleystown. In 1881 the coaches were drawn by horses on a rail system; by 1887, the line was acquired by the Central Transit Company and was operated by electric cable.

Chapter XX. Trip to Europe

1. Phoenix Park, the largest enclosed public park in Europe, covers 1,760 acres and contains the President's Residence and one of the world's oldest zoological gardens, founded in 1830. The "Phoenix Park murders," mentioned often in James Joyce's *Ulysses,* occurred there on May 6, 1882, just four months before Thomas Mellon's visit. At that time, Lord Cavendish, the chief secretary of Ireland, and Mr. Burke, his undersecretary, were stabbed to death by members of the Invincibles, a radical nationalist group.

2. Dublin Castle, built in 1204 by King John on the site of a former Viking fortress, was the seat of English rule for more than seven hundred years.

3. After the United Irish Rebellion of 1800, the English merged the Irish Parliament with their own and the building was sold to the Bank of Ireland on the condition that all reminders of the Irish Parliament be effaced. The curved walls and pillars of the current exterior were built around the original structure, which is considerably smaller than the outward appearance suggests.

4. The statue of Daniel O'Connell, a democratic politician of the early nineteenth century and the first Catholic Lord Mayor of Dublin, stands at the head of O'Connell Street, which also has monuments to John Stewart Parnell and labor champion Jones Larkin.

5. The White Hart Hotel was still operating in 1918 when Matthew Mellon made his first visit to Omagh and Camp Hill, but it has since been replaced by the local post office. The courthouse remains on the hill at the end of Main Street.

6. The current road from Omagh to Camp Hill is direct, a distance of about two miles. Given the locations of the Cappaigh Church, Cross Roads Meeting House, Cappaigh Bridge, Montjoy's estate, the Cappaigh Episcopal Church, and the Catholic church, Thomas Mellon would have had to follow a very circuitous route to pass them by on the way to his homestead in Lower Castletown. Though many old gravestones remain in the yard of the Cappaigh Episcopal Church, there are none marking those who fell in the rebellion of 1641.

7. Now designated the Church of Ireland.

8. The Cross Roads Meeting House is now a local civic building. Because of its importance to the Mellon family, a replica has been built in the Ulster-American Folk Park, which includes the Mellon farmstead in Camp Hill.

9. The Cappaigh Bridge, now called locally the Stone Bridge, is still an important crossing on the Strule, and though Thomas Mellon remembers it as having ten arches, only half a dozen are in evidence.

10. On clear days, Bessy Bell and Mary Gray, both in the Sperrin Mountain range some ten miles away, are visible from Camp Hill.

11. Built between 1614 and 1619, the walled medieval city of Derry has four main streets leading from the old gateways—Bishop's Gate, Ferryquay Gate, Shipquay Gate and Butcher's Gate. St. Columbra's Cathedral (1633) was the first built in Britain and Ireland after the Reformation. In its chapter house are relics of James II's 105-day siege of Derry in 1689 and a part of MaCaulay's manuscript for the *History of England*.

12. Located at the mouth of the River Ayr on the Irish Sea, Ayr became a thriving market town and holiday resort during the nineteenth century. Popular for tourists are the Tam O'Shanter Inn, now a museum, a Burns statue in the town center by G. A. Lawson (1891), the Auld Kirk with its Kirkyard and Martyrs Monument, and the Auld Brig, the subject of Burns's poem, "The Brigs of Ayr."

In Alloway, now a suburb of Ayr only a ten-minute drive from the railway station, is the Alloway Kirk where Tam was frightened by witches, and the Brig o'Doon, with the monument commemorating Burns, Tam, and Souter Johnnie nearby, which opened in 1823.

13. "Talkative idler"; Thomas Mellon included this and subsequent translations of Burns's dialect in his original edition.

14. "Epistle to a Young Friend" is one of Burns's most famous poems from his early period when he wrote primarily in the Scottish dialect, and an obvious favorite of Thomas Mellon, who had each of his sons memorize it when they were children. The "young friend" was Andrew Hunter Aiken, son of Robert Aiken of Ayr, who later became English consul at Riga. Although the poem has a somewhat cynical view of the human race, it emphasizes the importance of conscience, honor, and decency, not for the sake of public opinion, but for the personal satisfaction that is its own reward, a moral strain consistent with Mellon's own.

15. "strange"

16. "much"

17. "Who have no . . ."

18. "poverty"

19. "peep"

20. "flame"

21. "wealth"

22. "advice"

23. The Gothic structure of Glasgow Cathedral is the only cathedral left intact after the mid-sixteenth-century Scottish Reformation. Beneath the cathedral is Laigh Kirk, the last remnant of the original twelfth-century building, which houses the tomb of St. Mungo, patron saint of Glasgow.

24. Holyrood Palace served as the home of Mary Queen of Scots and remains the official residence of the English monarch in Scotland. Nearby is Holyrood Park and the peak of Arthur's Seat (elev. 823 ft.), an exposed volcanic summit.

25. Melrose Abbey, at the center of the tiny village of Melrose, was begun in 1136, rebuilt in an ornate Gothic style, and then decimated during the Reformation in 1543. Two miles west of Melrose is the mock-Gothic Abbotsford estate, where Sir Walter Scott wrote his Waverly novels. Dryburgh Abbey, where Scott is buried, is five miles southeast of Melrose.

Chapter XXI. Changes of a Lifetime

1. Thomas Mellon's thinking on education was deeply influenced by the writings of Herbert Spencer (1820–1903). In chapter 10, "The Study of Law," he advised his descendants to read Spencer's book on education, published in 1860, because he knew of no other source that offered "so much wise and practical advice." In addition to Spencer's educational and political theory, Mellon also seems to have read some of his work on sociology, as is evident later in this section. Spencer published *Descriptive Sociology; or, Groups of Sociological Facts, Classified and Arranged by*

Herbert Spencer in 1873, and was the editor of *Principles of Sociology*, a quarterly journal, 1874–1897.

Afterword

1. Unpublished letters of Thomas Mellon.
2. Unpublished letter to Richard B. Mellon, January 16, 1885.
3. Mellon and Sparkes, *Judge Mellon's Sons*, p. 129.
4. Hendrick, "Andrew William Mellon," ch. 3, p. 11.
5. Ibid., ch. 4, p. 12.
6. Ibid., ch. 4, p. 15.
7. Ibid., ch. 4, p. 18.

Family History
Chapter I. Name and Nationality

1. Brackets in original text. For context, see *Plutarch's Lives*, p. 357.

2. Modern variants in Ulster include O'Mallon, Mallon, Malone, as well as Mellon, though none of the modern Mellons are related to the descendants of Thomas Mellon.

3. Although the Greek etymology is correct, the connection Mellon draws between the Greek and Scotch-Irish etymology is obscure.

4. The Clan na-Gael, founded in New York in 1867, was an oath-bound Irish-American nationalist organization. The Molly Maguires, named after a widow who led a group of Irish anti-landlord agitators in the 1840s, was a secret organization of coal miners supposedly responsible for acts of sabotage and terrorism in the anthracite coal fields of Pennsylvania and West Virginia from 1862 to 1876.

5. The bloody rebellion of 1641—the Ulster Rising—was a turning point in Irish history that scarred the memory of both Protestants and Catholics. About 2,000 lives were lost, but over the years bitter memories of the event increased those numbers to legendary proportions. Thomas Mellon was fascinated by Irish history throughout his life, which never diminished his strident sympathies with the Ulster Protestants.

Chapter II. Ancestry

1. In order to bring Ireland under effective English rule, Queen Elizabeth had pursued a policy of introducing English "plantations" there, and this policy was continued by her successors. Land was taken from the native Irish and given to English and Scottish settlers. This policy helped provoke the rebellion that started in Ulster in 1641. After Ireland was subdued by Cromwell and other English generals between 1649 and 1652, the policy of dispossessing the native Irish in favor of English and Scottish settlers was enforced even more severely.

2. The Fairy Water is a small river near Omagh that eventually runs into the Strule River. Thomas Mellon's great grandfather, Samuel, one of Archibald's three sons, inherited a farm on the Fairy Water when the other two sons, Archibald and Mark, were given the Castletown family homestead in the Strule valley a few miles away. Samuel's son Archibald (Thomas Mellon's grandfather) eventually purchased the Castletown property from the descendants of Mark Mellon, where he lived until he emigrated in 1816.

3. Samuel's surviving sons, John and Archibald, emigrated to western Pennsylvania. In 1796, John settled in Unity Township in Westmoreland County near Latrobe, and later moved north to Crawford County, where his family came to be known as the Crawford County branch of the Mellons. It is John's grandson, Alexander, whom Thomas Mellon recalls in the following anecdote.

4. Thomas Mellon's notion that his mother's family descended from the Dutch may be true,

but is more likely a matter of family legend. The name Wauchob has a long history in Scotland, especially in the neighborhood of Edinburgh, but it was and is uncommon in Northern Ireland. In Black's *The Surnames of Scotland,* the name Wauchob (Wauchope) appears as early as 1203 among families who were tenants of a baron and had tenants and vassals of their own. Two branches of the family settled in Ulster in the seventeenth century, one in County Down and one in County Donegal. The earliest reference to the Kinkitt Wauchobs is a May 1, 1663 land lease record. Their family tradition is that they descended from three brothers who came to Ireland as "Cromwellian Soldiers" and settled in County Tyrone.

Chapter III. My Grandfather Mellon's Family

1. Sir Edward Michael Pakenham was Commander of the British expedition in the Battle of New Orleans (January 8, 1815), the final engagement of the War of 1812, in which he died.

Chapter V. The Negley and Winebiddle Families

1. Thomas and Sarah Jane Negley Mellon named their second son James Ross after the Negley family benefactor.

2. The Negley family is of Swiss origin, its earliest known ancestor another Jacob Negley, who was a disciple of Ulrich Zwingli (1484–1531), the first Protestant reformer of Switzerland, whose leadership established Zurich as the second major center of the Reformation, next to Wittenburg.

3. The present East Liberty Presbyterian Church, the fifth structure on the original site of Jacob Negley's log schoolhouse-church, was built in 1931–35, a family memorial gift from Mr. and Mrs. Richard B. Mellon. The Mellons donated Tiffany art glass from the older structure for the remodeling of the Unity Presbyterian Church in Unity Cemetery, Westmoreland County (1937), where early family members worshipped and nineteen are buried.

Bibliography

Alexander, Edwin P. *On the Main Line: The Pennsylvania Railroad in the Nineteenth Century.* New York: Clarkson N. Porter, Inc., 1971.

Banks and Bankers of the Keystone State. Pittsburgh: The Finance Company in Pittsburgh, 1905.

Boucher, John N. *History of Westmoreland County, Pennsylvania.* New York: The Lewis Publishing Company, 1906.

Brackenridge, Henry Marie. Three unpublished letters to Thomas Mellon, 1849, 1851, 1859. Darlington Library, University of Pittsburgh.

Couser, G. Thomas. *American Autobiography: The Prophetic Mode.* Amherst: University of Massachusetts Press, 1979.

Denton, Frank. *The Mellons of Pittsburgh.* New York: The Newcomen Society of England, 1948.

Dickens, Charles. *American Notes.* Paris: A. and W. Golignani and Co., 1842.

Donehoo, George P., ed. *Pennsylvania: A History.* New York: Lewis Historical Publishing Company, Inc., 1926.

Foster, R. F. *Modern Ireland, 1600–1972.* London: Penguin Books, 1989.

Franklin, Benjamin. *The Autobiography of Benjamin Franklin.* 1794. Ed. Leonard W. Labaree, Ralph L. Ketcham, Helen C. Boatfield, and Helen Fineman. New Haven: Yale University Press, 1964.

Harper, Frank C. *Pittsburgh: Forge of the Universe.* New York: Comet Press Books, 1957.

Harvey, George. *Henry Clay Frick: The Man.* New York: Charles Scribner's Sons, 1928.

Hendrick, Burton. "Andrew William Mellon." Unpublished manuscript, courtesy of Paul Mellon.

Hersh, Burton. *The Mellon Family.* New York: William Morrow and Company, Inc., 1978.

History of Pittsburgh and Environs. New York: The American Historical Society, Inc., 1922.

Leyburn, James G. *The Scotch-Irish: A Social History.* Chapel Hill: The University of North Carolina Press, 1962.

Lorant, Stefan. *Pittsburgh: The Story of an American City.* Lenox, Mass.: Authors Edition, Inc., 1988.

Lundberg, Ferdinand. *America's Sixty Families.* New York: The Vanguard Press, 1937.

McCullough, C. Hax, Jr. *One Hundred Years of Banking.* Privately printed, Pittsburgh, 1969.

McEvoy, John. *County of Tyrone, 1802: A Statistical Survey.* Belfast: Friar's Bush Press, 1991.

McKinsey, Elizabeth. *Niagara Falls: Icon of the American Sublime.* Cambridge, Eng.: Cambridge University Press, 1985.

McKnight, Robert. Unpublished diaries, 1842, 1846, 1847. Darlington Library, University of Pittsburgh. Includes observations on the courtroom quarrel between Thomas Mellon and Samuel W. Black.

Mellon, James Ross. *Letters, 1862–1895.* Privately printed, Pittsburgh, 1928.

Mellon, Matthew T. Taped interview with John Gilmour, Ulster-American Folk Park, Camp Hill, Northern Ireland, 1980.

———. *War Log: 1917–1918.* Privately printed, 1975.

———. *Watermellons.* Privately printed, 1974.

Mellon, Paul, with John Baskett. *Reflections in a Silver Spoon.* New York: William Morrow and Company, Inc., 1992.

Mellon, Rachel Hughey (Larimer). *The Larimer, McMasters, and Allied Families.* Comp. and ed. Rachel H. L. Mellon. Philadelphia: Printed for private circulation by J. B. Lippincott, 1903.

Mellon, Thomas. *Thomas Mellon and His Times.* Privately printed, Pittsburgh: Wm. G. Johnston & Co., 1885. Rpt. New York: Kraus Reprint Co., 1969. Abridged ed., selected and ed. Matthew T. Mellon, Belfast: Stanhope House, 1968.

_____. Unpublished letters and copy book, courtesy of Paul Mellon.

Mellon, Thomas, and William B. Negley. "Day-book, Pittsburgh 1853–1860." Darlington Library, University of Pittsburgh. Lists amounts received for legal services, with signatures by Mellon or Negley indicating which handled each case, plus receipts with signatures of various parties.

Mellon, William Larimer, and Boyden Sparkes. *Judge Mellon's Sons.* Privately printed, 1948.

Mellon National Bank: A Brief Historical Sketch of the Bank, Beginning with Its Founding by Thomas Mellon in 1869. Privately printed, Pittsburgh, 1944.

Miller, Kerby A. *Emigrants and Exiles: Ireland and the Irish Exodus to North America.* New York: Oxford University Press, 1985.

Montgomery, Eric. *The Ulster-American Folk Park: How It All Began.* Omagh: The Scotch-Irish Trust of Ulster, 1991.

Moorhead, Elizabeth. *Whirling Spindle: The Story of a Pittsburgh Family.* Pittsburgh: University of Pittsburgh Press, 1942. Includes letters of Moorhead's grandfather, Samuel W. Black.

Murphy, Charles J. V. "The Mellons of Pittsburgh." *Fortune Magazine* (October, November, and December, 1967).

O'Connor, Harvey. *Mellon's Millions.* New York: John Day, 1933.

Parkinson, Tom E. *The Street Railways of Pittsburgh, 1859–1967.* Privately printed, no date.

Plutarch's Lives, trans. Bernadotte Perrin. Vol. 5. London: William Heinemann, 1917.

Rook, Charles Alexander, ed. *Western Pennsylvanians: A Work for Newspaper and Library Reference.* Pittsburgh: Western Pennsylvania Biographical Association, 1923.

Ross, James. "Reminiscences of Hon. James Ross" [1896]. *Western Pennsylvania Magazine* 3 (1920), pp. 103–08.

Rosters, History, Routes, and Other Data on Pittsburgh Railway Companies. Privately printed, 1947.

Rothman, Ellen K. *Hands and Hearts: A History of Courtship in America.* New York: Basic Books, 1984.

Smith, Helene. *Export: A Patch of Tapestry Out of Coal Country America.* Greensburg, Pa.: McDonald/Sward Company, 1986.

Smith, Helene, and George Swetnam. *A Guidebook to Historic Western Pennsylvania.* Pittsburgh: University of Pittsburgh Press, 1991.

Spencer, Herbert. *Education: Intellectual, Moral, and Physical.* New York: D. Appleton, 1860.

Spencer, Herbert. *Descriptive Sociology; or, Groups of Sociological Facts, Classified and Arranged by Herbert Spencer.* New York: D. Appleton & Company, 1873.

Swetnam, George. *Pittsylvania Country.* New York: Duell, Sloan & Pearce, 1951.

Starrett, Agnes Lynch. *One Hundred and Fifty Years: The University of Pittsburgh.* Pittsburgh: University of Pittsburgh Press, 1937.

Two Hundred Years in Ligonier Valley, 1758–1958. Ligonier, Pa.: The Ligonier Bicentennial Association, Inc., 1958.

Walton, Rachel Larimer Mellon. Taped interview with Mary Louise Briscoe, Pittsburgh, March 1, 1993.

White, Edward. *A Century of Banking in Pittsburgh.* Pittsburgh: The Index Company, 1903.

"Thomas Mellon." *Magazine of Western History* 3, no. 5 (March 1886), pp. 520–27.

Index